Perspectives on Close Relationships

Ann L. Weber
University of North Carolina at Asheville

John H. Harvey
University of Iowa

Allyn and Bacon
Boston • London • Toronto • Sydney • Tokyo • Singapore

Editor-in-Chief, Social Sciences: Susan Badger
Editorial Assistant: Laura Ellingson
Production Administrator: Ann Greenberger
Editorial-Production Service: Progressive Typographers
Cover Administrator: Suzanne Harbison
Composition Buyer: Linda Cox
Manufacturing Buyer: Megan Cochran

Library of Congress Cataloging-in-Publication Data

Perspectives on close relationships / edited by Ann L. Weber,
  John H. Harvey.
    p. cm.
  Includes bibliographical references, index, and name index.
  ISBN 0-205-13964-7 ✓
  1. Emotions. 2. Interpersonal relations. 3. Intimacy
(Psychology) I. Weber, Ann L. II. Harvey, John H., 1943–
BF511.P46 1994
158'.2—dc20   93-5202
                                                    CIP

Printed in the United States of America

10 9 8 7 6 5 4 3 2 1   98 97 96 95 94 93

*To the memory of three writers whom we lost too soon, but
who left us their work, and lifetimes of insights
into close relationships:*

*Laurie Colwin (1944–1992)
Raymond Carver (1938–1988)
Merle Shain (1935–1989)*

*. . . Pleasure requires high and loving spirits and energy, but
living in the world—being battered by it—having your heart
pierced, sharpens everything. I had grown up without knowing
it, and now I knew. I knew that you might believe in rapture,
but you had to earn the right to feel it. You had to pay for it
with grief and loss, and it was worth it. I knew what it was
like to be ultimately close to your best friend on earth, to someone you had waited to know, had watched and calculated, someone well loved and intelligible to you. . . . It was relief, and it
was terrifying.*

—*Laurie Colwin,* Shine On Bright & Dangerous Object
(1975), p. 118

Contents

Preface

To the Student

The authors of these chapters have written this volume for *you*. The field of close relationships is at once too personal and too scientific: too personal and real for us to pretend we have not ourselves been caught up in the dance of intimacy; and too scientifically "knowable" to justify much complaining and wondering without eventually trying to find answers. The tension between these two extremes—the personally subjective and the scientifically objective—tugs us back and forth, and will challenge you to follow and track us as we weave between these extreme perspectives on attraction and disillusionment, love and loss, intimacy and public life.

What emerges from this volume is not a polished portrait of a homogenized collection of scholars, but a snapshot of a work in progress—almost a noisy, colorful event full of devoted, chattering party-goers. We welcome you to share our interests and our dedication to the study of close relationships. We hope and expect you will be glad you joined us.

To the Teacher

One of the paradoxes of teaching about close relationships is encouraging students to read others' perspectives without suggesting that books are a viable substitute for life experience. We think the ideas and processes presented in these pages will be recognizably familiar and relevant to most students. At those points where the connections seem most clear, your students will reach into their own memories, lessons, and observations, rather than into the wisdom of this or other written works. Your challenge—not an impossible or unpleasant one—is to foster a *balance* between the many personal worlds your students have brought to this learning experience and the more formal presentation of this text. No, it's not a fair competition—a live person is a much more appealing model than a closed book. Therefore, don't *close* this book! Urge your students to keep the book "open," both literally and figuratively. Use the margins to record personal observations and arguments; mull over the questions that seem to you to be most worth answering, and plot your research strategy, similar to or different from the methods of present company.

The authors who represent their work between these covers *are* alive and lively people, active as researchers and teachers, and accessible to students and colleagues. You and your students are invited to contact the chapter authors about their work, and to send feedback to us editors about this book as well as your concerns with the field of close relationships. We sincerely hope and intend that, for you and your students, the last page of this book might become the first page in a congenial correspondence among colleagues. Thanks in advance for your hard work, and for bringing us along for the endeavor.

Acknowledgments

In addition to the contributions and support provided by our co-authors, our editors at Allyn & Bacon, the staff at Progressive Typographers, our friends and colleagues, we are grateful to the following people for specific assistance: Carol Fleming, research librarian at the D. Hiden Ramsey Library, UNC at Asheville; Adela Griffith, in the Psychology Department, UNC at Asheville, for secretarial support throughout the course of this project; Christina Davidson, who assisted in compiling and producing the Subject Index; John Quigley, who compiled the citations for the Names Index; and Peggy Gardner, who produced the penultimate draft of the Names Index.

We are grateful that these people were there when we needed help—usually on short notice and at inconvenient moments! We editors take full responsibility for the flaws and shortcomings of this work. Credit and thanks for the successes of this volume we happily share with these talented and generous individuals.

Ann L. Weber
John H. Harvey

Introduction

We started this volume in a humble fashion. Specifically, the two editors of this volume were sitting on the second editor's sofa, in the spring of 1989, amusing and communing with two cats, Precious Memory and Red Dukes. These cats have been in on many a scholarly conversation. Also present was our long-time friend and collaborator Terri Orbuch. The discussion turned to texts for the field of close relationships. We knew then of a few, but none were very comprehensive. Those that we had been using in our classes were usually coupled with one or more specific supplementary works on close relationships, such as a book on some particular topic, or a set of readings—including newspaper or magazine articles. We wondered what it would be like to try to write such a text. That idea was soon discarded because it would take a long time for any small team of writers to cover in a sufficient way this vast and mushrooming field of inquiry. Maybe someday for one or both of us, but not just then.

We then hit on the idea of multi-authored text, with a team of literally dozens of experts representing the field. Could it be done? The second editor had seen it done, with a fair degree of success, for the broad field of social psychology (see Conclusion chapter). The first editor believed that such a project might be feasible for this field since many colleagues also believed that a more comprehensive text was needed. Further, we had an outstanding network of scholars available from which to invite coverage of interesting, representative topics. The first editor also had the courage to believe that these invited chapters could be edited to coordinate in format and to complement one another in content. Whether that bold decision, in the midst of cat games, was one of folly is now for you the reader to determine.

By inviting contributions and working with writers, our main objectives for this text were to develop a work that reflected part of the diversity of topics and disciplines represented in our field. We also tried to gauge the text at a level that would make it useful both for undergraduate and graduate classes on relationships and related phenomena. To pursue these goals, we have now collaborated with over 30 authors in this undertaking. We believe that the present text is the first one to be authored by more than a score of scholars in the field of close relationships. The fields represented include communication studies, clinical psychology, environmental psychology, family studies, social psychology, and sociology. This list is by no means exhaustive of the different disciplines in our field. We began with a fantasy list of topics, and then sought expert scholars we knew to write original chapters on these subjects. In the harsh light of day, some of our fantasies had to be overhauled. To our disappointment, we were never able to secure a chapter exclusively devoted to the topic of friendship, for example. On the other hand, we were able to obtain contributions on such nontraditional topics as betrayal and the environmental context of close relationships. So we comfort ourselves, and we hope the reader as well, with the rationale that this collection, if not comprehensive, is nonetheless rich and provocative.

Once we had secured our committed scholars and their repertoire of topics, we asked each author or team of authors to approach their chapters with a view to instruction and invitation. We asked them to imagine having the opportunity to present a single lecture on their topic within the context of the multidisciplinary field of close relationships. We asked them to pitch their presentations to an interested student audience, providing research evidence, theory, and illustrations—anything the authors felt was necessary to display the vitality and relevance of their favorite subjects. Our authors took to this charge as labors of love.

However, in developing a book that is detailed, but not encyclopedic, we have made some compromises. Each chapter presents a brief glimpse of the author's particular discipline, but no one had the space to explain his or her field in depth. As we have mentioned, some basic topics like friendship are not dealt with in separate chapters—although several chapters do touch on the processes and principles of those missing topics. Finally, this is a very personal collection, revealing a scholar's view of the field of close relationships, related in a teacher's voice through most of these pages. While this is a book designed for use as a course text rather than a reader, it is not meant to be comprehensive or all-purpose. Indeed, the instructor who uses this text will want to customize it for a particular presentation, and may want to tag on other works and readings to represent his or her tastes and perspectives.

What do we hope that students will learn from reading this text? We hope that readers will discover that there is a plethora of work on the close relationships phenomena being done by scholars representing several disciplines. In a later chapter on the multidisciplinary nature of this field, Duck elaborates on its characteristics, including the different methods that are being developed to investigate relationships, and how different disciplines are synergistically collaborating in this pursuit. Further, we hope that the reader learns quite a bit about our various topics: from the bright side of relating, such as how and why people love, support, engage in sexual relations, and make long-term commitments; to the dark side of relating, such as how and why people become jealous, engage in betrayal or conflict, sometimes part ways, and even deal with abuse in their close relationships. Finally, we hope that the reader will consider carefully some of the research strategies that have evolved in the field, as they are discussed in the methods chapter by Ickes.

We urge the reader not to stop with this text in her or his pursuit and enjoyment of reading about close relationships. We hope this volume will serve as a stimulus for the reader to delve into favorite topics in more depth through the various types of written and other media. There is figuratively an iceberg out there of relevant material on close relationships. This volume, we know, has merely chipped out a little piece of that iceberg.

The two of us have collaborated on a number of works during the last fifteen years. That is quite a record given how frequently some authors' and editors' relationships dissolve after a couple of works together. We are the best of friends across dimensions of living, and that helps enormously in giving perspective to these projects. Perhaps, too, we owe our feline friends, Precious and Red, and their North Carolina cousin Minerva (Nervie), a huge vote of thanks for some of the social support that has kept us not only task-oriented, but also sufficiently positive in mood and will, that we could weather whatever happened—with the development and production of this book. We owe our friend Terri Orbuch much gratitude for supporting this project at its inception point. We owe our many authors thanks and a vote of confidence for their diligent work to bring this volume to fruition. We also thank our editor, Susan Badger, at Allyn & Bacon, who believed in this project from the start and, unlike the two of us, never seemed to doubt its value or eventual successful completion. Finally, we appreciate the support and good humor of John Quigley and Christina Davidson, who gave us the quiet confidence that whatever we were doing, we would get it done—as well as the blessed opportunity to spend some time not working on a project!

To complete this introduction, we offer a favorite quote from the profound writer and poet W. H. Auden. We share these lines with you as you embark on the task of examining this book, and we move on to still other scholarly toils—work that really will know no end or completion. That indeed was Auden's point, as he spoke of the abiding fragility and incompleteness of the creative enterprise.[1]

> *In the eyes of others, a man is a poet if he has written one good poem. In his own, he is only a poet at the moment when he is making his last revision to a new poem. The moment before, he was still a potential poet; the moment after, he is a man who has ceased to write poetry, perhaps forever.*

ALW
JHH

---

[1]W. H. Auden, *Collected Poems*, ed. Edward Mendelson, 1976 (New York: Random House), p. 12.

Chapter 1

Close Relationships Over Time

ROSEMARY BLIESZNER

Department of Family and Child Development and Center for Gerontology
Virginia Polytechnic Institute and State University

Outline

Dimensions of Time in the Study of Close Relationships
 Individual Development
 Life Course Stages and Social Structure
 Relationship Phases and Processes
 Historical Perspectives

Theory and Methods in the Study of Close Relationships Over Time
 Life-Span Development and Life-Course Analysis
 Methodological Implications

Research Findings: Sample Case of Friendship
 Toward a Life-Span View of Friendship
 Findings from Contemporary Studies

Conclusion and Summary

When Lucy was a child, her best friend was Tanya, who lived next door. They were inseparable until Tanya's family moved to another town some miles away. The distance was not great, but the girls were too young to drive and didn't write letters, so after only a few months they lost touch. Lucy didn't have another best friend until high school when she spent all her time with Jody and Lynnette. The girls were a tight threesome and their parents joked that they were physically connected because they seemed to do everything together: attending games and dances, visiting and shopping, even dating and making plans for college.

After graduation the threesome broke up because Lynnette chose a college out of state, while Lucy and Jody decided to attend the state university and room together. During their freshman year Lucy and Jody were still close, but they also found other friends—different friends. Lucy, majoring in engineering, spent time talking and collaborating on projects with women and men she met in class. Jody, a music major, seemed always to be rehearsing or attending a concert somewhere. By their sophomore year, Lucy and Jody decided to find other roommates, although they still considered themselves friends.

After college, Lucy attended graduate school in another city, while Jody got a job teaching in their hometown. In a way, this helped Lucy stay close to Jody; they could visit together whenever Lucy went home to see her family. However, in another sense, Lucy felt she and Jody no longer had much in common. Lucy wanted to try new things, live in different places far from home, and pursue her career as far as she could. In Lucy's opinion, Jody was settling for less by going back home and looking for an undemanding job and a husband.

As the years passed, the women stayed friendly but no longer considered themselves close friends. Lucy developed close ties with some of the women and men she worked with. She continues to correspond with old friends from college and graduate school, and she exchanges holiday greetings with lots of acquaintances. Sometimes when Lucy looks back on her life, she wonders how she could have lost touch with people who were once so important to her—first Tanya, then Lynnette, and finally Jody. How can you be so close to someone at one time in your life, and end up so different? Can you count on keeping old friends and even making new ones all through life?

Dimensions of Time in the Study of Close Relationships

Just as people grow and change over time, yet possess certain enduring characteristics, so do close relationships. The intersection of close relationships and time can be described in terms of four domains: personal (development of personality, cognitive and social abilities, and other attributes over the life span), social (life course stages such as infancy, childhood, adolescence, adulthood, and old age, and the roles and statuses associated with each), relational (beginning, middle, or end of a close relationship, for instance), and historical (ancient philosophers' views of relationships compared to contemporary perspectives and the influence of historical events on cohorts of people and on their relationships). The focus of this chapter is on the ways in which these intersecting dimensions of time affect close relationships in people's lives, using friendship as an illustrative case.

Compared to dating and marriage, friendship is a close relationship that has received relatively little scholarly attention. In the past, for instance, researchers often distinguished family from other types of relationships but did not study the other categories separately, implying that friends, neighbors, coworkers and others are all alike. More recently, studies focusing specifically on friendship have revealed that defining friendship can be tricky. On the one hand, almost anyone can say what "friend" means and even articulate differences between best, close, and casual friends. Most people believe that friendship involves sharing and caring—evidence of similarity and emotional closeness. Most people assume that friends are chosen voluntarily (whereas relatives are not chosen and we typically have less choice about coworkers and neighbors than about friends) and that friendships are egalitarian. In contrast to the legal relationships that exist between spouses and between parents and children, no laws govern friendships.

On the other hand, investigators of friendship are demonstrating that some assumptions about it are not necessarily accurate. Friends may be freely chosen, but the choice occurs within the context of a social structure that provides opportunities to meet some kinds of people and limits chances to meet others, making friendship not entirely voluntary. Notice, for example, that Lucy's new friends in college came from her major—the situation that commanded most of her time and energy. Not all friendships are intimate and egalitarian, either. Some people use friendships to advance themselves socially, economically, or politically.

Friendship, like other close relationships, exists within contexts of both stability and change. Friendship is stable in the sense that people have friends throughout their lives and probably enact friendships fairly similarly over the life course according to their personality characteristics and social skills. Also, friendships change as people seek out different kinds of friends at different life stages or as particular friendships grow emotionally closer or more distant. Consider the various changes in Lucy's relationships with Tanya, Lynnette, and Jody. History reveals that conceptions of friendship change over time. The following sections elaborate on these intersecting influences of time on friendship. More details can be found in a book that I wrote with Rebecca Adams (1992).

Individual Development

Like Lucy, most people have friends from earliest childhood to the last of life. Looking over the years of a person's life reveals that friendship varies according to individual developmental characteristics such as personality, level of cognition, social skills, and needs. Stephanie Tesch's 1983 analysis of friendship across the life span showed, for instance, that the meaning of friendship changes with age as children and adolescents gradually add new dimensions to their definitions of "friend." Shared activity emerges as an important aspect of friendship in childhood and continues through adolescence and adulthood. Loyalty and mutual aid become key elements of friendship to preadolescents. Teenagers place less value on the mutual benefits of friendship than children do, and they become capable of sharing intimate information with their friends. The influence of friends on one's self-concept is probably strongest during the adolescent years. Adults focus less on similarity and more on uniqueness among friends than teenagers do. Expectations of continued intimacy and reciprocal dependability among friends endure throughout adulthood. Old age seems to be the time when interaction with friends contributes more to life satisfaction than contact with family members. (For other reviews of research on the connection between individual development and friendship over the life cycle, see chapters by Douglas Kimmel, published in 1979, and by Wenda Dickens and Daniel Perlman, published in 1981.)

Note that the interaction between friendship and individual development is two way: experiences that people have with friends can affect their personal development. To give an example of research that demonstrates this point, in 1986 Kenneth Tokuno examined the ways friends influence the transition from adolescence to young adulthood. Based on indepth interviews, he identified five categories that summarize the processes involved. First, friends serve as role models. They perform actions that alter one's own behavior or self-concept; they report on their experiences from which one can learn vicariously; or they model behavior that alters one's conception of categories of people. Second, friends are active agents of change or development. They give advice, guidance, and information; they encourage one to participate in joint activities that may influence one's habits or interests; and they attempt to convince one to pursue a course of action. Third, friends react to one's decisions and give support, encouragement, and reassurance that enables one to act or maintain a decision. Fourth, friends encourage personal growth by requesting help for themselves and by engaging in discussions of different points of view. This process emphasizes the reciprocal nature of friendship. Finally, friends influence development passively when they make themselves available to listen uncritically, when they are understanding, and when they provide a reference group that offers a sense of belonging.

Robert Hays, writing in 1988, pointed out that all through life people must restructure their friend networks to correspond to their changing identities and life situations. In fact, a person's development may be enhanced by letting go of certain friendships. Hays found, for example, that college freshmen adapted better when they incorporated new friends who were college students into their social networks. Those who clung to their old high school and neighborhood friends who were not college students found it more difficult to adjust to college.

Life Course Stages and Social Structure

Friendship varies with a person's life course stage and position in the structure of society. With respect to life course stage, in an interesting 1990 essay, B. Bradford Brown postulated that infancy is a time of orientation to friendship involving joint exploration of the environment among babies. Childhood serves as a stage of socialization into the friendship role as children try out many ways of being friendly with many different age mates. Adolescence functions as a time of investment in friendship as teenagers broaden emotional commitment from the family exclusively to same- and cross-sex peer relationships. In turn, young adulthood represents a stage of adjustment to friendship in the context of other close relationships and emerging responsibilities, middle age harbors a term of selective maintenance of core friendships in the face of competing obligations in multiple social roles, and old age signifies a period of reinvestment in friendship made possible by decreased family and work responsibilities.

People's social structural characteristics also affect their friendships. As discussed in the book that I wrote with Rebecca Adams (published in 1992), opportunities for and constraints on forming and maintaining friendships vary with the roles that people play in society, with their gender, racial/ethnic characteristics, socioeconomic class, marital and employment status, and with other social features. For example, college students like Lucy have many opportunities to meet other students of approximately their same age, but relatively fewer chances to make friends with young adult nonstudents or with people who are older or younger than they are. Married couples tend to establish joint couple friendships and limit their friendships with individuals, especially those of the opposite sex. People who are retired may miss the built-in contact with friends that work affords, or they may relish the free time that enables them to make friends with people in new groups and activities. Friendships tend to be homogeneous across gender, racial/ethnic, and class lines because people usually spend time with others who are like themselves, live in similar neighborhoods, and enjoy the same activities.

Relationship Phases and Processes

Friendships are not static, but rather, have beginnings, periods of endurance and change, and endings. Each phase of friendship is varied and complex, with many possibilities for how it is played out. Change from one phase to another—for instance, from first impression to closest friendship—can occur rapidly or slowly. The length of each phase—building, sustaining, declining—varies across people and circumstances. Movement from one phase to another is sometimes deliberate and sometimes occurs by happenstance. Not all phases occur in all friendships; some never move beyond the early "just acquaintance" stage, others become deeply intimate and endure for decades with no sign of ending.

Friendship phases occur as a result of processes—thoughts, feelings, and behaviors—in which partners engage. Cognitive or thought processes can be about the self, the friend, and the friendship. Examples include the definitions of "friend" that people hold and how they evaluate their own and their friends' performances of the friend role, assess the stability of the friendship, explain events that occur in the friendship, interpret either partner's intentions or needs, or judge characteristics such as attractiveness and similarity. Affective processes encompass emotional reactions to friends and friendship, such as trust, loyalty, satisfaction, indifference, anger, or jealousy. Behavioral processes are the action components of friendship, including, for instance, communication, help and support, displays of affection, conflict, manipulation, or betrayal (see Blieszner & Adams 1992, for more details).

Friendship phases and processes interact with individual development and stage of the life course. It should be obvious that level of maturity and associated social roles affect what processes partners will use in developing their friendship and what phases the friendship will go through. Preschoolers have fleeting friendships based on momentary sharing of interests and activities; adults can employ cognitive and social skills to cultivate friendships that are mutually satisfying, can weather separation or conflict, and meet many different types of needs.

Historical Perspectives

Conceptions of friendship—what it is and how friends should act—change over historical periods. Looking back to the ancient philosophers, William Sahakian noted in 1974 that early ideas about friendship were rooted in philosophical questions about the relationship between social justice and personal happiness. Early Greek and Roman philosophers held the conviction that wholesome biological and psychological development resulted in spiritual or moral character. For example, according to Mark Snyder and Dave Smith's review in 1986, Plato viewed true friendship as deriving from basic human needs and wants, such as striving toward goodness, desiring to be affiliated with others, seeking self-understanding, and needing to love and be loved. Aristotle elaborated on the notion of ideal versus illusory friendship by defining three types of friends, each of which serves different functions. Friendship for the sake of utility and friendship for the sake of pleasure are imperfect types, because the primary motive is to benefit the person forming the friendship. In contrast, perfect friendship, which benefits both partners, occurs between people who admire each other's qualities of goodness, mutually value the benefits of the friendship, and take pleasure in each other's presence. Cicero's typology of friendship included two forms, a superficial type between dissimilar persons who affiliate for self-beneficial reasons and a deeper type between partners who are similar with respect to character and virtue. (Michael Pakaluck provided, in 1991, an extensive collection of excerpts on friendship from many classical thinkers).

In a contemporary test of Aristotle's typology of friendship among college students, William Bukowski and his colleagues reported in 1987 that goodness was, indeed, more central to friendship than enjoyableness or utility. That is, friendships characterized by goodness tend also to feature enjoyableness and utility, but friendships characterized by either enjoyableness or utility will not necessarily feature the other properties. They also found that male students were more likely than female students to differentiate between same-sex and opposite-sex friends on the basis of goodness and enjoyableness, suggesting that men and women use affective dimensions, or feelings, differently when rating their friendships. The results of this research show that in a general sense, modern students' perceptions of friendship are in accord with Aristotle's philosophical discourse.

Other analyses of friendship, based on consideration of changes in its enactment and functions over historical periods, have appeared recently. Helena Lopata published one such summary in 1990. From primitive to medieval times, people spent their days in close association with relatives and many other community members, presumably having many friend relationships. As commerce developed in medieval Europe, social activity took place in the streets and markets, and friendships existed across sex, age, and class distinctions. As more emphasis was placed on privacy in the nuclear family and work was separated from the home setting, friendships became less central in people's lives and were limited to others of similar sex, age, and class. Later, industrialization resulted in little time for leisurely social contacts, again diminishing the perceived importance of friendship.

Stacey Oliker's 1989 examination of gender differences in notions and styles of friendship revealed that the eighteenth and nineteenth century patterns described previously existed more for men than for women. Women's friendships with each other were highly romanticized, providing a counterpoint to the romantic, companionate ideal in marriage that was difficult to acquire in a society that increasingly separated the spheres of men and women. Later, when romantic friendships were viewed with suspicion, women were encouraged to intensify their emotional involvement in marriage, and their friendships became less romantic in tone.

In contrast to Lopata's assessment that the emergence of the market economy led to the decline of intimate relationships outside the family, Allan Silver argued in 1990 that commercial society actually enabled friendship based on sympathy and affection (instead of on commercial interests) to emerge. Industrialization resulted in the separation of impersonal, market-based relationships from more personal friendships that excluded notions of exchange and utility. In 1989 Eugene Litwak likewise asserted that the unique characteristics of friendships, as compared to kin, coworker, or neighbor relations, give them special roles to play in people's lives. For instance, because of similarity of age and life style, friends are often better than anyone else at helping with figuring out one's identity, reminiscing, giving advice, providing socialization for new roles, and sharing leisure activities. These historical analyses of friendship illustrate the enduring nature of friendship as a close and supportive relationship despite differences in social expectations of friends over the eras.

Theory and Methods in the Study of Close Relationships Over Time

As evident in the previous section, friendship has many characteristics in common with other close relationships. In fact, it is not unusual to hear a person say, "My wife [or husband or sister] is my best friend," blurring the distinction between kinship and friendship. Some unique features of friendship were high-lighted earlier, but on the other hand, all types of close relationships change over time, affect the partners involved in them, occur as a result of processes, and serve important support functions in people's lives. In fact, scholarly writing about social and emotional support demonstrates the similarities between friendship and other close relationships—people obtain such sustenance from a variety of significant others. Because friends are selected and are not bound by legalities, most people consider them to be special relationships. To give just one example, Greg Arling (1977) found that friends (and neighbors) were more beneficial to the morale of older widows than family members were—perhaps because friends are usually peers who share similar interests and values.

Life-Span Development and Life-Course Analysis

What behavioral science perspectives underpin the analysis of the intersection of close relationships and dimensions of time? Two major theoretical traditions, life-span developmental psychology and life-course analysis in sociology, are influential. The life-span development approach had its origins in biologically-based developmental psychology. It emerged when researchers discovered that stage-oriented, fixed-sequence, hierarchical principles of development, although useful for describing and explaining children's growth patterns, do not apply well to the diversity observed in adulthood and old age. Instead, a more flexible model of development is needed, one that takes into account the overlapping influences of biological, social, and historical factors. Users of the life span development approach typically focus on aspects of individual development such as personality and cognition.

Life-course analysis in sociology evolved as researchers acknowledged that historical and cultural changes affect social structure, which in turn influences the trajectories of people's lives. Initial work within the life-course perspective was concerned, for example, with the effects of age stratification on individual opportunity or the influence of history and culture on status achievement. Both approaches address differences within and between people over time and attempt to explain how, when, and why change occurs and how individuals adjust to it. (For more detail on these perspectives, see an article published by Paul Baltes in 1987 on life-span developmental psychology, one written by Gundhild Hagestad in 1990 on the life course, and one by Rosemary Blieszner and Jay Mancini from 1992 on a developmental perspective of close relationship loss.)

Recently, social scientists who study close relationships have become aware of their dynamic nature and of myriad influences on them. They realize that both life-span and life-course conceptions of development and change can be applied to the analysis of close relationships, including friendship. For example, friendships exist for various periods of time and their length is likely to affect the processes that take place between friends and the outcomes they experience. Moreover, the life stage, concurrent roles, cognitive capacity, personality traits, and other characteristics of individuals are also likely to influence the experience of friendship, as is the historical period in which the friends live. Thus it is possible and desirable to study close relationships from a temporal and multidisciplinary perspective, combining such an approach with theoretical propositions from traditional scholarly fields such as social and clinical psychology, communications, family studies, and sociology.

The following chapters of this book provide many examples of traditional theory as applied to close relationships. Relevant questions to ask in each case, from the life-span and life-course points of view, are: Do the principles of close relationship behavior under consideration vary across people's developmental stages? Do they vary among different subgroups of the population? Do they operate similarly in new and more established relationships? Have they changed over historical time?

To take an example from the domain of psychology, cognitive theories such as attribution (e.g., the ways that people explain events that occur in the relationship) and self-monitoring (e.g., how concerned people are about the image they project to others) have been used in friendship studies. From the perspective of this chapter, it would be inappropriate to assume that such cognitive processes operate in the same manner across the entire life span or across all phases of friendship development. Rather, determination of whether they are similar or different, and identification of predictors of similarities or differences across age or other groups, are examples of the empirical focus that researchers using a multidisciplinary life-span/life-course perspective would take.

One of the limitations of close relationship research, including friendship research, is that studies typically have been conducted with only a narrow range of respondents (often college students) without replication among other groups or in different decades. Thus, the data needed to answer the previously-mentioned questions, such as the same assessments from multiple age and social groups, typically do not exist.

Methodological Implications

Early research on social relationships often was conducted in laboratory settings, using experimental techniques to discover, for instance, the effects of people's physical appearance on perceptions of whether or not they wanted to get to know each other better. The problem with much of that research is that the interactions were usually quite short and often took place between people who had just met in the lab setting. Thus, although the results were informative for understanding certain aspects of what attracted people to each other, they were less useful for analyzing characteristics of enduring relationships. Recognition of the dynamic and multidimensional nature of close relationships has led to an expanding array of research methods employed to study them. Researchers have focused on actual ongoing partnerships and have used participant observation, survey, indepth interview, daily interaction diary, and focus group techniques to gain insights into what affects interaction patterns among friends and other close persons.

Because they acknowledge the influence of time on people's lives, full application of the life span and life course perspectives to close relationship research requires short- and long-term longitudinal designs. Repeated measurements of the same persons and relationships are necessary to address questions about whether and how friendships change as people age, as relationships endure over time, and as historical periods pass. Longitudinal studies in the friendship literature have been fairly short, ranging from a few weeks to about four years in duration. So far, then, data exist on stability and change within particular friendships but not on aging or cohort (historical period) effects.

Research Findings: Sample Case of Friendship

Toward a Life-Span View of Friendship

Early empirical research on friendship centered on children. Many studies of children's peer relationships and friendships were conducted in the 1920s and 1930s by psychologists, sociologists, and educators. According to Steven Asher and John Gottman, who edited a book on children's friendship in 1981, these scientists contributed to the advancement of research methods, including sociometric techniques, observation strategies, and the use of experimental research designs in field settings. Their studies were not developmental, however, typically focusing on one age group but not attempting to examine changes in friendships over time, as noted by Peter Renshaw in 1981. After several decades of focusing more on parent-child relationships than on peer relationships, the 1970s brought a renewed interest in studying children's social skills and peer relationships. Topics included children's definitions of friendship, expectations of friendship, and meanings attached to friend interactions. Other research focused on developmental issues such as the link between childhood social relations and psychological outcomes in adulthood, according to Kenneth Rubin and Hildy Ross, 1982, and Stephanie Tesch, writing in 1989.

As the emphasis on understanding adolescent development increased, scholars began to recognize both that the nature of friendship was likely to change as youth confronted new developmental tasks and that friends could influence the course of a teenager's development (refer to the earlier discussion of Tokuno's 1986 study). Subsequent studies of childhood and adolescent friendship provided theoretical and methodological background for the development of research on adult friendship.

In contrast to the fairly long history of research on child and teenage friendship, systematic study of adult friendship only began in the last twenty-five years. Before that, the record shows scattered descriptive studies. For example, in 1934 Raymond Cattell, a psychologist, identified personality and temperament traits associated with being chosen as a friend; in 1959 Robin Williams, a sociologist, studied the functions of friendship; and in 1969 Robert Paine, an anthropologist, grappled with distinguishing friendship conceptually from kin and other social relationships. Then in 1972 Beth Hess published a major review of the friendship studies from the 1940s through the 1960s. Her analysis of the connections among age, life course stage, and friendship structure and processes set the stage for a developmental perspective of friendship as defined in this chapter.

Although research on the connection between friendship and the structure of the adult life course and on certain friendship processes has a somewhat longer history, most studies of the ways adult friendships are formed and change over time are less than a decade old. There are few investigations of how adult friend relationships contribute to an individual's development. Yet, the value of studying friendship across the adult years is apparent given an increased awareness of the effects of early life experiences on later development, demographic trends leading to the graying of the population, changes in family ties in our mobile society, and public policy emphasis on informal sources of support for servicing the needs of older adults.

Findings from Contemporary Studies

Although the literature does not contain examples of studies that account for friendship across multiple stages of individuals' lives and across historical periods, researchers have examined various phases of friendship in several different age groups. The results illustrate the dynamic nature of friendship.

For example, in a series of reports on short-term longitudinal studies with college students presented in 1984 and 1985, Robert Hays described attitudinal and other behavioral changes as partners moved from acquaintanceship to close friendship. The friendships that became closer over time, compared to those that did not, increased in amount and breadth of interaction and moved from fairly superficial to increasingly intimate levels of behavior exchange. A similar description of friendship initiation appeared in research by Leslie Baxter and William Wilmot in 1986. Thus, multiplex relationships, those that include a variety of shared interests and activities, seem to be important for friendship development among college students. Despite some decline in interaction frequency, growing friendships were rated increasingly higher on intimacy over time, showing that friendship bonds were more dependent on affection than on frequency of contact. Respondents whose friendships grew, compared to nonfriends, reported more relationship benefits and increasing benefits over time. The two groups did not differ on perceived costs, implying that benefits are more important than costs in friendship development.

In terms of predictors of friendship initiation and development, John Berg reported in 1984 on a longitudinal study of dyads who began the academic year as unacquainted roommates and ended it by deciding whether or not to live together the following year. Students who chose not to continue living together had decreased in liking and satisfaction with the friendship over time, reported a decrease in help received from their roommates, saw themselves as dissimilar to their roommates, and evaluated their current living arrangement less favorably than alternatives. Like Hays (1984), Berg found that the decision about whether to continue the friendship was made fairly early in the relationship.

Turning to friendship initiation among elderly persons, several studies are available. First, Sarah Matthews provided, in her 1986 book, indirect evidence suggesting that friendship formation occurs throughout life. By means of retrospective interviews about respondents' life histories, Matthews identified three styles of friendship behavior reflecting patterns that had emerged over their lives. Members of the group she termed acquisitive were more likely than others to continue to make new friends in the later years. These individuals reported that their friend networks increased in size as they experienced life events such as job changes, relocation, or changes in marital status.

Direct evidence about friendship initiation in old age appears in an article by Laurie Shea, Linda Thompson, and Rosemary Blieszner, published in 1988. We investigated friendship development among strangers who moved into a newly-constructed retirement community all at the same time. Within five months of becoming acquainted, respondents differentiated among their old and new friends on both subjective and behavioral measures. They reported more liking, loving, and commitment for friends who grew closer than for those who became less close.

At the beginning of the study, old friends, acquaintances who eventually became friends, and acquaintances who did not become friends did not differ on the perceived likelihood or actual frequency of exchanging resources such as favors, information, and so on. But five months later, old friends and new ones who became closer received higher scores on the likelihood and frequency of exchange measures than did friends who became more distant. Thus, both affective and behavioral variables are important contributors to the evolution of new friendships in old age. In the respondents' own words, "Our feelings are so much closer and more intense because of the time spent together, enjoying each other," "We are now more open with admiration and compliments," "She's the first one I go to with a problem . . . it's nice to have a friend who will tell me the truth and give me good advice," "She helps me now . . . she knows I appreciate it . . . I wish I could do more for her—but there was a time when I helped her a lot too. That's how friendships are. You help each other when the other is in need."

What people do to keep their friendships going has also been the focus of research with various groups of adults. One way that partners maintain their friendships, according to Michael Argyle and Monika Henderson's 1984 research, is to follow the normative rules of friendship concerning behavioral exchanges, intimacy, relations with respect to third parties outside the dyad, and coordination of interaction. Of course, the ability to keep the rules depends on both knowing them and possessing the requisite social skills to follow them. Several researchers found that the strategies used to maintain friendships varied by level of closeness. For example, Argyle and Henderson (1984) observed that some rules were kept more often in close than in casual friendships. Keeping casual friends as opposed to close or best friends required more physical proximity but less affection, whereas retention of close and best friendships required at least some expressed affection and a great deal of interaction, according to a study by Susanna Rose and Felicisima Serafica in 1986. Robert Hays's 1989 study also showed that, compared to casual friends, close friends interacted more frequently, interacted across a greater range of settings, felt that their interactions were more exclusive and provided more benefits, and weighted costs of friendship less heavily.

What factors contribute to the endurance of closeness over time? Em Griffin and Glenn Sparks published a report in 1990 indicating that they were better able to predict male-male closeness after four years than female-female closeness. Significant predictors of male-male friendship closeness as measured at the beginning of the study were perceived status similarity, shared knowledge, being roommates, and fewer taboo topics of conversation. Another important predictor was geographic distance after four years, with those living closer together being emotionally closer as well. Overall, similarity seemed to be important for continued closeness, at least for male friends.

Several researchers have looked at friend retention strategies of older adults. For example, Matthews (1986) found that some friendships endured due to favorable social circumstances, such as visits to the home town or school reunions, rather than to respondents' explicit efforts to maintain them. Other friendships continued over time because the partners engaged in letter writing, telephoning, and visiting, or they selected a retirement community near their friends or went on vacations together. These more active versus rather passive styles of friendship maintenance seemed to be linked both to individual personality characteristics and to lifelong friend interaction styles.

Elderly people may use different maintenance strategies for old than for new friends (Shea et al. 1988). Respondents took expressions of affection as givens in old friendships, whereas new ones required displays of affection to aid in their growth and maintenance. Conveying esteem for each other was crucial for both ongoing and fairly new friends. Respondents valued advice from their old friends and engaged in reminiscing and self-disclosure with them, but the information they shared with new friends focused more on current day-to-day events and less personal topics. Old friends exchanged various forms of services and assistance as needed, and study participants appreciated the help and support that old friends had provided over the years. Exchange of services was not, however, a significant part of relationship maintenance between new friends, and those who did do favors for each other had a concern about reciprocity that was not evident in the discussions of old friendships.

By studying a unique population, Glen Elder and Elizabeth Clipp (1988) uncovered other influences on friendship maintenance. They examined social bonding among old male veterans of the Armed Forces. Having shared intense combat experiences and losses of comrades, veterans retained strong ties to service friends because "the act of remembering a life period or event maintains contact with people who were important at the time. Such memories perpetuate social bonds and are, in turn, sustained by them" (p. 193). Such ties can serve a very beneficial purpose by helping veterans overcome the long-term stresses associated with combat experience.

Friend networks not only endure throughout life, they also can change in old age just as at any other stage. Adams (1987) observed this in a three-year investigation of older women and their networks. When study participants had been freed from the constraints on their friendships imposed by obligations to family, community, and work during middle age, they became liberated from their old patterns and developed different networks.

Friendships, like other close relationships, do not always last indefinitely, though. Argyle and Henderson (1984) found that friendships fell apart when one of the partners violated general rules of friendship such as keeping confidences and not criticizing one's friend in public. Lack of social skills, inappropriate forms of self-disclosure, inability to express feelings, failure to conform to resource exchange expectations, and having less time to spend together because one of the partners established a romantic relationship are other causes of friendship decline, according to Steve Duck (1981) and Suzanna Rose (1984). Also, a friendship might lapse if either partner's criteria for what they like in a friend change, or if a friend changes in directions that lead to display of traits or behaviors that the partner dislikes (Hays 1988; Rose 1984).

College students invoke varied ways of terminating friendship. Argyle and Henderson (1984) discovered that, just as relationship rules affect friendship initiation and maintenance, they also operate to structure the disengagement process when friendship lapses. At such a time, partners uphold general informal social rules but not specific friendship rules about intimacy and support, thus maintaining the social norm of commitment to the ideal of a relationship despite lack of closeness. In Rose's (1984) study, some students ended friendships via physical separation, such as failing to exchange addresses when one partner moved away. Others simply replaced old friends with new ones, often under amiable circumstances. Individuals tended to be less direct in disengaging from friendships than from romantic liaisons, as discussed by Leslie Baxter in 1985.

In Matthews's (1986) research on older adult friendships, it appeared that friendships just faded away due to diverging lifestyles and pathways over the years; few individuals actively terminated friendships. Some friendships deteriorated because one of the partners became ill or moved away. Because these friendships had not ended in disharmony, respondents felt they could revitalize them if circumstances should permit—unlike the assumption of a permanent rift that younger adults tend to hold when a friendship disintegrates.

As pointed out earlier and illustrated by this sample of research results, it is difficult to compare friendship phases across age groups because different aspects of friendship have been examined in the various studies. Nevertheless, the findings reveal that individuals actively seek out friendships, work to keep them going, and, sometimes, must cope with friendship loss. Understanding of the particular processes that underlie each phase of friendship awaits application of specific theoretical propositions associated with the thoughts, feelings, and actions of the relationship partners, as discussed in subsequent chapters of this book.

Conclusions and Summary

The story of Lucy's life, seen through the lens of changing friendship experiences, illustrates the importance of close relationships to people of all ages. Theories about and methods of studying close relationships over time as described previously can be applied to the whole life span, to many kinds of relationships besides friendship, and to multiple phases of relationships. If detailed information about all sorts of close relationships were available for children, youth, and adults, a greater understanding of how people negotiate close relationships, how such relationships affect partners, and how to help those with relationship problems would be possible. This is an important goal for future close relationship research.

As shown in this chapter and throughout this book, many descriptions of friendship and other close relationships exist, and many variables have been correlated with aspects of close relationships. Most of this research has been conducted from the researcher's point of view, with only a few investigators starting from the perspective of everyday people when developing their theory or designing their research. Thus, relatively little is known about the meaning that people ascribe to different kinds of close relationships; how that meaning might change over the course of the partners' lives, over the duration of the relationship itself, and over historical eras; and how that meaning affects the development of those who are involved together. Thus, another important goal for future studies is investigation of the connection between the meaning of relationships and the multiple dimensions of time that can affect them.

References

Adams, R. G. 1987. Patterns of network change: A longitudinal study of friendships of elderly women. *The Gerontologist*, 27:222–27.

Argyle, M., and M. Henderson. 1984. The rules of friendship. *Journal of Social and Personal Relationships*, 1:211–37.

Arling, G. 1977. The elderly widow and her family, neighbors and friends. *Journal of Marriage and the Family*, 38:757–68.

Asher, S. R., and J. M. Gottman, ed. 1981. Editorial preface. *The development of children's friendships*, xi–xiv. Cambridge: Cambridge University Press.

Baltes, P. B., 1987. Theoretical propositions of lifespan developmental psychology: On the dynamics between growth and decline. *Developmental Psychology*, 23:611–26.

Baxter, L. A. 1985. Accomplishing relationship disengagement. In *Understanding personal relationships*, ed. S. Duck and D. Perlman, 243–65. London: Sage.

Baxter, L. A., and W. W. Wilmot. 1986. Interaction characteristics of disengaging, stable, and growing relationships. In *The emerging field of personal relationships*, ed. R. Gilmour and S. Duck, 145–159. Hillsdale, NJ: Erlbaum.

Berg, J. H. 1984. Development of friendship between roommates. *Journal of Personality and Social Psychology*, 46:346–56.

Blieszner, R., and R. G. Adams. 1992. *Adult friendship*. Newbury Park, CA: Sage.

Blieszner, R., and J. A. Mancini. 1992. A lifespan developmental perspective on relationship loss. In *Close relationship loss: Theoretical ap-*

proaches, ed. T. L. Orbuch, 142–54. New York: Springer-Verlag.

Brown, B. B. 1990. A life-span approach to friendship. In *Friendship in context*, ed. H. Z. Lopata and D. R. Maines, 23–50. Greenwich, CT: JAI Press.

Bukowski, W. M., B. J. Nappi and B. Hoza. 1987. A test of Aristotle's model of friendship for young adults' same-sex and opposite-sex relationships. *The Journal of Social Psychology*, 127:595–603.

Cattell, R. B. 1934. Friends and enemies: A psychological study of character and temperament. *Character and Personality*, 3:54–63.

Dickens, W. J., and D. Perlman. 1981. Friendship over the life-cycle. In *Personal relationships 2: Developing personal relationships*, ed. S. Duck and R. Gilmour, 91–122. London: Academic Press.

Duck, S. 1981. Toward a research map for the study of relationship breakdown. In *Personal relationships 3: Personal relationships in disorder*, ed. S. Duck and R. Gilmour, 1–29. London: Academic Press.

Elder, G. H., Jr., and E. C. Clipp. 1988. Wartime losses and social bonding. *Psychiatry*, 51:177–98.

Hagestad, G. O. 1990. Social perspectives on the life course. In *Handbook of aging and the social sciences*, 3rd ed., ed. R. H. Binstock and L. K. George, 151–68. San Diego: Academic Press.

Hays, R. B. 1984. The development and maintenance of friendship. *Journal of Social and Personal Relationships*, 1:75–98.

———. 1985. A longitudinal study of friendship development. *Journal of Personality and Social Psychology*, 48:909–24.

———. 1988. Friendship. In *Handbook of personal relationships*, ed. S. W. Duck, 391–408. Chichester, England: Wiley.

———. 1989. The day-to-day functioning of close versus casual friendships. *Journal of Social and Personal Relationships*, 6:21–37.

Hess, B. B. 1972. Friendship. In *Aging and society*, ed. M. W. Riley, M. Johnson, and A. Foner, vol. 3, 357–393. New York: Russell Sage.

Griffin, E., and G. G. Sparks. 1990. Friends forever: A longitudinal exploration of intimacy in same-sex friends and platonic pairs. *Journal of Social and Personal Relationships*, 7: 29–46.

Kimmel, D. C. 1979. Relationship initiation and development: A life-span developmental approach. In *Social exchange in developing relationships*, ed. R. L. Burgess and T. L. Huston, 351–377. New York: Academic Press.

Litwak, E. 1989. Forms of friendships among older people in an industrial society. In *Older adult friendship*, ed. R. G. Adams and R. Blieszner, 65–88. Newbury Park, CA: Sage.

Lopata, H. Z. 1990. Friendship: Historical and theoretical introduction. In *Friendship in context*, ed. H. Z. Lopata and D. R. Maines, 1–22. Greenwich, CT: JAI Press.

Matthews, S. H. 1986. *Friendships through the life course*. Beverly Hills: Sage.

Oliker, S. J. 1989. *Best friends and marriage*. Berkeley, CA: University of California Press.

Pakaluck, M. 1991. *Other selves: Philosophers on friendship*. Indianapolis, IN: Hackett.

Paine, R. 1969. In search of friendship: An exploratory analysis in "Middle-class" culture. *Man*, 4:505–24.

Renshaw, P. D. 1981. The roots of peer interaction research: A historical analysis of the 1930s. In *The development of children's friendships*, ed. S. R. Asher & J. M. Gottman, 1–25. Cambridge: Cambridge University Press.

Rose, S. M. 1984. How friendships end. *Journal of Social and Personal Relationships*, 1:267–77.

Rose, S., and F. C. Serafica. 1986. Keeping and ending close and best friendships. *Journal of Social and Personal Relationships*, 3:275–88.

Rubin, K. H., and H. S. Ross. 1982. Some reflections on the state of the art: The study of peer relationships and social skills. In *Peer relationships and social skills in childhood*, ed. K. H. Rubin & H. S. Ross, 1–8. New York: Springer-Verlag.

Sahakian, W. S. 1974. *Systematic social psychology*. New York: Chandler.

Shea, L., L. Thompson, and R. Blieszner. 1988. Resources in older adults' old and new friendships. *Journal of Social and Personal Relationships*, 5:83–96.

Silver, A. 1990. Friendship in commercial society: Eighteenth-century social theory and modern sociology. *American Journal of Sociology,* 95:1474–1504.

Snyder, M., and D. Smith. 1986. Personality and friendship: The friendship worlds of self-monitoring. In *Friendship and social interaction,* ed. V. J. Derlega and B. A. Winstead, 63–80. New York: Springer-Verlag.

Tesch, S. A. 1983. Review of friendship development across the life span. *Human Development,* 26:266–76.

———. 1989. Early-life development and adult friendship. In *Older adult friendship,* ed. R. G. Adams and R. Blieszner, 89–107. Newbury Park, CA: Sage.

Tokuno, K. A. 1986. The early adult transition and friendships: Mechanisms of support. *Adolescence,* 21:593–606.

Williams, R. 1959. Friendship and social values in a suburban community. *Pacific Sociological Review,* 2:3–10.

Chapter 2

Methods of Studying Close Relationships

WILLIAM ICKES
University of Texas at Arlington

Outline

Something unusual is happening here. For as long as you have known them, your best female friend Janice and your best male friend Don have simply not gotten along. As much as you like them as individuals, and as often as you have tried to bring them together, they have always seemed to get on each other's nerves. You can feel the tension between them whenever they are in the same room, and you have often wondered why it is that two people whom you like so much don't seem to like each other.

But what's really got you wondering lately is this: Why, three days after Janice broke off her engagement to her fiance, Bobby, did you see Don's car parked in front of her apartment as you drove by on your way to class? And why, after calling Janice last night and discovering that her line was busy, did it happen that when you tried to call Don, you discovered that his line was busy too? Could it be that Janice and Don are not as uncomfortable around each other as you thought? Could it be that the tension you have felt between them in the past was not the "push" of magnetic poles that repel each other but the "pull" of magnetic poles that attract?

Naturally, as nosy as you are, you won't be able to rest until you find out for sure, one way or the other . . .

How Do We Learn About Close Relationships in Our Everyday Lives?

But where do you go from here? If you really want to know if (and when, and how, and why) the relationship between Janice and Don has changed, what options are available to you for obtaining this information? You quickly run through a mental list, which, if you took the time to organize it, might look something like this:

1. Ask Janice to tell me what is going on.
2. Ask Don to tell me what is going on.
3. Get them both together and confront them with my suspicions.
4. Get them both together, but play it cool and observe them closely.
5. Ask around and see if our mutual friends know anything.
6. Put a tap on Janice's telephone line. Ditto Don's.
7. Intercept Janice's mail. Ditto Don's.
8. Sneak a long look at Janice's diary. Don's too, if he has one.
9. Hire private detectives to follow them around and report back.
10. Bug their apartments with listening devices.
11. Bug their persons with locating devices.
12. Hide video cameras in their apartments to record their behavior.
13. Sit them down side-by-side, hooked up to a Libido Meter.
14. If all else fails, read their minds.

With the possible exception of items 13 and 14, which suggest that you were beginning to drift off into Fantasyland, the items in this list appear to provide a useful summary of the different methods you could use to investigate Janice and Don's relationship. Some of these methods are more exotic and complicated than others, but they all represent ways that people can and do use to investigate relationships in everyday life. Indeed, it may not surprise you to learn that social scientists have drawn from a highly similar list of methodological options in their more formal and systematic attempts to study close relationships. But which of these methodological options should you choose? And how should you decide?

Like the social scientists who study relationships, you must choose one or more of these options based on a comparative analysis of the relative advantages and disadvantages (e.g., the pros and cons) associated with each. Moreover, this comparison of the different methods' advantages and disadvantages must be made within the context of your own goals as a researcher. In other words, like more formally trained students of close relationships, you will have to begin by dealing with what we will call the trade-off problem.

The Trade-Off Problem

Whenever you settle on a single method for studying any phenomenon, including a close relationship, you simultaneously gain some things and lose others. The choice you make represents a complex trade-off in which the combined strengths and weaknesses of the method that you decide to use are weighed against the combined strengths and weaknesses of any alternative method(s) that you decide not to use. Some of the trade-offs that are commonly encountered in the study of close relationships are described below.

Choosing One Perspective Over Another

If you choose Option 1 from your list ("Ask Janice to tell me what's going on"), you may stand a good chance of getting Janice to give you her perspective on her relationship with Don. However, if Option 1 is the only option you choose, you will obtain Janice's perspective at the expense of the perspectives that you might have obtained if you had selected Option 2 ("Ask Don") or Option 5 ("Ask our mutual friends") instead. In deciding to seek one perspective at the expense of some other(s), you are implicitly making judgments about whose perspective is likely to be the most accurate, unbiased, uncensored, perceptive, fully informed, and so on. If you choose to seek the wrong perspective—one that is inaccurate, uninformed, biased, or misleading—you risk coming to the wrong conclusion about Janice and Don's relationship.

Choosing One Level of Analysis Over Another

If you choose either Option 1 ("Ask Janice") or Option 2 ("Ask Don"), the information you obtain from each person as an individual may be different from the information you would obtain if you chose Option 4 and studied Janice and Don together, as a couple. For example, when interviewed separately, Janice and Don might deny that they have any romantic interest in each other; however, their verbal or nonverbal reactions when you observe them together might tell you just the opposite. If you choose to inquire about their relationship at the "wrong" level of analysis (e.g., at the individual, rather than the dyadic, level), you may again risk reaching a conclusion that is misleading or incorrect.

Choosing an Obtrusive Method Over an Unobtrusive One

Some of the methods in your list (in particular, Options 1, 2, and 3) are obtrusive in that they blatantly convey to Janice and Don your interest in their relationship. All of the remaining methods are somewhat more unobtrusive in that they seek to obtain the same information without alerting Janice and Don of your interest. If you think that Janice and Don are motivated to lie to you or mislead you, an obtrusive method is likely to fail to tell you what you really want to know. On the other hand, the use of an unobtrusive method incurs certain risks as well. For example, what would happen if Janice and Don discover that you have been "spying" on them by listening in on their conversations (Options 6 and 10), reading their private thoughts and feelings (Options 7 and 8—and 14!), or covertly monitoring their behavior (Options 9, 11, and 12). At best, they might become more suspicious and guarded around you in the future; at worst, they might sue you for invading their privacy!

Because unobtrusive methods involve some form of spying, there are potential ethical and practical costs associated with them. From an ethical standpoint, these methods can violate the subjects' right to privacy and reveal things about them and their relationships that they would prefer to keep to themselves. From a practical standpoint, these methods can be costly to implement as well. Installing a phone tap, purchasing video equipment, or retaining the services of a private detective can be expensive ways to find out what you want to know. These costs, like the others just mentioned, must also be considered when you choose among the various options on your list.

Choosing an Ethically Questionable Method Over an Ethically Safe One

Let's face it—some of the methods in your list are either ethically questionable (Options 8 and 9, for example) or downright illegal (Options 6 and 7). Given the high potential costs associated with such ethically questionable methods (losing the trust of the people you are studying, being arrested, getting sued, and so on), when—and why—would you ever consider using them?

In general, you probably would not consider using them. Your society holds you accountable for your unethical behavior in the same way that various legal, professional, and social institutions hold social scientists accountable for their unethical behavior. In fact, social scientists typically have to submit descriptions of their proposed research projects for approval by Institutional Review Boards (IRBs) before they can even begin to collect their data. These review boards are charged with the task of ensuring that any research projects they approve are ethically defensible and involve only a minor and acceptable level of risk to any potential subject's well-being.

However decisions of this type are not always easy to make. Ethical considerations such as invasion of the subjects' privacy must be balanced against the importance to society of the knowledge to be gained from the research. An assessment of the method's informativeness and freedom from self-presentation bias must also be weighed against its potential threat to the subjects' privacy and well-being. Finally, it should be recognized that a given research method may be more or less ethically defensible, depending on the circumstances in which it is applied. If, for example, subjects sign a consent form notifying them at the outset that certain behaviors may be observed and recorded unobtrusively, they have effectively granted their permission to allow some limited invasion of their privacy to occur. Even in cases such as this, however, the subjects' privacy is in a larger sense still protected by the researcher's pledge to keep their identities confidential and to use their data "for statistical purposes only."

Choosing a Method Reflecting One "Philosophy" versus Another

So far, this discussion of the trade-off problem has sounded like a cost-benefit analysis that takes no account of the researcher's own philosophy and theoretical commitments. It is time to correct that impression. The researcher's choice of a method is strongly (and, in some cases, perhaps entirely) determined by her theoretical and philosophical assumptions about the phenomenon being investigated. As Steve Duck (1992, personal communication) has noted:

> For instance, no one would do diary and interaction record studies who did not believe that subjects could recall or introspect about their personal relationships with a certain degree of acceptable accuracy. By contrast, someone who does observational studies is usually of the opinion that people can be biased and mistaken when they report on their behavior, and are influenced by psychological dynamics that do not corrupt an outside observer. In other words, the selection of methods is not necessarily an intellectually neutral enterprise, but instead involves the implicit adoption of a perspective from which to see things—and an implicit set of values as well.

Solutions to the Trade-Off Problem

We will consider many more of these trade-off issues in the remainder of this chapter and in the chapters to follow. Before we do, however, it may be useful to consider the most obvious and common sense solution to the trade-off problem: using multiple methods that complement each others' strengths and compensate for each others' weaknesses.

For example, instead of seeking only Janice's perspective (Option 1), you might invest the extra time and effort required to seek Don's perspective (Option 2) and the perspective of your mutual friends (Option 5) as well. Although more costs are involved in obtaining these additional sources of data, some potential benefits may also result. In the ideal case, all three sources of data would agree, increasing your confidence that Janice and Don's relationship really has changed, consistent with your hypothesis. But even if all three sources of data do not converge on the same conclusion, the overall pattern of data may still provide you with greater insight into what is actually happening. Suppose that your mutual friends all agree that Don has fallen in love with Janice, but that neither Janice or Don is willing to acknowledge that this is true. Considering (a) that Janice has just broken up with Robby, and may be feeling confused about whom she really loves—Robby or Don, and (b) that Don may be feeling guilty about being the cause of their breakup, you may be able to conclude that Janice and Don's relationship really has changed, although neither of them is yet willing to publicly acknowledge that it has.

Similarly, by complementing Janice and Don's individual accounts (Options 1 and 2) with information about how they relate to each other when they are observed together (Option 4), you may again be able to conclude that their relationship really has changed, but that neither of them is yet willing to publicly acknowledge it. Obtaining more unobtrusive measures of Janice and Don's behavior (Options 6 through 12) may further confirm your suspicions, despite their public denials. In other words, the convergence or triangulation of data obtained by different methods or from different sources is likely to provide a more complete and accurate view of the relationship than is any single type of data taken by itself (Duck, 1990).

How Do Social Scientists Learn About Close Relationships?

As the example of Janice and Don suggests, social scientists learn about close relationships in essentially the same ways that we do in our everyday lives. The methods that social scientists use are similar to ours, only more systematic, and in some cases, more sophisticated. In the sections to follow, we will briefly review these methods, which include self-report, peer report, observational, life-event archival, experimental, and physiological methods, along with eclectic approaches in which multiple methods are combined. Beginning in most cases with a representative research example, we will examine the purposes and procedures of each method and consider the kinds of questions that are typically used for study. We will then turn to a discussion of the trade-off problem in close relationship research, and explore a range of possible solutions to this problem. As we will see, these solutions implicate both the methods that social scientists use and the theories that they apply in their study of close relationships.

Self-Report Methods

Self-report methods have been used more frequently than any other type of method to study close relationships. These methods require one or more of the relationship members to serve as respondents, providing data in the form of verbal or written information about the relationship. This information is assumed to be subjective to the extent that it reflects the particular viewpoint of the respondent who provided it. Self-report methods in close relationship research include

(a) questionnaire studies,
(b) face-to-face or telephone interview studies,
(c) diary and account studies,
(d) interaction record studies, and
(e) epistolary studies of written correspondence.

Questionnaire Studies

Leanne Lamke (1989) conducted a questionnaire study to determine how the gender-role orientations of married couples were related to their marital adjustment and satisfaction. In her study, nearly 300 couples living in rural Alabama were mailed paper-and-pencil survey questionnaires that about a third of these couples completed and returned. By having both husbands and wives complete the Personal Attributes Questionnaire (Spence, Helmreich, and Stapp 1975), Lamke was able to measure the extent to which each partner reported having such "feminine" traits as nurturance, caring, gentleness, and kindness, and such "masculine" traits as assertiveness, dominance, and decisiveness. And, by having both husbands and wives complete the Spanier Dyadic Adjustment Scale (Spanier 1976), Lamke was able to measure the extent to which each partner was satisfied with the marital relationship.

Lamke found that the wives' marital satisfaction was not predicted by their husbands' masculine traits such as dominance and decisiveness ($r = .05$), but was instead predicted by their husbands' more feminine traits such as being kind, affectionate, and caring ($r = .43$). Similarly, the husbands' marital satisfaction was not predicted by their wives' masculine traits ($r = .10$), but was strongly predicted by their wives' feminine traits ($r = .51$). For both husbands and wives, it appears that "happiness is having a feminine marriage partner" (Ickes 1985, p. 200).

Lamke's questionnaire study is typical in that it attempted to relate one or more predictor variables (self-reported masculine and feminine traits) to one or more criterion variables (self-reported marital satisfaction). Most questionnaire studies of close relationships are of this type. They seek to relate external predictors such as demographic characteristics (e.g., age, ethnicity), personality traits (e.g., shyness, femininity), and situational factors (e.g., employment status, incidence of neighborhood crime) to the respondents' subjective perceptions about one or more aspects of their close relationship (e.g., satisfaction, conflict resolution). The typical goal of this research is to increase our understanding of how individuals' social identities, personalities, and life circumstances affect the way their close relationships are experienced and described (Harvey, Hendrick, and Tucker 1988).

Not all questionnaire studies are conducted by mail however. College-age respondents are often asked to respond to research questionnaires in classroom or laboratory settings (e.g., Simpson and Gangestad 1991). They may enter their responses into a computer or mark them down on computer-scorable answer sheets instead of writing them directly on the questionnaire itself. While mail-out surveys can be a useful way to sample the responses of people in the community at large, such people can also be reached through survey questionnaires published in local or national newspapers and magazines (e.g., Shaver and Rubenstein 1983).

As Susan and Clyde Hendrick (1992) have noted, "the development of relationship-oriented [questionnaire] measures has greatly increased in recent years, so that now there are measures for love (e.g., Hendrick and Hendrick 1986), intimacy (e.g., Lund 1985), romantic beliefs (e.g., Sprecher and Metts 1989), self-disclosure (e.g., Miller, Berg, and Archer 1983), and a host of other concepts" (p. 11).

Interview Studies

Self-report data can also be collected through either face-to-face or telephone interview studies. For example, John Antill and his students used face-to-face interviews to collect the same type of data that Lamke (1989) later collected by mailing out questionnaires (Antill 1983). After recruiting potential subjects at various shopping centers in the metropolitan area of Sydney, Australia, Antill's research assistants conducted in-home interviews with 108 married couples. During these interviews, both spouses independently provided responses to the Bem Sex-Role Inventory (Bem 1974) and the Spanier Dyadic Adjustment Scale (Spanier 1976). Like Lamke (1989), Antill (1983) found that marital satisfaction for both husbands and wives was uniquely predicted by the degree to which their partners were seen as having the traditionally feminine traits of being kind, considerate, and emotionally supportive.

It is possible that the same data could have been collected through telephone interviews as well. However, Antill's decision to conduct face-to-face interviews probably reflected his belief that subjects who were interviewed by telephone would have been less cooperative in providing a large number of responses about a highly personal matter (i.e., their marital satisfaction) to an anonymous caller.

Diary and Account Studies

Paul Rosenblatt, while doing research on romantic love, came across the diary of Mollie Dorsey Sanford (1959) and was so fascinated by it that he spent several years "tracking down unpublished nineteenth century diaries with material on close relationships." He soon realized that "grief was the most common aspect of the close relationships that was represented in the diaries. A few diaries dealt with marital disenchantment, a few with courtship, a few with problems in childrearing; but many dealt with deaths and separation" (Rosenblatt 1983, p. vii).

Rosenblatt's analysis of these diaries addressed a range of issues regarding the grief process, including the time course and patterning of grief, the events and occasions that re-invoke it, and the ways that individuals and family systems attempt to cope with it. Diary studies have not been frequently used in the study of close relationships, and they represent a rich and largely untapped source of data. It may be possible, for example, to compare the size and diversity of individuals' social networks through the data available in their diaries, with *The Diary of H. L. Mencken* providing a prototypical example.

Accounts of close relationships can be found in a variety of forms. "Naturalistically, they may appear in diary form or in recordings, letters and notes, and even videotapes" (Harvey et al. 1988, p. 108). In one recent study, subjects were asked to provide a running commentary on their conversation with a co-participant on a microcomputer network (Daly et al. 1989). The typical focus of most account studies focus is the differences that are found when separate accounts of the same relational event(s) are compared. For example, the accounts of marriage partners can reveal differences so striking that it appears "as if there are two different relationships cohabiting in one marriage" (Mansfield and Collard 1988, p. 39). Even the accounts of the same individual can differ substantially as time passes and the benefits of hindsight accumulate (Burnett 1987; Harvey et al. 1988).

Interaction Record Studies

The use of interaction record studies in relationship research is based on the assumption that people can monitor their social life while they are in the process of living it. To appreciate this assumption, imagine that as you interact with various people during the course of a typical day, you take mental notes on each of these interactions. You remember the time of day each interaction occurred, how long it lasted, the number of people you were with, the gender of these interaction partners, how pleasant or unpleasant the interaction was, and so on. Periodically, you retrieve these interaction records from your memory and convert them into written form. The data in these written records are subsequently analyzed to determine what your general pattern of social interaction looks like: whether you have many social contacts or only a few, whether your interactions are mostly with members of the same sex or with members of the opposite sex, how much you self-disclose and to whom, and so on.

Interest in this research method was stimulated by a series of studies conducted by Ladd Wheeler, John Nezlek, Harry Reis, and their colleagues at the University of Rochester (Reis and Wheeler 1991). In these studies, college-age subjects used the Rochester Interaction Record (RIR)—a standardized form depicted in Figure 2–1—to make a record of each of their social interactions that lasted 10 minutes or longer. The subjects were asked to keep these records for an extended period of time (typically, 10–14 days) in order to adequately sample their general pattern of social activity. To date, the RIR has been used to study a range of topics that include loneliness (Wheeler, Reis, and Nezlek 1983), adaptation to the college environment (Wheeler and Nezlek 1977), the impact of physical attractiveness on one's social life (Reis, Nezlek, and Wheeler 1980), and the tendency to withdraw from other relationships during the later stages of courtship (Milardo, Johnson, and Huston 1983).

More recently, Steve Duck and his colleagues at the University of Iowa have developed the Iowa Communication Record (ICR) to permit a more focused and

DATE _____ TIME _____ AM _____ LENGTH: _____ HRS _____ MIN _____
PM _____

INITIALS _____ _____ _____   IF MORE THAN 3 OTHERS:

SEX _____   # OF FEMALES _____ # OF MALES _____

INTIMACY:	SUPERFICIAL	1	2	3	4	5	6	7	MEANINGFUL
I DISCLOSED:	VERY LITTLE	1	2	3	4	5	6	7	A GREAT DEAL
OTHER DISCLOSED:	VERY LITTLE	1	2	3	4	5	6	7	A GREAT DEAL
QUALITY:	UNPLEASANT	1	2	3	4	5	6	7	PLEASANT
SATISFACTION:	LESS THAN EXPECTED	1	2	3	4	5	6	7	MORE THAN EXPECTED
INITIATION:	I INITIATED	1	2	3	4	5	6	7	OTHER INITIATED
INFLUENCE:	I INFLUENCED MORE	1	2	3	4	5	6	7	OTHER INFLUENCED MORE

NATURE: WORK   TASK   PASTIME   CONVERSATION   DATE

FIGURE 2–1   The Rochester Interaction Record

intensive study of the conversations that take place between interaction partners (Duck 1991). The ICR contains questions about the content of the conversation, the context in which it occurred, and its perceived quality, purpose, and impact on the participants' relationship. Steve Duck, Kris Pond, and Geoff Leatham (1991) have used the ICR in a recent study in which each pair of subjects was videotaped interacting for five minutes while a second pair of subjects observed their interaction. The results indicated that active participants (insiders) and passive observers (outsiders) have different views of the interaction, particularly with regard to its perceived quality and intimacy, even though they have presumably attended to the same behavioral cues. For research suggesting a similar conclusion, see Abbey (1982) and Floyd and Markman (1983).

Interaction record studies using the RIR and the ICR are event-contingent—requiring respondents to report their experience each time an appropriate event (e.g., an interaction at least 10 minutes long) has occurred. In contrast, other interaction record studies have been interval-contingent—requiring respondents to report at regular, predetermined intervals, or signal-contingent—requiring respondents to report whenever signalled by the researcher (Wheeler & Reis, 1991). For example, Dirk Revenstorf and his colleagues used an interval-contingent interaction record study when they asked couples involved in marital therapy to make daily ratings of six aspects of their relationship (Revenstorf et al. 1984).

These data were subsequently analyzed using time series statistics in order to assess the changes that occurred in the couples' relationships over time.

Signal-contingent studies require subjects to complete an interaction record whenever the experimenter signals them by means of a telephone call or the beeping of an electronic pager. In an elegant study using telephone calls both to signal the subjects and record their responses, Ted Huston and his colleagues phoned married couples nine times during a two- or three-week period. During these calls, each spouse was asked to report on activities in the past twenty-four hours that included household tasks, leisure activities, positive and negative interaction events, conflict, and conversations (Huston et al. 1987). In a study which sampled the day-to-day experiences of 170 high school students, Maria Mei-Ha Wong and Mihaly Csikszentmihalyi (1991) used preprogrammed electronic pagers to signal their teenage subjects to complete a behavioral self-report measure at randomly determined intervals. One of their strongest findings was that the girls spent more time with friends and less time alone than the boys.

Epistolary Studies

An analysis of letters (e.g., epistles) and other forms of written correspondence (e.g., electronic mail) represents another way in which self-report data can be used to study relationships. As Catalin Mamali has noted in his epistolary study of the relationship between Theodore Dreiser and H. L. Mencken, the letters which two people exchange can provide coherent, chronological records of interpersonal cognitions, emotions, accounts, communications, and actions (Mamali 1991). They can be very useful in documenting a consistent style of relating to others, as evidenced by the relentlessly irreverent letters of Groucho Marx (1987). Because written correspondence is also a mode of relating to others, epistolary studies may also have much to teach us about the dynamics of personal relationships as they are expressed in this as well as in other modes (Mamali 1992).

Peer Report Methods

Peer report methods have rarely been used in the study of close relationships. These methods require one or more knowledgeable informants to serve as respondents, providing data in the form of verbal or written information about the relationship(s) of people with whom they are acquainted.

In contrast to research using self-report methods, which frequently seeks evidence of differences in the viewpoints of the individual relationship members, research using peer report methods frequently seeks evidence of agreement or consensus among the set of peer respondents in their perceptions of a given relationship. Whereas self-report research tends to focus on the different subjective reactions of the individual members of a relationship, peer report research tends to focus on the shared intersubjective reactions of a set of peers who all view the relationship from the outside, as observers and knowledgeable informants. Theoretical interest in the agreement or consensus of peer reports is based on the assumption that such consensus is not coincidental, but points instead to genuine relational phenomena that are potentially worthy of study.

In theory, peer report methods in relationship research can take the same forms as self-report methods:

(a) questionnaire studies,
(b) face-to-face or telephone interview studies,
(c) diary and account studies,
(d) interaction record studies, and
(e) epistolary studies of written correspondence.

In practice, however, close relationship researchers have seldom attempted to collect peer report data—even though they are the kind of data that are routinely collected by biographers and social historians (see, for example, Jean Stein's (1982) biography of Andy Warhol's protege Edith Sedgwick—a biography composed entirely of excerpts from the conversational accounts of people who knew Edie, or knew of her). Still, if researchers are willing to invest the time and effort required, they could probably learn much by asking knowledgeable observers of a given relationship to complete questionnaires, answer interview questions, provide written accounts, keep interaction records, or allow their own correspondence about the relationship to be examined.

Observational Methods

There is a simple way to distinguish peer report studies from observational studies in relationship research. Peer report studies, in the strictest sense of the term, involve verbal or written reports made by observer-acquaintances whose insights are based on their cumulative knowledge of the relationship members and the history of their relationship. In contrast, observational studies involve summary judgments or behavioral records made by trained raters who typically have no prior knowledge of the relationship members or the history of their relationship. An important consequence of this distinction is that peer report studies are extremely rare in close relationship research whereas observational studies are relatively common.

As Ickes and Tooke (1988) have noted, the range of relationships that have been studied by observational methods is impressively large:

> To cite just a few representative examples, the observational method has been applied to the study of children's quarrels (Dawe 1934) and children's friendships (Gottman and Parker 1986). It has been used to explore the interactions of poker players (Hayano 1980), police officers (Rubenstein 1973), prison inmates (Jacobs 1974) distressed and nondistressed married couples (Gottman 1979), and the families of schizophrenics (Cheek and Anthony 1970). In clinical and counseling psychology, its most common application has been to the study of therapist-client relationships (Jones, Reid, and Patterson 1975; Scheflen 1974). (p. 80)

The range of behaviors that can be observed and recorded is also impressively large, and may be limited only by the researcher's imagination. According to Karl Weick (1968), researchers may study nonverbal behaviors such as facial expressions, directed gazes, body movements, and interpersonal distance; extralinguistic behaviors such as the pitch, amplitude, and rate of speech; and linguistic behaviors such as giving suggestions, expressing agreement, or asking for an opinion or evaluation. In some studies, researchers may examine only one behavior, such as the eyeblinks that people display when they are observed in natural settings (Ponder and Kennedy 1927). In other studies, researchers may examine several behaviors, such as the talking, smiling, gazing and gesturing of opposite-sex strangers (Garcia et al. 1991). Researchers may also explore more extensive patterns of behavior, such as the reciprocation of negative feelings during conflict by distressed versus nondistressed married couples (Gottman 1979).

Although many observational studies are conducted in laboratory settings (e.g., Gottman, Markman, and Notarius 1977; Ickes 1984), many others are conducted in real world settings as diverse as an auction (Clark and Halford 1978), a party (Riesman and Watson 1964), a high school (Barker and Gump 1964), a hospital delivery room (Leventhal and Sharp 1965), a police station (Holdaway 1980), a subway train (Fried and DeFazio 1974), and the United Nations building (Alger 1966). Whatever setting is chosen, it is important that the observation itself be as unobtrusive as possible. Recording the subjects' interaction by means of a hidden video camera for later analysis (Ickes 1983; Ickes et al. 1990) provides one means of ensuring that the subjects' behavior will not be biased by the presence of trained raters on the scene. Having college roommates start an audio tape recorder in their dormitory room whenever they begin a conversation is also a relatively unobtrusive way to study their naturally occurring interactions (Ginsberg and Gottman 1986). However, putting directional microphones in subjects' faces and requiring them to interact in front of a camera crew or in the presence of trained raters will virtually guarantee that their behavior will be altered or interfered with by the recording process itself.

Life-Event Archival Methods

Some of the problems explored by relationship researchers can be studied by means of life-event data that are publicly available in archival sources. A good example is the archival study by Frank Trovato of the relationship between divorce and suicide in Canada (Trovato 1986, 1987; Trovato and Lauris 1989). Susan and Clyde Hendrick (1992, pp. 14–15) have described this study as follows:

> *Trovato used census-type demographic data from all the Canadian provinces to assess the impact of divorce on suicide, taking into consideration the effects of other variables such as educational level, religious preferences, marriage rates, and geographical mobility between provinces. He determined that divorce has a substantial effect on suicide rate (1986), and he did this without administering a single questionnaire or making even one behavioral observation.*

Trovato's findings were similar to those of Steven Stack, who used the same kinds of archival data to test the relationship between divorce and suicide in the United States (Stack 1980; 1981) and in Norway (Stack 1989). As this set of studies illustrates, data concerning major live events can be obtained from national agencies that compile statistics from official records such as divorce decrees and birth, marriage, and death certificates. Researchers such as Stack and Trovato can then use these archival data to test important hypotheses about personal relationships without having any direct contact with the subjects of their research. Of all of the methods available for conducting relationship research, the archival methods are the least obtrusive. For this reason, they are the least likely to be biased by the subjects' reactions to the researcher.

Experimental Methods

Experimental methods in relationship research are used to determine whether changes in the level of certain independent variables cause corresponding changes to be observed in the level of one or more dependent variables. In any application of the experimental method, the independent variables are the ones that are systematically manipulated by the experimenter, whereas the dependent variables are the ones that are subsequently measured by the experimenter. For a study to qualify as a true experiment, two criteria must be met. First, the experimenter must manipulate, or systematically vary, the level of the independent variable (the specific treatment that subjects receive) across the set of experimental conditions. Second, the experimenter must randomly assign the subjects (as individuals, dyads, groups, etc.) to each of the experimental conditions.

For example, William Ickes, Miles Patterson, D. W. Rajecki, and Sarah Tanford (1982) conducted a study in which one member of each pair of male strangers (the perceiver) was randomly assigned to receive one of one of three different kinds of pre-interaction information about the other member (the target). Specifically, some perceivers were led to expect that their target partners would act very friendly, others were led to expect that their partners would act very unfriendly, and a third (control) group was given no expectancy information. Of course, the information the perceivers received was in no case based on what their interactional partners were actually like; it was instead manipulated independently by the experimenters.

The results of the study converged to suggest that, relative to the no-expectancy perceivers, the friendly-expectancy perceivers adopted a reciprocal interaction strategy (one designed to reciprocate the friendly behaviors they expected their partner to display), whereas the unfriendly-expectancy perceivers adopted a compensatory interaction strategy (one designed to compensate for the unfriendly behaviors they expected their partner to display). Because the experimenters determined what kind of expectancy information the perceivers received, and the subjects (perceivers and targets) were randomly assigned to the three expectancy conditions, the differences in the perceivers' behavior in the three conditions could be attributed to the different expectancies that were created rather than to differences in the types of subjects assigned to the three conditions. In other words, the only plausible cause of the difference in the perceivers' behavior in the three conditions was the difference in the expectancies which the experimenters had established.

As this example suggests, researchers who use the experimental method in relationship research often seek to identify those independent variables whose manipulation establishes the varying conditions in which different types of relational phenomena (for example, reciprocity versus compensation) will be observed. Occasionally, however, experimenters may pursue the opposite goal of manipulating the presence or absence of certain relational phenomena in order to assess their effects on subjects' perceptions of the relationship (e.g., Clark 1985; Clark and Mills 1979).

Physiological Methods

Perhaps the most fanciful option in our list of ways to discover Janice and Don's true feelings about each other is Option 13: "Sit them down side-by-side, hooked up to a Libido Meter." This option may be more realistic than it sounds, however. A growing number of relationship researchers are using physiological methods to determine how their subjects respond to others at the visceral level, that is, the level at which various bodily reactions are measured. Men's sexual arousal, for example, is often assessed by means of a mercury-in-rubber strain gauge which measures changes in penile tumescence (i.e., degree of erection). If we could somehow persuade Don to wear the penile gauge while reading two sexual scenarios—one in which he made love to Janice and one in which he made love in the same way to his ex-girlfriend, Linda—we might expect his "Libido Meter" to reveal greater sexual arousal in response to Janice than to Linda.

It is important to realize, however, that the same method we might use to assess Don's passionate love for Janice could be used to assess socially undesirable forms of sexual arousal as well. As Neil Malamuth (1986) has noted, a measure called the penile tumescence rape index has proven useful in distinguishing rapists from nonrapists. Research with this index suggests that men whose maximum penile tumescence in response to a rape scenario is greater than their maximum tumescence to a consensual sex scenario may have a predisposition to rape (Quinsey et al. 1987).

Physiological methods have also been used to demonstrate that a high level of physiological arousal during marital conflict is strongly correlated with a long-term decline in marital satisfaction. Robert Levenson and John Gottman (1983, 1985) arranged to have 30 married couples argue about high-conflict issues in the laboratory while their physiological reactions (heart rate, skin conductance, etc.) were monitored. When they contacted the couples three years later, they found that the couples whose marital satisfaction had declined the most were the same couples who had displayed the greatest physiological arousal during the laboratory conflict. In fact, "the correlation between the husband's heart rate during the conflict discussion and decline in marital satisfaction was .92"

(Gottman and Levenson 1986, p. 41). Apparently, having a marital partner who makes your heart beat faster is not always a good thing!

Eclectic Approaches

In contemporary research on relationships, it is becoming increasingly common for researchers to use eclectic approaches which combine two or more of the types of methods described above. The researcher's goal in these cases is to combine the different methods in such a way that they build on each other's strengths and compensate for each other's weaknesses. A useful example of the eclectic approach is the unstructured dyadic interaction paradigm developed by William Ickes (who feels weird referring to himself in the third person) and his colleagues (who feel weird being referred to as "et al.") (Ickes 1983; Ickes and Tooke 1988; Ickes et al. 1990).

The general procedure is as follows: the members of each dyad—who can be strangers, acquaintances, or intimates, depending on the purposes of the study—are led into a waiting room and left there together in the experimenter's absence. During this time in which the subjects are ostensibly waiting for the experiment to begin, their verbal and nonverbal behaviors are unobtrusively audio- and videotaped. When the experimenter returns at the end of the observation period, the subjects are partially debriefed and asked for their signed consent to release the videotape of their interaction for use as data. They are also asked to participate in a second part of the study that concerns the specific thoughts and feelings they had during the interaction.

If their signed consent is given, the subjects are then seated in separate but identical cubicles where they are each instructed to view a videotaped copy of the interaction. By stopping the videotape with a remote start/pause control at those points where they remember having had a specific thought or feeling, each subject makes a written, time-logged listing on a standardized form (see Figure 2–2, left) of these actual thought-feeling entries. The subjects are then instructed to view the videotape a second time, during which the tape is stopped for them at each of those points at which their interaction partner reported a thought or feeling. The subject's task during this pass through the tape is to infer the content of their partner's thoughts and feelings and provide a written, time-logged listing on a second, standardized form (see Figure 2–2, right) of these inferred thought-feeling entries. When both subjects have completed this task, they are asked to complete a posttest questionnaire assessing their perceptions of themselves and their partner during the interaction. They are then debriefed more completely, thanked, and released.

The unstructured dyadic interaction paradigm combines a number of the methods already described in this chapter. First, the observational method is used when the participants' interaction behavior is unobtrusively recorded on audio- and videotape for later analysis. Second, the subjects are cued by the events recorded on the videotape to make an event-contingent self-report interaction record of their own thoughts and feelings during the interaction. Third, they are then cued by the same videotape to make an event-contingent peer-report inter-action record of the inferred thoughts and feelings of their interaction partners. Fourth, the subjects complete a posttest questionnaire in which they provide additional self-report and peer-report data. Fifth, in some cases the experimental method can be incorporated into this procedure, as illustrated by the previously-described study in which one male dyad member was randomly designated to

DATE _____
NUMBER _____
M   F

TIME	THOUGHT OR FEELING	+, 0, −	
	☐ I was thinking: ☐ I was feeling:	+ 0 −	
	☐ I was thinking: ☐ I was feeling:	+ 0 −	
	☐ I was thinking: ☐ I was feeling:	+ 0 −	
	☐ I was thinking: ☐ I was feeling:	+ 0 −	
	☐ I was thinking: ☐ I was feeling:	+ 0 −	
	☐ I was thinking: ☐ I was feeling:	+ 0 −	
	☐ I was thinking: ☐ I was feeling:	+ 0 −	
	☐ I was thinking: ☐ I was feeling:	+ 0 −	
	☐ I was thinking: ☐ I was feeling:	+ 0 −	
	☐ I was thinking: ☐ I was feeling:	+ 0 −	

DATE _____
NUMBER _____
M   F

TIME	THOUGHT OR FEELING	+, 0, −	
	☐ He/she was thinking: ☐ He/she was feeling:	+ 0 −	
	☐ He/she was thinking: ☐ He/she was feeling:	+ 0 −	
	☐ He/she was thinking: ☐ He/she was feeling:	+ 0 −	
	☐ He/she was thinking: ☐ He/she was feeling:	+ 0 −	
	☐ He/she was thinking: ☐ He/she was feeling:	+ 0 −	
	☐ He/she was thinking: ☐ He/she was feeling:	+ 0 −	
	☐ He/she was thinking: ☐ He/she was feeling:	+ 0 −	
	☐ He/she was thinking: ☐ He/she was feeling:	+ 0 −	
	☐ He/she was thinking: ☐ He/she was feeling:	+ 0 −	
	☐ He/she was thinking: ☐ He/she was feeling:	+ 0 −	

FIGURE 2–2   Standardized forms for recording actual and inferred thoughts and feelings.

receive false feedback about the friendliness or unfriendliness of the other male dyad member before their interaction took place (Ickes et al. 1982, Experiment 1).

To further illustrate the eclecticism of this procedure, imagine that we are able to study Janice's and Don's relationship using the unstructured dyadic interaction paradigm. By means of the posttest questionnaire data, we can ask straightforward questions about Janice's view of the relationship (Option 1 of our original list) and about Don's view of the relationship (Option 2). By means of the unobtrusive audiotaping and videotaping procedure (Options 10 and 12), we can observe Janice and Don closely while they are left alone together (Option 4). By means of the thought/feeling records they are later asked to create, we can read their private thoughts and feelings as directly as if we were reading their personal diaries (Option 8)—and almost as directly as if we were reading their minds (Option 14!). And, by comparing the content of Janice's actual thoughts and feelings with the content of Don's inferences about her thoughts and feelings (and vice versa), we can even determine how good they are at reading each other's minds (Ickes et al. 1990; Ickes et al. 1990; Stinson and Ickes 1992)!

The Trade-Off Problem in Close Relationship Research

Earlier in this chapter it was noted that any choice of method for studying relationships represents a complex trade-off—one in which the combined strengths and weaknesses of the method that the researcher decides to use are weighed against the combined strengths and weaknesses of any alternative method(s) that the researcher decides not to use. What are the strengths and weaknesses of the various methods we have reviewed above? What kinds of trade-offs do researchers typically make when choosing to use one method instead of another? In what ways can different methods be combined so as to complement each others' strengths and compensate for each others' weaknesses?

Strengths and Weaknesses of the Various Methods

Each type of method used by relationship researchers is characterized by its own distinctive strengths and weaknesses. Following are summaries of these strengths and weaknesses:

Self-Report Methods

According to John Harvey and his colleagues (Harvey, Christenson, and McClintock 1983; Harvey et al. 1988), there are at least three major advantages of using self-report methods to study relationships. First, self-reports are relatively easy, efficient, and inexpensive to obtain from the participants in the relationships. Second, they represent the only way researchers currently have to access purely subjective events, such as the participants' thoughts, feelings, perceptions, expectancies, and memories. Third, they enable researchers to obtain the participants' reports of certain overt behaviors that are typically private, and that might otherwise remain inaccessible to study (for example, conflict and sexual behavior).

Contrasted with these strengths are a variety of weaknesses (Duck and Sants 1983; Harvey et al. 1983, 1988; Huston et al. 1987; Wheeler and Reis 1991). First, participants may not understand the researchers' questions, or may interpret them differently from the way the researchers intended. Second, the participants' self-reports may be biased by:

(a) poor, selective, or distorted memory,
(b) reactions against what are perceived to be invasive and inappropriate questions by the researcher,
(c) egocentric reactions that fail to give appropriate weight to the relational perceptions of one's interaction partners,
(d) egodefensive reactions designed to promote a favorable view of oneself and one's actions, and
(e) "errors in the calculation of events, questionnaire response biases, and so on" (Harvey et al. 1988, p. 110).

Third, any single participant's view of the relationship is necessarily incomplete, and there is no guarantee that combining the individual views of all the participants will produce an image that is any more coherent than that of the blind men's views of the elephant. Fourth, the degree to which the researcher is perceived by the participants as an insider or outsider may not only affect their trust and willingness to self-disclose but can also alter the dynamics of the relationship itself (Levinger 1977).

Of course, some types of self-report methods are less susceptible than others to the problems described earlier. For example, misunderstanding or misinterpreting the researchers' questions is not an issue that is relevant to diary and epistolary studies. And memory-based biases can be reduced, if not eliminated, in interaction record studies if relational events are recorded as soon as possible after they occur (Huston et al. 1987; Wheeler and Reis 1991). Other forms of bias may be difficult to eliminate, however, and collectively may constitute the greatest potential threat to the validity of any methods that rely exclusively on the participants' self-reports.

Peer Report Methods

Peer report data can be used to obtain information about the subjective thoughts and feelings of relationship participants which they have confided to peer respondents. In addition, such data can provide some insight into private behaviors, such as sex and conflict, which the relationship members may have confided to their peers. However, peer report data are not as easily and inexpensively obtained as self-report data, because they require the researcher to identify knowledgeable peer respondents and persuade them to provide information about the relationship of people who, if still living, may regard their cooperation in the research enterprise as both an invasion of privacy and a breach of trust. They are also susceptible to many of the same biases as self-report data, although some of the biases of individual respondents may be cancelled out when their data are combined with those of other respondents.

Observational Methods

At their best, observational data can have the weight of objectively recorded facts. To the extent that they were obtained in an unobtrusive, nonreactive manner and are based on representative samples of the participants' behavior, observational data may be among the most valid types of data available. On the other hand, observational data are expensive and inconvenient to obtain. In most cases, they require sophisticated electronic equipment to record the succession of events that unfold over time in the relationships being studied. In nearly all cases, they require the presence of trained raters to code and often re-code various aspects of the participants' behavior from the resulting behavioral records. Moreover, the analyses of such data are typically complicated by the between-dyad and within-dyad interdependence of the participants' responses (Bissonnette 1992; Kenny 1988; Kenny and Kashy 1991). Finally, observational methods may require that the participants' privacy be invaded, and may raise other ethical questions as well (Middlemist, Knowles, and Matter 1976, 1977; Koocher 1977).

Life-Event Archival Methods

As noted earlier, life-event archival methods have a number of advantages. They do not require researchers to collect original data, allowing them to rely instead on statistical information about major life events (births, marriages, divorces, etc.) that have previously been compiled by various public agencies. Moreover, because archival methods do not require researchers to have any direct contact with the subjects of their research, they are among the most unobtrusive and nonreactive methods available. On the other hand, archival data can display some serious limitations as well. For example, "because of idiosyncrasies and/or shortcomings in methods of reporting," different institutions (different cities, counties, states, etc.) may provide data that differ substantially in their accuracy, their completeness, and the criteria used in compiling them (Cox, Paulus, and McCain 1984, p. 1149). In addition, relationships based on summary statistics for large populations "may not accurately reflect the actual experience" of the individuals who comprise the summary statistics (Baum and Paulus 1987, p. 541).

Experimental Methods

The major advantage of using experimental methods to study relationships is the ability of well-designed experiments to establish causal relationships between independent variables that are manipulated by the experimenter and dependent variables that are measured by the experimenter. There are three major disadvantages of using experimental methods, according to Charles Tardy and Lawrence Hosman (1991). First, many laboratory studies create interaction situations that may strike the participants as being somewhat artificial or unnatural—a criticism that is less often applied to field experiments conducted outside of the lab. Second, the typical experiment confronts the participants with a psychologically strong situation that encourages them to behave as passive reactors rather than as active agents (Ickes 1982; Snyder and Ickes 1985). Third, because the specific conditions established in the experiment may not match the real-world conditions of the participants' everyday lives, the results of experiments may lack ecological validity and may not always generalize well to other settings.

Physiological Methods

The most obvious and unique strength of using physiological measures to study relationships is their potential to measure people's visceral reactions to each other. Countering this strength, however, are certain barriers which John Cacioppo and Richard Petty have described as impeding the application of physiological procedures to the study of important social processes. Perhaps the most daunting of these barriers is the extensive "physiological background, technical sophistication, and elaborate instrumentation that are necessary of collecting, reducing, and analyzing interpretable psychophysiological data in already complex social-psychological paradigms" (Cacioppo and Petty 1986, p. 649). Other obstacles include the high cost (in time, equipment, and trained personnel) of conducting this type of research, the participants' reactivity to certain kinds of physiological measures, and the fact that some physiological measures may be perceived as highly invasive (the strain gauge measure of penile tumescence, for example!).

Typical Trade-Offs in the Choice of a Method

What kinds of trade-offs do researchers typically make when choosing to use one method instead of another? In general, researchers who rely exclusively on self-report data benefit from the convenience of collecting such data and from the insights the data offers into the subjective experience and private behaviors of the relationship members. On the other hand, these researchers run the risk that their self-report data may be biased in any of a number of ways described previously. Moreover, unless they assess the subjective perceptions of all of the participants in the relationship, these researchers may run the risk of obtaining a very one-sided view that, in the worst case, represents the egocentric perceptions of only a single respondent. Finally, unless the researchers' self-report data takes the form of interaction records, they may fail to learn much, if anything, about the specific behaviors on which their subjects' perceptions are presumably based.

Researchers who rely on peer report data will typically make the same kinds of trade-offs, but the problems will be magnified because their respondents are not the actual participants in the relationships being studied, but are instead peer informants. Because these peer informants may differ greatly in how much knowledge they actually have about the relationship, and how willing they are to report gossip and hearsay as fact, it is even more important than in the case of self-report data that the researchers seek evidence of convergence and consensus in their informants' responses.

Researchers who use observational, physiological, and life-event archival methods will typically benefit by obtaining information about the behavior of the relationship participants that is objective, reliable, and free from many of the sources of bias that can plague self-report research. On the other hand, researchers who rely exclusively on these methods may find it difficult to determine the meaning these behaviors have for the relationship members (Harvey et al. 1988). In order to establish this meaning, the objective recording of behavior must be supplemented by the participants' own self-reports.

Finally, researchers who rely exclusively on experimental methods will typically benefit from being able to identify specific causal relationships. The trade-off, however, is they will often incur the risk that these relationships may not generalize well beyond the specific conditions established within the experiment itself.

Combining Methods as a Solution to the Trade-Off Problem

Increasingly, relationship researchers have begun to use eclectic approaches as a solution to the trade-off problem. Their general strategy, as illustrated by the unstructured dyadic interaction paradigm described earlier in this chapter, is to combine different methods in such a way that they build on each other's strengths and compensate for each other's weaknesses. When this strategy is successfully applied, the integration of different methods within a single research project may enable researchers to demonstrate a convergence or triangulation of results across the various methods. It may also broaden the researchers' view of the relational phenomena they are studying in ways that can help them to account for any discrepancies in the patterns of results obtained by one method versus another. Obtaining these important advantages also requires a trade-off however, in that eclectic approaches often require a greater investment of time, effort, and other resources than single-method approaches require.

Conclusions and Summary

What have you learned to this point? Well, you learned this morning from your friend Chris that Janice and Don eloped late last night, and that they are heading for Las Vegas where they plan to be married before continuing on to Lake Tahoe for a two-week honeymoon. Ironically, despite all of your interest, they didn't even bother to tell you; and, as it turns out, you are one of their last friends to know. Not only are you stuck here while they are out in Nevada celebrating the commitment they have made to their relationship; you have to learn the material in this chapter well enough so that you can be tested over it later. No wonder you are sitting here feeling a little depressed and more than a little uninformed.

Don't despair—I have some good news for you. To boost your confidence and to help you to remember the material in this chapter, I offer the following summary statement: "This chapter has reviewed the different research methods by which social scientists have INQUIRED about PEOPLE'S relationships." If you can remember even two words of this summary statement (guess which two words), you should also be able to remember the different types of methods that relationship researchers have used. As you might have guessed, these two words are mnemonic devices or memory aids. More specifically, they are acrostic-anagrams that are formed by taking the first letters of the different types of methods and then re-ordering these letters to form the words INQUIRED and PEOPLE'S.

The second word, PEOPLE'S, is an acrostic-anagram that gives you the first letters of the major types of methods used by relationship researchers. These, in their newly scrambled order, are Peer report, Experimental, Observational, Physiological, Life-event archival, Eclectic, and Self-report. The first word, INQUIRED, is an acrostic-anagram that gives you the first letters of the different subcategories of self-report methods that relationship researchers have used. These letters should help to remind you of INterview studies, QUestionnaire studies, Interaction Record studies, Epistolary studies of written correspondence, and Diary and account studies. In the interest of ensuring that our author-reader relationship will live on in your memory (at least until your exam is over), I leave these two words with you.

References

Abbey, A. 1982. Sex differences in attributions for friendly behavior: Do males misperceive females' friendliness? *Journal of Personality and Social Psychology*, 42:830–38.

Alger, C. F. 1966. Interaction in a committee of the United Nations General Assembly. *Midwest Journal of Political Science*, 10:411–47.

Antill, J. K. 1983. Sex role complementarity versus similarity in married couples. *Journal of Personality and Social Psychology*, 45:145–55.

Barker, R. G., and P. V. Gump. 1964. *Big school, small school: High school size and student behavior*. Stanford, CA: Stanford University Press.

Baum, A., and P. B. Paulus. 1987. Crowding. In *Handbook of Environmental Psychology*, ed. D. Stokols and I. Altman, 533–70. New York: John Wiley and Sons.

Bem, S. L. 1974. The measurement of psychological androgyny. *Journal of Consulting and Clinical Psychology*, 42:155–62.

Bissonnette, V. L. 1992. Interdependence in dyadic gazing. Unpublished doctoral dissertation, University of Texas at Arlington.

Burnett, R. 1987. Reflection in personal relationships. In *Accounting for relationships: Explanation, representation, and knowledge*, ed. R. Burnett, P. McGhee, and D. D. Clarke. London: Methuen.

Cacioppo, J. T., and R. E. Petty. 1986. Social processes. In *Psychophysiology: Systems, processes, and applications*, ed. M. G. H. Coles, E. Donchin, and S. W. Porges, 646–79. New York: The Guilford Press.

Cheek, F. E., and R. Anthony. 1970. Personal pronoun usage in families of schizophrenics and social space utilization. *Family Process*, 9:431–48.

Clark, M. S. 1985. Implications of relationship type for understanding compatibility. In *Compatible and incompatible relationships*, ed. W. Ickes, 119–40. New York: Springer-Verlag.

Clark, M. S., and J. Mills. 1979. Interpersonal attraction in exchange and communal relationships. *Journal of Personality and Social Psychology*, 37:12–24.

Clark, R. E., and L. J. Halford. 1978. Going . . . going . . . gone: Some preliminary observations on 'deals' at auctions. *Urban Life,* 7:285–307.

Cox, V. C., P. B. Paulus, and G. McCain. 1984. Prison crowding research: The relevance for prison housing standards and a general approach regarding crowding phenomena. *American Psychologist,* 39:1148–60.

Daly, J. A., D. J. Weber, A. L. Vangelisti, M. Maxwell, and H. Neel. 1989. Concurrent cognitions during conversations: Protocol analysis as a means of exploring conversations. *Discourse processes,* 12:227–44.

Dawe, H. C. 1934. An analysis of two hundred quarrels of pre-school children. *Child Development,* 5:139–57.

Duck, S. 1990. Relationships as unfinished business: Out of the frying pan and into the 1990s. *Journal of Social and Personal Relationships,* 7:5–29.

Duck, S. 1991. Diaries and logs. In *Studying interpersonal relationships,* ed. B. M. Montgomery and S. Duck, 141–61. New York: The Guilford Press.

Duck, S., K. Pond, and G. Leatham. 1991. Remembering as a context for being in relationships: Different perspectives on the same interaction. Paper presented at the Third Conference of the International Network on Personal Relationships, Normal/Bloomington, Illinois.

Duck, S., and H. K. A. Sants. 1983. On the origin of the specious: Are personal relationships really interpersonal states? *Journal of Social and Clinical Psychology,* 1:27–41.

Floyd, F., and H. Markman. 1983. Observational biases in spouse interaction: Toward a cognitive/behavioral model of marriage. *Journal of Consulting and Clinical Psychology,* 51:450–57.

Fried, M. L., and V. J. DeFazio. 1974. Territoriality and boundary conflicts in the subway. *Psychiatry,* 37:47–59.

Garcia, S., L. Stinson, W. Ickes, V. Bissonnette, and S. Briggs. 1991. Shyness and physical attractiveness in mixed-sex dyads. *Journal of Personality and Social Psychology,* 61: 35–49.

Ginsberg, D., and J. M. Gottman. 1986. Conversations of college roommates: Similarities and differences in male and female friendship. In *Conversations of friends,* ed. J. M. Gottman and J. G. Parker, 241–91. New York: Cambridge University Press.

Gottman, J. M. 1979. *Marital interaction: Experimental investigations.* New York: Academic Press.

Gottman, J. M., and R. W. Levenson. 1986. Assessing the role of emotion in marriage. *Behavioral Assessment,* 8, 31–48.

Gottman, J. M., H. Markman, and C. Notarius. 1977. The topography of marital conflict: A study of verbal and nonverbal behavior. *Journal of Marriage and the Family,* 39:461–77.

Gottman, J. M., and J. G. Parker. eds. 1986. *Conversations of friends.* New York: Cambridge University Press.

Harvey, J. H., A. Christensen, and E. McClintock. 1983. Research methods. In *Close relationships,* ed. H. H. Kelley, E. Berscheid, A. Christensen, J. H. Harvey, T. L. Huston, G. Levinger, E. McClintock, L. A. Peplau, and D. R. Peterson, 449–85. New York: W. H. Freeman.

Harvey, J. H., S. S. Hendrick, and K. Tucker. 1988. Self-report methods in studying personal relationships. In *Handbook of personal relationships: Theory, research, and interventions,* ed. S. Duck, D. F. Hay, S. E. Hobfall, W. Ickes, and B. M. Montgomery, 99–113. Chichester: John Wiley and Sons.

Hayano, D. M. 1980. Communicative competency among poker players. *Journal of Communication,* 30: 113–20.

Hendrick, C., and S. Hendrick. 1986. A theory and method of love. *Journal of Personality and Social Psychology,* 50:392–402.

Hendrick, S., and C. Hendrick. 1992. *Liking, loving and relating: Second edition.* Pacific Grove, CA: Brooks/Cole.

Holdaway, S. 1980. The police station. *Urban Life,* 9:79–100.

Huston, T. L., E. Robins, J. Atkinson, and S. M. McHale. 1987. Surveying the landscape of marital behavior: A behavioral self-report approach to studying marriage. In *Family processes and problems: Social psychological aspects. Applied Social Psychology Annual,* ed. S. Oskamp, 7:46–71. Newbury Park, CA: Sage.

Ickes, W. 1982. A basic paradigm for the study of personality, roles, and social behavior. In *Personality, roles, and social behavior*, ed. W. Ickes and E. S. Knowles, 305–41. New York: Springer-Verlag.

Ickes, W. 1983. A basic paradigm for the study of unstructured dyadic interaction. In *New directions for methodology of social and behavioral science: Naturalistic approaches to studying social interaction*, ed. H. T. Reis, 15:5–21. San Francisco: Jossey-Bass.

Ickes, W. 1984. Compositions in black and white: Determinants of interaction in interracial dyads. *Journal of Personality and Social Psychology*, 47:330–41.

Ickes, W. 1985. Sex-role influences on compatibility in relationships. In *Compatible and incompatible relationships*, ed. W. Ickes, 187–208. New York: Springer-Verlag.

Ickes, W., V. Bissonnette, S. Garcia, and L. Stinson, 1990. Implementing and using the dyadic interaction paradigm. In *Review of Personality and Social Psychology: Vol. 11, Research Methods in Personality and Social Psychology*, ed. C.Hendrick and M. Clark, 16–44. Newbury Park, CA: Sage.

Ickes, W., M. L. Patterson, D. W. Rajecki, and S. Tanford. 1982. Behavioral and cognitive consequences of reciprocal versus compensatory responses to pre-interaction expectancies. *Social Cognition*, 1:160–90.

Ickes, W., L. Stinson, V. Bissonnette, and S. Garcia. 1990. Naturalistic social cognition: Empathic accuracy in mixed-sex dyads. *Journal of Personality and Social Psychology*, 59:730–742.

Ickes, W., and W. Tooke. 1988. The observational method: Studying the interaction of minds and bodies. In *Handbook of personal relationships: Theory, research and interventions*, ed. S. Duck, D. F. Hay, S. E. Hobfall, W. Ickes, and B. M. Montgomery, 79–97. Chichester: John Wiley and Sons.

Jacobs, J. B. 1974. Participant observation in prison. *Urban Life Culture*, 3:221–40.

Jones, R. R., J. B. Reid, and G. R. Patterson. 1975. Naturalistic observations in clinical assessment. In *Advances in Psychological Assessment*, ed. P. McReynolds, vol. 3. San Francisco: Jossey-Bass.

Kenny, D. A. 1988. The analysis of data from two-person relationships. In *Handbook of personal relationships: Theory, research and interventions*, ed. S. Duck, D. F. Hay, S. E. Hobfall, W. Ickes, and B. M. Montgomery, 57–77. Chichester: John Wiley and Sons.

Kenny, D. A., and D. A. Kashy. 1991. Analyzing interdependence in dyads. In *Studying interpersonal relationships*, ed. B. M. Montgomery and S. Duck, 275–85. New York: The Guilford Press.

Koocher, G. P. 1977. Bathroom behavior and human dignity. *Journal of Personality and Social Psychology*, 35:120–21.

Lamke, L. K. 1989. Marital adjustment among rural couples: The role of expressiveness. *Sex Roles*, 21:579–90.

Leventhal, H., and E. Sharp. 1965. Facial expressions as indicators of distress. In *Affect, cognition, and personality*, ed. S. S. Tompkins and C. E. Izard, 296–318. New York: Springer.

Levenson, R. W., and J. M. Gottman. 1983. Marital interaction: Physiological linkage and affective exchange. *Journal of Personality and Social Psychology*, 45:587–97.

Levenson, R. W., and J. M. Gottman. 1985. Physiological and affective predictors of change in relationship satisfaction. *Journal of Personality and Social Psychology*, 49:85–94.

Levinger, G. 1977. Re-viewing the close relationship. In *Close relationships*, ed. G. Levinger and H. L. Raush. Amherst, MA: University of Massachusetts Press.

Lund, M. 1985. The development of investment and commitment scales for predicting continuity of personal relationships. *Journal of Social and Personal Relationships*, 2:3–23.

Malamuth, N. M. 1986. Predictors of naturalistic sexual aggression. *Journal of Personality and Social Psychology*, 50:953–62.

Mamali, C. 1991. The dynamic of personal relationships between Dreiser and Mencken: The correspondentogram of a dyadic epistolary space (1907–1945). Paper presented at the Third Conference of the International Network on Personal Relationships, Normal/Bloomington, Illinois.

Mamali, C. 1992. Correspondence and the reconstruction of social dynamics: The correspondentogram of a nuclear family. Paper presented at the Workshop on Theoretical Analysis, Department of Sociology, University of Iowa, Iowa City, Iowa.

Mansfield, P., and J. Collard. 1988. *The beginning of the rest of our life: A portrait of newly-wed marriage.* London: MacMillan.

Marx, G. 1987. *The Groucho letters: Letters from and to Groucho Marx.* New York: Fireside.

Mencken, H. L. 1991. *The diary of H. L. Mencken.* New York: Vintage Books.

Middlemist, R. D., E. S. Knowles, and C. F. Matter. 1976. Personal space invasions in the lavatory: Suggestive evidence for arousal. *Journal of Personality and Social Psychology,* 33:541–46.

Middlemist, R. D., E. S. Knowles, and C. F. Matter. 1977. What to do and what to report: A reply to Koocher. *Journal of Personality and Social Psychology,* 35:122–24.

Milardo, R. M., M. P. Johnson, and T. L. Huston. 1983. Developing close relationships: Changing patterns of interaction between pair members and social networks. *Journal of Personality and Social Psychology,* 44:964–76.

Miller, L. C., J. H. Berg, and R. L. Archer. 1983. Openers: Individuals who elicit intimate self-disclosure. *Journal of Personality and Social Psychology,* 44:1234–44.

Ponder, E., and W. P. Kennedy. 1927. On the act of blinking. *Quarterly Journal of Experimental Physiology,* 18:89–110.

Quinsey, V. L., T. C. Chaplin, A. M. Maguire, and D. Upfold. 1987. The behavioral treatment of rapists and child molesters. In *Behavioral approaches to crime and delinquency: Application, research, and theory,* ed. E. K. Morris and C. J. Braukmann, 363–82. New York: Plenum.

Reis, H. T., J. Nezlek, and L. Wheeler. 1980. Physical attractiveness in social interaction. *Journal of Personality and Social Psychology,* 38:604–17.

Reis, H. T., and L. Wheeler. 1991. Studying social interaction with the Rochester Interaction Record. In *Advances in experimental social psychology,* 24:269–318. New York: Academic Press.

Revenstorf, D., K. Hahlweg, L. Schindler, and H. Kunert. 1984. The use of time series analysis in marriage counseling. In *Marital interaction: Analysis and modification.* ed. K. Hahlweg and N. S. Jacobson, 199–231. New York: Guilford.

Riesman, D., and J. Watson. 1964. The sociability project: A chronicle of frustration and achievement. In *Sociologists at work,* ed. P. E. Hammond, 235–321. New York: Basic Books.

Rosenblatt, P. C. 1983. *Bitter, bitter tears: Nineteenth-century diarists and twentieth-century grief theorists.* Minneapolis: University of Minnesota Press.

Rubenstein, J. 1973. *City police.* New York: Ferrar, Strauss, and Giroux.

Sanford, M. D. 1959. *Mollie: The journal of Mollie Dorsey Sanford in Nebraska and Colorado Territories, 1857–1866.* Lincoln: University of Nebraska Press.

Scheflen, A. E. 1974. *How behavior means.* Garden City, NJ: Anchor.

Shaver, P., and C. Rubenstein. 1983. Research potential of magazine and newspaper surveys. In *New directions for methodology of social and behavioral science: Naturalistic approaches to studying social interaction* ed. H. T. Reis, 15:75–92. San Francisco: Jossey-Bass.

Simpson, J. A., and S. W. Gangestad. 1991. Individual differences in sociosexuality: Evidence for convergent and discriminant validity. *Journal of Personality and Social Psychology,* 60:870–83.

Snyder, M. and W. Ickes. 1985. Personality and social behavior. In *The handbook of social psychology: Third edition.* ed. G. Lindzey and E. Aronson, 2:883–947. New York: Random House.

Spanier, G. 1976. Measuring dyadic adjustment: New scales for assessing the quality of marriage and similar dyads. *Journal of Marriage and the Family,* 38:15–28.

Spence, J., R. Helmreich, and J. Stapp. 1975. Ratings of self and peers on sex role attributes and their relation to self-esteem and conceptions of masculinity and femininity. *Journal of Personality and Social Psychology,* 32:29–39.

Sprecher, S., and S. Metts. 1989. Development of the "Romantic Beliefs Scale" and examination of the effects of gender and gender-role orientation. *Journal of Social and Personal Relationships,* 6:387–411.

Stack, S. 1980. The effects of marital dissolution on suicide. *Journal of Marriage and the Family,* 42:83–91.

———. 1981. Divorce and suicide: A time series analysis, 1933–1970. *Journal of Family Issues,* 2:77–90.

———. 1989. The impact of divorce on suicide in Norway, 1951–1980. *Journal of Marriage and the Family,* 51:229–38.

Stein, J. 1982. *Edie: An American biography.* New York: Dell.

Stinson, L., and W. Ickes. 1992. Empathic accuracy in the interactions of male friends versus male strangers. *Journal of Personality and Social Psychology, 62:* 787–797.

Tardy, C. H., and L. A. Hosman, 1991. Experimentation. In *Studying interpersonal relationships,* ed. B. M. Montgomery and S. Duck, 219–35. New York: The Guilford Press.

Trovato, F. 1986. The relation between marital dissolution and suicide: The Canadian case. *Journal of Marriage and the Family,* 48:341–48.

Trovato, F. 1987. A longitudinal analysis of divorce and suicide in Canada. *Journal of Marriage and the Family,* 49:193–203.

Trovato, F., and G. Lauris. 1989. Marital status and mortality in Canada: 1951–1981. *Journal of Marriage and the Family,* 51:907–22.

Weick, K. 1968. Systematic observational methods. In *The handbook of social psychology: Second edition,* ed. G. Lindzey and E. Aronson II, 357–451. Reading, MA: Addison-Wesley.

Wheeler, L., and J. Nezlek, 1977. Sex differences in social participation. *Journal of Personality and Social Psychology,* 35:742–54.

Wheeler, L., and H. T. Reis, 1991. Self-recording of everyday life events: Origins, types, and uses. *Journal of Personality,* 59:339–54.

Wheeler, L., H. T. Reis, and J. Nezlek. 1983. Loneliness, social interaction, and sex roles. *Journal of Personality and Social Psychology,* 45:943–53.

Wong, M. M., and M. Csikszentmihalyi. 1991. Affiliation motivation and daily experience: Some issues on gender differences. *Journal of Personality and Social Psychology,* 60:154–164.

Chapter 3

Interpersonal Attraction

JEFFRY A. SIMPSON
Texas A&M University

BETTY A. HARRIS
Texas A&M University

Outline

Introduction

In recent weeks, Susan has been thinking about starting a new romantic relationship. Although she is neither lonely nor depressed, Susan's high needs for intimacy and affiliation have not been satisfied by her current group of friends and acquaintances. Since moving to a new apartment complex three months ago, she has had casual yet repeated contact with a man named John who recently moved into an apartment two doors down from her. While Susan has exchanged little more than formal greetings and pleasant glances with John, she has begun to find him increasingly more attractive. Similar to Susan, John is a sociable and physically attractive person. In light of his attractiveness, Susan assumes that he must be a warm, self-confident, and talented individual.

The following week, Susan and John separately attend a large party for residents of the apartment complex. The party is held in a dimly lit, cool room filled with soft, pleasant music. Despite the fact that Susan and John happen to be in very good moods, both are somewhat apprehensive about having to meet and interact with new people. After getting up the nerve, Susan approaches John and starts a conversation. From the outset, her nonverbal behavior toward him is very positive; she maintains eye contact, smiles, laughs, and adopts a relaxed, open body posture. Within minutes, she discovers that John is indeed a very warm and interesting person, someone whom she both likes and respects. As they pass the evening together, Susan learns that she and John have similar attitudes, personality characteristics, personal backgrounds, and leisure interests. Moreover, Susan senses that John likes her just as much as she likes him. By the end of the night, they have embarked on a new relationship.

This scenario highlights many of the factors that are known to increase interpersonal attraction during the initial stages of relationship formation. As this example illustrates, interpersonal attraction is best conceptualized as a dynamic process that unfolds over time and is governed by a myriad of different precipitating events. Two aspects of this vignette are worth emphasizing. First, even though the precise sequence of events that produce attraction can vary depending on the nature of the relationship and the circumstances under which it develops (Berscheid and Graziano 1978), interpersonal attraction often does not commence unless a person: wants to initiate a relationship; is in close enough physical proximity with an individual to establish and sustain interaction; and has the social skills necessary to initiate and maintain the relationship. Once these prerequisites have been met, features associated with the other person (John) and the unique fit between the two interactants (John and Susan) can influence the attraction process. Second, contrary to popular wisdom, the extent to which a given perceiver (Susan) is attracted to another person (John) often depends as much on the attributes of the perceiver (e.g., Susan's current needs, desires and social skills), the environment in which the initial interaction takes place, and the unique fit between the perceiver and the other (e.g., the degree to which Susan and John are similar) as it does on the quality of attributes possessed by the other (John).

Interpersonal attraction, therefore, is much more than merely the sum of positive features associated with the object of attraction.

Every relationship can be traced back to its beginning, a point in time when partners first met and the relationship was not close. To date, most research on interpersonal attraction has focused on why people initially become attracted to one another during the early stages of relationship formation. Considerably less attention has been devoted to examining what kinds of factors maintain attraction during the latter stages of relationship development. Given these circumstances, the present chapter will predominantly focus on factors known to increase or decrease attraction between people involved in the early stages of relationship formation, usually prior to the development of pronounced closeness.

In reviewing the attraction literature, we will draw from several different disciplines, including anthropology, sociology and social psychology. The primary perspective guiding our review, however, will be social psychology. Social psychologists "attempt to understand and explain how the thought, feeling, and behavior of individuals are influenced by the actual, imagined, or implied presence of others" (Allport 1954, pp. 5). Hence, we will seek to understand how the actual, imagined, or implied actions of one person affect the feelings, thoughts, and behaviors of another person as the attraction process unfolds.

We first present a formal definition of interpersonal attraction and explain how the construct traditionally has been measured. We then describe a general model of relationship closeness proposed by Harold Kelley and his colleagues (Kelley et al. 1983) into which most of the major variables known to facilitate attraction can be classified. Next, we selectively review the interpersonal attraction literature, highlighting how existing research on attraction can be organized within the Kelley et al. model. Whenever possible, we specify what kinds of psychological theories or principles have been invoked to explain why certain variables influence interpersonal attraction. In the final section, we speculate about where conceptual and empirical gaps exist in the field of interpersonal attraction, and we suggest some possible avenues for future research.

Interpersonal Attraction: Definition, Measurement, and a Model

Interpersonal attraction can be defined as a motivational state in which an individual is predisposed to think, feel, and usually behave in a positive manner toward another person (Berscheid 1985). Over the years, the attraction construct has been operationalized and measured in different ways. Most frequently, it has been assessed by simply asking perceivers to provide self-reports of how much they like, respect, have positive feelings toward, and/or harbor positive thoughts about someone else. Somewhat less often, the construct has been measured by peer-reports (provided by friends, siblings or parents) designed to index the degree to which two people appear to be attracted to each other and by life record data (e.g., permanent records of who marries whom). On relatively rare occasions, attraction has been inferred from behavioral measures of who chooses to be with whom and/or the quality and emotional tone of interaction that transpires between two people.

Interpersonal attraction can and often does begin in the absence of direct contact. Yet attraction typically cannot progress beyond rudimentary stages unless two people eventually interact. Indeed, positive regard for someone usually occurs between, and is shaped by the quality of interactions that transpire between, two people (Berscheid 1985). Drawing on this premise, Kelley et al. (1983) have developed a model of relationship closeness which contends that the nature and quality of interactions two people have are influenced by four casual conditions: P variables (attributes specific to the person evaluating the other: e.g., Susan); E variables (factors that characterize the physical and social environment in which the relationship begins and is embedded); O variables (attributes specific to the other who serves as the target of evaluation: e.g., John); and P x O variables (*emergent* variables that are unique to the relationship between P and O: e.g., the fit between Susan and John).

These four sets of precipitating conditions and the variables that constitute them are dynamic and interactive in nature (Gifford and Gallagher 1985; Wright, Ingraham, and Blackmer 1985). For example, the kinds of attributes that P brings to an initial encounter can drastically alter what P values in O as well as whether P and O have—or can develop—common interests. Similarly, the environmental context in which an initial interaction takes place can profoundly affect whether P finds O appealing and, hence, whether P and O interact long enough to identify their similarities or feelings of mutual attraction.

To simplify our presentation, we have classified each of the major variables known to heighten or diminish attraction into one of the four categories identified by Kelley et al. (1983). Because interpersonal attraction typically begins with the attributes that P brings to an initial encounter, we first review variables associated with P that tend to promote or inhibit the initial stages of the attraction process. We then examine how features of the environment (E) influence attraction, especially during the early stages of relationship formation (first encounters). Following this, we review what sorts of attributes possessed by O affect interpersonal attraction. We conclude by exploring how the unique fit between P and O influences attraction.

P Variables

Susan's attraction to John was facilitated from the outset by her specific motives, predispositions, and social skills. She had strong needs for intimacy and affiliation that were not being met by her existing social network. She was neither lonely nor depressed, and she approached John expecting that he was warm, would like her, and would reciprocate her warmth and positive feelings. Past research has shown that the type of social motives, social deficiencies and interpersonal expectancies a person brings to a social encounter can dramatically affect the degree to which a person is attracted to another individual.

Social Motives

People typically seek out relationships to satisfy their needs for affiliation and/or intimacy (McClelland 1951; McAdams 1982). Individuals who have a strong need to affiliate with others tend to establish and maintain a large number of social contacts. To meet this need, they adopt an active and controlling orientation toward relationships in which breadth and quantity of social ties assume paramount importance (McClelland 1985). Persons high in need for affiliation tend to spend more time talking to other people (McClelland 1985), are more self-confident (Crouse and Mehrabian 1977), and make more friends during the school year (Greendlinger and Byrne 1985).

Conversely, persons with a high need for intimacy prefer a smaller number of close, warm, and intimate relationships. As a result, they tend to adopt a more passive and less controlling style in which depth and quality of relationships are stressed. People high in need for intimacy usually are more trusting, confide more in others, and experience greater subjective well-being (McAdams and Bryant 1987; McAdams, Healy, and Krause 1984).

Individuals who have strong intimacy needs tend to display better long-term psychological adjustment than do those who possess strong needs for affiliation (McAdams and Vaillant 1982). This implies that attraction which is based on the quality of relationships might yield greater long-term happiness and personal satisfaction than attraction that stems from sheer quantity of social contacts.

Social Deficiencies

Three major types of social deficiencies impede social interaction and, therefore, hinder the development of interpersonal attraction: social anxiety, loneliness, and depression. Social anxiety involves feelings of discomfort and awkwardness when in the presence of others (Leary 1983). Even though it can have many different origins (Leary 1987), acute social anxiety frequently emanates from concerns about proper self-presentation in social settings (Schlenker and Leary 1982), and it is closely linked to chronic shyness (Zimbardo 1977). Extreme anxiety thwarts initial attraction by trapping people in a cycle of negative social interactions in which social withdrawal on the part of P is interpreted as rejection by O. This leads O to rebuff P, thereby justifying and thus perpetuating P's high level of anxiety (Jones and Carpenter 1986). These events are compounded by the fact that highly anxious persons are more likely to over-interpret or misinterpret innocuous events that occur in their interactions (Maddox, Norton, and Leary 1988), further exacerbating their timid, reclusive nature.

Loneliness is perhaps the most common social deficiency. It typically occurs during important life transitions (e.g., moving away to college) and major life disruptions (e.g., the loss of a long-term romantic partner). Perlman and Peplau (1981) define loneliness as a feeling of deprivation originating from unsatisfactory social relations with others. Two distinct types of loneliness have been identified (Weiss 1973): social isolation (which is felt when social contacts are too infrequent); and emotional isolation (which is experienced when in-depth, emotionally close relationships are lacking). Loneliness impedes social interaction in much the same way as does acute anxiety. During social encounters, lonely individuals tend to be less responsive to, less sensitive to, and less intimate with their interaction partners. Consequently, they are perceived by others as being less socially competent (Sloan and Solano 1984; Spitzberg and Carney 1985).

Depression also can generate interaction styles that sharply curtail the development of attraction. Depressed people often reject and dismiss others, have awkward and inadequate social skills, and are rejected by others in turn (Hokanson, et al. 1986; Strack and Coyne 1983).

These three deficiencies oftentimes are witnessed simultaneously in a given individual (Jones and Carpenter 1986). In fact, the presence of one deficiency can induce the others. Chronic social anxiety, for instance, often elicits social rejection from others. Over time, repeated rejection can produce loneliness and, in extreme cases, depression. What links these deficiencies together is that all three impede interpersonal attraction by making people more socially cautious when communicating with others (Pietromonaco and Rook 1987; Vaux 1988). By avoiding situations that pose the threat of social rejection, persons who harbor these deficiencies perpetuate their isolation and cannot progress to latter stages of the attraction process.

Interpersonal Expectancies

It has long been known that, prior to meeting someone, the mere anticipation of interaction can heighten attraction to them (Darley and Berscheid 1967). In recent years, researchers have begun to identify how specific expectancies that a person brings to an initial encounter can alter the degree of attraction experienced toward others. Two of the most important expectancies are perceptions of others, physical attractiveness and beliefs concerning whether they initially like us.

Mark Snyder and his colleagues have shown that when men think they are talking to an attractive woman over a phone (independent of her actual appearance), women behave in a more friendly, sociable, and skilled manner than when men are led to believe that the woman is unattractive (Snyder, Tanke, and Berscheid 1977). That is, expectancies about another person's level of physical attractiveness can channel interactions between men and women such that men bring out positive attributes in women whom they believe are attractive and negative attributes in women whom they presume are unattractive. These different styles of interaction affect the extent of attraction interactants feel for each other.

Furthermore, when people enter an interaction believing that their partner likes them, they disclose more, disagree less, adopt a warmer attitude, and talk in a more pleasant tone of voice (Curtis and Miller 1986). This behavior elicits reciprocal warmth from the partner. Thus, perceptions of liking—even if they are not true—can stimulate positive communication and increase attraction.

E Variables

One of the primary reasons why Susan initially became attracted to John was his close proximity to her, a situation that allowed for frequent (albeit informal and fleeting) contact. Moreover, when Susan approached John to strike up a formal conversation at the party, the physical and social environment was highly conducive for fostering attraction: the room was dimly lit, cool, and filled with soft, pleasant music. Despite the fact that Susan was in a good mood, she approached John feeling a diffuse sense of arousal and excitement. More than three decades of research has revealed that all of these factors tend to fuel interpersonal attraction.

Physical Proximity

Perhaps the best predictor of whether two people eventually will like one another is the sheer amount of contact they have. Needless to say, individuals must meet and interact for attraction to fully blossom. This point is most eloquently illustrated in a classic study by Leon Festinger and his colleagues. Festinger, Schachter, and Back (1950) studied friendship patterns in a large student housing complex where apartments were assigned randomly (i.e., on a first come, first served basis). The strongest predictor of who eventually became friends with whom was the location of their apartments. Persons who lived close together and came in contact with each other more often were more likely to become friends. Indeed, close proximity has been found to increase attraction among soldiers assigned to bomber crews (Kipnis 1957), college students assigned to alphabetized seats in their classes (Segal 1974), senior citizens randomly placed in high-rise apartment complexes (Nahemow and Lawton 1975), and homeowners in new subdivisions (Whyte 1956). In each case, persons who are closer to and have more frequent contact with each other tend to become better friends.

The effects of proximity, of course, are not always positive. Some of the people we dislike the most also tend to live nearby (Ebbesen, Kjos, and Konecni 1976). Thus, proximity provides the opportunity for interaction; it does not determine its quality.

Why does proximity generally increase attraction? Five plausible reasons exist. First, Zajonc (1968) has argued that repeated exposure to objects or people produces increased liking because familiar things are presumed to be safe and, hence, comforting. Although there are limits to this mere exposure effect (Harrison 1977; Perlman and Oskamp 1971; Swap 1977), it serves as one of the primary means through which proximity increases attraction. Even relatively infrequent exposure to a person (e.g., seeing someone briefly once a week) can increase attraction (Saegert, Swap, and Zajonc 1973). Second, frequent interaction typically enhances perceptions of the similarity between people, thereby facilitating attraction (Moreland and Zajonc 1982). Third, frequent contact allows people to explore their actual similarities and sense reciprocal liking for each other (Insko and Wilson 1977), permitting them to see themselves as a social unit (Arkin and Burger 1980). Fourth, regular interaction leads people to anticipate future contact which, in turn, enhances liking (Darley and Berscheid 1967). Anticipation of interaction generates liking because, by presuming that others will be pleasant, people can maximize any rewards that might emerge from the forthcoming interaction (Knight and Vallacher 1981; Tyler and Sears 1977). Fifth, individuals in close proximity are more readily accessible and available. Hence, they can provide rewards without inflicting the costs of time, effort, and money associated with persons who are not nearby.

Features of the Physical and Social Environment

Various features of the physical environment in which an interaction takes place can have subtle yet dramatic effects on interpersonal attraction. When people are evaluated in hot, humid rooms (Griffitt 1970) or in the presence of unpleasant music (May and Hamilton 1980), they tend to be seen as less attractive. Similarly, if raters have just witnessed a distressing event (e.g., a sad movie [Gouaux 1971]) or heard bad news (Veitch and Griffitt 1976), they usually rate others more harshly.

What accounts for these effects? According to the Reinforcement-Affect Model (Clore and Byrne 1974), positive emotion is generated when an individual experiences pleasant physical and/or social environments, while negative emotion is produced when environments are unpleasant. This positive or negative affect, in turn, is unwittingly and often unconsciously associated with persons who are present when the affect is experienced. Clore and Byrne conjecture that positive emotion produces attraction to others, whereas negative emotion results in repulsion.

Certain aspects of the social context in which an interaction occurs also can promote attraction. In an ingenious study, Dutton and Aron (1974) arranged for men to meet an attractive woman after walking over either a low-lying, stable bridge or an unstable bridge situated over a deep ravine. Men who had just crossed the wobbly bridge rated the woman as more attractive than did those who walked across the stable one. Although their interpretation of this finding has been the subject of debate (Kenrick and Cialdini 1977; Kenrick, Cialdini, and Linder 1979), Dutton and Aron argue that the intense arousal associated with traversing the unstable bridge was mistakenly attributed to strong liking for the woman, a misattribution that produced greater attraction.

Working from a different perspective, Stanley Schachter (1959) has shown that situationally-induced fear can heighten attraction toward others who must confront the same threatening situation, especially in individuals who were born first in their families. Events that provoke stress and fear, however, produce greater attraction only when affiliation with others can reduce the negative impact of the stressor (Rofe 1984). Stressful situations do not yield greater attraction when others cannot reduce or ameliorate their unpleasantness (Sarnoff and Zimbardo 1961).

The extent to which a person is seen as attractive also is contingent on whether the person is evaluated in relation to highly attractive others (e.g., models), when during the course of a social evening evaluations are made, and whether parents or authority figures approve of the relationship. Douglas Kenrick and his colleagues have found that men rate their dating partners as less physically attractive (Kenrick and Gutierres 1980) and report less love for them (Kenrick, Gutierres, and Goldberg 1989) after viewing highly attractive female models. Male patrons of country-and-western bars tend to rate women as more attractive as the night wears on (Pennebaker et al. 1979). And borrowing an idea from the play *Romeo and Juliet*, Driscoll, Davis, and Lipatz (1972) have demonstrated that interference by parents in their son's or daughter's dating relationship breeds greater mutual attraction and commitment among young lovers.

What psychological principle explains some of these effects? One viable candidate is reactance theory (Brehm 1966). Psychological reactance is a negative motivational state that begins to operate when individuals feel that their freedom to behave as they want to is unfairly restricted. One means by which people attempt to reinstate their freedom is to distort the attractiveness of the objects on which restrictions have been imposed. Thus, as closing time draws near, all of the women suddenly become more appealing. And as interference by parents escalates, one's lover is perceived as more desirable.

O Variables

Susan was also drawn to John because of the positive attributes he possessed. To begin with, he was a physically attractive person. On the basis of his attractiveness, Susan implicitly assumed that he possessed a host of other admirable characteristics, an assumption that subtly altered Susan's conversational behavior toward John and elicited positive verbal and nonverbal behavior from him at the party. While conversing with him, Susan learned that John's personal attributes were just as stellar as was his physical appearance; John conveyed the impression of being highly likable and a person worthy of admiration and respect. Empirical studies have shown that all of these features enhance attraction.

Physical Attractiveness

Physical attractiveness differs from other personal attributes in that it serves as the first and sometimes only characteristic of others that individuals can evaluate in the absence of direct contact. In light of this fact, physical attractiveness is unique among attributes of O because it can strongly influence interpersonal attraction during the earliest stages of the attraction process (Berscheid and Walster 1974; Hatfield and Sprecher 1986). Most other personal attributes (e.g., O's personality, attitudes, and values) can be inferred only after direct interaction has taken place. As a result, attributes other than physical attractiveness tend to play a more important role during later stages of attraction.

Why does physical attractiveness facilitate global attraction? Attractive people usually reward those with whom they associate in at least four different ways. First, attractive people are more aesthetically pleasing to look at. Second, they tend to be more socially skilled (Goldman and Lewis 1977) and, therefore, more rewarding as interaction partners. Third, individuals can reap benefits by associating with highly attractive others (Waller 1937). Friends of attractive same-sex peers, for example, are rated by others as more attractive simply through their association with attractive peers (Geiselman, Haight, and Kimata 1984; Kernis and Wheeler 1981). In addition, men who date attractive women are evaluated more highly than men who do not (Sigall and Landy 1973), although women do not accrue similar benefits from dating attractive men (Bar-Tal and Saxe 1976). Fourth, people tacitly assume that attractive people are good people (Dion, Berscheid, and Walster 1972). Regardless of their actual attributes, attractive people are believed to be more poised, interesting, sociable, independent, exciting, and sexually warm than their less attractive counterparts (Brigham 1980). Attractive persons also are considered to be more intelligent, more successful, and happier (Hatfield and Sprecher 1986). Less attractive individuals, on the other hand, are presumed to be more deviant in terms of psychopathology, their political views, and their sexual lifestyle (Jones, Hannson, and Phillips 1978; Unger, Hilderbrand, and Madar 1982).

This "beautiful-is-good" stereotype facilitates attraction in two ways. First, by believing that attractive people have a variety of desirable features, the aesthetic rewards associated with being in their presence increase. Second, by harboring this stereotype, individuals behave in ways that actually elicit good deeds, attributes, and actions from attractive people (Langlois 1986).

In general, however, this stereotype is not completely true. While physically attractive persons do tend to be more socially skilled (Chaiken 1979; Goldman and Lewis 1977), more socially assertive (Jackson and Huston 1975), less prone to psychological disorders (Hatfield and Sprecher 1986), more successful at attaining higher levels of education, income, and occupational status (Umberson and Hughes 1984), and have more satisfying interactions with others (Reis, Nezlek, and Wheeler 1980), they do not possess all of the positive features embodied in the stereotype. Most individuals, however, treat attractive persons as if they do. Because of this, these desirable features are elicited from attractive people during social interaction, heightening their global appeal (Langlois 1986).

Perceptions of what makes a person physically attractive vary from person to person (Berscheid and Walster 1974) and from culture to culture (Hatfield and Sprecher 1986). Nevertheless, investigators have begun to identify what kinds of physical features make faces attractive to most people. Contrary to popular conceptions, Langlois and Roggman (1990) have found that people are most strongly attracted to faces whose features conform to the average of the population. Individuals with facial features that do not deviate too much from what is normal might be perceived as more attractive if such features were associated with other attributes that were adaptive during evolutionary history.

Research also has begun to identify what specific kinds of facial features men and women find differentially attractive. Women who have youthful, immature facial features such as relatively large eyes, small noses, small chins, and broad smiles tend to be rated as more attractive by men (Cunningham 1986). Men who have a mixture of immature features (large eyes), mature features (prominent cheek bones and large chins), and expressive features (broad smiles) are viewed as more attractive by women (Cunningham, Barbee, and Pike 1990). Adopting an evolutionary perspective, Cunningham argues that youthful features in women are more attractive because they indicate fertility and high reproductive potential in women. A mixture of mature, immature, and expressive features in men may be perceived as more attractive to the extent that maturity signifies higher status and greater capacity to provide resources, while immaturity and expressiveness convey personal warmth and lack of threat. In line with these speculations, men who display non-aggressive, socially dominant behaviors during social interactions are viewed as more physically attractive than those who do not (Sallada, Kenrick, and Vershure 1987).

Personality

Certain personality attributes tend to be universally valued in others, regardless of the idiosyncratic needs of perceivers. When it comes to choosing friends, for example, sincerity is valued most highly, whereas being a liar and phoniness are most abhorred (Anderson 1968). With regard to mate selection, both men and women prefer mates who are good companions, considerate, honest, affectionate, dependable, intelligent, kind, understanding, interesting to converse with, and loyal (Buss and Barnes 1986).

Two major components of personality appear to influence global attraction: feelings of affection for another based on warmth, and feelings of respect based on competence (Lydon, Jamieson, and Zanna 1988; Rubin 1973). These two dimensions have relatively independent effects on attraction. More specifically, people who score high on both dimensions are rated as most attractive, whereas those who score low on both dimensions are seen as least attractive.

Warmth is communicated by expressing positive attitudes toward other people, objects, or events in general (Folkes and Sears 1977). It also is conveyed by nonverbal behaviors such as smiling at others, paying attention to them, and openly expressing one's emotion (Friedman, Riggio, and Casella 1988; Simpson, Gangested, and Biek 1992).

Competence is expressed through intelligence, social skills, and knowledge. Too much competence can sometimes reduce global attraction, particularly if observers feel threatened by excessive talent. If highly competent people occasionally make minor blunders, however, such pratfalls can enhance their attractiveness in the eyes of observers (Aronson, Willerman, and Floyd 1966).

Finally, individuals also perceive as more attractive persons who are relatively dominant (Palmer and Byrne 1970), competitive (Riskind and Wilson 1982), personally agreeable (Kaplan and Anderson 1973), and those who mutually disclose personal information (McAllister and Bregman 1983).

$P \times O$ Variables

Once Susan began talking with John, she learned that they shared many similarities. For instance, they held similar views on important issues, they had relatively similar personalities and personal backgrounds, and they liked to do many of the same leisure activities. In essence, their personal attributes and preferences seemed to match up and mesh fairly well. As these commonalties emerged, John and Susan began to sense that their liking for one another was mutual. Research suggests that all of these factors promote attraction.

Similarity between P and O

One of the strongest predictors of interpersonal attraction is similarity; people who are similar on important attributes and personal preferences tend to experience greater attraction. The tendency for similar people to be attracted to each other has been documented in five areas: attitudes, personality, demographic characteristics, behavioral styles, and physical attractiveness.

The bulk of research has been done on attitude similarity (Byrne 1971). At base, two kinds of attitudinal similarity can affect attraction: actual similarity and perceived similarity. In one of the finest interpersonal attraction studies ever conducted, Theodore Newcomb (1961) provided a small group of male undergraduates with room and board in exchange for the opportunity to observe how same-sex friendships develop over time. After information on several attitudinal, personality, and demographic variables was collected, members of the boarding house were randomly assigned to roommates. Men who initially thought they held similar opinions on important issues liked each other more at the beginning of the semester. Once students got to know each other, however, actual attitudinal similarity became a better predictor of who liked whom. That is, men who had similar attitudes were more likely to become friends at the end of the semester. This effect has been replicated among men confined to a small fallout shelter (Griffitt and Veitch 1974), among women in their preferences for college roommates (Hill and Stull 1981), and in a computer dating study (Byrne, Ervin, and Lamberth 1970). Recent research suggests that attitude similarity may be more important in enhancing respect, whereas similarity of personal interests might be more critical in generating liking (Lydon et al. 1988).

Personality similarity tends to be a weaker predictor of interpersonal attraction compared to attitudinal similarity. Nevertheless, individuals do prefer others who are similar to themselves in their standing on traditional versus non-traditional sex-role orientation, masculinity versus femininity, sensation-seeking, and cognitive style (Antill 1983; Barry 1970). For personality dimensions on which similarity does not actually exist, friends frequently assume that it does (Feinberg, Miller, and Ross 1981).

Persons who are similar on salient demographic characteristics also experience greater mutual attraction (Newcomb 1961). Best friends in high school, for instance, tend to be similar with respect to their grade in school, age, sex, race, religion, and social class (Kandel 1978). College dating couples typically are similar on age, IQ, educational plans, religion, race, and even height (Hill, Rubin, and Peplau 1976).

People who adopt similar behavioral styles also are drawn to one another. Individuals who are similar in the frequency with which they make personal self-disclosures tend to like each other more (Daher and Banikiotes 1976). People also like those who imitate their positive behaviors and make the same decisions that they do (Roberts et al. 1981; Thelen et al. 1981). Finally, friends typically are similar in how often they engage in deviant behavior (e.g., drug use: Kandel, Single, and Kessler 1976).

Persons involved in relationships usually are matched in their level of physical attractiveness (Feingold 1988). This is true of marriages (Price and Vandenberg 1979), dating relationships (Berscheid et al. 1971), and even same-sex friendships (Cash and Derlega 1978). Why is this so? Even though most people ideally would like to be in relationships with persons who are maximally attractive (Walster et al. 1966), the most attractive individuals tend to pair-off, resulting in a narrowed pool of eligibles for those who are less attractive. Accordingly, individuals typically form relationships with others who are similar to themselves in attractiveness.

 Similarity clearly breeds attraction on many different dimensions. What accounts for this? According to Byrne and Clore (1970), similarity to others is rewarding because it reassures, confirms, and validates people's views about the world. It also promotes anticipatory reciprocity (Aronson and Worchel 1966). Indeed, as we will discuss later, expectations about whether someone will like us can have stronger effects on attraction than the perceived similarity of their attitudes (Condon and Crano 1988).

Of course, similarity does not always lead to attraction. Situations do arise in which dissimilar persons are preferred over similar ones. People are more attracted to dissimilar others when such individuals offer new information (Gormly 1979), reduce uncertainty or confusion in unfamiliar settings (Russ, Gold, and Stone 1980), or make us feel special or unique (Snyder and Fromkin 1980). Dissimilar others also are preferred when being similar to someone is threatening (e.g., when the similar other is mentally ill: Novak and Lerner 1968) and when individuals are assured from the outset that dissimilar others will like them (Walster and Walster 1963).

Complementarity

Some theorists (e.g., Winch 1958) have suggested that opposites should be most strongly attracted to one another. According to this view, people should be drawn to others who can maximally gratify their specific needs. As a result, they should gravitate toward those with complementary needs. Dominant individuals, for instance, should be attracted to submissive persons toward whom dominant actions can be directed, and vice versa. Although complementarity of needs can operate in well established, long-term relationships (Kerckhoff and Davis 1962), it appears to influence such relationships on only a few dimensions and in a limited number of situations (Levinger, Senn, and Jorgensen 1970). Generally speaking, need compatibility (a form of similarity) is a much stronger force in generating attraction between two people than is need complementarity.

Despite the fact that little evidence has been marshaled for Winch's theory at the level of personality, attitudes, and demographic characteristics (Berscheid and Walster 1978; Buss 1984), complementarity principles may operate in some domains. Behavioral complementarity (Strong et al. 1988) and complementarity that occurs with regard to abilities and areas of personal achievement (Tesser 1988) both can increase attraction to another person. Moreover, different types of resources that individuals have or own can be exchanged in a complementary way (Foa 1971). In personal ads run by dating services, for example, women often highlight their relative youth and attractiveness, while men request this information. Men, on the other hand, commonly offer security and provide financial information, whereas women seek these attributes (Green, Buchanan, and Heuer 1984; Harrison and Saeed 1977). In fact, when complementarity occurs, it often is witnessed in romantic relationships (Buss 1985).

Reciprocal Liking

As a general rule, people like others who like them and say nice things about them (Sachs 1976). Indeed, one person's liking for another individual is strongly predicated on reciprocal liking (Kenny and Nasby 1980). When people enter new relationships, they tacitly absume that those they like will like them in return (Curry and Emerson 1970). Merely being told that someone either likes us or evaluates us highly produces feelings of reciprocal affection (Berscheid and Walster 1978). How is reciprocal liking generated? Individuals who anticipate that an interaction partner likes them disclose more, disagree less, and exude a warmer demeanor, all of which elicit warmth and reciprocal affection from their partner (Curtis and Miller 1986).

Even though people tend to be attracted to those who like them, there are limits to the reciprocity effect. If praise is too extreme or unwarranted, it may be seen as ingratiation driven by ulterior motives (Jones 1964). Under such circumstances, excessive flattery may result in the loss of respect for, and decreased attraction to, the flatterer (Shrauger 1975). Individuals who lavish too much praise on others often have their praise either taken for granted (Aronson and Linder 1965) or are perceived as undiscriminating and less intelligent (Amabile 1983), attributes that undermine attraction. On the whole, people are most strongly attracted to those whose praise and affection is either directed selectively to them (Walster et al. 1973) or who are moderately difficult to attract (Wright and Contrada 1986).

Conclusion and Summary

 Interpersonal attraction is a complicated and dynamic process that occurs over time and is influenced by a wide array of different factors. The vignette describing Susan and John epitomizes how this process frequently unfolds. Prior to meeting John, Susan was prepared to develop a new relationship. The environmental conditions surrounding their relationship—both before and during their first formal conversation—were highly conducive to the development of rapid intimacy and strong attraction. While John's physical attractiveness initially drew Susan's attention, his positive personal attributes substantially increased her liking for him once they started conversing. Within a matter of minutes, they began to identify their similarities and to sense strong, mutual attraction.

We are not suggesting that attraction invariably unfolds in this precise sequence. Sometimes it follows different paths. Furthermore, we do not mean to imply that the variables discussed always increase or decrease attraction to others. People occasionally do enter new relationships even though they are not optimally prepared to do so; relationships sometimes do blossom under highly aversive environmental conditions; people can be attracted to others who are physically unattractive (by most people's standards) or who have negative personal attributes; and, in rare cases, individuals sometimes are drawn to persons with whom they share few similarities. These anomalies, however, are exceptions to the general principles discussed.

Where should future research on interpersonal attraction be directed? Four possible avenues come to mind. First, considering that attraction is a process that emerges over time, past research has been notoriously static in nature. It typically has isolated and studied only one stage of the attraction process at a time, with a disproportionately large amount of attention having been devoted to O and P x O factors at the expense of E and P factors. More longitudinal research needs to be conducted in which the independent and interactive effects of P, E, O, and P x O variables on interpersonal attraction are studied within relationships as they develop. Attention also should focus on how attraction changes over time within the same relationship.

Second, most research to date has studied attraction during the early stages of relationship formation. Less work has examined how attraction is maintained once a relationship becomes close and committed. Johnson and Rusbult (1989) have shown that individuals who are more committed to their romantic relationships devalue and derogate potential alternative partners more strongly than do less committed individuals, especially when alternatives are highly attractive and pose a clear threat to the relationship. On a more general level, Simpson, Gangested, and Lerma (1990) have found that people involved in exclusive dating relationships perceive young, opposite-sex persons to be less physically and sexually attractive compared to people who are not dating someone exclusively. This effect may reflect the operation of psychological mechanisms that buffer established relationships from dissolution. At present, however, only a limited number of studies have investigated relationship maintenance processes. Future work should explore how attraction is maintained in long-term relationships.

Third, since the needs of P can strongly influence whether the attraction process initiates and how it evolves, far too little attention has been allotted to understanding how the needs of P interact with E, O, and P x O variables to produce strong attraction. Future research should focus more explicitly on the role that personal needs, motives, and drives play in the attraction process.

Finally, the majority of research on attraction has centered on same-sex friendships and romantic relationships. Much less attention has been paid to other types of relationships (e.g., gay relationships, relationships between younger and older persons). Future research should redress this shortcoming.

Observant readers will note that most of the research cited in this chapter was conducted prior to the early 1980s. What has happened to research on interpersonal attraction during the past decade? Guided by Kelley et al.'s (1983) model of relationship closeness, research has gradually shifted from studying how important variables in the interpersonal attraction process affect relationship initiation to studying how they influence what transpires in close, long-term relationships. Nevertheless, interpersonal attraction research remains alive and well; it now is simply being conducted in the context close relationships.

References

Allport, G. W. 1954. The historical background of modern social psychology. In *The handbook of social psychology,* ed. G. Lindzey, vol. 1, 3–56. Cambridge, MA: Addison-Wesley.

Amabile, T. M. 1983. Brilliant but cruel: Perceptions of negative evaluators. *Journal of Experimental Social Psychology,* 19:146–156.

Anderson, N. H. 1968. Likeableness ratings of 555 personality-trait words. *Journal of Personality and Social Psychology,* 9:272–79.

Antill, J. K. 1983. Sex role complementarity versus similarity in married couples. *Journal of Personality and Social Psychology,* 45:145–55.

Arkin, R. M., and J. M. Burger. 1980. Effects of unit relation tendencies on interpersonal attraction. *Social Psychology Quarterly,* 43:380–91.

Aronson, E., and D. Linder. 1965. Gain and loss of esteem as determinants of interpersonal attractiveness. *Journal of Experimental Social Psychology,* 1:156–71.

Aronson, E., B. Willerman, and J. Floyd. 1966. The effect of a pratfall on increasing inter-personal attractiveness. *Psychonomic Science,* 4:227–28.

Aronson, E., and S. Worchel. 1966. Similarity versus liking as determinants of interpersonal attractiveness. *Psychonomic Science,* 5:157–58.

Bar-Tal, D., and L. Saxe. 1976. Perceptions of similarly and dissimilarly attractive couples and individuals. *Journal of Personality and Social Psychology,* 33:772–81.

Barry, W. A. 1970. Marriage research and conflict: An integrative review. *Psychological Bulletin,* 73:41–54.

Berscheid, E. 1985. Interpersonal attraction. In *The handbook of social psychology,* ed. G. Lindzey and E. Aronson, 413–484. New York: Random House.

Berscheid, E., K. Dion, E. Walster, and G. Walster. 1971. Physical attractiveness and dating choice: A test of the matching hypothesis. *Journal of Experimental Social Psychology,* 7:173–89.

Berscheid, E., and W. Graziano. 1978. The initiation of social relationships and interpersonal attraction. In *Social exchange in developing relationships*, ed. R. L. Burgess and T. L. Huston, 31–60. New York: Academic Press.

Berscheid, E., and E. Walster. 1974. Physical attractiveness. In *Advances in experimental social psychology*, ed. L. Berkowitz, vol. 7, 157–215. New York: Academic Press.

———. 1978. *Interpersonal attraction*, 2nd ed. Reading, MA: Addison-Wesley.

Brehm, J. W. 1966. *A theory of psychological reactance*. New York: Random House.

Brigham, J. C. 1980. Limiting conditions of the "physical attractiveness stereotype": Attributions about divorce. *Journal of Research in Personality*, 14:365–75.

Byrne, D. 1971. *The attraction paradigm*. New York: Academic Press.

Byrne, D., and G. L. Clore. 1970. A reinforcement model of evaluative responses. *Personality: An International Journal*, 1:103–28.

Byrne, D., C. R. Ervin, and J. Lamberth. 1970. Continuity between the experimental study of attraction and real life computer dating. *Journal of Personality and Social Psychology*, 16:157–65.

Buss, D. M. 1984. Toward a psychology of person-environment (PE) correlation: The role of spouse selection. *Journal of Personality and Social Psychology*, 47:361–77.

———. 1985. Human mate selection. *American Scientist*, 73:47–51.

Buss, D. M., and M. Barnes. 1986. Preferences in human mate selections. *Journal of Personality and Social Psychology*, 50:559–70.

Cash, T. F., and V. J. Derlega. 1978. The matching hypothesis: Physical attractiveness among same-sexed friends. *Personality and Social Psychology Bulletin*, 4:240–43.

Chaiken, S. 1979. Communicator physical attractiveness and persuasion. *Journal of Personality and Social Psychology*, 37:1387–97.

Clore, G. L., and D. Byrne. 1974. A reinforcement-affect model of attraction. In *Foundations of interpersonal attraction*, ed. T. L. Huston, 143–170. New York: Academic Press.

Condon, J. W., and W. D. Crano. 1988. Inferred evaluation and the relation between attitude and similarity and interpersonal attraction.

Journal of Personality and Social Psychology, 54:789–97.

Crouse, B. B., and A. Mehrabian. 1977. Affiliation of opposite-sex strangers. *Journal of Research in Personality*, 11:38–47.

Cunningham, M. R. 1986. Measuring the physical in physical attractiveness: Quasi-experiments on the sociobiology of female facial beauty. *Journal of Personality and Social Psychology*, 50:925–35.

Cunningham, M. R., A. P. Barbee, and C. L. Pike. 1990. What do women want? Facialmetric assessment of multiple motives in the perception of male facial physical attractiveness. *Journal of Personality and Social Psychology*, 59:61–72.

Curry, T. J., and R. M. Emerson. 1970. Balance theory: A theory of interpersonal attraction? *Sociometry*, 33:216–38.

Curtis, R. C., and K. Miller. 1986. Believing another likes or dislikes you: Behaviors making the beliefs come true. *Journal of Personality and Social Pycology*, 51:284–90.

Daher, D. M., and P. G. Banikiotes. 1976. Interpersonal attraction and rewarding aspects of disclosure content and level. *Journal of Personality and Social Psychology*, 33:492–96.

Darley, J. M., and E. Berscheid. 1967. Increasing liking as a result of the anticipation of personal contact. *Human Relations*, 20:29–39.

Dion, K. K., E. Berscheid, and E. Walster. 1972. What is beautiful is good. *Journal of Personality and Social Psychology*, 24:285–90.

Driscoll, R., K. W. Davis, and M. E. Lipetz. 1972. Parental interference and romantic love. *Journal of Personality and Social Psychology*, 24:1–10.

Dutton, D. G., and A. P. Aron. 1974. Some evidence for heightened sexual attraction under conditions of high anxiety. *Journal of Personality and Social Psychology*, 30:510–17.

Ebbesen, E. B., G. L. Kjos, and V. J. Konecni. 1976. Spatial ecology: Its effects on the choice of friends and enemies. *Journal of Experimental Social Psychology*, 12: 505–18.

Feinberg, R. A., F. G. Miller, and G. A. Ross. 1981. Perceived and actual locus of control similarity among friends. *Personality and Social Psychology Bulletin*, 7:85–9.

Feingold, A. 1988. Matching for attractiveness in romantic partners and same-sex friends: A meta-analysis and theoretical critique. *Psychosocial Bulletin*, 104:226–35.

Festinger, L., S. Schachter, and K. W. Back. 1950. *Social pressures in informal groups: A study of human factors in housing*. New York: Harper & Brothers.

Foa, U. G. 1971. Interpersonal an economic resources. *Science*, 71:345–54.

Folkes, V. S., and D. O. Sears. 1977. Does everybody like a liker? *Journal of Experimental Social Psychology*, 13:505–19.

Friedman, H. S., R. E. Riggio, and D. F. Casella. 1988. Nonverbal skill, personal charisma, and initial attraction. *Personality and Social Psychology Bulletin*, 14:203–11.

Geiselman, R. E., N. A. Haight, and L. G. Kimata. 1984. Context effects in the perceived physical attractiveness of faces. *Journal of Experimental Social Psychology*, 20:409–24.

Gifford, R., and T. M. B. Gallagher. 1985. Sociability: Personality, social context, and physical setting. *Journal of Personality and Social Psychology*, 48:1015–23.

Goldman, W., and P. Lewis. 1977. Beautiful is good: Evidence that the physically attractive are more socially skillful. *Journal of Experimental Social Psychology*, 13:125–30.

Gormly, A. V. 1979. Behavioral effects of receiving agreement or disagreement from a peer. *Personality and Social Psychology Bulletin*, 5:405–8.

Gouaux, C. 1971. Induced affective states and interpersonal attraction. *Journal of Personality and Social Psychology*, 20:37–43.

Green, S. K., D. R. Buchanan, and S. K. Heuer. 1984. Winners, losers, and choosers: A field investigation of dating initiation. *Personality and Social Psychology Bulletin*, 10:502–11.

Greendlinger, V., and D. Byrne. 1985. *Propinquity and affiliative needs as joint determinants of classroom friendships*. Unpublished manuscript, SUNY at Albany.

Griffit, W. 1970. Environmental effects on interpersonal affective behavior: Ambient effective temperature and attraction. *Journal of Personality and Social Psychology*, 15:240–44.

Griffitt, W., and R. Veitch. 1974. Preacquaintance attitude similarity and attraction revisited: Ten days in a fall-out shelter. *Sociometry*, 37:163–73.

Harrison, A. A. 1977. Mere exposure. In *Advances in experimental social psychology*, ed. L. Berkowitz, vol. 10, 39–83. New York: Academic Press.

Harrison, A. A., and L. Saeed. 1977. Let's make a deal: An analysis of revelations and stipulations in lonely hearts advertisements. *Journal of Personality and Social Psychology*, 35:257–64.

Hatfield, E., and S. Sprecher. 1986. *Mirror, mirror . . . The importance of looks in everyday life*. Albany, New York: State University of New York Press.

Hill, C. T., Z. Rubin, and L. A. Peplau. 1976. Break-ups before marriage: The end of 103 affairs. *Journal of Social Issues*, 32(1):147–68.

Hill, C. T., and D. E. Stull. 1981. Sex differences in effects of social and value similarity in same-sex friendship. *Journal of Personality and Social Psychology*, 41:488–502.

Hokanson, J. E., D. A. Loewenstein, C. Hedeen, and M. J. Howes. 1986. Dysphoric college students and roommates: A study of social behaviors over a three-month period. *Personality and Social Psychology Bulletin*, 12:311–24.

Insko, C. A., and M. Wilson. 1977. Interpersonal attraction as a function of social interaction. *Journal of Personality and Social Psychology*, 35:903–11.

Jackson, D. J., and T. L. Huston. 1975. Physical attractiveness and assertiveness. *Journal of Social Psychology*, 96:79–84.

Johnson, D. L., and Rusbult, C. E. 1989. Resisting temptation: Devaluation of alternate partners as a means of maintaining commitment in close relationships. *Journal of Personality and Social Psychology*, 57:967–80.

Jones: E. E. 1964. *Ingratiation: A social psychological analysis*. New York: Appleton-Century-Crofts.

Jones, W. H., and B. N. Carpenter. 1986. Shyness, social behavior, and relationships. In *Shyness: Perspectives on research and treatment*, ed. W. H. Jones, J. M. Cheek, and S. R. Briggs. New York: Plenum.

Jones, W. H., R. Hannson, and A. L. Phillips. 1978. Physical attractiveness and judgements of psychotherapy. *Journal of Social Psychology*, 105:79–84.

Kandel, D. B. 1978. Similarity in real life adolescent friendship pairs. *Journal of Personality and Social Psychology*, 36:306–12.

Kandel, D. B., E. Single, and R. C. Kessler. 1976. The epidemiology of drug use among New York high school students: Distribution, trends, and change in rates of use. *American Journal of Public Health*, 66:43–53.

Kaplan, M. F., and N. H. Anderson. 1973. Information integration theory and reinforcement theory as approaches to interpersonal attraction. *Journal of Personality and Social Psychology*, 28:301–12.

Kelley, H. H., E. Berscheid, A. Christensen, J. H. Harvey, T. L. Huston, G. Levinger, E. McClintock, L. A. Peplau, and D. R. Peterson. 1983. *Close relationships*. New York: Freeman.

Kenny, D. A., and W. Nasby. 1980. Splitting the reciprocity correlation. *Journal of Personality and Social Psychology*, 38:249–56.

Kenrick, D. T., and R. B. Cialdini. 1977. Romantic attraction: Misattribution versus reinforcement explanations. *Journal of Personality and Social Psychology*, 35: 381–91.

Kenrick, D. T., R. B. Cialdini, and D. E. Linder. 1979. Misattribution under fear-producing circumstances: Four failures to replicate. *Personality and Social Psychology Bulletin*, 5:329–34.

Kenrick, D. T., and S. E. Gutierres. 1980. Contrast effects and judgements of physical attractiveness: When beauty becomes a social problem. *Journal of Personality and Social Psychology*, 38:131–40.

Kenrick, D. T., S. E. Gutierres, and L. L. Goldberg. 1989. Influence of popular erotica on judgements of strangers and mates. *Journal of Experimental Social Psychology*, 25:159–67.

Kerckhoff, A. C., and K. E. Davis. 1962. Value consensus and need complentarity in mate selection. *American Sociological Review*, 27:295–303.

Kernis, M. H., and L. Wheeler. 1981. Beautiful friends and ugly strangers: Radiation and contrast effects in perceptions of same-sex pairs. *Personality and Social Psychology Bulletin*, 7:617–20.

Kipnis, D. M. 1957. Interaction between members of bomber crews as a determinant of sociometric choice. *Human Relations*, 10:263–70.

Knight, J. A., and R. R. Vallacher. 1981. Interpersonal engagement in social perception: The consequence of getting into the action. *Journal of Personality and Social Psychology*, 40:990–99.

Langlois, J. H. 1986. From the eye of the beholder to behavioral reality: Development of social behaviors as a function of physical attractiveness. In *The Ontario Symposium, Volume 3: Physical appearance, stigmata, and social behavior*, ed. C. P. Herman, M. P. Zanna, & E. T. Higgins, 23–51. Hillsdale, NJ: Erlbaum.

Langlois, J. H., and L. A. Roggman. 1990. Attractive faces are only average. *Psychological Science*, 1:115–21.

Leary, M. R. 1983. *Understanding social anxiety: Social, personality, and clinical perspectives*. Beverly Hills, CA: Sage.

———. 1987. A self-presentational model for treatment of social anxieties. In *Social processes in clinical and counseling psychology*, ed. J. E. Maddux, C. D. Stoltenberg, and R. Rosenwein, 126–138. New York: Springer-Verlag.

Levinger, G., D. J. Senn, and B. W. Jorgensen. 1970. Progress towards permanence in courtship: A test of the Kerckhoff-Davis hypothesis. *Sociometry*, 33:427–43.

Lydon, J. E., D. W. Jamieson, and M. P. Zanna. 1988. Interpersonal similarity and the social and intellectual dimensions of first impressions. *Social Cognition*, 6:269–86.

Maddux, J. E., L. W. Norton, and M. R. Leary. 1988. Cognitive components of social anxiety: An investigation of the integration of self-presentation theory and self-efficacy theory. *Journal of Social and Clinical Psychology*, 6:180–90.

May, J. L., and P. A. Hamilton. 1980. Effects of musically evoked affect on woman's interpersonal attraction toward and perceptual judgements of physical attractiveness of men. *Motivation and Emotion*, 4:217–28.

McAdams, D. P. 1982. Intimacy motivation. In *Motivation and society*, ed. A. J. Stewart, 133–171. San Francisco, CA: Jossey-Bass.

McAdams, D. P., and F. B. Bryant. 1987. Intimacy motivation and subjective mental health in a nationwide sample. *Journal of Personality*, 55:395–414.

McAdams, D. P., S. Healy, and S. Krause. 1984. Social motives and friendship patterns. *Journal of Personality and Social Psychology,* 47:828–38.

McAdams, D. P., and G. E. Vaillant. 1982. Intimacy motivation and psychosocial adjustment: A longitudnal study. *Journal of Personality Assessment,* 46:586–93.

McAllister, H. A., and N. J. Bregman. 1983. Self-disclosure and liking: An integration theory approach. *Journal of Personality,* 51:202–12.

McClelland, D. C. 1951. *Personality.* New York: Holt, Rinehart & Winston.

———. 1985. How motives, skills, and values determine what people do. *American Psychologist,* 40:812–25.

Moreland, R. L., and R. B. Zajonc. 1982. Exposure effects may not depend on stimulus recognition. *Journal of Personality and Social Psychology,* 37:1085–89.

Nahemow, L., and M. P. Lawton. 1975. Similarity and propinquity in friendship formation. *Journal of Personality and Social Psychology,* 33:205–13.

Newcomb, T. M. 1961. *The acquaintance process.* New York: Holt, Rinehart & Winston.

Novak, D. W., and M. J. Lerner. 1968. Rejection as a consequence of perceived similarity. *Journal of Personality and Social Psychology,* 9:147–52.

Palmer, J., and D. Byrne. 1970. Attraction toward dominant and submissive strangers: Similarity versus complimentarity. *Journal of Experimental Research in Personality,* 4:108–15.

Pennebaker, J. W., M. A. Dyer, R. J. Caulkins, D. L. Litowitz, P. L. Ackreman, D. B. Anderson, and K. M. McGraw. 1979. Don't the girls get prettier at closing time: A country and western application to psychology. *Personality and Social Psychology Bulletin,* 5:122–25.

Perlman, D., and S. Oskamp. 1971. The effects of picture context and exposure frequency on evaluations of negroes and whites. *Journal of Experimental Social Psychology,* 7:503–14.

Perlman, D., and L. A. Peplau. 1981. Toward a social psychology of loneliness. In *Personal relationships 3: Personal relationships in disorder,* ed. S. Duck and R. Gilmore, 31–56. New York: Academic Press.

Pietromonaco, P. R., and K. S. Rook. 1987. Decision style in depression: The contribution of

perceived risk versus benefits. *Journal of Personality and Social Psychology,* 52:399–408.

Price, R. A., and S. S. Vandenberg. 1979. Matching for physical attractiveness. *Personality and Social Psychology Bulletin,* 5:398–400.

Reis, H. T., J. Nezlek and L. Wheeler. 1980. Physical attractiveness in social interaction. *Journal of Personality and Social Psychology,* 38:604–17.

Riskind, J. H., and D. W. Wilson. 1982. Interpersonal attraction for the competitive person: Unscrambling the competition paradox. *Journal of Applied Social Psychology,* 12:444–52.

Roberts, M. C., S. K. Wurtele, R. Boone, V. Metts, and V. Smith. 1981. Toward a reconceptualization of the reciprocal imitation phenomenon: Two experiments. *Journal of Research in Personality,* 15:447–59.

Rofe, Y. 1984. Stress and affiliation: A utility theory. *Psychological Review,* 91:235–50.

Rubin, Z. 1973. *Liking and loving.* New York: Holt, Rinehart & Winston.

Russ, R. C., J. A. Gold, and W. F. Stone. 1980. Opportunity for thought as a mediator of attraction to a dissimilar stranger: A further test of an information seeking interpretation. *Journal of Experimental Social Psychology,* 16:562–72.

Sachs, D. H. 1976. The effects of similarity, evaluation, and self-esteem on interpersonal attraction. *Representative Research in Social Psychology,* 7:44–50.

Saegert, S., W. Swap, and R. B. Zajonc. 1973. Exposure, context, and interpersonal attraction. *Journal of Personality and Social Psychology,* 25:234–42.

Sallada, E. K., D. T. Kenrick, and B. Vershure. 1987. Dominance and heterosexual attraction. *Journal of Personality and Social Psychology,* 52:730–38.

Sarnoff, I., and P. Zimbardo. 1961. Anxiety, fear, and social affiliation. *Journal of Abnormal and Social Psychology,* 62:356–63.

Schachter, S. 1959. *The psychology of affiliation: Experimental studies of the sources of gregariousness.* Stanford, CA: Stanford University Press.

Schlenker, B. R., and M. R. Leary. 1982. Social anxiety and self-preservation: A conceptualization and model. *Psychological Bulletin,* 92:641–69.

Segal, M. W. 1974. Alphabet and attraction: An unobtrusive measure of the effect of propinquity in a field setting. *Journal of Personality and Social Psychology,* 30:654–57.

Shrauger, J. S. 1975. Responses to evaluation as a function of initial self-perceptions. *Psychological Bulletin,* 82:581–96.

Sigall, H., and D. Landy. 1973. Radiating beauty: The effects of having a physically attractive partner on person perception. *Journal of Personality and Social Psychology,* 28:218–24.

Simpson, J. A., S. W. Gangestad, and M. Biek. 1992. Personality and nonverbal social behavior: The Dating Game revisited. Unpublished manuscript, Texas A&M University.

Simpson, J. A., S. W. Gangestad, and M. Lerma. 1990. Perception of physical attractiveness: Mechanisms involved in the maintenance of romantic relationships. *Journal of Personality and Social Psychology,* 59:1192–1201.

Sloan, W. W., Jr., and C. Solano. 1984. The conversational styles of lonely males with strangers and roommates. *Personality and Social Psychology Bulletin,* 10:293–301.

Snyder, C. R., and H. L. Fromkin. 1980. *Uniqueness: The human pursuit of difference.* New York: Plenum Press.

Snyder, M., E. D. Tanke, and E. Berscheid. 1977. Social perception and interpersonal behavior: On the self-fulfilling nature of social stereotypes. *Journal of Personality and Social Psychology,* 35:656–66.

Spitzberg, B. H., and D. J. Carney. 1985. Loneliness and relationally competent communication. *Journal of Social and Personal Relations,* 2:387–402.

Strack, S., and J. C. Coyne. 1983. Social confirmation of dysphoria: Shared and private reactions to depression. *Journal of Personality and Social Psychology,* 44:798–806.

Strong, S. R., H. J. Hills, T. C. Kilmartin, H. DeVries, K. Lanier, B. N. Nelson, D. Strickland, and C. W. Meyer. 1988. The dynamic relations among interpersonal behaviors: A test of complementarity and anticomplementarity. *Journal of Personality and Social Psychology,* 54:798–810.

Swap, W. C. 1977. Interpersonal attraction and repeated exposure to rewarders and punishers. *Personality and Social Psychology Bulletin,* 3:248–51.

Tesser, A. 1988. Toward a self-evaluation maintenance model of social behavior. In *Advances in experimental social psychology,* ed. L. Berkowitz, vol. 21, 181–227. New York: Academic Press.

Thelen, M. H., N. M. Frautschi, M. C. Roberts, K. D. Kirkland, and S. J. Dollinger. 1981. Being imitated, conformity, and social influence: An integrative review. *Journal of Research in Personality,* 15:403–26.

Tyler, T. R., and D. O. Sears. 1977. Coming to like obnoxious people when we must live with them. *Journal of Personality and Social Psychology,* 35:200–11.

Umberson, D., and M. Hughes. 1984. The impact of physical attractiveness on achievement and psychological well-being. *Social Psychology Quarterly,* 50:227–36.

Unger, R. K., M. Hilderbrand, and T. Madar. 1982. Physical attractiveness and assumptions about social deviance: Some sex-by-sex comparisons. *Personality and Social Psychology Bulletin,* 8:293–301.

Vaux, A. 1988. Social and personal factors in loneliness. *Journal of Social and Clinical Psychology,* 6:462–71.

Veitch, R., and W. Griffitt. 1976. Good news-bad news: Affective and interpersonal effects. *Journal of Applied Social Psychology,* 6:69–75.

Waller, W. W. 1937. The rating and dating complex. *American Sociological Review,* 2:727–37.

Walster, E., V. Aronson, D. Abrahams, and L. Rottman. 1966. The importance of physical attractiveness in dating behavior. *Journal of Personality and Social Psychology,* 4:508–16.

Walster, E., and G. W. Walster. 1963. Effects of expecting to be liked on choice of associates. *Journal of Abnormal and Social Psychology,* 67:402–04.

Walster, E., G. Walster, J. Piliavin, and L. Schmidt. 1973. "Playing hard to get": Understanding an elusive phenomenon. *Journal of Personality and Social Psychology,* 26:113–21.

Weiss, R. S. 1973. *Loneliness.* Cambridge, MA: MIT Press.

Whyte, W. H., Jr. 1956. *The organization man.* New York: Simon & Schuster.

Winch, R. F. 1958. *Mate selection: A study of complementary needs.* New York: Harper & Row.

Wright, R. A., and R. J. Contrada. 1986. Dating selectivity and interpersonal attraction: Toward a better understanding of the "elusive phenomenon." *Journal of Social and Personal Relationships,* 3:131–48.

Wright, T. L., L. J. Ingraham, and D. R. Blackmer. 1985. Simulaneous study of individual differences and relationship effects on attraction. *Journal of Personality and Social Psychology,* 47:1059–62.

Zajonc, R. B. 1968. Attitudinal effects of mere exposure. *Journal of Personality and Social Psychology Monograph Supplement,* 9:1–27.

Zimbardo, P. G. 1977. *Shyness.* New York: Jove.

$Chapter$ 4

Communication in Close Relationships

BARBARA M. MONTGOMERY
Office of Academic Affairs
University of New Hampshire

Outline

Introduction

Sample Dialogue

She Guess what! The library has a secretarial opening. Will you help me fill out the application form? I want to get it in tomorrow.

He The library . . . I thought you were happy with your job downtown, and I thought you were happy with the money it brought in.

She I know that a campus job will pay a lot less, but this is a chance to get back to the university. It would make it easier to take a course or two, part-time; finish my degree sooner; get on with things instead of spending half my time commuting downtown every day.

He I don't think that we can afford it. You agreed that we would concentrate on getting me through school first, and then you. We need your income to do that.

She When we agreed that you would go to school full-time, we never said I couldn't go part-time. As a university employee, I won't have to pay tuition. It would be cheaper in the long run.

He What are we supposed to do for food and rent money in the meantime? Fine time you pick to get bored with a little commute!

No matter how we communicate with friends, family, and loved ones, most of us wish from time to time that we did it better, especially when we have a conversation like the one earlier. Typically, we come away from such encounters wishing that we had fewer arguments, or had our feelings hurt less often, or experienced less misunderstanding with our partner. As much as we would like these things to happen, though, most of us find them a challenge to bring about. This is because there are no simple answers to the problems of interpersonal communication—no "10 Easy Steps for Good Communication in Close Relationships." Research studies tell us that to understand communication between intimates we must develop a complex sensitivity to the people involved, their relationship, their situational circumstances, and, most importantly, the nature of the social process that ties all of these elements together. This chapter explores these issues from the disciplinary perspective of interpersonal communication.

Definitions and Disciplines

A discipline is a structure recognized within academic circles for its identifying assumptions, methods of study, and accumulated understandings about the nature of something. At colleges and universities, disciplines like communication, psychology, and sociology, to name just a few, are typically associated with undergraduate majors, curriculum plans, and departmental divisions. In the broader scholarly community, disciplines are represented by professional associations and journals that promote the work of the discipline's members.

Communication is such a discipline. Its unique focus is on how, why, and with what effects people create meaning together. Members of the communication discipline—students and scholars—study the creation of meaning as it occurs in circumstances like mass mediated events (e.g., television, film, newspapers), public presentations (e.g., speeches), organizational contexts (e.g., business meetings, office newsletters), and interpersonal settings (e.g. friend talking to friend, parent talking to child). The latter encompasses most instances of communication between close relationship partners, and so it is relevant to this text.

Interpersonal communication can be formally defined as *a process in which at least two people behaviorally interact and interpret that interaction in meaningful ways.* The behaviors may be verbal, such as a statement or a question, or they may be nonverbal, such as a smile or a body stance, and they may be exhibited momentarily or at length. However, the behaviors must be interactionally interdependent. That is, they must show some level of behavioral responsiveness so that the actions of one person are related to the actions of the other: John smiles and Mary reciprocates; Mary talks while John listens; John says, "How are you?" and Mary says, "Fine." Communication, then, involves the exchange of interrelated behaviors—action and reaction, question and answer, request and response.

Further, the interactants assign meanings to their behavioral exchanges. A touch, a glance, a statement, a tone of voice—all can be interpreted to mean something. It is not necessary for the interactants to share the exact same meanings for communication to occur; in fact, rarely are one person's interpretations more than an approximation of the other person's. This is because each person brings to a communication event a life-time of experiences that are different than anyone else's and which serve as references in interpreting behavior. It is, therefore, more helpful to think about communication involving the coordination of meaning (Pearce and Cronen 1980). Coordination occurs when behavioral exchanges cohere to define a social episode that makes sense to each of the participants and when that episode is affected by what each of the participants does. From this perspective, the husband and wife's argument that began this chapter would constitute communication even though he thought they were arguing about money (or the lack of it) and she thought that they were arguing about equity issues.

Interpersonal communication has two important functions in close relationships: an instrumental function and a substantive function. The instrumental function refers to the role communication plays as the vehicle for relating; it is the method, the means, the instrument by which people come together into a social unit. Any number of separate individuals are transformed into a social unit—a friendship, a romantic couple—when they communicate with each other. Further, whether the relationship continues or ends is determined by the presence or absence of communication between its members. In the instrumental sense, then, communication is the glue of social bonds; it is the means for relating.

The second function of communication is to provide the substantive meanings of a relationship. The meanings associated with partners' communicative acts, both verbal and nonverbal, define relationship events like arguments, lovemaking, flirtations, play, discussions, apologies, and so forth. It is in and through the extensive range of such interpersonal events that partners develop a sense of what their relationship is like—its nature and character. These meanings, then, constitute the matter and material—the substantive stuff—of all relationships.

This discussion suggests some commonalities and some differences between communication and other social science disciplines. Communication scholars study many of the traditional building blocks of relationships that have interested psychologists and sociologists: individuals with their characterizing traits, attitudes and cognitive patterns and situational and cultural contexts with their accompanying roles, rules and social scripts. But communication scholars place an extraordinary emphasis on the temporal aspects of relationships. For them, relationships exist in communication behaviors and interpreted meanings, both of which unfold over time. Therefore, communication studies focus on the rhythms and tempos, durations and cycles, pasts, presents, and futures of relationships. The interest is in describing how relationships come into being and are changed, reinforced, or affected by the sequences of behaviors that are enacted between their members and by the meanings that are created in that process. Whereas a psychological perspective focuses more on understanding how relationships are associated with individual well-being, especially cognitive and emotional well-being, and whereas a sociological perspective focuses more on understanding relationships as broad-based social structures, a communication perspective focuses more on understanding how relationships are associated with the process of generating meaning in the exchange of messages.

The study of interpersonal communication in close relationships has centered on two questions more than any others: (1) How are relating and communicating associated with each other—that is, what role does communication play in the very existence and nature of relationships? and (2) What is competent communication in close relationships? Answers to each of these questions are explored in the remainder of this chapter.

Communicating and Relating

Two individuals must achieve a significant level of dyadic coordination in order to act together as a couple. While it may not be necessary for partners to think about or to describe their relationship in exactly the same way, it is important that their actions fit together in a way that both find meaningful. Communication is the key to how couples do this. Through their interpersonal communication, couples: (1) learn about and adopt social norms for relating; (2) establish a unique relational culture, and (3) signal their coupleness to others (Montgomery 1992).

Social Norms and Communication

One way that partners achieve coordination is to act as other couples act in similar relationships. In acting normatively, couples achieve a kind of coordination that emanates from the social order of the culture. Partners follow communication scripts and play interactive roles that have been tested by others and found to work.

For instance, researchers have provided considerable detail about the social script for beginning and developing romantic relationships. In general, that script includes the following sequence of behaviors:

1. meeting;
2. small talk;
3. one person calling the other;
4. a formal date;
5. physically showing affection;
6. sharing time together;
7. disclosing personal information;
8. sexual intercourse;
9. meeting each other's parents;
10. exchanging tokens like gifts and flowers;
11. expressing interest in each other's life goals and plans;
12. talking about a long-term relationship;
13. getting married (Honeycutt, Cantrell, and Greene 1989).

The most well known theoretical model of this script is that of Irwin Altman and Dalmas Taylor (1973), who coined the phrase "social penetration" to describe the process in which partners share more aspects of their personal selves as their relationship, whether it be a romance or a friendship, develops. Verbally and nonverbally, partners move from superficial, sometimes confusing and uncoordinated exchanges about narrowly limited topics, which are characteristic of initial encounters, to much more spontaneous, open, efficient and expansive interactions.

Altman and Taylor suggest that stages exist in this movement. The orientation stage consists of impersonal exchanges of only the most superficial information. Partners act in conventional, polite, restrained ways. The overall tone of the interaction is cautious and tentative. During the exploratory affective exchange stage, communication becomes more spontaneous, relaxed, and casual, although the topics remain at the periphery of the partners' personal selves. This stage is characteristic of casual acquaintances and friendly neighbors; indeed, most relationships do not progress past this stage. Those that do, though, enter the third stage of affective exchange. During this period, partners center their disclosures on more personal information and feelings, including feelings about each other. Interaction is expansive and less restrained, although it is still guarded about extremely private matters. Finally, the stable exchange phase, which is reached in only a very few relationships, begins when the partners' disclosures are so intimate as to allow them to predict each other's feelings and responses very well.

Over the years, researchers have added refinements to this script. One of the most important is the conclusion that direct, open, and disclosing communication in developing relationships does not happen with great frequency, but rather occurs in highly selective and special instances that are embedded in a dominant pattern of indirectness (Baxter 1987; Duck et al. 1991). As Altman and Taylor's model predicts, partners do not openly disclose their interest in each other as they begin a relationship. Rather, they depend upon very indirect and often subtle communication strategies: they give compliments, do favors, often happen to be in the same place at the same time, emphasize their similar interests, and test the waters with jokes and hints (Baxter and Philpott, 1982). While partners in more developed relationships are less restricted and more expressive in their communication, they are still cautious about how and when they share private thoughts and feelings (Altman et al. 1981). For instance, research indicates that even close partners rarely talk directly about the state of their relationship, but rather are more likely to employ secret tests to discern each other's feelings and commitment level (Baxter and Wilmot 1984). They devise endurance tests to see if the partner will remain committed even when times are tough; they contrive triangle tests by monitoring how a partner acts with an attractive rival; they stage separation tests to see if the partner will then initiate a reuniting.

Other communication-based scripts exist for relating. One, which has been called the "norm of reciprocity," calls for matching the intimacy of your partner's personal revelations by following with your own—very soon after if you are just beginning a relationship or after a delay if you are in a long-term relationship (Taylor 1979). Other scripts guide people's behavior as they ask another out for a date and go on a first date (Pryor and Merluzzi 1985). Still another script presents men in the initiator role with regard to sexual intimacy and women in the regulator role of controlling the actual occurrence of sexual activity. Both roles emphasize the use of indirect, ambiguous behavior like nonverbal posturing and verbal hints to minimize the risks of interpersonal hurt and rejection (Cupach and Metts 1991).

Partners learn such scripts and roles from a variety of sources, but the three most prominent are social institutions, cultural artifacts, and social networks. Social institutions associated with education, religion, recreation, business, government and leisure provide laws, rules, customs, rituals, and ceremonies that teach and reinforce social scripts. For instance, across a variety of cultures the legal and religious ceremonial aspects of getting married reflect the culture's expectations for how the partners will behave toward one another well beyond their wedding day. Consider the traditional Javanese ceremony, which stresses the subordination of the wife to the husband by having the bride wash the groom's feet and by having both bride and groom throw betel nuts at one another, with the understanding that the one who first hits the other will be in control in the relationship; not surprisingly, the groom always wins (Altman et al., 1992) These customs sharply contrast with modern ceremonies in the United States that emphasize the equality between the bride and groom: often they walk together into the church and down the aisle; both may contribute equally to paying the wedding expenses; neither are likely to take vows to obey the other. As different as the symbolic messages of these two ceremonies are, both define and reinforce role prescriptions for the husband and wife.

Cultural artifacts like books, films, magazines, videos, sculpture, television, newspapers and the like reflect a strong fascination with close relationships and regularly present texts structured around the basic themes of relating. Analyses of romance novels and soap operas, for instance, indicate that they have broad audiences for which their fictional dialogues may well serve as models for how romantic talk should ensue in actual relationships, especially for women (Alberts 1986; Hubbard 1987; Livingstone 1987).

Finally, the partners' parents, siblings, colleagues, acquaintances, friends, spouses, and children—their social network—affects the scripts and roles that the partners learn. Relationship beginnings and endings as well as the activity in between have been linked to influential characteristics of the overarching social network (Altman et al., 1992; Surra 1988). Parents, relatives, teachers, and peers socialize children about how people act in close relationships (Honeycutt, Cantrill and Greene 1989), the characteristics of a good relationship, and the qualities a partner should have (Romberger 1986; VanLear 1992). These teachings are reinforced by the network with a system of social rewards and costs that continue to be applied through adulthood (See Gottlieb, Chapter 15).

Establishing a Relational Culture

Couples do not always follow normative scripts and role prescriptions. Over time, partners work out more and more ways of relating that are particularly effective for them and them alone. They adapt to each other and their circumstances, negotiating their expectations about appropriate ways to act. Partners also can develop unique interpretations of communication events. Private meaning systems can emerge that often bear little resemblance to public language rules (Gottman 1979; Montgomery 1988). A simple example is the use of endearing nicknames, which often seem anything but endearing to outsiders (e.g. belly-pot, spinach-man, broad). Other kinds of non-normative interpretations often are developed by partners for facial expressions ("When he smiles, it means he's frustrated"), eye movements ("When she looks me right in the eye I know she's a mile away in her thoughts"), and postures ("When he slowly crosses his right leg over his left, be prepared for an emotional explosion").

These unique understandings and ways of relating make up what has been called a relational culture (Wood 1982). As with cultures in general, a relational culture arises when a couple develops unique ways of engaging in, interpreting, and evaluating communication behavior that represent and reinforce the special identity of the couple in comparison with others.

Linda Harris and her associates (Harris and Sadeghi 1987; Masheter and Harris 1986) explain the potential couples have to create relational cultures with the example of Sue and Fred, for whom such statements as "Your cooking smells" and "So does your breath" count as acts of affection. In this example, Sue and Fred are able to ignore social norms for assigning meaning to their statements and create new meanings. As Masheter and Harris note, " . . . interpretation of the remark, 'Your cooking smells,' as a compliment is what becomes the fact of the compliment. Interpretation of the same remark as an insult brings about the fact of insult" (p. 179). This happens in much the same way that national cultures develop as large groups of people attach special meanings to various symbols, giving rise to unique languages, cultural rituals, and national emblems.

Leslie Baxter's (1987) research about the development of relationship symbols has added other examples of unique meaning systems in close relationships. Baxter and her associates interviewed over 100 college students about objects, places, and sayings that held unique meanings within their relationships with either friends or romantic partners. The college students identified 500 such symbols, ranging from a game of hiding stuffed hearts, which signaled affection, to the use of codewords for sexual matters, to places like a resort that evoked tender feelings because of a perfect ski weekend.

Jointly held symbols like these carry an overlaid message that the relationship is special, unique, and different from other relationships. The main character in Kurt Vonnegut's *Mother Night* refers to this private and special world shared by close relationship partners as *"Reich der Zwei"* or "a country of two." Less poetically but still powerfully, partners in the Baxter (1987) study corroborate the importance of sharing a unique meaning system by reporting that relationship-based symbols represent the closeness, intimacy, and affection in their relationships, promote togetherness and sharing, and provide a sense of privacy or exclusivity.

Signalling Coupleness to Others

An important part of relating is having outsiders acknowledge the existence of a close relationship and act appropriately in relation to it. Much of the couple's behavior in public carries potentially meaningful information for outsiders in this regard. For instance, a wedding ceremony not only legally, socially, and emotionally binds partners together, it also broadcasts new limits on the relationships others may have with the spouses. In Western cultures a wedding marks the exclusivity of the partners, discouraging outsiders from engaging them in some kinds of interactions—romantic encounters, for instance—and encouraging other kinds of interactions—encounters with couples rather than individuals, for instance.

Irving Goffman (1971) has referred to such behavior as tie-signs, which he defines as behavioral evidence as to the type and nature of a relationship. He illustrates with the example of a couple arriving at a party where they will be mingling separately. They may, just before they part, smile warmly at each other or touch hands. Not only does such a display reinforce the intimacy they feel for each other, it also serves "to provide the gathering with initial evidence of the relationship and what it is that will have to be respected" (p. 203).

The public use of private meaning systems, discussed earlier, can function as a tie-sign. When partners use special nicknames for each other or tell a private joke or use codewords in public, outsiders are likely to notice that the partners seem to interpret messages differently from the others who are present and, therefore, have a special relationship. Other examples of this kind of tie-sign are the explicit discussion of partners' shared experiences and jointly held attitudes and memories (e.g., "You'll have to ask Margaret more about our trip to Venice; she's the designated keeper of our romantic memories") (see Wegner, Giuliano, and Hertel 1985). Jennifer Mandelbaum's (1987) research on partners' joint story-telling activity provides still another example of tie-signs. The unusually high level of interpersonal coordination required to interactively initiate, develop and emphasize an unfolding story signals not only that the partners have shared in a past experience that can be turned into a narrative, but also that they share in the present experience of the telling as well. For the observer, the unusualness of the latter, particularly, is likely to foster a sense of identity for the couple.

This chapter section has focused on the association between communicating and relating. The instrumental function of communication, the ability to tie two (or more) people together into a single social unit—is evident when partners coordinate their being together by using normative, scripted interactive behavior, by developing private message systems as part of their relational culture, and by using communication to signal their relationship to others. These communicative activities establish and reinforce the very existence of a personal relationship, knowable to the partners themselves and to those around them. The substantive function of communication is also evident in this discussion, in that the nature of a relationship—its character or personality—emerges in the choices partners make about which social scripts to follow, what themes to stress in their developing relational culture, and how they wish to portray their relationship to others. Thus, communicating and relating are inherently tied together as social phenomena. Two people cannot initiate or define a close relationship without communicating with one another.

Competent Communication in Close Relationships

How good you might judge the communication to be in any particular relationship depends upon whose standards you use in making the judgement (Montgomery 1988). Societal standards are norms and traditions that define what is good communication for the typical relationship. These describe traditions that a society values as ideals or models for most couples, but rarely are they whole-heartedly embraced by any particular couple. Rather, couples create relational standards by adapting and modifying normative social standards, custom fitting them to their own unique needs and circumstances. Finally, each partner develops idiosyncratic individual standards for judging the quality of communication in his or her relationship. Each of these sets of standards is discussed below.

Societal Standards

Society's notions about what makes for a good relationship have changed over the years. In the 1950s it was thought that people's happiness depended almost entirely upon how well they fulfilled their role obligations as wife or husband or mother or father or friend. Each role had tasks and duties mandated by social norms, and a good relationship was one in which the people in it carried out those expected tasks. By the late 1970s, though, people in western cultures were placing more importance on interpersonal or interactional sources of happiness. Mace (1979) suggested that marriages, for instance, were evolving to where they were held together more by internal cohesion rather than by external coercion. Externally designated roles became less important and internal, communication-based characteristics became more important. Society began distinguishing between real communication and mere talk (Katriel and Philipsen 1981), stressing that people could only become intimate through the special verbal and nonverbal behavior involved in the former. Although a large number of communication behaviors have been associated with real communication, three sets have gained more attention from scholars than any others. These are behaviors associated with positiveness, intimacy, and communication management.

Positive and Negative Behaviors

As children, we are taught that "if you can't say anything nice, don't say anything at all." This sentiment represents a particularly strong ideal for how to communicate in close relationships. People in our culture consistently assume that positiveness (as opposed to negativeness) is connected with high satisfaction levels in most friendships, marriages and romantic relationships.

In general, research findings have confirmed such a link. People happy in their relationships communicate with more positive behaviors, and people unhappy in their relationships communicate with more negative behaviors (Gottman 1979; Stafford and Canary 1991; Ting-Toomey 1983). Table 4–1 lists a sample of positive and negative behaviors that have been studied.

The research of John Gottman and his associates (Gottman 1979) has particularly expanded our understanding of the impact of positive and negative communication behaviors on relationships. Gottman videotaped married couples in the laboratory and at home as they talked about a wide variety of topics like how their day went, the nutritional value of certain foods, marital problems in general, and specific problems in their relationship. He and his associates then coded the couples' verbal and nonverbal behaviors into categories like those presented in Table 4–1.

The analyses of these data indicated that the presence or absence of negative behaviors was related more strongly to the quality of couples' relationships than the presence or absence of positive behaviors. Positiveness and negativeness are not mutually exclusive; increasing one does not automatically decrease the other. For instance, simply getting couples to increase their positive behaviors does not affect the relationship as much as getting them to decrease their negative behaviors.

Gottman also found that negative, nonverbal behaviors had more impact than negative, verbal behaviors. For instance, in many of his studies he found no differences between distressed and undistressed couples in how much disagree-

TABLE 4–1   A Sample of Positive and Negative Communication Behaviors

Positive Behaviors	Negative Behaviors
Verbal	
Agreement	Disagreement
Confirmation	Insults
Integration	Slurs
Constructive problem solving	Threats
Pleasing behaviors	Demands
Compliments	Criticisms
Politeness	
Expresses forgiveness	
Nonverbal	
Smile	Frown
Empathetic expression	Glare
Head nod	Sneer
Caring or concerned or affectionate voice	Cold, hard voice
Cheerful or happy or joyful voice	Accusing or blaming voice
Open arms	Pointing or jabbing
Relaxed posture	Arms akimbo
Forward lean	

(Behaviors identified in studies by: Gottman 1979; Riskin and Faunce 1970; Ting-Toomey 1983; Rusbult, Johnson and Morrow 1986; Stafford and Canary 1991; Wills, Weiss and Patterson 1974.)

ment (i.e., negative, verbal behavior) they expressed; but he found significant differences in how much negative nonverbal behavior they expressed.

Another important finding was that distressed couples tended to string a number of negative behaviors together more than undistressed couples did. If one partner in a distressed relationship complained, the other was likely to reciprocate the complaint, which would be followed by another complaint from the first partner; Gottman calls this a cross-complaining loop. He found the same kind of pattern for negative nonverbal behaviors. This is not to say that nondistressed couples do not have arguments or disagreements in which they exchange negative behaviors; they do. But the data indicate that they emerge more quickly from such negative cycles than do distressed couples, and, interestingly, that it is typically the wife who breaks the negative cycle.

Intimate Behaviors
The ideal of intimacy has become a major theme in the scholarly study of interpersonal communication. The cornerstone for social penetration theories like Altman and Taylor's and others (Berger and Bradac 1982; Knapp 1984; Miller and Steinberg 1975) is that competent communication in close relationships includes high levels of intimate, personally expressive exchanges. By and large research

findings support this notion by finding that the more close partners are open with one another, the happier, more satisfied they are with their relationship (Davidson, Balswick, and Halverson 1983; Hendrick 1981). However, the research also has produced some important qualifications to this general trend.

First, while verbal self-disclosure may have significant impact in close relationships, it does not occur with great frequency even between the happiest of partners. Studies in which partners kept detailed records of their conversations over extended time periods show that everyday communication is mundane and undistinguishable from communication in non-close relationships (Duck et al. 1991). In fact, it may be that the very ordinary nature of most of the talk in close relationships helps to solidify and routinize the bond between partners (Bochner 1982; Duck and Pond 1989), an important function in the maintenance of close relationships. Related to this point, Leslie Baxter and Bill Wilmot (1984) have found that partners in close relationships identity taboo topics that are perceived to be too risky or threatening to disclose and discuss. The topic most often cited as an example was the state of the relationship. Other taboo topics included activities outside the relationship, prior romantic relationships, sexual norms, and known issues of disagreement.

Second, while the verbal expression of intimate feelings and thoughts through self-disclosure is important to relationship quality, the nonverbal expression appears to be more important. In general, people rely more on nonverbal than verbal cues to interpret messages (Archer and Akert 1977; Argyle, Alkema, and Gilmour 1971; Burgoon 1985). The nonverbal behaviors that typically communicate about intimacy include: proximity, body lean, body orientation, touch, gaze, vocal variation, gesturing, and time spent together. These kinds of nonverbal behaviors have been found to better predict relationship quality than do verbal expressions of intimacy (Chelune et al. 1979).

Third, the association between relationship quality and intimate expressions vary considerably over time. Verbal self-disclosure, for instance, has been found to be more impacting in beginning stages of relationships than in later stages. Altman, Vinsel and Brown (1981) address the variability of intimate expressions in a revision of social penetration theory by suggesting that even in the healthiest relationships, partners naturally cycle between being open in their communication and being closed. Recent research has found strong evidence for such cycles in the interaction between growing acquaintances, friends, romantic partners and spouses (VanLear 1991). This cycling helps meet personal and situational needs for both privacy and togetherness, for both separateness and integration (Baxter 1990). Analyses of the interactions between close relationship partners confirm this explanation (VanLear 1991: Wiseman 1986; Rawlins 1983). Even very close partners feel susceptible to being hurt when they disclose private information and, therefore, often will cycle in and out of periods of restraint and cautiousness.

Fourth, frequently both partners do not disclose at equal levels. In heterosexual relationships, women are more likely to carry the major responsibility for expressing personal feelings and thoughts, both verbally (Dosser, Blaswick, and Halverson 1983) and nonverbally (Notarius and Johnson 1982). This difference between the sexes may signal that there are two competing ideals concerning intimacy. The first values open, expressive communication in close relationships, but the second values behavior consistent with stereotypical sexual roles which specify that males are unemotional and restrained and females are emotional and expressive.

A fifth qualification is that the presentation style of personal disclosures has important effects on the quality of close relationships. That is, how intimacy is expressed is as important to the relationship as the fact that it is expressed. Berg (1987) for instance, reports the importance of responsive behaviors like addressing the same topic as the partner, matching the intimacy level of a self-disclosure, and various listener cues like eye contact, smiles, and head nods. Norton and Montgomery (1982) describe similar behaviors with the concept of an open communicator style. An open presentational style is typically interpreted to mean that a message is representative of a person's felt emotions, beliefs, or opinions. Such a style is pronounced in the communication between partners in satisfying close relationships (Honeycutt 1986).

Finally, not all expressive messages are equally linked to high quality in personal relationships. Consistent with the ideal of positiveness discussed earlier, the expression of positive as opposed to negative facts and feelings is more indicative of good relationships (Chelune et al. 1984; Levinger and Senn 1967). This was underscored by a study of how individuals deal with the revelation of unexpected, significant information from friends or romantic partners (Planalp and Honeycutt 1985). The researchers found that learning that a partner had lied, cheated, or engaged in other kinds of negative activities increased the uncertainty people felt about their relationships, resulted in negative emotional reactions towards the partner, and, for about sixty percent of the people in the study, led to decreases in the quality of their relationships. Evidently, the dictum "to know a person is to love a person" is truer when what we know is positive.

Communication Management

Members of our society prize personal relationships in which they actively shape their own futures, direct their own destinies, and manage their own fates (Miller et al. 1986). Partners value the notion of consciously and directly working on their relationships (Katriel and Philipsen 1981). The assumption is that good relationships are not the product of luck or happenstance, but rather are the result of the abilities and efforts of their members. In particular, partners feel that they need to control their communication rather than letting it control them.

One sign of this control is the production of coherent conversations: comments are cogent and clear, topics are introduced smoothly and expanded appropriately, actions are synchronized and spontaneous. In short, partners cooperate to construct an orderly conversation. Indeed, research shows that partners in lower quality relationships do not do these things well. Gottman (1979; Gottman et al. 1976) found that conversations of couples in distressed marriages as opposed to nondistressed ones are characterized by distinct patterns of verbal mismanagement, which are summarized in Table 4–2. He suggests that in well managed conversations, partners ask each other for feedback about their reactions and interpretations, they listen carefully to each other, and they communicate that the other's position is reasonable, even if they cannot agree with it.

Another aspect of managing communication is coordinating nonverbal behavior. Coordination requires that partners mutually adjust to each other's interaction-regulating behaviors like speech rate, pause length, eye gaze, body

---

TABLE 4–2   Distinctive Communication Patterns in Distressed Relationships

Cross-complaining: Exchanging a series of criticisms rather than focusing comments on one issue at a time:

> *She:* "You could have called to say you were going to be late."
> *He:* "And you could have cooked something for dinner other than the same old thing."

A better alternative is to focus on one complaint at a time to try to understand each other's point of view:

> *She:* "You could have called to say your were going to be late."
> *He:* "The budget meeting went on and on and on; I couldn't get away, and pretty soon it was 6:00."
> *She:* "So what can we do to make sure that our dinner isn't ruined when you have late meetings?"
> *He:* "How about next time that we have one of these afternoon budget meetings on the schedule, I'll let you know ahead of time."

Kitchen-sinking: Introducing a number of topics into the conversation at the same time: "Can't we skip the annual boring holiday dinner at your parents this year, and while we're at it, how about telling your sister to stop counting on us as free babysitters every other Saturday."

A better alternative, similar to the one for cross-complaining, is to focus on one topic at a time.

Mindreading: Assuming knowledge about the partner's thoughts, feelings, opinions: "I know that you like being with the Davises, so I've invited them to dinner Thursday."

A better alternative is to directly ask how the other feels or thinks: "Are you interested in inviting the Davises for dinner on Thursday?"

Yes-butting: Consistently finding something wrong with the partner's viewpoint:

> *She:* "I think we're spending too much money on eating out."
> *He:* "Yes, but with both of us working, who has time to cook?"

A better alternative is to give feedback and ask questions in an attempt to better understand the partner's point of view:

> *She:* "I think we're spending too much money on eating out."
> *He:* "How much are we spending?"
> *She:* "Last week we spent $60 and the week before we spent $75."
> *He:* "I didn't realize we were spending so much. How much do you think our budget can afford?"

orientation, and physical distance (Cappella 1984). In well-managed interactions partners' regulating behaviors mesh to produce a smoothly synchronized exchange of messages. Uncoordinated interactions in which behaviors do not mesh can signal relationship problems and dissatisfactions (Cappella 1985; Noller 1980).

Partners in distressed relationships also engage in more metacommunication or reflexive talk (i.e., talk about talk) aimed at clarifying meanings and intentions (Gottman 1979). These couples become much more absorbed with this kind of communication, chaining reflexive messages together at the expense of the original topic of conversation. Apparently, while some talk about talk can counter misunderstandings, extensive metacommunication stymies conversational progress. Partners stand in place by cycling their comments around one idea: "What you seem to be saying is . . . "; "What I meant to say was . . . "; "No, I heard you say that . . . "; "Well, what I really meant was. . . . "Preoccupation with this kind of communication is more likely to resort in mismanaged interactions.

Finally, the extent to which partners concur in their interpretations of messages is related to relationship quality. Shared meanings are not necessary for communication to occur, but they help improve the chances of having a satisfying close relationship (Sillars and Scott 1983). For instance, dissatisfied married partners experience more discrepancies between the message one spouse attempts to send and the message the other spouse receives. Moreover, this discrepancy is biased towards assigning negative interpretations to messages with neutral or positive intent (Kahn 1970; Gottman 1979). This trend is even more disquieting when one considers that dissatisfied partners express more confidence that their interpretations of each other's messages are accurate (Noller and Venardos 1986). Thus, these couples are both less accurate in their communication and also less aware of their inaccuracy.

Relational Standards

Not only do societies develop standards for judging communication in close relationships, so too do relationship partners. Partners develop their own set of beliefs about and behaviors for relating well to each other. This set of relational standards is part of their unique relationship culture, which was discussed earlier.

Relational standards are distinguished by some key characteristics. First, they are the products of negotiation. In day-to-day interaction, partners make claims and counterclaims about the way they should conduct their relationship. This negotiation process continues until some level of consensus is achieved. Second, these claims and counterclaims are more often communicated implicitly in the patterns of behavioral exchanges that take place rather than explicitly as a subject of conversation. One friend is not likely to say to another "Talking about travel is good for our relationship, so we should do it more often." However, two friends might well arrive at that very same conclusion through repeatedly talking about their travels with each other and encountering positive responses. Third, relational standards are unique for each partnership. They are developed entirely within the confines of a particular relationship. Relational standards can contradict, add to, and substitute for social standards, but they are always different from social standards. That difference may be slight, as when two friends are happy being open about everything except their families. Or the difference may be extreme, as when a married couple defies the ideal of positiveness by counting insults as signs of the high quality of their relationship (Masheter and Harris 1986). Considerable possibilities exist within these bounds. Partners may count arguing as caring, rejection as teaching, lying as saving face for the partner, or put-downs as attentiveness. A good relationship may be one which requires little of one's physical and emotional resources; or a good relationship may be one which requires the commitment of vast resources.

Because relational standards are, by definition, unique for each relationship, they are difficult to summarize. However, research by Mary Ann Fitzpatrick (1988) on patterns of interaction between married couples has shed light on a few prominent patterns. Fitzpatrick distinguishes among traditional, independent, and separate couples. Briefly, traditionals follow society's norms for good communication in their relationships. They espouse conventional beliefs and values concerning marriage, and their interaction closely mirrors socially accepted and endorsed roles and scripts. Independents and separates, on the other hand, appear to be guided much more by relational standards for communication. Independents epitomize the complex modern marriage. Their interaction reflects a commitment to working things out as they occur and being attentive to the demands of the moment. There is no one script that they consistently follow. They value intimacy and personal freedom, control and change, positiveness and confrontation. Separates are most noted for their emphasis on detachment. They value being physically and emotionally separate from each other.

Comparisons of the relationship quality for the three couple types indicate that, as a group, traditional couples tend to be the most satisfied, although some couples in all of the types report above average levels of happiness and satisfaction. Further, the pattern of findings suggest that all three couple types represent functional or workable marriages. For instance, independents average exceptionally high in interpersonal understanding, a characteristic they particularly value in relationships (Sillars et al. 1983). Also, more satisfied separates are more likely than less satisfied separates to communicate less emotionally and be less talkative, a violation of the social ideal for intimate communication. These differences for independents and for separates are related to the behavioral patterns uniquely valued by the two couple types, and therefore, suggest the existence of unique relational standards.

Negotiating a shared and unique standard for communication as part of a private message system is undoubtedly very rewarding for partners. Simply sharing in the same meaning system is a positive experience for most. Interactions are coordinated and interpretations are confirmed. Additionally, creating a unique standard helps partners realize a specialness in their relationship. Not only is their standard different, but it is specifically tailored to accommodate their relational circumstances. Couples exercise the freedom to define what counts within the confines of their relationship. The only significant constraint on this process is that the standard must not adversely affect people outside the relationship. Otherwise, social pressure is likely to be brought to bear on the couple to more closely conform to society's standards.

Individual, Idiosyncratic Standards

Besides societal and relational standards, individuals also develop communication standards for quality relationships. These individual standards are idiosyncratic in that they are peculiar and unique to a specific person. They are custom-made and different from the standards advocated by the society or negotiated by the relational unit.

An extended example may help to differentiate among these three types of standards. The intimacy ideal, one aspect of society's standards, advises dating couples to be open, share feelings, and disclose information about themselves. A particular dating couple, though, may have found that they are happier if they exclude some topics from this general expectation for expressiveness, say his drinking and her past loves. This discovery might have come through repeated arguments, hurt feelings, misunderstandings, or awkward silences whenever these topics were introduced. No matter how this conclusion developed, it represents a relational standard of communication that affects the quality of their relationship: if they both avoid the drinking and past loves topics, both are happier and more satisfied in the relationship. In addition, though, both partners may have developed idiosyncratic notions about expressiveness that are not shared but do affect each individual's happiness. For instance, he may most value infrequent but long, late-night, soul-searching, open discussions in which they tackle the problems of the world. She may most value the fifteen-minute chats they have while fixing dinner in which they share synopses of their respective days. The couple may engage in both kinds of intimacy expressions. But since they are not similarly valued, neither probably happens as often nor as well as the partner who prizes that particular kind would like. The crucial aspect of these two individual preferences for intimacy expression is that each carries meaningfully different weights in affecting each partner's satisfaction in the relationship. This is the essential characteristic of idiosyncratic standards.

There are clinical implications of idiosyncratic communication standards, in that an individual may develop values that are not only different from those others hold, but may be disruptive to the larger social order or to the relational culture. Dryden (1981), for example, shows how the standards of depressed persons can be so unfathomable to their friends or spouses that the relationships suffer.

However, individual standards are applied regularly by people in the general population as well. For instance, research indicates that people vary considerably in how they react to expressions of jealousy from their partner, with some indicating that such expressions affect the quality of their relationship a great deal, with some indicating that such expressions have no effect, and with most aligning in between (Sabatelli 1984). This high level of variability in reactions indicates the presence of individual standards. A similar pattern is suggested by studies of how people react to the notion of lying (McCornack and Levine 1990), especially to protect a partner's feelings (Metts 1989).

Conclusion

Scholars in the communication discipline are exploring through their research a great many diverse questions about close relationships. The two discussed in this chapter—"How are communicating and relating associated?" and "What constitutes effective communication in close relationships?"—are among the most prevalent. The answers that are emerging provide notable kernels of insight that this chapter has attempted to describe. Taken together, these answers suggest that:

1. Communicating and relating are interdependent processes; one cannot be done without the other;
2. Communicating in close relationships is different from communication in relationships that are not close; among the major differences are the greater quantity and quality of information available to close partners and their heightened concerns for the quality of their relationships;
3. The ways partners say something is at least as important if not more important to their relationships than what they say;
4. The ways partners communicate change as their relationships develop;
5. Partners follow social norms in their communication with each other, but they also develop communication patterns that are uniquely suited to their particular relationship and its relational culture and to their individual selves.

Summary

This chapter has considered close relationships from a communication perspective, emphasizing how meanings are generated in the behavioral interactions of relationship partners. Through a wide variety of communication sources, from churches to films to parents, partners learn about the prevailing' social norms for relating—how society expects them to act together in their relationship. Over time, though, partners also develop distinctive ways of interacting that signal the emergence of a unique relational culture. These communication activities establish, reinforce, and give identity to their relationship, both as the partners know it and as others around them observe it.

The quality of partners' communication is associated with the quality of their relationship. In our particular society, partners are generally happier when their communication is characterized more by positive behaviors than negative behaviors, when they are open and expressive, and when they engage in coherent, smoothly coordinated conversations. However, partners, together and individually, have considerable latitude to develop ideals for good communication that differ markedly from and can even contradict society's norms. These creative relational and individual standards for good communication often become more dominant than society's norms in influencing how couples communicate within the context of their relationship.

References

Alberts, J. 1986. The role of couples' conversations in relational development: A content analysis of courtship talk in Harlequin romance novels. *Communication Quarterly*, 34:127–42.

Altman, I., B. Brown, B. Staples, and C. Werner. 1992. A transactional approach to close relationships: Courtship, weddings, and place-making. In *Person-Evironment Psychology*, ed. B. Walsh, K. Craik, and R. Price. Hillsdale, NJ: Erlbaum.

Altman, I. and D. Taylor. 1973. *Social Penetration: The Development of Relationships*. New York: Holt, Rinehart and Winston.

Altman, I., A. Vinsel, and B. B. Brown. 1981. Dialectic comparisons in social psychology: An application to social penetration and privacy regulation. In *Advances in experimental social psychology: Volume 14*, ed. L. Berkowitz, 107–160. New York: Academic Press.

Archer, D. and R. Akert. 1977. Words and everything else: Verbal and nonverbal cues in social interpretation. *Journal of Personality and Social Psychology*, 35:443–49.

Argyle, M., F. Alkema, and R. Gilmour. 1971. The communication of friendly and hostile attitudes by verbal and nonverbal signals. *European Journal of Social Psychology*, 1:385–402.

Baxter, L. 1987. Cognition and communication in the relationship process. In *Accounting for Relationships: Explanation, Representation and Knowledge*, ed. R. Burnett, P. McGhee and D. Clarke. London: Methuen.

———. 1990. Dialectical contradictions in relationship development. *Journal of Social and Personal Relationships*, 7:69–88.

Baxter, L. and J. Philpott. 1982. Attribution-based strategies for initiating and terminating relationships. *Communication Quarterly*, 30:217–24.

Baxter, L. and W. Wilmot. 1984. Secret tests: Social strategies for acquiring information about the state of the relationship. *Human Communication Research*, 11:171–201.

Berg, J. H. 1987. Responsiveness and self-disclosure. In *Self-Disclosure: Theory, Research, and Therapy*, ed. V. Derlega and J. Berg. New York: Plenum.

Berger, C. R. and J. J. Bradac. 1982. *Language and social knowledge: Uncertainty in interpersonal relations*. London: Edward Arnold.

Bochner, A. 1982. On the efficacy of openness in close relationships. In *Communication Yearbook 5*, ed. M. Burgoon. New Brunswick: Transaction.

Burgoon, J. K. 1985. Nonverbal signals. In *Handbook of Interpersonal Communication*, ed. M. Knapp,& G. R. Miller. Beverly Hills: Sage.

Cappella, J. N. 1984. The relevance of the microstructure of interaction to relationship change. *Journal of Social and Personal Relationships*, 1:239–64.

———. 1985. The management of conversations. In *The Handbook of Interpersonal Communication*, ed. M. L. Knapp and G. R. Miller. Beverly Hills: Sage.

Chelune, G. J. and associates. 1979. *Self-disclosure: Origins, patterns, and implication of openness in interpersonal relationships*. San Francisco: Jossey-Bass.

Chelune, G. J., E. Waring, B. Yosk, F. Sultan, and J. Ogden. 1984. Self-disclosure and its relationship to marital intimacy. *Journal of Clinical Psychology*, 40:216–19.

Cupach, W. R. and S. Metts. 1991. Sexuality and communication in close relationships. In *Sexuality in Close Relationships*, ed. K. McKinney and S. Sprecher. Hillsdale, NJ: Lawrence Erlbaum.

Davidson, B., J. Balswick, and C. Halveson. 1983. Affective self-disclosure and marital adjustment: A test of equity theory. *Journal of Marriage and the Family,* 45:93–102.

Dosser, D. A., Jr., J. O. Blaswick, and C. F. Halverson, Jr. 1983. Situational context of emotional expressiveness. *Journal of Counseling Psychology,* 30:375–87.

Dryden, W. 1981. The relationship of depressed persons. In *Personal Relationships 3: Personal Relationships in Disorder,* ed. S. W. Duck and R. Gilmour. London: Academic Press.

Duck, S. W. and K. Pond. 1989. Friends, Romans, countrymen, led me your retrospective data: Rhetoric and reality in personal relationships. In *Review of Social Psychology and Personality, Vol. 10: Close Relationships,* ed. C. Hendrick. Newbury Park, CA: Sage.

Duck, S. W., D. Rutt, M. H. Hurst, and H. Strejc. 1991. Some evident truths about conversations in everyday relationships: All communications are not created equal. *Human Communication Research,* 18:228–67.

Fitzpatrick, M.A. 1988. *Between husbands and wives: Communication in marriage.* Newbury Park, CA: Sage.

Goffman, E. 1971. *Relations in public.* New York: Basic.

Gottman, J. 1979. *Marital interaction: Experimental investigations.* New York: Academic Press.

Gottman, J., C. Notarius, and H. Markman. 1976. *A couple's guide to communication.* Champaign, IL: Research Press.

Harris, L. and A. Sadeghi. 1987. Realizing: How facts are created in human interaction. *Journal of Social and Personal Relationships,* 4:480–95.

Hendrick, S. S. 1981. Self-disclosure and marital satisfaction. *Journal of Personality and Social Psychology,* 40:1150–59.

Honeycutt, J. 1986. A model of marital functioning based on an attraction paradigm and social-penetration dimensions. *Journal of Marriage and the Family,* 48:651–67.

Honeycutt, J., J. Cantrill, and R. Greene. 1989. Memory structures for relational escalation: A cognitive test of the sequencing of relational actions and stages. *Human Communication Research,* 16:62–90.

Hubbard, R. 1987. Relationship styles in popular romance novels 1950 to 1983. *Communication Quarterly,* 33:113–25.

Kahn, M. 1970. Nonverbal communication and marital satisfaction. *Family Process,* 9:449–56.

Katriel, T. and G. Philipsen. 1981. "What we need is communication": "Communication" as a cultural category in some American speech. *Communication Monographs,* 48:301–17.

Knapp, M. 1984. *Interpersonal communication and human relationships.* Boston: Allyn and Bacon.

Levinger, G. and D. Senn. 1967. Disclosure of feelings in marriage. *Merrill-Palmer Quarterly,* 13:237–49.

Livingstone, S. 1987. The representation of personal relationships in television drama: Realism, convention and morality. In *Accounting for Relationships,* ed. R. Burnett. London: Methuen.

Mace, D. 1979. Marriage and family enrichment—a new field. *The Family Coordinator,* 28:409–19.

Mandelbaum, J. 1987. Couples sharing stories. *Communication Quarterly,* 35:144–70.

Masheter, C. and L. Harris. 1986. From divorce to friendship: A study of dialectic relationship development. *Journal of Social and Personal Relationships,* 3:177–90.

McCornack, S. A. and T. R. Levine. 1990. When lies are uncovered: emotional and relational outcomes of discovered deception. *Communication Monographs,* 57:119–38.

Metts, S. 1989. An exploratory investigation of deception in close relationships. *Journal of Social and Personal Relationships,* 6:159–80.

Miller, G. R. and M. Steinberg. 1975. *Between people: A new analysis of interpersonal communication.* Chicago: Science Research Associates.

Miller, P., H. Lefcourt, J. Holmes, E. Ware, and W. Seleh. 1986. Marital locus of control and marital problem solving. *Journal of Personality and Social Psychology,* 51:161–69.

Montgomery, B. 1988. Quality communication in personal relationships. In *Handbook of Personal Relationships: Theory, Research and Interventions,* ed. S. Duck, D. Hay, S. Hobfoll, W. Ickes, and B. Montgomery. Chichester: John Wiley.

———. 1992. Communication as the interface between couples and culture. In *Communication*

Yearbook 15, ed. S. Deetz. Newbury Park, CA: Sage.

Noller, P. 1980. Gaze in married couples. *Journal of Nonverbal Behavior,* 5:115–29.

Noller, P. and C. Venardos. 1986. Communication awareness in married couples. *Journal of Social and Personal Relationships,* 3:31–42.

Norton, R. W. and B. M. Montgomery. 1982. Style, content and target components of openness. *Communication Research,* 9:399–431.

Notarius, C. I. and J. S. Johnson. 1982. Emotional expression in husbands and wives. *Journal of Marriage and the Family,* 44:483–89.

Pearce, W. B. and V. E. Cronen. 1980. *Communication, action, and meaning: The creation of social realities.* New York: Praeger.

Planalp, S. and J. M. Honeycutt. 1985. Events that increase uncertainty in personal relationships. *Human Communication Research,* 11:593–604.

Pryor, J. B. and T. V. Merluzzi. 1985. The role of expertise in processing social interaction scripts. *Journal of Experimental Social Psychology,* 21:362–79.

Rawlins, W. 1983. Openness as problematic in ongoing friendships: Two conversational dilemmas. *Communication Monographs,* 50:1–13.

Riskin, J. and E. Faunce. 1970. Family interaction scales, III. Discussion of methodology and substantive findings. *Archives of General Psychiatry,* 22:527–37.

Romberger, B. 1986. "Aunt Sophie always said . . . ": Oral histories of the commonplaces women learned about relating to men. *American Behavioral Scientist,* 29:342–67.

Rusbult, C. E., D. J. Johnson, and G. D. Morrow. 1986. Impact of couple patterns of problem solving on distress and nondistress in dating relationships. *Journal of Personality and Social Psychology,* 50:744–53.

Sabatelli, R. 1984. The marital comparison level index: A measure for assessing outcomes relative to expectations. *Journal of Marriage and the Family,* 46:651–61.

Sillars, A., G. Pike, T. Jones, and K. Redmon. 1983. Communication and conflict in marriage. In *Communication Yearbook 7,* ed. R. Bostrom. Beverly Hills: Sage.

Sillars, A. and M. Scott. 1983. Interpersonal perception between intimates: An integrative review. *Human Communication Research,* 10:153–76.

Stafford, L. and D. Canary. 1991. Maintenance strategies and romantic relationship type, gender and relational characteristics. *Journal of Social and Personal Relationships,* 8:217–43.

Surra, C. 1988. The influence of the interactive network on developing relationships. In *Families and Social Networks,* ed. R. Milardo. Newbury Park, CA: Sage.

Taylor, D. 1979. Motivational bases. In Self-Disclosure, ed. G. Chelune and associates. San Francisco: Jossey-Bass.

Ting-Toomey, S. 1983. An analysis of verbal communication patterns in high and low marital adjustment groups. *Human Communication Research,* 9:306–19.

Wegner, D. M., T. Giuliano, and P. Hertel. 1985. Cognitive interdependence in close relationships. In *Compatible and Incompatible Relationships,* ed. W. J. Ickes. New York: Springer-Verlag.

Wills, T., R. Weiss, and G. Patterson. 1974. A behavioral analysis of the determinants of marital satisfaction. *Journal of Consulting and Clinical Psychology,* 42:802–11.

Wiseman, J. 1986. Friendship: Bonds and binds in a voluntary relationship. *Journal of Social and Personal Relationships,* 3:191–212.

Wood, J. 1982. Communication and relational culture: Bases for the study of human relationships. *Communication Quarterly,* 30:75–83.

VanLear, C. A. 1991. Testing a cyclical model of communication openness in relationship development: Two longitudinal studies. *Communication Monographs,* 58:337–62.

———. 1992. Marital communication across the generations: Learning and rebellion, continuity and change. *Journal of Social and Personal Relationships,* 9:103–23.

Toward Understanding Emotions in Intimate Relationships

PARASTU MEHTA
Carnegie Mellon University

MARGARET S. CLARK
Carnegie Mellon University

Outline

Introduction

Some Examples

Have you ever had experiences like the following ones? You are home from school for the summer and have not yet found a summer job. You feel very discouraged about the prospects of finding a job, much less one you will like or that will look good on your resume when you finish school. You feel depressed and are now lying on your bed staring at the ceiling. Your sister walks in. You think to yourself that she is pretty inconsiderate to simply barge into your room unannounced. She is cheerful and you find her cheerfulness to be irritating. You reject her suggestion to go to a movie. She comments that perhaps she ought to get out of your way, and she leaves the room.

Picture quite a different situation—one in which you are not feeling any particular emotion. You have just transferred to a new college and have been assigned a new roommate. You walk into your new room to meet her for the first time. She does not see you at first because she is talking on the phone leaving a message on someone's answering machine. You notice her cheerful tone and the fact that she is humming a happy tune. She is smiling. Her emotional state had nothing to do with you, yet it leads you to like her and think that you will get along easily with her.

Finally, consider the following. It is your birthday. A person who has expressed some interest in going out with you, but in whom you have absolutely no interest, appears at the door. This person hands you a nicely wrapped gift. You get a sinking feeling in your stomach and you feel both distressed about the situation and a bit angry. The person leaves. As you sit there depressed, your best friend walks in. Your friend too has a gift in hand. This time you look up and your mood brightens. You are pleased that your friend remembered. With a smile, you accept the gift.

All three situations have something to do with the role of emotions in relationships. In the first case, you are in a negative mood—a mood which has nothing at all to do with your relationship with your sister. Yet, it has an important impact on your interactions with her. In the second case, you are not in any particular mood, yet a person with whom you hope to develop a close relationship is in a happy mood. Her emotional state has an impact on your impressions of her. In the third case you have one emotional reaction to receiving a gift from someone with whom you would rather not have a close relationship and a very different reaction to receiving a gift from someone with whom you have an established close relationship.

Our chapter deals with the role of emotions in intimate relationships. Following some brief introductory comments, it is organized into three sections corresponding to the three scenarios just presented. The first section deals with research on how the emotions we bring to interactions with others who are close to us influence our own behavior in those interactions. The second section deals with research on how the emotions which others bring to their interactions with us influence our interactions with them. The third and final section deals with how the nature of our relationship with others may influence the emotional expressions and reactions which occur within that relationship.

We bring a particular perspective to this chapter. That is, we have chosen to focus on experimental social psychological theory and research. There is much other work on emotion in relationships done from other perspectives. In a brief chapter it is impossible to deal with all this research. Yet, since this other work is also important, at the end of this chapter we will mention some additional work which the interested student might wish to read.

When Do We Experience Emotion?

Much of the emotion we experience in everyday life arises in the context of our social relationships (DeRivera 1984; Scherer, Wallbott, and Summerfield 1986; Schwartz and Shaver 1987; Trevarthen 1984). For example, Csikszentmihalyi and his colleagues gave adolescents and adults electronic pagers. These researchers asked their subjects to report on a number of different aspects of their lives each time they were randomly beeped during the day. They found that both adolescents and adults were more likely to report feeling happy when they were with friends than when they were alone (Csikszentmihaly and Larson 1984; Larson, Csikszentmihalyi, and Graef 1982). Other researchers have found that joy and anger are much more likely and sadness somewhat more likely to occur in social than in non-social contexts (Babad and Wallbott 1986).

Despite the fact that our emotional life is closely intertwined with our social life, there is still little research on how emotions influence relationship structure and processes as well as little research on how relationship structure and relationship processes influence emotions. To a large extent this is due to the fact that social psychologists have long had a penchant for doing laboratory studies in which their variables are well controlled. Thus, to study attraction and interpersonal relations, a common strategy has been to bring together people who do not know one another and who probably do not expect to see one another again, to vary just one or two things about one person (a target person) and to observe how the other reacts to that target person. While this has resulted in clean, well controlled studies, it has also meant that we have tended not to study real, ongoing, intimate relationships. Since it is precisely such relationships in which most emotions appear to be experienced and expressed, emotion in relationships has been a relatively neglected topic. However, things are changing. Research on emotion in relationships is rapidly increasing. While much remains to be done, enough has been done to give the reader a feel for the role of emotions in relationships and we have taken that as our goal for this chapter.

In this chapter we discuss research dealing with the experience and expression of emotion in relationships. The particular emotions that have received the most empirical attention with respect to relationships have been anger, sadness, and happiness, and those will be the emotions we will focus upon most in this chapter.

Some Influences of Emotion on Behavior

How Do Emotions People Bring to their Relationship Influence their Behavior in those Relationships?

Considerable evidence from controlled laboratory studies suggests that the emotions we bring to the interactions with people close to us influence our perceptions of them, our feelings towards them, and also our behaviors toward them. In particular, researchers have used a number of techniques in the laboratory to create moods of sadness, happiness or anger, including having subjects read stories, view films, and receive feedback about performance. Results most often indicate that the induced emotions influence subjects' impressions of others such that those impressions become more congruent with their current mood state (e.g. Fiedler, Pampe, and Scherf 1986; Forgas and Bower 1987; Forgas, Bower, and Krantz 1984; Forgas and Moylan 1987; Schiffenbauer 1974).

An example of a field study in which the role of emotion in every day situations was examined is one by Forgas and Moylan (1987). These researchers interviewed Australian moviegoers attending films previously classified as being predominantly happy (e.g., Beverly Hills Cop, Brewster's Millions), predominantly sad (e.g., Mask, Killing Fields), or predominantly aggressive (e.g., First Blood, Rambo). Subjects were approached prior to the movie or immediately after the movie either in the theatre lobby or on the street in front of the exit. They were asked if they would participate in a brief survey requesting their judgments on a number of issues. It would only take a few seconds to complete. Subjects' judgments on a number of diverse topic areas, including their ratings of satisfaction with two prominent political figures—the prime minister and the leader of the opposition—were collected. These subjects' judgments were found to be more positive, lenient and optimistic after they had viewed a happy film than after they had viewed a sad or an aggressive film. (They also rated their moods as being more positive after happy than after sad or aggressive films.) It is important to add that these effects seem not to be due to different types of people choosing to go to different films. Subjects in control groups who completed the identical questionnaire before they entered the various movie theaters showed no differences in the overall positivity of judgments across the three film categories and no differences in self ratings of mood.

Similar results have been found in laboratory studies as well. Fiedler, Pampe and Scherf (1986) found that after inducing a positive mood, subjects formed more favorable impressions of target persons with respect to a number of categories of social behavior (e.g., sociability, altruism, honesty, creativity), and Forgas and Bower (1987) found that happy subjects formed more favorable impressions and made more positive judgments of target persons than did sad subjects. These studies suggest that our affective states can and often do influence the judgments we make about our relationships and about others involved in those relationships with us. The first example presented at the beginning of this chapter was chosen to illustrate this type of effect. In that example your own depressed mood over the lack of prospects of finding a summer job had an impact on your view of your own sister. You judged your sister to be inconsiderate, and found her cheerfulness to be irritating and her suggestion to go to a movie to be uninteresting.

In addition to influencing our liking of others, there is also evidence suggesting that a person's emotional state affects his or her judgments of the emotional state of others. One example of such a study is provided by Schiffenbauer (1974). He manipulated subjects' emotional states by tape-recorded messages. He found that an aroused subject was more likely to judge the facial expressions of others as consistent with the emotion he or she was feeling than was a non-aroused or a differently aroused subject. The implications of these results are that perhaps if we are happy, we see others as happy and look forward to interacting with them. However, if we are sad or angry, we may judge the other's mood to be like ours and may decide to refrain from an interaction with the other.

Other researchers have shown that merely feeling physiologically aroused as a result of exercise can also influence our judgments of other's positive emotions such that those judgments become more congruent with our own internal state. Specifically, Clark, Milberg and Erber (1984) found in each of two studies that subjects who had just exercised were more likely than subjects who had not exercised to interpret another person's positive statements and positive facial expressions as indicating joy (a high arousal emotion) than as indicating serenity (a low arousal emotion).

Still other studies have found that the emotions we bring to a relationship not only influence our impressions of other people, they also influence our behavior toward others. For instance, moods have been shown to influence prosocial behaviors such as helping or self-disclosure (Cialdini and Kenrick 1976; Cialdini, Baumann, and Kenrick 1981; Cunningham 1988a; 1988b; Isen 1970; Isen and Levin 1972; Levin and Isen 1975). Being in a positive mood, that is, feeling happy, has very consistently been shown to lead to increased helping (e.g. Cunningham, Steinberg, and Grev 1980; Isen 1970; Isen and Levin 1972; Isen, Clark, and Schwartz 1976; and see Carlson, Charlin, and Miller 1988 for a review). This finding has been demonstrated using a wide variety of manipulations of positive mood and a wide variety of measures of helpfulness. Just to give a few examples, Isen et al. (1976) manipulated mood by having an experimenter go door-to-door in suburban neighborhoods handing out free samples of stationery (or merely demonstrating the stationery) to the residents. Meanwhile another experimenter was calling these same subjects (as well as some others who had not been contacted by the first experimenter). The second experimenter used a prearranged schedule so as to reach the subjects at specified times after they had received (or not received) free stationery. When she contacted these people she asked for Victor and was inevitably told that she had reached the wrong number. Then she stammered a bit, and expressed dismay. She was in a phone booth and had just used her last dime to make the call. She asked the subject to make a call to her brother who was supposed to be at Victor's house. If the subject agreed she gave the subject a phone number to call. Calls to that number were monitored. In two separate studies using largely the same procedure, subjects who had received a free gift recently were significantly more likely to make the call than were subjects who had either not been contacted at all or subjects who had merely seen the stationery demonstrated to them. The researchers' results further suggested that the effect dissipated by the time twenty minutes had passed. If that amount of time had passed between subjects receiving free stationery (and presumably having been put in a good mood), they were no more likely than the "no contact" or the demonstration subjects to help.

An earlier study which also supported the idea that positive moods will enhance our tendency to help others was conducted by Isen (1970). She found that people who had just succeeded on a task were more likely to donate to an unrelated charity than were those who had not succeeded. What accounts for this link between feeling good and helping? Perhaps it is due to good mood causing people to view the possibility of helping more positively (Clark and Waddell 1985; Isen, Shalker, Clark, and Karp 1978), due to people wanting to maintain their good mood state (Isen and Simmonds 1978) or due to some other process (see Carlson et al. 1988 for a review). In any case, it is one of the most consistently reported effects in social psychology.

Negative moods have also been shown to have an impact on helping compared to being in no particular mood. Most studies have shown that being in a negative mood is also related to helping others more (e.g, Carlsmith and Gross 1969; Cialdini, Darby, and Vincent 1973; Donnerstein, Donnerstein, and Munger 1975), and a number of different explanations have been set forth for why this may occur. The results of many of these studies have been explained by assuming that we are socialized to think of helping as a good thing and that we come to feel good about ourselves after helping. Thus, helping is something we can do to alleviate guilt feelings (Carlsmith and Gross 1969) or to alleviate sadness (see Cialdini, Kenrick, and Baumann 1982). Interestingly, the studies which have shown the opposite effect (i.e., negative moods leading to less helping) have been conducted with children who may not yet have been sufficiently socialized to think of helping as a way to get out of a negative mood state (e.g., Moore, Underwood, and Rosenhan 1973; Underwood et al. 1977).

As a final example of research showing how the emotions we bring to our relationships with others can influence our behavior toward others, consider some recent work by Cunningham (1988a; 1988b). In two studies he found that positive moods were associated with more intimate self-disclosure, while negative moods were associated with sitting and thinking, being alone, as well as lower interest in social and leisure activities.

The evidence we have cited that the positive and negative moods we bring to our interactions with others influence behavior in those interactions has not been collected in the context of actual ongoing close relationships. Nonetheless, we think it is clearly of relevance to understanding the role of emotion in forming and in maintaining close relationships. Consider relationship formation first. Certainly self-disclosing to others and helping others are ways to initiate close relationships with those others (see for instance, Cohen, Sherrod, and Clark 1986 for evidence that self-disclosure predicts both the development of social support and of friendship, or Reis and Shaver's 1988 discussion of how a sense of intimacy comes to be established between two persons). Moreover we would be very surprised if self-disclosure and helping were not similarly important to maintaining such relationships.

In addition to the evidence demonstrating that the moods and emotions we experience can increase certain prosocial behaviors toward others, there is support for the notion that our emotions can affect our feelings towards others and that we can misattribute our emotions to feelings toward the other (e.g., White, Fishbein, and Rutstein 1981). In two studies, White, Fishbein and Rutstein (1981) found evidence that misattribution of arousal can facilitate romantic arousal. In one study they demonstrated that the misattribution effect can be obtained under conditions of neutral arousal (physical exercise). They observed that arousal and a confederate's attractiveness combined such that attraction was enhanced when the male subjects were aroused and the female confederate was attractive, whereas attraction was decreased when the subjects were aroused and the confederate was unattractive. Their explanation was that subjects misattributed their arousal to the confederate. If the confederate was attractive, subjects presumably attributed their arousal to liking for her. If she was unattractive they attributed their arousal to feelings of distaste. The results of a second study in which arousal was induced by having subjects listen to a positive (comedy tape) or negative (mutilation tape) or nonarousing tape (textbook excerpt) replicated the effects found in the first study. That is, regardless of valence of the source of arousal, aroused subjects liked the attractive confederate more and the unattractive confederate less than did unaroused subjects. The authors suggest that salience of plausible labels for arousal mediates the misattribution effect.

Consider how arousal might influence attraction in a common, everyday situation. Imagine that you have been running, and so you are physiologically aroused. You stop exercising and arousal drops somewhat, but not to baseline levels. In any case, you stop focusing on your arousal. A short time later you encounter an attractive other. You may also notice that at that moment your heart is beating faster than it normally does. You may think to yourself, "My heart must be beating fast because I am attracted to this individual," and you may misattribute your exercise-induced arousal to this attraction. Alternatively perhaps you are at a scary movie. After watching a frightening scene your arousal increases. Soon afterwards, during a more boring part of the movie, you look across the aisle and notice an attractive person also watching the movie. You note that your heart is beating fast and assume that the reason must be your attraction toward this other person, forgetting for the moment that you are at a horror movie which is the true cause of your enhanced arousal.

Again while the research on misattribution of arousal was not conducted in the context of ongoing close relationships, these results have implications for the effects of arousal which a person brings to any relationship. However, there is still a need to show whether, and if so how, these effects generalize to what occurs in close ongoing relationships. We turn next to the question of how the other's emotions may influence our interactions with that other.

How Do the Emotions Others Bring to our Relationships Influence our Behavior in those Relationships?

Recall the example given earlier about the cheerful roommate who gives you the impression she is a person with whom it will be easy to get along. There is evidence suggesting that both the short and long term emotions the other expresses can influence our perceptions of that other, of our relationship with that other, and our behavior toward the other.

Sommers (1984) found that among college students, target persons who were described as experiencing predominantly positive emotions were seen as more sociable, conventional, popular, and likable than target persons who supposedly were not experiencing these emotions. Expressions of predominantly negative moods caused people to be viewed as less likable, social, and popular. Interestingly, Sommers' results also revealed that females who expressed negative emotion were seen as more unsociable and unpopular than males who expressed the same negative affect. These results certainly suggest that the expression of emotions by the other can influence our desire to form, maintain or terminate a relationship with the other. Consider our example of the cheerful roommate who appears likable and with whom you think you will get along easily. Her cheerfulness may well enhance your motivation to form a close relationship with her. Suppose she was angry after getting off the phone, or maybe sad or distressed. Your impression of her would undoubtedly be more pessimistic, and that in turn might well cause you to behave more negatively toward her.

Another's expression of emotion can also influence our judgments regarding another's more specific personality traits. For instance, in a study by Chrisman and Clark (1991), the emotion of another person was revealed to the subject as being sad or angry or neutral. It was found that another's anger increased his or her perceived dominance as well as decreased his or her perceived likability. Also, another's sadness increased the perceived dependency of that person.

Certainly these more specific effects of another's expression of emotion should also have predictable effects on social interaction in close relationships. We may make fewer requests of others if they are angry, or we may give into their requests more often precisely because we do see them as dominant. We may be more likely to help sad others precisely because they do seem more dependent. A recent study by Clark (1992) supports this latter speculation. That is, Clark has shown that if we perceive that another person is sad we will be more likely to help that person. Perceiving them to be feeling angry or happy did not influence helping. Presumably we help sad people more than others because they seem more needy than others.

Interestingly, however, a study by Clark et al. (1987) suggests that the effects of another's sadness on the likelihood of helping them is a bit more complex than it might seem at first. Specifically, Clark et al. noted that in some relationships, called communal relationships, people feel more responsibility for the needs of the other than they do in other relationships, called exchange relationships. Communal relationships are often exemplified by the relationships that exist between friends and romantic partners. For half the subjects in a study, Clark et al. created desire for a communal relationship by having college students find out about a quite attractive opposite-sex other who was said to be eager to meet new people. Exchange relationships are often exemplified by relationships that exist between strangers meeting for the first time who have no reason to expect future interactions or acquaintances. For the remaining half of the subjects, Clark et al. created a desire for an exchange relationship by having subjects find out about an attractive opposite-sex other who happened to be married and busy and therefore not available for a friendship or a romantic relationship. This other appeared to be sad (for half the subjects in each relationship condition) or in no particular mood (for the remaining half the subjects in each relationship condition). Then the subjects had a chance to help the other. Not surprisingly, subjects helped more in the communal than in the exchange conditions. Interestingly for the present discussion, the other's sadness increased the amount of help given when a communal relationship was desired but not when an exchange relationship was desired. While sadness makes others seem needy and dependent, it may only increase helping when we feel a special desire to establish or maintain a communal relationship with that other.

In addition to the evidence which suggests that short term emotions expressed by others can influence our impressions and behavior toward another, there exists a body of research which reveals that emotions expressed over a long term can also have important influences on our thoughts, moods, and behaviors toward the person expressing the emotion—influences that do not always parallel the impact of similar short term emotions on our impressions of others. Coyne (1976a; 1976b), for instance, showed that in brief encounters, depressed persons induce negative moods such as hostility, depression and anxiety in others. In addition, these negative feelings appear to result in rejection of the depressed person. These reactions from others may perpetuate negative mood states and even contribute to the development and persistence of more severe mood disturbance in the depressed individuals. Studies by Coyne and his colleagues using severely depressed patients as well as mildly unhappy persons yield results which show that these negative moods elicit negative social responses. Specifically, Strack and Coyne (1983) have found that nondepressed subjects who had talked with depressed people or even mildly unhappy people came to feel more hostile, depressed, anxious, and also were less willing to interact with their partner in the future. These findings suggest that persons who are clinically depressed or even mildly unhappy will influence the impressions and behaviors of their partners and potential partners, quite likely driving these others away from them and perhaps leading to an undesired sense of isolation and more depression.

What Happens when Both People Bring Emotional States to their Interaction? How Will They Interact?

In addition to how the emotion of one person affects his or her own perceptions and behaviors or the perceptions and behaviors of the other person in the relationship, it is important to examine the effects of the combined emotions that members of a relationship pair bring to their interaction. A recent study examined the joint effects of emotion brought to an interaction episode by two people. In this study (Locke and Horowitz 1990), depressed and nondepressed people interacted with people of similar or dissimilar mood. People in homogeneous dyads (both partners were unhappy or both partners were not unhappy) were more satisfied, and their satisfaction increased as the conversation proceeded. People in mixed dyads were less satisfied, perceived each other as colder, and spoke about increasingly negative topics. These results are consistent with other research showing that similarity leads to liking (Byrne 1969; Byrne, Griffitt and Stefaniak 1967; Hendrick and Page 1970). The determinant of satisfaction with the conversation in this study was neither the mood of the subject nor the partner, but their similarity in mood. The authors proposed a number of mechanisms through which similarities and differences in the moods people bring to their interactions may influence their satisfaction with that interaction. One possibility is that partners in homogeneous dyads validate each other's feelings causing both to be satisfied with the interaction while this does not occur in heterogeneous dyads. Another possibility is that members of homogeneous dyads are more likely to like their partners than are members of heterogeneous dyads. Clearly more investigation into why people in similar moods are more satisfied with their interactions is needed.

Other work also looking at the influence of mutual emotional expression has focused on how specified patterns of emotional expression influence people's judgments about the relationship. For instance Beall, Barnes, and Salovey (1991) examined the influential role of positive emotional expression in perceptions of power, vulnerability, and liking. Characters in written scenarios who expressed similar amounts of positive emotion directed at one another were perceived to have equal amounts of power. Greatest perceived power was attributed to characters who expressed little positive emotion while their partner expressed much positive emotion; least perceived power was attributed to characters who expressed much emotion while their partner expressed little emotion. Partners who returned high levels of emotions (regardless of the character's initial expression) were viewed as less interested in ending the relationship, more likely to be upset if the relationship ended, and less likely to become romantically interested in someone else than did partners who returned low amounts of emotion. The results also revealed that characters who expressed high levels of emotion or returned high levels of emotion were more likable than less expressive characters. Further research should examine whether these results will hold for expressions of negative emotions as well.

Before leaving this section on how we react to others' expressions of emotion, we would note that most of the research we have cited examines how we react to others' emotion that is not directed at us. That is, the other is not sad or happy because of something we have done or is not angry at us. Future investigations in this area should systematically examine and differentiate between: a) our reactions to others' expressed emotion when that emotion is the result of something we did (e.g., the other is happy because we gave him or her a gift) versus when it was not (e.g., the other is happy because he or she received a gift from someone else), and b) reactions to others' expressed emotion when it is directed at us (e.g., another is angry at us) versus when it is not directed at us (e.g., the other is angry because of something someone else did). Reactions to expressed emotion undoubtedly will be quite different in these different types of situations.

Some Influences of Relationship Structure on Emotion

Recall the example given earlier about the negative reaction of distress and anger you had upon receiving a birthday gift from a person in whom you had no romantic interest and the opposite, positive reaction of joy upon receiving a gift from your best friend. Clearly, something about the differing natures of these relationships caused these different reactions. Several social psychological theories have found evidence that the structure of the relationship influences either the experience of emotion or reactions to emotion in the relationship.

Among those we will discuss here are Berscheid's (1983) theory of emotional interdependence, Clark and Mills' (1979; Mills and Clark 1982) distinction between communal and exchange relationships, Tesser's (1988) theory of self-evaluation maintenance processes, and Shaver and Hazan's (1988) application of attachment theory to adults. A brief explanation of each will help illustrate how the structure of the relationship affects both our own emotions and how we react to others' expressions of emotion.

Berscheid's Theory of Interdependence

Berscheid's theory of emotional interdependence in the context of ongoing relationships is based on Kelley et al.'s (1983) notion of a relationship, according to which a relationship exists between a person (P) and an other (O) if the thoughts, affect, and actions of one person influence and are influenced by the thoughts, affect, and actions of another person. The interdependence of thoughts, affect and actions (the causal connections in both directions) between P and O constitute a relationship. For Berscheid and her colleagues, a close relationship is one characterized by members who have frequent and strong impact on each other in diverse activities across time (Berscheid, Snyder, and Omoto 1989).

Berscheid notes that emotion can arise due to the combination of the arousal caused by interruptions in well-practiced action sequences and a cognitive appraisal of that arousal. Berscheid suggests that emotion is directly related to the nature of the interdependence in a relationship. If two people are not organized action sequences tend to be independent such that neither ..as much ability to interrupt the other. Therefore little emotion occurs in that relationship. In contrast, in close relationships, members' action sequences are very intertwined. There is considerable potential of each interrupting the other's well-practiced action sequences and eliciting arousal and emotion. According to this model, in highly interdependent relationships many interruptions may take place, leading to much emotion. However, interruptions may not occur, and if they do not, there is little emotion. Berscheid explains that emotions are labeled as negative when interruptions hinder goal attainment, and positive when they facilitate the attainment of goals or when the interruptions are under our control.

The term emotional investment in a relationship, for Berscheid, refers to the extent to which there exists the potential for the two members of that relationship to experience emotion in the context of their relationship. One may think of a person's emotional investment in a relationship as the extent to which that person is vulnerable to interruptions from events in the other person's thoughts, affect and behavior. Emotional investment must be high for much emotion to be generated based on the processes Berscheid discusses. However, it is important to note that just because emotional investment is high does not necessarily mean emotion will occur frequently. If interruptions do not occur, neither will emotion.

Think back to our birthday gift example. The emotions experienced in this example can be explained in terms of Berscheid's theoretical ideas. First, you receive a gift from the person for whom you have no romantic feelings. The arrival of the gift is unexpected and interrupts a normal sequence of events. Because the interruption hinders your goal attainment, which in this case is to convey to this individual that you are not romantically interested in this individual, you experience negative emotions. The receiving of a gift from your best friend, on the other hand, while still a surprise that interrupts the normal sequence of actions between you and your best friend, facilitates the attainment of your goals which may be to maintain a mutually caring and giving relationship with your best friend. Thus you interpret the action positively and experience happiness.

Simpson (1987) has empirically tested some of Berscheid's ideas using a relationship closeness inventory based on Berscheid's concept of interdependence. This inventory records the frequency with which people influence each other, the diversity of ways in which they influence each other, and the strength of the impact that each person's behaviors, emotions, and thoughts have on the other's behaviors, emotions and thoughts (Berscheid, Snyder, and Omoto 1989). First Simpson determined the length and closeness of ongoing relationships, relationship satisfaction, and perceived ease of finding new relationships in premarital couples. Three months later, he assessed emotional distress among those whose relationships had ended. The greater the interdependence (as indicated by closeness and length) and perceived difficulty of replacement, the greater the emotional distress. Specifically, individuals who were close to their former partner, who had dated the former partner for a long time, and who believed that they could not easily acquire a desirable alternative tended to experience more pronounced distress following dissolution. This supports Berscheid's idea that interruptions in closely intertwined relationships will generate considerable emotion. Interestingly and although it may seem counterintuitive, Simpson's findings also revealed that earlier feelings of satisfaction with the relationship did not predict emotional distress—a finding also consistent with Berscheid's theory. After all, Berscheid argues one can be satisfied in a relationship that is not very interdependent. When such a relationship breaks up there should be minimal disruption of routines, little arousal and consequently little distress. Similarly one can be very unsatisfied in a highly interdependent relationship yet still experience many interruptions and arousal when it breaks up, and label that arousal as distress over the breakup. For both these reasons, Berscheid's theory suggests that feelings of satisfaction in a relationship may not predict emotional distress upon break-up.

Clark and, Mills' Communal/Exchange Distinction

The existence of communal and exchange norms can also shape the emotional experiences in a relationship. As mentioned earlier, Clark and Mills (1979; Clark 1985; Mills and Clark 1982) have distinguished communal from exchange relationships. In communal relationships, members feel a general obligation to be concerned about the other's welfare. Thus, they pay attention to the other's needs (Clark, Mills, and Corcoran 1989; Clark, Mills, and Powell 1986), they give the other benefits in response to those needs (Clark, Ouellette, Powell, and Milberg 1987), and they feel good when they have helped the other (Williamson and Clark 1989). In contrast, in exchange relationships, members do not feel a special obligation to be concerned about the other's welfare. Thus, they keep track of who does what in their relationship (Clark 1984; Clark and Waddell 1985), they give benefits with the expectation of receiving comparable benefits in return or in payment for benefits previously received (Clark 1981; 1984; Clark and Mills 1979, Clark and Waddell 1985), and they are not especially responsive to the other's needs (Clark, Mills, and Powell 1986; Clark et al. 1987; Clark, Mills, and Corcoran 1989).

Distinguishing relationship types has implications for people's expressions of emotions and also their reactions to the expression of emotions by others. Expressing emotions conveys information about one's needs to others (Scherer 1984). Since having information about needs should be central to being able to adhere to the communal norm of meeting the other's needs, we should be more willing to express emotion to others in communal than in exchange relationships. We should also react more positively to other's expressions of emotion in communal than in exchange relationships. Clark and Taraban (1991) have provided evidence for both these ideas. In a first study they led half of their college student subjects to desire a communal relationship with another by choosing a physically attractive other and conveying that she was available for and interested in meeting new others. The remaining half of the subjects were led to desire an exchange relationship by conveying that the other was married, busy, and seemingly not interested in new communal relationships. Subjects discovered either that the other was feeling no particular emotion, or that the other was sad, happy or irritable. Then the subjects formed first impressions of the other. When no emotion was expressed there were no differences in the positivity of impressions of the other. However, when any emotion was expressed (sadness, happiness or irritability), impressions were more positive when a communal than when an exchange relationship was desired.

Clark and Taraban (1991) explain the more positive reaction to expressing emotion in communal relationships by noting that emotion communicates information about one's needs—something that is important and appropriate when a communal relationship in which members will feel a mutual responsibility for one another's needs is desired. However, in an exchange relationship members do not feel a mutual responsibility for one another's needs. Indeed they would probably rather not know about one another's needs. Therefore expressing emotion is seen as less appropriate and less desirable when exchange relationships are desired.

In another study, which we already mentioned earlier in this chapter, Clark et al. (1987) provided additional evidence that expressions of emotion will be reacted to more positively when communal than when exchange relationships are desired. Specifically, they found that subjects desiring communal relationships with another, but not those desiring exchange relationships increased the amount of help given to another in response to the other's sadness.

A second study by Clark and Taraban (1991) examined willingness to express emotion to the other. Subjects were paired with a friend or a stranger and were asked to have a discussion on one of a number of topics they were given. Friends ranked emotional topics (e.g., your fears, things that make you sad) as significantly more desirable than did strangers.

Going beyond issues of reacting to others' expressions of emotion and being willing to express emotions ourselves, the communal/exchange distinction can also inform us about how we will react emotionally to some of our own and to some of other people's behavior. For instance, the difference in norms suggests that we should feel better after helping someone with whom we have or desire a communal relationship (because the behavior fits the norm and should help to develop or maintain the relationship) than we will feel after helping someone with whom we have or desire an exchange relationship. Two studies by Williamson and Clark (1989, study 3; 1992) have confirmed that our moods do improve more after helping someone with whom we desire a communal relationship than after helping someone with whom we desire an exchange relationship. Indeed, Williamson and Clark (1992) actually found that choosing to help in an exchange relationship causes mood to become less positive (presumably because helping is not only unnecessary but creates a distressing inequity in the relationship). Finally, the communal/exchange distinction suggests that our moods should deteriorate more when we fail to help in a communal relationship than when we fail to help in an exchange relationship—an idea recently confirmed by Williamson et al. (1992).

What about reacting to others' behavior? Clearly we should experience positive emotions when the appropriate norms are followed and experience negative emotions when the norms are violated. This notion can be used to explain the emotional reactions described in one of the scenarios used at the beginning of this chapter. Specifically, why might we be happy when our friend gives us a gift for our birthday, but distressed when a stranger does so? The communal/exchange distinction suggests a clear answer. In communal relationships we want people to be concerned about our welfare. Moreover, receiving a benefit does not create a specific debt to repay the other. Instead it should serve to solidify the relationship. Therefore we ought to welcome the gift from our friend and we should feel good. In sharp contrast, in exchange relationships the other is not supposed to be especially concerned about our welfare. Assuming that we do not want to develop a communal relationship with someone with whom we have an exchange relationship, we are likely to react negatively to receiving a gift from that other. This may either signal that the other desires a type of relationship which we do not desire or that we are indebted to return a comparable benefit to that other as soon as possible. No wonder receiving such a gift may put us in a negative mood!

Tesser's Self-Evaluation Maintenance Theory

Self-evaluation theory can also be used to predict much about emotional experiences in intimate relationships (Pleban and Tesser 1981; Tesser and Campbell 1980; Tesser, Millar, and Moore 1988). Tesser and his colleagues have provided a model of social behavior called self-evaluation maintenance (SEM). It emphasizes the role of social circumstances in producing emotions. The model assumes that people are motivated to maintain a positive self-evaluation and that their self-evaluation is determined, at least in part, by two social psychological processes -social comparison and reflection.

In Tesser's theory social comparison simply refers to comparing one's own performance in a domain relevant to one's identity with that of another person. According to the theory, when another outperforms the self on a task high in relevance to the self, social comparison will take place and one will experience a threat to one's self esteem. The closer the relationship with the other, the greater the threat to self-evaluation. (In Tesser's work, closeness refers to being seen as belonging with the other—being in what social psychologists have called a unit relationship.) The threat to self-esteem will arouse negative affect. Thus one can predict that being outperformed by a close other (e.g., one's sister) in a relevant domain will generate more negative affect than being outperformed by someone who is not as close (e.g., an acquaintance).

Social reflection involves feeling that another's performance in a domain which is not very relevant to one's identity reflects upon one. According to Tesser's theory, when another with whom one is associated outperforms the self on a task low in relevance to the self one can experience a gain in self-evaluation through reflection. Such gains should arouse positive affect. The closer the rela-

tionship the greater the gain should be. Thus, one can predict that being outperformed by a close other (e.g., one's sister) in a domain not relevant to one's
self-esteem should result in greater jumps in positive affect than being outperformed in the same domain by a person who is not close (e.g., an acquaintance).
Tesser and his colleagues have presented evidence that being outperformed by a
close other in either domains relevant or irrelevant to one's identity result in
greater arousal than being outperformed by a distant other (Tesser, Millar, and
Moore 1988). Presumably when subjects were outperformed in relevant domains
this arousal was indicative of the negative affect associated with social comparison processes; when they were outperformed in an irrelevant domain this arousal
was indicative of positive affect associated with reflections processes. (Indeed,
other findings reported by these authors which are too complex to describe here
do support these assumptions about the presumed affective tone of the arousal.)

To get a better understanding of how the social comparison process may
influence emotional reactions, consider how you might feel in the following
situation. Both you and your friend care a great deal about doing well in school.
Both you and your friend have studied for an exam together and taken it. You
both feel you will probably get B's. Now you get the exams back. Yours is handed
back first and you have a B. You feel okay about that. Then your friend gets hers
back. You look over at her exam. She has an A. You feel terrible. Why? You feel
bad because she is a similar, relevant person with whom to compare yourself, and
she did better.

To get a better understanding of the reflection process, consider a close other
performing well on a task that is not terribly relevant to you. Your brother, for
instance, might be an avid and competitive skier while you just ski occasionally
for recreation. Now imagine that he wins a national championship. Your mood
will probably brighten and you may derive considerable pleasure in telling others
about his accomplishment. You feel good because a person close to you did well
and you believe that it reflects positively upon you. You do not feel bad because
skiing is not central to your identity while it is to his.

Tesser's theory is important for purposes of understanding emotional experiences in relationships. It is especially noteworthy for demonstrating that closeness and similarity do not always have positive implications for the experience of
emotion in relationships.

Attachment Theory

Yet another social psychological theory related to emotions in relationship is
attachment theory. Bowlby (1969, 1973, 1980) described the attachment, separation, and loss processes by which affectional bonds are developed and broken. He
explored how infants become emotionally attached to their primary caregivers
and emotionally distressed when separated from them. In recent years, laboratory
and naturalistic studies of infants and children (summarized by Maccoby 1980)
have provided considerable support for the attachment theory which was proposed by Bowlby and elaborated upon by several other investigators.

On the basis of their observations, Ainsworth et al. (1978) have identified three styles or types of attachment often called secure, anxious/ambivalent and avoidant. In their descriptions of these styles, Ainsworth and her colleagues refer to styles of caretaking and to infants' resulting expectations concerning their mothers' accessibility and responsiveness. Securely attached infants have primary caregivers who are generally available and responsive to the infant's needs. Such infants appear to be generally happier, more relaxed and adventuresome, and easier to comfort when distressed than are other infants. Anxious/ambivalent attachment characterizes infants whose primary caregiver is also anxious and seemingly out of step with the infant's needs, being sometimes available and responsive, but at other times unavailable and intrusive. When the primary caregiver is around, the child clings to him or her. These children are easily frightened but not easily comforted. They are without a secure base from which to venture forth and, in turn, they are not nearly as adventurous as the secure child. The third style, avoidant attachment, is characteristic of infants whose primary caregiver is generally unresponsive if not outright rejecting. These infants become socially closed and avoid their parents and strangers alike. While not particularly confident or adventurous, they are quite independent.

More recently, Hazan and Shaver (1987; 1990; Shaver and Hazan 1988, Shaver, Hazan, and Bradshaw 1988) suggest that romantic love among adults is an attachment process (a process of becoming attached) which is experienced somewhat differently and is associated with different emotions by different people because of variations in their attachment histories. According to these authors, the process of becoming emotionally attached to an adult romantic partner is somewhat similar to the way an infant becomes attached or bonded to its primary caregiver. Attachment theory includes attempts to predict and to explain both negative and positive emotion. In addition the theory also attempts to explain how loneliness and love are related. (See Chapter 7 in this volume.)

In two studies by Hazan and Shaver (1987), subjects provided descriptions of childhood relationships with parents, descriptions of themselves and others, and also of their most important romantic love experiences. These studies have shown that the relative prevalence of the three attachment styles is roughly the same in adulthood as in infancy. The proportions are approximately 56% secure, 23% avoidant, and 19% anxious/ambivalent (Hazan and Shaver 1987). The three kinds of adults differ predictably in the way they experience romantic love. More specifically, they hold different beliefs about the course of romantic love, availability, trustworthiness of love partners, and their own love-worthiness. Secure subjects describe their relationships with parents as generally warm and supportive; they appear to be confident and open, and they describe their most important love relationships in terms of friendship, trust and happiness. In contrast, anxious/ambivalent subjects describe their parents as unpredictable (sometimes responsive and sometimes not); they lack self-confidence and they describe their most important love relationship in terms of jealousy, desire for reciprocation, emotional highs and lows, and intense sexual desire. Avoidant subjects describe their parents as demanding, disrespectful, critical and uncaring. They characterize themselves as independent and disliked by others, and describe their most important love relationship in terms of fear of closeness, emotional highs and lows and lack of acceptance (Shaver and Hazan 1988). These findings suggest that securely attached persons may be especially likely to experience joy and love in their romantic relationships. On the other hand, anxious/ambivalent and avoidant persons may be especially likely to experience anger, fear, and sadness in their relationships.

Conclusion and Summary

To summarize, we have pointed out three ways in which one might think about the general topic of emotion in close relationships. First, you can think about how the emotions you bring into the relationship from the outside influence your interactions with others. Second, you can think about how your reactions to others' emotions influence your interactions with them, and finally you can think about how the very nature or structure of one's relationships will influence experiences of emotion in that relationship including what the antecedents and consequences of various emotions will likely be. We have tried to show that some social psychologists have taken each of these approaches and that a reasonable body of knowledge relevant to understanding the role of emotion in close relationships has emerged.

Clearly more work is needed. In addition to hoping that more social psychological, theory-driven research is done to illuminate the roles which emotions play in intimate relationships, we would also like to see tests of whether many of our currently existing findings will generalize to what happens in naturally occurring, ongoing intimate relationships.

Before closing, we would like to re-emphasize a point we made briefly in the introduction to this chapter. That is, we have left out some important, non-social-psychological research on emotion in close relationships due to space constraints. There is now a moderately sized literature which takes an exploratory, observational approach to understanding emotion in intimate relationships and which has yielded some interesting findings. We cannot go into detail regarding those studies here, but let us just note one intriguing finding. Gaelick, Bodenhausen and Wyer (1985), in examining emotional interdependence in marital relationships, found evidence that men (but not women) interpret their partners' failure to express love as an indication of hostility, whereas women (but not men) interpret their partners' lack of hostility as an indication of love. In other words, in this study women exhibited a positive bias in interpreting ambiguous communication whereas men exhibited a negative bias. Interestingly these same biases were evident in a study of decoding errors in non-verbal communication which was reported by Noller (1980). We cannot be sure why these gender differences exist but they are intriguing and potentially of great practical significance to people such as marital therapists who might wish to try to find ways of avoiding these biases and their potentially negative consequences for relationships. There are other such intriguing findings as well in the literature. We would urge the reader interested in pursuing more knowledge about the role of emotion in intimate relationships to read the original versions of studies such as those reported by Gaelick, Bodenhausen, and Wyer (1985), Noller (1980), and others (e.g., Gottman 1979; 1980; Levenson and Gottman 1983; 1985).

References

Ainsworth, M. D. S., M. C. Blehar, E. Waters, and S. Wall. 1978. *Patterns of attachment: A psychological study of the strange situation.* Hillsdale, NJ: Erlbaum.

Babad, E. Y., and H. G. Wallbott. 1986. The effects of social factors on emotional relations. In *Experiencing Emotion: A Cross-cultural Study,* ed. Scherer, K. R., Wallbott, H. G., and Summerfield, A. B., 154–172. Cambridge, England: Cambridge University Press.

Beall, A. E., M. Barnes, and P. Salovey. 1991. Emotional expressions influence one's power, vulnerability, and likability in romantic relationships. Poster presented at American Psychological Society conference.

Berscheid, E. 1983. Emotion. In *Close Relationships,* ed. H. H. Kelley, E. Berscheid, A. Christensen, J. H. Harvey, T. L. Huston, G. Levinger, E. McClintock, L. A. Peplau, and D. R. Peterson, 110–168. New York: W. H. Freeman.

Berscheid, E., M. Snyder, and A. M. Omoto. 1989. The relationship closeness inventory: assessing the closeness of interpersonal relationships. *Journal of Personality and Social Psychology,* 57: 792–807.

Bowlby, J. 1969. *Attachment and loss: Vol. 1. Attachment.* New York: Basic Books.

Bowlby, J. 1973. *Attachment and loss: Vol. 2. Separation: Anxiety and anger.* New York: Basic Books.

Bowlby, J. 1980. *Attachment and loss: Vol. 3. Loss.* New York: Basic Books.

Byrne, D. 1969. Attitudes and attraction. *Advances in experimental social psychology,* vol. 4. New York: Academic Press.

Byrne, D., W. Griffitt, and D. Stefaniak. 1967. Attraction and similarity of personality characteristics. *Journal of Personality and Social Psychology,* 5: 82–90.

Carlsmith, J. and A. Gross. 1969. Some effects of guilt on compliance. *Journal of Personality and Social Psychology,* 11: 232–39.

Carlson, M., V. Charlin, and N. Miller. 1988. Positive mood and helping behavior: A test of six hypotheses. *Journal of Personality and Social Psychology,* 55: 211–29.

Chrisman, K., and M. S. Clark. 1991. Anger increases perceived dominance and decreases likability; sadness increases perceived dependency. Paper presented at the American Psychological Society convention, Washington, D.C.

Cialdini, R. B., D. J. Baumann, and D. T. Kenrick. 1981. Insights from sadness: A 3 step model of the development of altruism as hedonism. *Developmental Review,* 1: 207–23.

Cialdini, R. B., B. L. Darby, and J. E. Vincent. 1973. Transgression and altruism: A case for hedonism. *Journal of Experimental Social Psychology,* 9: 502–16.

Cialdini, R. B., and D. T. Kenrick. 1976. Altruism as hedonism: A social development perspective on the relationship of negative mood state and helping. *Journal of Personality and Social Psychology,* 34: 907–14.

Cialdini, R. B., D. T. Kenrick, and D. J. Baumann. 1982. Effects of mood on prosocial behavior in children and adults. In *The development of prosocial behavior,* ed. N. Eisenberg-Berg, 339–59. New York: Academic Press.

Clark, M. S. 1981. Noncomparability of benefits given and received: A cue to the existence of friendship. *Social Psychology Quarterly,* 44: 375–81.

———. 1984. Record keeping in two types of relationships. *Journal of Personality and Social Psychology,* 47: 549–57.

———. 1985. Implications of relationship type for understanding compatibility. In *Compatible and Incompatible Relationship*, ed. W. Ickes 119–140. New York: Springer-Verlag.

———. 1992. Effects of a potential recipient's anger, sadness and happiness on the likelihood of receiving help. Unpublished manuscript, Carnegie Mellon University, Pittsburgh, PA.

Clark, M. S., S. Milberg, and R. Erber. 1984. Effects of arousal on judgments of others' emotions. *Journal of Personality and Social Psychology*, 46: 551–60.

Clark, M. S., and J. Mills. 1979. Interpersonal attraction in exchange and communal relationships. *Journal of Personality and Social Psychology*, 37: 12–24.

Clark, M. S., J. Mills, and D. Corcoran. 1989. Keeping track of needs in communal and exchange relationships. *Personality and Social Psychology Bulletin*, 15: 533–42.

Clark, M. S., J. Mills, and M. Powell. 1986. Keeping track of needs in communal and exchange relationships. *Journal of Personality and Social Psychology*, 52: 333–38.

Clark, M. S., R. Ouellette, M. Powell, and S. Milberg. 1987. Relationship type, recipient mood, and helping. *Journal of Personality and Social Psychology*, 53: 94–103.

Clark, M. S., and C. Taraban. 1991. Reactions to and willingness to express emotion in communal and exchange relationships. *Journal of Experimental Social Psychology*, 27: 324–36.

Clark, M. S., and B. Waddell. 1985. Perceptions of exploitation in communal and exchange relationships. *Journal of Social and Personal Relationships*, 2: 403–18.

Cohen, S., D. R. Sherrod, and M. S. Clark. 1986. Social skills and the stress-protective role of social support. *Journal of Personality and Social Psychology*, 50: 963–73.

Coyne, J. C. 1976a. Depression and the response of others. *Journal of Abnormal Psychology*, 85: 186–93.

———. 1976b. Toward an interactional description of depression. *Psychiatry*, 39: 28–40.

Csikszentmihalyi, M., and R. Larson. 1984. *Being Adolescent: Conflict and Growth in Teenage Years*. New York: Basic Books.

Cunningham, M. R. 1988a. Does happiness mean friendliness?: Induced mood and heterosexual self-disclosure. *Personality and Social Psychology Bulletin*, 14: 283–97.

———. 1988b. What do you do when you're happy or blue?: Mood, expectancies, and behavioral interest. *Motivation and Emotion*, 12: 309–30.

Cunningham, M. R. , J. Steinberg, and R. Grev. 1980. Wanting to and having to help: Separate motivations for positive mood and guilt-induced helping. *Journal of Personality and Social Psychology*, 38: 181–92.

DeRivera, J. 1984. The structure of emotional relationships. In *Review of Personality and Social Psychology: Emotions, Relationships, and Health*, ed. P. Shaver, 116–145. Beverly Hills: Sage.

Donnerstein, E., M. Donnerstein, and G. Munger. 1975. Helping behavior as a function of pictorially induced moods. *Journal of Social Psychology*, 97: 221–25.

Fiedler, K., H. Pampe, and U. Scherf. 1986. Mood and memory for tightly organized social information. *European Journal of Social Psychology*, 16: 149–65.

Forgas, J. P., and G. H. Bower. 1987. Mood effects on person perception judgments. *Journal of Personality and Social Psychology*, 53: 53–60.

Forgas, J. P., G. H. Bower, and S. E. Krantz. 1984. The influence of mood on perceptions of social interactions. *Journal of Experimental Social Psychology*, 20: 497–513.

Forgas, J. P., and S. Moylan. 1987. After the movies: transient mood and social judgments. *Personality and Social Psychology Bulletin*, 13: 467–77.

Gaelick, L., G. V. Bodenhausen, and R. S. Wyer. 1985. Emotional communication in close relationships. *Journal of Personality and Social Psychology*, 49: 1246–65.

Gottman, J. 1979. *Marital Interaction: Experimental Investigations*. New York: Academic.

———. 1980. Consistency of nonverbal affect and affect reciprocity in marital interaction. *Journal of Consulting and Clinical Psychology*, 48: 711–17.

Hazan, C., and P. R. Shaver. 1987. Romantic love conceptualized as an attachment process.

Journal of Personality and Social Psychology, 52: 511–24.

———. 1990. Love and work: An attachment-theoretical perspective. *Journal of Personality and Social Psychology*, 59: 270–80

Hendrick, C., and H. Page. 1970. Self-esteem, attitude similarity, and attraction. *Journal of Personality*, 38: 588–601.

Isen, A. M. 1970. Success, failure, attention, and reaction to others. *Journal of Personality and Social Psychology*, 15: 294–301.

Isen, A. M., M. Clark, and M. F. Schwartz. 1976. Duration of the effect of good mood on helping: "Footprints on the sands of time." *Journal of Personality and Social Psychology*, 34: 385–93.

Isen, A. M., and P. F. Levin. 1972. Effect of feeling good on helping: Cookies and kindness. *Journal of Personality and Social Psychology*, 21: 384–88.

Isen, A. M., T. E. Shalker, M. Clark, and L. Karp. 1978. Affect, accessibility of material in memory, and behavior: A cognitive loop? *Journal of Personality and Social Psychology*, 36: 1–12.

Isen, A. M., and S. F. Simmonds. 1978. The effect of feeling good on a helping task that is incompatible with good mood. *Social Psychology*, 41: 346–49.

Kelley, H. H., E. Berscheid, A. Christensen, J. H. Harvey, T. L. Huston, G. Levinger, E. McClintock, L. A. Peplau., and D. R. Peterson. 1983. *Close Relationships*. W. H. Freeman: New York.

Larson, R., M. Csikszentmihalyi, and R. Graef. 1982. Time alone in daily experience: Loneliness or renewal? In *Loneliness: A Sourcebook of Current Theory, Research and Therapy*, ed. L. A. Peplau and D. Perlman. New York: Wiley-Interscience.

Levenson, R. W., and J. M. Gottman. 1983. Marital interaction: Physiological linkage and affective exchange. *Journal of Personality and Social Psychology*, 45: 587–97.

———. 1985. Physiological and affective predictors of change in relationship satisfaction. *Journal of Personality and Social Psychology*, 49: 85–94.

Levin, P. F., and A. M. Isen. 1975. Further studies on the effect of feeling good on helping. *Sociometry*, 38: 141–47.

Locke, K. D., and L. M. Horowitz. 1990. Satisfaction in interpersonal interactions as a function of similarity in level of dysphoria. *Journal of Personality and Social Psychology*, 58: 823–31.

Maccoby, E. E. 1980. *Social development: Psychological growth and the parent-child relationship.* New York: Harcourt Brace Jovanovich.

Mills, J., and M. S. Clark. 1982. Exchange and communal relationships. In *Review of Personality and Social Psychology*, ed. L. Wheeler, 121–144. Beverly Hills: Sage.

Moore, B. S., B. Underwood, and D. L. Rosenhan. 1973. Affect and altruism. *Developmental Psychology*, 8: 99–104.

Noller, P. 1980. Misunderstandings in marital communication: a study of couple's nonverbal communication. *Journal of Personality and Social Psychology*, 44: 310–21.

Pleban, R., and A. Tesser. 1981. The effects of relevance and quality of another's performance on interpersonal closeness. *Social Psychology Quarterly*, 44: 278–85.

Reis, H. T., and P. Shaver. 1988. Intimacy as an interpersonal process. In *Handbook of personal relationships: Theory, relationships and interventions*, ed. S. Duck. Chichester, England: Wiley.

Scherer, K. R. 1984. On the nature and function of emotion: A component process approach. In *Approaches to emotion*, ed. K. R. Scherer and P. Ekman. Hillsdale, NJ: Erlbaum.

Scherer, K. R., H. G. Wallbott, and A. B. Summerfield, eds. 1986. *Experiencing Emotion: A Cross-Cultural Study.* Cambridge: Cambridge University Press.

Schiffenbauer, A. 1974. Effect of observer's emotional state on judgments of the emotional state of others. *Journal of Personality and Social Psychology*, 30: 31–5.

Schwartz, J. C., and P. R. Shaver. 1987. Emotion and emotion knowledge in interpersonal relationships. In *Advances in Personal Relationships*, ed. W. Jones and D. Perlman. Greenwich, Conn: JAI Press.

Shaver, P. R., and C. Hazan. 1988. A biased overview of the study of love. *Journal of Social and Personal Relations,* 5: 473–501.

Shaver, P. R., C. Hazan, and D. Bradshaw. 1988. Love as attachment: The integration of three behavioral systems. In *The Psychology of Love,* ed. R. J. Sternberg and M. L. Barnes, 68–99. New Haven, CT: Yale University Press.

Simpson, J. A. 1987. The dissolution of romantic relationships: Factors involved in relationship stability and emotional distress. *Journal of Personality and Social Psychology,* 53: 683–92.

Sommers, S. 1984. Reported emotions and conventions of emotionality among college students. *Journal of Personality and Social Psychology,* 46: 207–15.

Strack, S., and J. C. Coyne. 1983. Social confirmation of dysphoria: shared and private reactions to depression. *Journal of Personality and Social Psychology,* 44: 798–806.

Tesser, A. 1988. Toward a self-evaluation maintenance model of social behavior. In *Advances in Experimental Social Psychology,* ed. L. Berkowitz, vol. 21, 181–227. New York: Academic Press.

Tesser, A., and J. Campbell. 1980. Self-definition: The impact of the relative performance and similarity of others. *Social Psychology Quarterly,* 43: 341–47.

Tesser, A., M. Millar, and J. Moore. 1988. Some affective consequences of social comparison and reflection processes: the pain and pleasure of being close. *Journal of F. Social Psychology,* 54: 49–61.

Trevarthen, C. 1984. Emotions in infancy tors of contact and relationships w. sons. In *Approaches to Emotion,* ed. K. S and P. Ekman. Hillsdale, N.J.: Erlbaum.

Underwood, B., J. F. Berenson, R. Berenson, . Cheng, D. Wilson, J. Kulik, G. Moore, and G. Wenzel. 1977. Attention, negative affect, and altruism: An ecological validation. *Personality and Social Psychology Bulletin,* 3: 54–8.

White, G. L., S. Fishbein, J. Rutstein. 1981. Passionate love and misattribution of arousal. *Journal of Personality and Social Psychology,* 41: 56–62.

Williamson, G. M., and M. S. Clark. 1989. Providing help and desired relationship type as determinants of changes in moods and self-evaluations. *Journal of Personality and Social Psychology,* 56: 722–34.

Williamson, G. M., and M. S. Clark. 1992. Impact of desired relationship type on affective reactions to choosing and being required to help. *Personality and Social Psychology Bulletin,* 18: 10–18.

Williamson, G. M, R. Schulz, M. S. Clark, L. Pegalis, and A. Behan. 1992. Affective consequences of helping and refusing to help in communal and exchange relationships: Underlying mechanisms and generalizability. Unpublished manuscript, University of Georgia, Athens, GA.

Chapter 6

Attachment

PHILLIP R. SHAVER
University of California, Davis

CINDY HAZAN
Cornell University

Outline

Introduction: Examples of Attachment Processes

A young wife, Angela, is awakened at 12:30 a.m. on a weeknight by a telephone call from the police. Her husband Bruce has been killed in a head-on collision while driving home from the evening shift at work. Over the next few months, Angela cries uncontrollably, suffers repeated nightmares about the accident, and when alone, sometimes calls Bruce's name pleadingly even though she knows he can't answer. Occasionally, she imagines hearing him downstairs while she is working upstairs; while falling asleep at night, she sometimes feels him lying next to her. For five years, two of dating and three of marriage, Angela had become closer and closer to Bruce, gradually accepting him as the most important person in her life. In the deepest layers of her being, she cannot accept that he is gone.

Gregory, a 1-year-old, plays in the park on a sunny April morning, turning a shiny, multi-colored rock over and over in his hands. All of a sudden, hearing a stir on the park bench where his mother has been sitting, he drops the rock, boosts himself up, and toddles anxiously toward the bench, while his mother, having just finished a magazine article, walks around and stretches to relieve her momentary stiffness. "Hi!" she exclaims brightly, "Whatcha doin'?" He stops, smiles, and plunks back down to examine more rocks. The impending crisis, "Mommy is leaving me!", has been averted.

Ken, a middle-aged man whose wife divorced him a year ago, cannot seem to get accustomed to living alone. He stays at his office way past closing time, stops for a beer at a neighborhood bar, and still feels anxious and lonely when he gets home. He keeps thinking about a woman he met at a conference last week. She seemed unusually attuned to his ideas and sense of humor, smiled at him frequently during group meetings, almost immediately called him by his first name, and chatted warmly during coffee breaks. He thinks maybe he will send her a pretty card revealing his romantic interest in her, but he is nervous about her reaction. A couple of other times since the divorce, he has suspected that women to whom he felt attracted—coworkers who seemed attentive and responsive—were also attracted to him, but when he started leaving them notes or sending flowers, all responded by explaining that although they liked Ken as a friend and colleague, they had no romantic interest in him. He is beginning to feel both vulnerable and desperate.

Can you see common themes in these examples? In each example, a person has become emotionally attached to someone or, in the third example, wishes to become attached. These real and longed-for attachments are the source of a wide range of emotions, including attraction, love, hope, grief, fear of abandonment, and loneliness—many of the topics discussed in other chapters of this book. It took the brilliance of British psychiatrist John Bowlby and his American collaborator, psychologist Mary Ainsworth, to notice and describe the attachment behavioral system that underlies the many emotions that arise in close relationships. Bowlby called the affectional bonds that develop in such dyads attachments, and he and Ainsworth created a theory to explain how attachment works in close relationships, especially those between infants and their caregivers. Subsequent investigators, us included, have extended the theory to adolescent and adult friendships and romantic relationships. The purpose of the present chapter is to summarize the vast and constantly growing literature on attachment.

A Brief Survey of Attachment Theory

Bowlby's Three-Volume Theoretical Work: Attachment and Loss

We will convey the heart of Bowlby and Ainsworth's theory in two ways, using key paraphrases from Bowlby's (1969/1982, 1973, 1980) three-volume series, *Attachment and Loss,* and a diagram from our own writings, based on Ainsworth, Blehar, Waters, and Wall (1978), which summarizes attachment dynamics.

In Bowlby's first volume, *Attachment,* he argued that human beings evolved biologically over tens of thousands of years so as to fear being alone, especially when in a novel, dark, or dangerous environment and when tired, injured, or ill. These conditions all signal that a person, especially during infancy and early childhood but at later ages as well, needs the protection and support of others, preferably others who have a special interest in the person's survival and well-being. Bowlby's central idea was that evolution solved the problem of people's needs for protection and support (not intentionally, of course, but through blind natural selection) by equipping each of us with an attachment behavioral system. An organized system of emotions and behaviors that increases the likelihood of establishing a close relationship—an attachment relationship in Bowlby and Ainsworth's terms. An attachment relationship serves as a safe haven in times of trouble and a secure base from which to venture out into the environment when the coast is clear. The first such relationship in most people's lives is the one with their mother, because in most societies mothers nurse or feed their children and take special care of them during the first few years of life. But an infant's primary attachment figure might also be the father, a grandparent, a daycare worker, an older sibling—anyone who regularly plays the role of caregiver and comforter. Attachment theorists use the term "primary" caregiver to suggest that there is a hierarchy of attachment figures, with one being preferred in times of trouble whereas others are welcome when the primary figure is unavailable.

In Bowlby's second volume, *Separation: Anxiety and Anger,* he used three propositions to explain the psychological significance of the quality of early attachment relationships. Here, we will shorten and paraphrase these propositions slightly in order to save space. First, if a person is confident that an attachment figure will be available whenever needed, the person will be much less prone to either intense or chronic fear than will a person who for any reason has no such confidence. In other words, self-confidence and freedom from anxiety are based, at least in part, on the quality of a person's present and past attachments. (Inherited temperament may also play a role, a possibility discussed later in this chapter.) In the beginning examples for this chapter, Angela was frightened and preoccupied because her primary attachment figure, her husband, was unavailable. Bowlby pointed out in his third volume, *Loss: Sadness and Depression*, that the mind naturally recoils from the idea that there is no attachment figure to rely on. When a primary attachment figure departs or dies, a person often grasps at alternatives such as mother, a coworker, or God. This helps explain why many young adults move back home following a divorce or the death of a spouse; why lonely adolescents and adults rush into ill-considered and ill-fated love affairs; and why people of all ages turn to God—in a sense, the ultimate attachment figure—for help during times of crisis. In our second example, baby Gregory became frightened when he thought he heard his mother leaving the park without him. As interested as he was in rocks, this interest did not begin to compare with his concern about his mother's availability. Our third example shows that adults like Ken can also be preoccupied with the wish for a romantic attachment figure, a warm and responsive partner who will fill the void created by a wife's departure.

Bowlby's second theoretical proposition is as follows: Confidence in the availability of attachment figures, or a lack of such confidence, is built up slowly during the years of immaturity—infancy, childhood, and adolescence—and whatever expectations are developed during those years tend to persist relatively unchanged throughout the rest of life. In other words, attachment relationships affect personality development, and insecure or abusive attachments can cause lasting psychological problems. When attempting to understand a person's feelings and behaviors in later love relationships, it is helpful to know what happened in earlier ones.

Finally, the expectations concerning attachment figures' accessibility and responsiveness that people develop during the years of immaturity are tolerably accurate reflections of the experiences those individuals have actually had. This is an extremely important claim. Bowlby, having trained as a psychoanalyst, became increasingly dissatisfied with the emphasis in psychoanalysis on fantasy. Through a combination of research and clinical work, he came to believe that people do not form impressions of close relationship partners on the basis of fantasy, although childish misunderstandings and parental misdirection may make certain beliefs seem unrealistic. Instead, fears and expectations are rooted in actual experiences with parents, grandparents, siblings, romantic partners, and other attachment figures. The problem for a therapist, therefore, is not to eliminate fantasies and discount a client's beliefs and feelings about past attachment figures, but rather to serve temporarily as a new and different, a more sensitive and responsive, attachment figure with whose help the client can explore and reconstruct his or her conscious and unconscious reality-based models of relationships. The problem with those models is not that they are based on fantasy but that they are rooted in atypical and misleading experiences which form a poor foundation for later relationships.

The notion of mental models, which Bowlby and other attachment researchers call internal working models to indicate their hidden but active role in

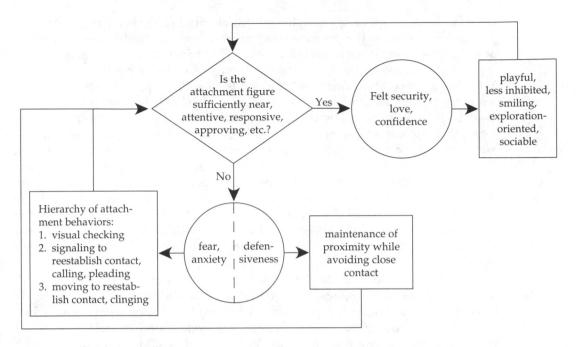

FIGURE 6–1   Flowchart representation of the attachment behavioral system.

interpreting experiences and initiating actions, brings us to a second set of ideas from Bowlby's second volume:

> *Confidence that an attachment figure is likely to be responsive can be seen to turn on at least two variables: (a) whether or not the attachment figure is judged to be the sort of person who in general responds to calls for support or protection; and (b) whether or not the self is judged to be the sort of person towards whom anyone, and the attachment figure in particular, is likely to respond in a helpful way. (1973, p. 238)*

Bowlby went on to explain that these two beliefs are often complementary and mutually confirming. "Thus, an unwanted child is likely not only to feel unwanted by his parents but to believe that he or she is essentially unwanted by anyone. Though logically indefensible [because certainly a child could be unwanted by parents and still be quite lovable to others], these crude over-generalizations are the rule. Once adopted, moreover, they are apt never to be seriously questioned." Hence, a child with a negative model of both self and attachment figures can become an adolescent or adult who implicitly distrusts relationship partners, expects them to be cruel, neglectful, or unpredictable, and feels unworthy of anyone's care. Looking on the bright side, a child who is consistently well treated by attachment figures can grow up feeling that relationship partners are likely to be trustworthy and responsive, and that the self is worthy of love. In short, self-esteem and healthy love of others go hand in hand, as many wise philosophers and religious teachers have noticed.

Attachment Dynamics

In our own work, we have summarized other scientists' writings about the attachment behavioral system using the flowchart in Figure 6–1. According to attachment theory, the human mind, beginning early in infancy, seems to asks the question shown in the diamond-shaped box in the flowchart: Is there an attachment figure who is sufficiently near, attentive, and responsive? A major assumption of the theory is that the human brain evolved to ask this question—an assumption supported by a large literature on attachment behavior in nonhuman primates and other mammals. In the human case, if the answer to the question is yes, certain emotions (represented by circles in the flowchart) and observable behaviors (represented by squares) arise naturally. When infants like Gregory notice that their attachment figure is available, interested, and responsive, they become more playful, less inhibited, visibly happier, and more interested in exploration. If adults like Ken find a compatible lover, they often behave in similar ways, feeling happier, sleeping better, smiling and laughing more easily, being more interested in creative activities and new experiences. This is one reason why, as the song says, "everybody loves a lover"—because the lover's intense joy, openness, and vitality are contagious.

If the answer to the flowchart's central question is no, on the other hand, fear and anxiety mushroom, and a hierarchy of increasingly intense attachment-related behaviors come into play: visually searching for the attachment figure, calling and pleading to re-establish contact, toddling or running to the figure, and clinging to him or her for dear life. These behaviors are familiar to anyone who has ever watched a young child, but they are painfully common in adults as well. Angela's calling out to her dead husband is one perfectly normal example; Ken's vigilant scanning of the women in his environment to see if any of them might care for him is another. Most of us are destined to play these painful parts in life's drama at one time or another.

There is a third important region of Figure 6–1—the lower right-hand portion, which deals with intimacy avoidance and detachment. If the hierarchy of attachment behaviors repeatedly fails to reduce anxiety, the mind is capable of deactivating the system, at least to some extent, and defensively attempting to become more self-reliant. This leads eventually to the condition Bowlby called detachment. We know that this state is defensive, as stated in the flowchart, rather than being a simple erosion of attachment (like a natural fading of memory), because it can quickly bounce back to a state of attachment-system activation if a person begins to believe that his or her temporarily lost or unresponsive attachment figure is available once again. Thus, a child whose mother has been away for a few weeks, on an important business trip, say, or caring for a sick relative in another part of the country, may seem to ignore her upon her return, as if the child has simply forgotten her. A heart-rate monitor would reveal, however, that the child's autonomic nervous system is responding mightily to mother's return (Sroufe and Waters, 1977). Moreover, after mother had been home for several days, indicating to the child that she really is back to stay, the child may suddenly burst into tears, cling to the mother's body, and refuse for several hours, if not days, to be physically separated from her. It is as if a torrent of attachment-related emotion had been held back to allow the child to cope with daily life, and it all comes pouring out when the defensive barrier is lifted.

Ainsworth's Classification Scheme: Three Patterns of Attachment

Figure 1 is meant to capture what all human beings have in common in the way of attachment dynamics. All of us come into the world with a capacity to monitor attachment figures, to become anxious when left alone, to make a fuss in order to assure proper care, and to defensively suppress the fussing if it causes more harm than good. Ainsworth's major contribution to attachment theory was to show how these universal dynamics interact with different caregiving environments to produce important personality differences. In a landmark study which has been replicated and extended many times, Ainsworth and her colleagues observed American mother-infant dyads at home during the first several months of the infants' lives and then brought them into a laboratory situation, dubbed the Strange Situation, to see how the infants would react to novel toys, an unfamiliar adult experimenter, and a temporary separation from mother. To make a long and fascinating story short (see Ainsworth et al., 1978, for details), Ainsworth documented the differences between three major kinds of dyads: secure, anxious-ambivalent, and avoidant.

Secure infant-mother dyads were characterized by all of the processes shown in the upper right-hand portion of Figure 1. That is, secure infants seemed to believe, even when their mother was temporarily out of sight, that she would be accessible and responsive if called upon for help. They were effective explorers of the novel play environment (the Strange Situation) and were quickly cuddled back into a relaxed and playful state when mother returned from an experimentally imposed 3-minute separation. This pattern of behavior was predictable from responsive mothering at home during the infant's first few months of life. Anxious-ambivalent dyads were characterized by all of the processes shown in the lower left-hand portion of the figure—that is, by attachment-system activation. Infants in this category were somewhat wary of the unfamiliar experimenter and the laboratory Strange Situation. They cried intensely when mother left the room and, perhaps surprisingly, threw a tantrum when she returned and tried to comfort them. Unlike secure infants, the anxious-ambivalent infants were not completely soothed or comforted by their mother's return and seemed angry and preoccupied with her whereabouts for the rest of the laboratory session. This pattern of behavior in the laboratory was predictable from home observations indicating the mother's own anxiety, self-preoccupation, and inconsistent availability and responsiveness. Evidently, the anxious-ambivalent infants had been inadvertently rewarded for vigilance and scolding, which probably seemed to them to be the key to their success in gaining access to their mother. Finally, infants in the avoidant category seemed prematurely independent and unconcerned about mother. They rarely cried when she left the room and actively avoided contact when she returned. This pattern was predictable from a home situation in which the mother appeared not to enjoy close bodily contact with the infant and instead consistently rebuffed the infant's attachment-related behaviors. Ainsworth suggested that these infants had learned to keep their attachment behaviors in check, perhaps as a way to get some of their needs met without experiencing the pain of repeated rejection.

The Continuity of Attachment Patterns During Childhood

The different patterns, or attachment styles, documented by Ainsworth in her studies of infant-mother dyads, would be interesting even if they did not presage later developments. They would make us more aware of the temporary suffering experienced by infants whose caretakers are, usually unwittingly, nonoptimally responsive. The main source of interest in Ainsworth's findings, however, and in attachment theory more generally, is the possibility that early attachment experiences provide the foundation for social aspects of children's later personalities. Scores of studies have been conducted to determine whether or not early attachment patterns foreshadow later outcomes. What follows is a brief summary of this literature.

In one of the earliest studies of continuity in attachment patterns during infancy, Waters (1978) found that forty-eight (or 96 percent) of fifty infants from middle class homes exhibited the same attachment style when assessed twice in the Strange Situation, once at twelve months of age and again at eighteen months. Studies of this kind have since been conducted with children of a wide variety of ages, with different subject samples (rich and poor, from majority and minority cultures, in different countries, etc.), and with different methods of assessment, which are required when children get beyond two or three years of age. Most of these studies suggest that around 80 percent of infants from middle class homes, whose environments tend to be fairly stable, show the same attachment pattern, or style, across time (say, up to age six). In economically less stable and more stressful homes, the figure drops to around 60 percent, which is still considerably higher than expected by chance. (See Rothbard and Shaver, in press, for a review of these and other studies summarized in this section.) This continuity supports Bowlby's idea that early attachment experiences help to shape children's personalities.

Some researchers, seeing the accumulated evidence for cross-age continuity in attachment style, have wondered whether the continuity might be due to inborn personality characteristics, collectively called temperament, rather than to interactions with attachment figures. The drop in continuity from 80 percent to 60 percent as a function of environmental stability is one sign that environment does matter: When parents are more stressed, their children tend to switch from a secure attachment style to one of the insecure styles (avoidant or anxious-ambivalent); when parents are less stressed (e.g., when a single mother develops a stable relationship or gains the full-time assistance of the child's grandmother), their children tend to switch from insecure attachment styles to the secure style. Another sign that relationships matter is that a child can exhibit different attachment styles in the Strange Situation with mother and with father, especially if the parents' own attachment styles (to be discussed later in this chapter) are measurably different. In other words, children seem to be able to develop any one of the three styles, depending on the treatment they receive from particular attachment figures. In an important study (Main, Kaplan, and Cassidy, 1985), children's attachment behavior at age six proved to be more predictable from Strange Situation assessments at age one involving mother than from Strange Situation assessments involving father. This difference was attributed to the fact that the typical American child spends many more hours each day with mother than with father during the first six years of life. Finally, direct studies of a possible connection between infant temperament and attachment classification have so far failed to find a correlation (e.g., Sroufe, 1985; Vaughn, Lafever, Seifer, and Barglow, 1989). For the moment, it seems reasonable to conclude that persisting differences between attachment styles are due at least in part to social experiences, not solely to whatever innate differences there may be between children.

Many studies (e.g., those reviewed by Eliciker, Englund, and Sroufe, 1992) have examined personality and behavioral differences between children who differed in Strange Situation behavior at age one. In general, the results reveal that secure children (at ages ranging from two to six years) are more socially responsive and competent, handle interpersonal conflict more effectively, are more competent problem solvers and explorers of their environment, perform better on age-appropriate cognitive tasks, have higher self-esteem (as indicated by behavioral observations in the case of the youngest children), show more empathy and positive emotion in social situations, and have more harmonious and happier friendships. Insecure children are more likely to exhibit symptoms of childhood depression and be involved in exploitative peer relationships, especially ones in which an avoidant child victimizes an anxious-ambivalent child. Moreover, children with different attachment styles induce teachers to respond differently to them; teachers treat secure children in a matter-of-fact but warm way, become angry more often with avoidant children, and show special consideration for anxious-ambivalent children's needy dependence.

The farthest reaching longitudinal study to date (Eliciker et al., 1992) followed children from age twelve months to eleven years. The investigators created a summer camp program for children, each session lasting four weeks. Besides playing and making friends, as children would do at any summer camp, these children were videotaped, interviewed, and rated (at the end) by their counselors. Here are some of the key findings, in the words of the authors: "Overall, camp counselors without prior information about the subjects saw those with secure attachment histories as more self-assured, emotionally healthy, and competent." "Children who had secure attachments [earlier in life] were found to spend more time with peers and less time with adults only or in isolation. In addition, those with secure attachment histories were observed more often in groups of three or more children than those with anxious [insecure] histories." "Children with [anxious-ambivalent] histories are not deficient in their level of understanding of others' internal states [based on interviews], but may have negative biases or anxieties with regard to peer relations. Those with avoidant histories may have both lower interpersonal understanding [than children with secure histories] and more negative social-evaluative biases." "Children with secure attachment histories were more likely to form friendships than those with [insecure] attachments," and the secure children spent more time with their friends. "Secure-secure [friendship] pairs were more likely to form than other combinations," and "seating charts showed that children more often sat next to others with the same, rather than different, attachment histories. "

Taken together, the vast majority of existing studies suggest that attachment patterns assessed at age one are useful predictors of later childhood social behavior and self-esteem. This led us to believe, in the mid-1980s, that it might be worthwhile to examine attachment styles in late adolescence and adulthood, where the styles might affect the formation and maintenance of romantic relationships. Around the same time, Mary Main and her students were developing an interview technique that could classify parents in terms of attachment history and predict the attachment behavior of their one-year-old children in the Strange Situation. In other words, the notion of adult attachment style was explored by two different research teams, with foci as different as romantic love and parenting behavior. These two lines of research have provoked scores of fascinating studies during the past few years, and it is to those studies that we now turn.

Early Measures of Adult Attachment Style

Hazan and Shaver's Measure

We (Hazan and Shaver, 1987; Shaver, Hazan, and Bradshaw, 1988) were interested in studying adolescent and adult loneliness and romantic love from an attachment perspective, and we had to invent measures for the purpose. Our approach was to look carefully at Ainsworth et al.'s descriptions of the three kinds of infants, secure, avoidant, and anxious-ambivalent, at the end of their 1978 book. This was the best summary available of all of the infant attachment studies conducted up until then. We wanted our parallel adult measure to be suitable for a brief questionnaire, because we had secured the consent of a local newspaper editor to publish the questionnaire in the paper. This is a good way to do exploratory research, because the subjects pay for their own questionnaires and reply envelopes! We decided to ask our respondents to think back across all of the romantic feelings and relationships in their lives and then decide which of the following descriptions (minus the labels we've added for your convenience) fit them best:

> *Avoidant. I am somewhat uncomfortable being close to others; I find it difficult to trust them completely, difficult to allow myself to depend on them. I am nervous when anyone gets too close, and often, love partners want me to be more intimate than I feel comfortable being.*

> *Anxious-ambivalent. I find that others are reluctant to get as close as I would like. I often worry that my partner doesn't really love me or won't want to stay with me. I want to get very close to my partner, and this sometimes scares people away.*

> *Secure. I find it relatively easy to get close to others and am comfortable depending on them. I don't often worry about being abandoned or about someone getting too close to me.*

We asked several additional kinds of questions, dealing with: each respondent's most important love relationship, his or her feelings of loneliness, beliefs (internal working models) about self and relationship partners, and memories of childhood attachment relationships with parents. The breakdown of attachment styles—55 percent secure, 25 percent avoidant, and 20 percent anxious-ambivalent—was similar to the breakdown in studies of American infants. (The proportions vary across cultures, avoidance being more common in Northern Germany, for example, and anxious-ambivalence being more common in Israel and Japan.) Secure respondents had more positive models of self and were more likely to say that other people are well-intentioned and good-hearted. This fits with expectations based on Bowlby's theory. Secure respondents were more likely to view their most important relationship as a trusting partnership, whereas anxious-ambivalent respondents talked about emotional ups and downs, greater jealousy, and more intense sexual passion, and avoidant respondents focused on fear of intimacy and expectations that love relationships are doomed to fail. On the average, the three groups of respondents remembered their relationships with parents differently, secure respondents viewing them largely favorably, with avoidant respondents emphasizing coolness and rejection, and anxious-ambivalent respondents emphasizing inconsistency, intrusiveness, and unfairness. These patterns also fit with Bowlby's theory and Ainsworth's observations of the kinds of parent-infant interactions that lead to different attachment styles.

The Adult Attachment Interview

While we were working on the study just described, Main et al. (1985) showed that parental attachment styles reflected in an Adult Attachment Interview (AAI) could predict with surprising accuracy (around 80 percent) how a parent's child would behave in the Strange Situation. The AAI focuses on parents' memories of their childhood experiences with attachment figures and is coded not only in terms of answer content but also in terms of defensive style. This result has since been replicated several times. In one study, Fonagy, Steele, and Steele (1991) showed that accurate predictions of infant attachment style could be based on interviews with pregnant mothers. In other words, a mother's attachment dynamics, as revealed by the AAI, could predict her baby's attachment style in the Strange Situation before the baby was born and some 15 months before the baby was tested.

In the remainder of this chapter, we will briefly review some of the many intriguing findings obtained by researchers who have used either the Hazan and Shaver measure (or one of many variants of it) or the AAI. In general, we will not focus on measurement or methodological details, but you should know that there are still many unresolved issues concerning the measurement of attachment in adulthood. We have examined these matters in a more advanced chapter (Shaver and Hazan, 1993) which you might tackle next if you find the topic interesting.

Adult Attachment: Recent Discoveries

Love and Work

Bowlby and Ainsworth paid a great deal of attention to the connections between attachment and exploration, because they thought the ability to move out from early caregivers to explore the environment, develop cognitive and other forms of competence, and make friends was partly a result of secure attachment. We (Hazan and Shaver, 1990) wondered whether these ideas, like the notion of attachment itself, might also apply to adults, many of whom exercise their need for exploration and develop their adult feelings of competence while at work. We therefore decided to conduct another large-scale newspaper survey, this time focusing on love and work.

We discovered that secure respondents report relatively high levels of satisfaction with job security, coworkers, income, and opportunity for challenge and advancement. In other words, once again, in a new domain, they show the affective positivity that has been associated with attachment security in every study involving research subjects from ages one to eighty. (Because our initial studies were conducted in a large-circulation newspaper, we received responses from adults of all ages.) Anxious-ambivalents, in contrast, are troubled by job insecurity, lack of appreciation and recognition from coworkers, and not getting desired and (according to the respondents) deserved promotions. In other words, anxious-ambivalents' complaint that coworkers and bosses do not love them enough echoes this group's earlier complaints that attachment figures are insufficiently close and comforting. Avoidants were dissatisfied with coworkers but similar to secures in being satisfied with job security and opportunities for learning.

To our surprise, anxious-ambivalents made significantly less money than secures and avoidants, even when possible confounding variables such as gender and education were controlled. Wondering if this was perhaps a fluke, one of Hazan's doctoral students, Michelle Hutt, conducted a more extensive study involving dairy farmers in upstate New York. She found that anxious-ambivalent farmers make less money than secure and avoidant farmers, and that the three groups have measurably different management styles which are consistent with attachment theory. Literally, it pays not to be excessively anxious-ambivalent.

Hazan and Shaver (1990) also found, concerning the effects of love on work and people's efforts to balance the two, that secures place the highest value on, and derive the most pleasure from, relationships rather than work. Anxious-ambivalents are most likely to claim that love-worries interfere with work. And avoidant respondents are most likely to emphasize the importance of work over love. (They were, in popular terms, workaholics.) Table 6–1 lists some of the items that distinguish between the anxious-ambivalent and avoidant groups' descriptions of their feelings and behavior at work. Anxious-ambivalents, perhaps because they are working primarily for recognition, approval, and appreciation, tend to daydream about how wonderful success would be and then slack off after praise. They like working with others, hate working alone, get overinvolved in tasks, have difficulty finishing them, and feel that their work efforts are misunderstood and unappreciated. Avoidants, in contrast, prefer to work alone, find vacations pleasureless, and seem generally satisfied with their discovery that work leaves no time for friends; they say that work is useful for avoiding social events.

Extensions of Hazan and Shaver's Studies

Feeney and Noller (1990, 1991) replicated our findings in Australia and made some additional discoveries: (a) Anxious/ambivalence is related to limerence (obsessive love; Tennov, 1979) and love addiction. From this category, come those fatal attractions and women who love too much that we hear so much about in popular books and movies. (b) People with either kind of insecure attachment,

TABLE 6–1 Characteristics That Distinguish Between Anxious-Ambivalent and Avoidant Workers

Items Associated with the Avoidant Style	Items Associated with the Anxious-Ambivalent Style
Vacations are pleasureless	Difficulty finishing projects
Work interferes with relationships	Work efforts misunderstood
Work is useful for avoiding social events	Work efforts unappreciated
Prefers to work alone	Works better with others
	Slacks off after praise
	Gets overinvolved in tasks
	Hates working alone
	Daydreams about success

avoidance or anxious-ambivalence, score lower than secure subjects on a range of self-esteem scales, supporting Bowlby's claim that the insecure groups continue to have negative internal models of self. (c) Attachment-style differences are detectable when people talk freely about their relationships and their partners (in other words, key results do not depend on questionnaire measures). This is an important finding, because before this study was completed it seemed possible that we might have somehow shaped our early findings by the way we wrote our initial closed-ended questions and response alternatives.

Collins and Read (1990) elaborated what we said about the connections between attachment styles and internal working models, and used more reliable and familiar measures of such beliefs and behaviors as trust, self-esteem, self-disclosure, and masculinity and femininity. They showed, in a study of dating couples, that couple members' attachment styles affect both their own and their partner's satisfaction and commitment. This is an important discovery because the cross-partner effects suggest that findings obtained in previous studies were not due simply to biases or connections within single individual's minds (a problem with many psychological findings based exclusively on questionnaires). Also, Collins and Read found that a person's attachment-related description of his or her opposite-sex parent is related to the partner's self-reported attachment style. People who view their opposite-sex parent as security-enhancing somehow hook up with dating partners who are relatively secure. This suggests that we should not think only in terms of mother's influence on later romantic attachments (mother more often being the primary caregiver), but that for women, feelings about their relationship with their father may also be important.

Mikulincer and Nachshon (1991) replicated our main findings in Israel and also studied self-disclosure preferences and behaviors associated with the three attachment styles. Secures generally liked other people who self-disclosed, and they self-disclosed appropriately themselves, in proportion to the nature of their relationship with a particular conversation partner. That is, secures were appropriate self-disclosers. Anxious-ambivalents also generally liked others who disclosed, but they themselves disclosed too readily and without much concern for their relationship with their conversation partner. In other words, their abundant self-disclosure was sometimes inappropriate. Avoidants tended not to like others who disclosed and not to be disclosers themselves. By now, it should be easy for you to see how these findings fit with Ainsworth's descriptions of the three attachment styles in infancy: Secures went to attachment figures for support when support was needed and went back to exploring toys after support was adequately provided; anxious-ambivalents kept track of attachment figures at the expense of full attention to toys, and they tried to hang on and express their feelings to their caregiver long after he or she had tried and failed to provide comfort; avoidants suppressed their feelings and their need for comfort, and avoided their caregiver even when the caregiver made an effort to establish contact.

Simpson (1990) studied college students' dating relationships over time and found that avoidant daters claimed to be less bothered when their relationships broke up. This is one of the first studies to begin to establish a connection between adult attachment styles and coping with loss, a topic that deserves further study. One thing we would like to know is whether avoidant people really do suffer less from breakups and losses or whether they merely say this, in a defensive way, while suffering indirect effects of stress, such as physical symptoms (e.g., headaches, muscle tension, susceptibility to flu). (See Hazan and Shaver, 1992, for more on attachment theory's approach to relationship loss.)

Senchak and Leonard (1992) interviewed hundreds of newlywed couples who were recruited into their study when the couples applied for a marriage license. These researchers documented a tendency for secure people to marry secure partners (similar to the findings for eleven-year-old summer campers' friendships, discussed earlier). Anxious-ambivalent men had shorter premarital relationships, a finding consistent with results obtained by other investigators indicating that anxious-ambivalent men's relationships are relatively short-lived (for reasons we do not yet understand). Perhaps the anxious-ambivalent men were trying to get married before another relationship came to an end! Avoidant men were more likely than secure and anxious men to be heavy drinkers, a finding compatible with Brennan, Shaver, and Tobey's (1991) discovery that avoidant college students are more likely to have grown up with one or two parents who themselves had drinking problems. (Drinking may be a coping strategy used by people who cannot share their fears and feelings of stress with attachment figures; alcohol may temporarily reduce unbearable feelings of tension.) Secure-secure couples were better off in a number of ways than couples involving one or two insecure people.

Most of the existing studies of adult attachment are based on self-report questionnaire measures rather than behavior (the self-disclosure study reviewed above being a rare exception). This choice of methods probably reflects researchers' wish to explore a new topic area in a relatively inexpensive and easy way, before investing the time and resources associated with more demanding methods. An interesting exception to the self-report rule is a recent study by Simpson, Rholes, and Nelligan (1992). These investigators brought dating couples into the lab, placed the partners in separate rooms and, unbeknownst to the male partner, told the female partner that later in the study she would undergo a painful and stressful procedure. Both partners were then sent back to what they thought was a simple waiting room, but which, without their knowledge, had been equipped with a hidden video camera. Later, with the subjects' permission, the videotapes were systematically coded, and the researchers discovered that the more anxious the female partner became (as indicated by her behavior), the more the distinction between secure and avoidant attachment mattered. Avoidant women withdrew from their partner's support as they became more anxious; avoidant men withdrew from supporting their partner as she became more anxious. These results parallel what has been found in studies of infants and their mothers: Avoidant infants are more noticeably avoidant when frightened, and avoidance-engendering mothers withdraw support from their infant when the infant becomes more distressed.

Attachment, God, and the Threat of Death

According to attachment theory, the reason for the existence of the attachment behavioral system in the first place is that it helped assure our ancestors' survival. Infants, children, and adults who recognized threats to life and health and effectively sought the protection and support of attachment figures were more likely to survive. This suggests that adults who are confronted with death will experience attachment-system activation, and that death anxiety and methods of coping with it will be systematically related to attachment style.

Mikulincer, Florian, and Tolmacz (1990), studying a sample of Israeli men, found that conscious death anxiety is high in anxious-ambivalent men and relatively low in secure and avoidant men. Moreover, anxious-ambivalent men conceptualize death as separation (as having to go somewhere without being accompanied by an attachment figure); avoidant men conceptualize death as stepping into the unknown but do not seem consciously concerned about stepping in alone. *Unconscious* death anxiety (measured by a projective test, the Thematic Apperception Test) is high among both anxious and avoidant people. (Interestingly, Dozier and Kobak, 1992, recently reported that skin conductance increases in avoidant adults when they deny, during the AAI, that they were rejected or hurt by parents—another sign that they are anxious in some sense without being fully aware of the reason.)

One possible implication of this study is that securely attached people, who seem not to be inordinately afraid of death, either consciously or unconsciously, feel confident that they will be securely situated in the hands of God when they die. In other words, perhaps people who have enjoyed secure attachments to their human caregivers also feel they have a secure attachment to God. A recent study by Kirkpatrick and Shaver (1992) supported this prediction.

Mikulincer, Florian, and Weller (1993) interviewed Israelis immediately following the Scud missile attacks that occurred during the Gulf War. As you may recall, several missiles were launched at Israel from locations in Iraq, and the United States asked Israel not to retaliate. Israelis were forced to create sealed rooms in their homes and workplaces, because it was thought that the Scuds might be equipped with deadly chemical warheads. Every time an air-raid siren sounded, Israelis had to scurry into their sealed rooms, taking with them family members, coworkers, and pets. The researchers studied stress reactions, coping techniques, and subjects' proximity to the Scud landings. Anxious/ambivalents reported the most intense distress and tended to use what stress researchers call emotion-focused coping techniques (trying to reduce the overwhelming feeling of stress). Avoidants reported more somatization (physical symptoms of stress), hostility, and trauma-related avoidance; they coped with stress by emotionally distancing themselves from thoughts of the threat (the same thing they do to avoid experiencing death anxiety). Secures used more social-support-seeking strategies and fared best in terms of stress levels. The attachment-style differences were stronger for people living closer to the danger, which parallels findings from Strange Situation studies of infants. Differences between the three kinds of infants get stronger as the Strange Situation is made increasingly more stressful, culminating in an episode in which both mother and stranger leave the infant all alone.

If these attachment-style differences in experiences and responses to life-threatening stress affect people's eagerness to turn to God as a safe haven, there should be attachment-style differences in various religious experiences and behaviors. Kirkpatrick and Shaver (1990) found that direct experiences of God (being born again, being touched by God, being spoken to by God) are much more common among people who grew up with an avoidance-producing mother. In adolescence, for example, 27.8 percent of such people had religious experiences, whereas only 0.9 percent of people with security-producing mothers had one (3.5 percent for people with anxious-ambivalence-producing mothers). Considering intense conversion experiences at any point in life, the corresponding figures were 44.4 percent, 9.4 percent, and 8.2 percent. Interestingly, among adults whose mothers were not religious, those with avoidance-producing mothers were more likely to believe in a personal God and be born again; but this was not so if the mother was religious. This suggests that God is not a viable attachment figure (or, at least, not one with whom a believer can be emotionally intimate) if God is too closely associated with a rejecting mother.

Future Directions

Despite considerable progress in the study of adult attachment, there are many problems, controversies, and questions yet to be resolved. One of the most important has to do with measurement. As mentioned earlier, we began our work with a simple self-report measure whereas Main and her coworkers developed the Adult Attachment Interview. In 1990, Kim Bartholomew published an insightful article which showed that our measure's definition of avoidance is not quite the same as the definition used in coding the AAI. This is too technical a matter to discuss in detail here, but suffice it to say that Bartholomew solved the problem by proposing a four-category rather than a three-category classification system; in the new system, there are two kinds of avoidance, dismissing (similar to the conception embodied in the AAI) and fearful (similar to the conception embodied in our measure). The four categories can be arrayed in a two-dimensional diagram, with one dimension being Model of Self (positive versus negative) and the other being Model of Others (positive versus negative). In the new system, secure people are those who hold positive models of both self and others; anxious-ambivalents hold positive models of others but negative models of self; dismissing avoidants hold negative models of others but positive models of self; and fearful avoidants hold negative models of both self and others. Bartholomew and Horowitz (1991) were the first to use the new scheme in a published study, and it proved to be predictably related to a number of theoretically relevant personality measures.

Once we entertain the possibility that adult attachment styles are definable in terms of two dimensions, it becomes important to figure out what those dimensions are. It seems unlikely that they will prove to be completely distinct from all of the other dimensions that personality researchers have measured over the years. In fact, the Self Model dimension is, as you might expect, highly similar to existing measures of self-esteem (on the positive- model side) and neuroticism or negative affectivity (on the negative-model side). A recent study by Shaver and Brennan (1992) showed that the Self Model dimension is highly correlated with a standard measure of neuroticism. It is more difficult to say what the Other Model dimension corresponds to, but surely it is related to existing measures of warmth, sociability, and intimacy avoidance.

If attachment styles are closely related to previously studied personality dimensions, we can begin to answer a question that has been difficult to answer in studies of infants: Are attachment styles innate to any significant degree? If so, it is a mistake to attribute insecure attachment entirely to caregiver behavior (which some skeptical authors call blaming mother—a misnomer in any case, because attachment theory sees the mother's behavior as just another step in an intergenerational chain for which no one is uniquely responsible). Because it is fairly easy to measure both attachment style and personality characteristics in adults, and to examine, in twin studies, the degree to which heredity influences both, we may be able to discover soon how much genes have to do with attachment styles. It has been difficult to accomplish the same trick in studies of infants, because it is difficult to measure personality during the first year of life.

Another important issue is change in attachment styles. We mentioned that attachment styles are fairly, but by no means perfectly, stable in childhood. A study by Hazan and her students, based on a random-sample survey of adults in an upstate New York town, suggests that adult attachment styles are also generally stable but not incapable of changing. Of adults who said they had changed, most attributed the change to important close relationships that violated expectations (in attachment terms, that altered internal working models of self and others). Hazan has also been studying the ways in which existing attachment figures (e.g., parents) are slowly relinquished in favor of new ones (e.g., close friends or romantic partners). It seems that people first seek proximity with potential attachment figures while relying on old ones to be safe havens and secure bases. If that first step goes well, the new figures gradually become safe havens (receiving one's intimate self-disclosures and providing social support), but not necessarily one's most secure base. As adolescents spend more and more time with peers and less and less time with parents, for example, they gradually rely on peers for social support; but if they encounter a really scary threat, they come running back to parents. As mentioned earlier, this may happen even after an adult child is married, and is especially likely to occur following a divorce. Perhaps parents are always, in Weiss's (1982) words, attachment figures in reserve.

Finally, further research needs to be done on internal working models. What are they, exactly? Are they mostly conscious or mostly unconscious? How do they determine a person's attachment-related feelings and behaviors? Fortunately, research on social cognition (Fiske and Taylor, 1991) has become very sophisticated in recent years, and it may provide the procedures necessary to add empirical flesh to the theoretical bones of one of attachment theory's central constructs. (See Collins and Read, in press, for a good start.)

Conclusion and Summary

Starting with ideas from psychoanalysis and evolutionary biology, John Bowlby forged a theory about certain kinds of close relationships which has great depth and range. His main goal was to explain why loss of mother has such a devastating effect on children's mental and physical health, but he also saw the need for a lifespan theory of attachment and loss, one that could explain adult loneliness and grief as well as infant separation anxiety. Mary Ainsworth provided an empirical approach to attachment and launched a research venture that now includes literally hundreds of studies. Although attachment theory continues to evolve as more investigators join the venture, the notion of an innate attachment behavioral system still seems central, as does the notion that important aspects of personality emerge as a person's social relationships push him or her into secure or insecure developmental pathways.

Attachment theory is by no means yet a complete theory of close relationships (Hazan and Shaver, in press). As Shaver et al. (1988) suggested in their initial theoretical account of an attachment-theoretical approach to romantic love, love consists, at least, in the integration of three behavioral systems: attachment, caregiving, and sex. Adolescent and adult lovers become attached to each other, serve as caregivers for each other, and are often sexual partners as well. Although matters of caregiving and sex are starting to receive attention in adult attachment studies (e.g., Brennan and Shaver, in press; Kunce and Shaver, in press), the surface has barely been scratched. One of our goals in writing this chapter is to recruit a new generation of attachment researchers. If you find the topic as interesting as we do, why not consider joining us. What could be more exciting than figuring out how human attachment, and the many emotions it engenders, work?

References

Ainsworth, M. D. S., M. Blehar, E. Waters, and S. Wall, 1978. *Patterns of attachment.* Hillsdale, NJ: Erlbaum.

Bartholomew, K. 1990. Avoidance of intimacy: An attachment perspective. *Journal of Social and Personal Relationships,* 7:147–78.

Bartholomew, K., and L. M. Horowitz, 1991. Attachment styles among young adults: A test of a four-category model. *Journal of Personality and Social Psychology,* 61:226–44.

Bowlby, J. 1969/1982. *Attachment and loss,* vol. 1: *Attachment,* 2nd ed. New York: Basic Books.

———. 1973. *Attachment and loss,* vol. 2: *Separation: Anxiety and anger.* New York: Basic Books.

———. 1980. *Attachment and loss,* vol. 3: *Loss: Sadness and depression.* New York: Basic Books.

Brennan, K. A., and P. R. Shaver, in press. Dimensions of attachment and the dynamics of romantic relationships. *Personality and Social Psychology Bulletin.*

Brennan, K. A., P. R. Shaver, and A. E. Tobey, 1991. Attachment styles, gender, and parental problem drinking. *Journal of Social and Personal Relationships,* 8:451–66.

Collins, N. L., and S. J. Read, 1990. Adult attachment, working models, and relationship quality in dating couples. *Journal of Personality and Social Psychology,* 58:644–63.

———. in press. Cognitive representations of adult attachment: The structure and function of working models. In *Advances in personal relationships,* ed. D. Perlman and K. Bartholomew, vol. 5. London, England: Jessica Kingsley.

Dozier, M., and R. R. Kobak, 1992. Psychophysiology and adolescent attachment interviews: Converging evidence for repressing strategies. *Child Development,* 63:1473–80.

Elicker, J., M. Englund, and L. A. Sroufe. 1992. Predicting peer competence and peer relationships in childhood from early parent-child relationships. In *Family-peer relations: Modes of linkage,* ed. R. Parke and G. Ladd, 77–106. Hillsdale, NJ: Erlbaum.

Feeney, J. A., and P. Noller, 1990. Attachment style as a predictor of adult romantic relationships. *Journal of Personality and Social Psychology,* 58:281–91.

———. 1991. Attachment style and verbal descriptions of romantic partners. *Journal of Social and Personal Relationships,* 8:187–215.

Fiske, S. T., and S. E. Taylor, 1991. *Social cognition* 2nd ed. New York: McGraw-Hill.

Fonagy, P., H. Steele, and M. Steele, 1991. Maternal representations of attachment during pregnancy predict the organization of infant-mother attachment at one year of age. *Child Development,* 62:891–905.

Hazan, C., and P. R. Shaver, 1987. Romantic love conceptualized as an attachment process. *Journal of Personality and Social Psychology,* 52:511–24.

———. 1990. Love and work: An attachment-theoretical perspective. *Journal of Personality and Social Psychology,* 59:270–80.

———. 1992. Broken attachments: Relationship loss from the perspective of attachment theory. In *Close relationship loss: Theoretical approaches,* ed. T. L. Orbach, 90–108. New York: Springer-Verlag.

———. in press. Attachment theory as an organizing framework for the study of close relationships. *Psychological Inquiry.*

Kirkpatrick, L. A., and P. R. Shaver, 1990. Attachment theory and religion: Childhood attachments, religious beliefs, and conversion. *Journal for the Scientific Study of Religion,* 29:315–34.

———. 1992. An attachment-theoretical approach to romantic love and religious belief. *Personality and Social Psychology Bulletin,* 18:266–75.

Kunce, L. J., and P. R. Shaver, in press. An attachment-theoretical approach to caregiving in romantic relationships. In *Advances in personal relationships,* ed. D. Perlman and K. Bartholomew, vol. 5. London, England: Jessica Kingsley.

Main, M., N. Kaplan, and J. Cassidy, 1985. Security in infancy, childhood, and adulthood: A move to the level of representation. *Monographs of the Society for Research in Child Development,* vol. 50, nos. 1–2, 66–104.

Mikulincer, M., V. Florian, and R. Tolmacz, 1990. Attachment styles and fear of personal death: A case study of affect regulation. *Journal of Personality and Social Psychology,* 58:273–80.

Mikulincer, M., V. Florian, and A. Weller, 1993. Attachment styles, coping strategies, and post-traumatic psychological distress: The impact of the Gulf War in Israel. *Journal of Personality and Social Psychology,* 64:817–26.

Mikulincer, M., and O. Nachshon, 1991. Attachment styles and patterns of self-disclosure. *Journal of Personality and Social Psychology,* 61:321–31.

Rothbard, J. C., and P. R. Shaver, in press. Continuity of attachment across the lifecourse: An attachment-theoretical perspective on personality. In *Attachment in adults: Theory, assessment, and treatment,* ed. M. B. Sperling and W. H. Berman, New York: Guilford.

Senchak, M., and K. E. Leonard, 1992. Attachment styles and marital adjustment among newlywed couples. *Journal of Social and Personal Relationships,* 9:51–64.

Shaver, P. R., and K. A. Brennan, 1992. Attachment styles and the "big five" personality traits: Their connections with each other and with romantic relationship outcomes.

Personality and Social Psychology Bulletin, 18:536–45.

Shaver, P. R., and C. Hazan, 1993. Adult attachment: Theory and research. In *Advances in personal relationships,* ed. W. Jones and D. Perlman, vol. 4, 29–70. London, England: Jessica Kingsley.

Shaver, P. R., C. Hazan, and D. Bradshaw, 1988. Love as attachment: The integration of three behavioral systems. In *The psychology of love* ed. R. J. Sternberg and M. L. Barnes, 68–99. New Haven, CT: Yale University Press.

Simpson, J. A. 1990. The influence of attachment styles on romantic relationships. *Journal of Personality and Social Psychology,* 59:971–80.

Simpson, J. A., W. S. Rholes, and J. S. Nelligan, 1992. Support-seeking and support-giving within couple members in an anxiety-provoking situation: The role of attachment styles. *Journal of Personality and Social Psychology,* 62:434–46.

Sroufe, L. A. 1985. Attachment classification from the perspective of infant-caregiver relationships and infant temperament. *Child Development,* 56:1–14.

Sroufe, L. A., and E. Waters, 1977. Heart rate as a convergent measure in clinical and developmental psychology. *Merrill-Palmer Quarterly,* 23:3–27.

Tennov, D. 1979. *Love and limerence.* New York: Stein and Day.

Vaughn, B. E., G. B. Lefever, R. Seifer, and P. Barglow, 1989. Attachment behavior, attachment security, and temperament during infancy. *Child Development,* 60:728–37.

Waters, E. 1978. The reliability and stability of individual differences in infant-mother attachment. *Child Development,* 49:483–94.

Weiss, R. S. 1982. Attachment in adult life. In *The place of attachment in human behavior,* ed. C. M. Parkes and J. Stevenson-Hinde, 171–84. New York: Basic Books.

Chapter *7*

Love

ARTHUR ARON
*State University of New York
at Stony Brook*

ELAINE N. ARON
*Pacific Graduate Institute
Carpinteria, CA*

Outline

Introduction—Goals and Assumptions

Terry meets Chris, is attracted to Chris, begins to feel something for Chris. Chris wonders, "Is this love?"

This chapter examines one of the questions we are most often asked about love: "How do I know if what I am experiencing is really love?" We will examine how people in general understand the meaning of love, how different people's understandings of love differ in terms of the aspects of love they emphasize, the actions and feelings that indicate love, how love is likely to develop over time, the relation of love and sex, the question of whether love can be really selfless, and the ideals our culture holds about love. We will conclude by attempting to integrate much of this material, using as a framework an aspect of what we call the self-expansion model. This model, our own approach to understanding love, we will also introduce along the way as it is relevant to the issues we consider.

Our emphasis in this chapter is on romantic love—that is, we do not explore love very much in the context of friendship or family relationships, except by way of contrast to romantic love. Also, to avoid repetition, we have minimized discussion of topics related to material discussed elsewhere in this text (such as in the chapters on attraction, emotion, attachment, sexuality, and jealousy). Finally, we want to make one point very clear: Most of what we have to say is based on research done in Western cultures, primarily the United States and Canada. This still makes the research very important to those of us in these cultures, but we cannot assume that these studies describe how or when love appears in other cultures, much less its universal qualities.

Lastly, we should add that our thinking about love is influenced by our disciplinary perspective as psychologists—Art as a social psychologist, Elaine as a personality and depth, clinical psychologist. This means our emphasis is primarily on the individual's experience and behavior, and much less on the relationship and the place of the person and relationship in society. It also means that our approach is based mainly on systematic, quantitative research, such as experiments and questionnaire surveys. However, Elaine's interest in depth psychology—as well as both of us having enjoyed a considerable exposure to Eastern psychology—has also made us open to ideas often seen by other psychologists as philosophical, or even mystical.

Is This What People Mean When They Use the Word "Love"?

Of Apples and Olives

When we ask what people mean by a particular concept, we are usually asking for the definition. Thus, when people identify a pattern as a triangle, it is probably the case that they mean it is a closed figure with three sides. This is called a classical definition. But for many concepts, people seem to be less systematic than logic teachers might like. For example, when people identify a particular object as a fruit, they are probably operating not using a botanist's definition, but rather are comparing what they see to a prototype fruit, such as an apple.

In 1973 Eleanor Rosch, who is mainly responsible for developing the theory of prototypes, found that it took people many milliseconds longer to verify the truth of a statement like "Olive is a fruit" than it did to verify a statement like "Apple is a fruit." One way to interpret that need to pause is that there are prototypical features of fruits—being sweet to the taste, growing on trees, being about tennis-ball size, and such—that are usually part of what people think of as fruits, and apples have more of these than olives. Naturally some of us who are social psychologists have wondered about the prototypical features of love.

The Prototypical Features of Love

Influenced by Rosch's (1973) prototype approach to concepts, in 1988 Beverley Fehr reported a series of studies to identify the prototypical features of love. In Fehr's first study she gave the following instructions to a group of undergraduates at the University of British Columbia (in Vancouver, Canada):

> *If you were asked to list the characteristics of a person experiencing terror you might write: possible danger occurs, heart beats quickly, may be imaginary like a ghost, hands tremble . . . Please make a similar list for the concept love.*

The students were each given three minutes to list as many features of love as came to mind.

Fehr then went through the various lists and came up with sixty-eight features that were included by two or more respondents. In a second study Fehr presented this list to a new group of students, and asked them to rate each for "how central is this feature to love?" There was considerable agreement among the ratings, so that certain features were consistently rated as quite central and others as relatively less so. Indeed, the features rated as most central tended to be those having the highest percentage of people listing them in the first study. All of this suggests that the way people understand love is organized in a structure with some features relatively central and others relatively peripheral (less central), and that this structure is quite similar over different people. The sixty-eight features and the average ratings of their centrality are shown in Table 7–1.

Fehr conducted several additional studies to demonstrate that this prototypical structure determines the way people process information about love—for example, central features as compared to peripheral features are more vivid in memory, are seen as more descriptive of love-type relationships (such as mar-

TABLE 7–1 Prototypical Features of Love and Average Ratings of their Centrality to the Concept of Love

Central Features		*Peripheral Features*	
Feature	Centrality	Feature	Centrality
Trust	7.50	Miss other when apart	5.99
Caring	7.28	Comfort other	5.95
Honesty	7.18	Attachment	5.89
Friendship	7.08	Sex appeal	5.87
Respect	7.01	Touching	5.82
Concern for other's well-being	7.00	Sexual passion	5.81
Loyalty	7.00	Need each other	5.80
Commitment	6.92	Mutual	5.78
Accept other the way s/he is	6.82	Contentment	5.77
Supportiveness	6.78	Put other first	5.70
Want to be with the other	6.78	Unconditional	5.70
Interest in the other	6.70	Wonderful feelings	5.62
Affection	6.68	Physical attraction	5.58
Closeness	6.65	Laughing	5.47
Understanding	6.61	Sacrifice	5.43
Sharing	6.58	Helping	5.42
Want best for other	6.58	Empathy	5.35
Forgiveness	6.55	Admiration	5.31
Intimacy	6.53	Positive outlook	5.28
Other is important	6.46	Kind	5.14
Openness	6.39	Protectiveness	5.11
Feel relaxed with other	6.37	Have a lot in common	5.11
Liking	6.34	Excitement	5.03
Compassion	6.31	Security	4.99
Devotion	6.28	Think about the other all the time	4.45
Giving	6.23	Energy	4.28
Happiness	6.22	Heart rate increases	4.26
Feel free to talk about anything	6.19	Euphoria	4.12
Do things for the other	6.14	Gazing at the other	4.10
Feel good about self	6.07	See only the other's good qualities	3.45
Responsibility	6.04	Butterflies in stomach	3.41
Warm feelings	6.04	Uncertainty	2.88
Patience	6.00	Dependency	2.81
Long-lasting	6.00	Scary	2.28

Centrality was rated on an 8-point scale from Data from 1 "extremely poor feature of love" to 8 "extremely good feature of love." (From Fehr 1988.)

riage) than nonlove-type relationships (such as work partners), and their absence is seen as more likely to be disruptive of a love relationship.

Since Fehr's pioneering work, several other researchers have repeated her procedures with other groups of subjects and found very similar results. For example, in 1990 Edward Rousar reported results of a study he conducted in which he found that ratings of centrality for Fehr's features were about the same for women and men; heterosexuals and homosexuals of both genders; and among young, middle, and older age adults.

Is This What I Mean by Love?

While people seem to share a general idea of what love is about, they do diverge as to its details. Thus, several researchers have explored the ways in which people differ in how they understand love. (One such difference of this kind has to do with what is called attachment style, and is discussed in detail in Chapter 6.) In this section we focus on two lines of thinking about individual differences in people's concept of love—individual differences in centrality of different prototypical love features, and love styles.

Individual Differences in Centrality of Prototypical Features of Love

In 1992 Arthur Aron and Lori Westbay analyzed the pattern of centrality ratings for Fehr's sixty-eight features given by several hundred college students. We used a statistical technique, called factor analysis, which locates groupings of items, called factors. Each factor is such that ratings of items within the factor are all similar (that is, people who rate any of the items high tend to rate them all high, people who rate any of the items low tend to rate them all low), and ratings of items in one factor are unrelated to ratings of items in other factors (that is, the fact that a person rates items in one factor as high or low tells nothing about how that person will rate items in other factors).

In this study we found that Fehr's sixty-eight features fell into a clear pattern of three factors. (We actually did the study twice—once to identify the factors and a second time, with new subjects, to cross-check the original finding.) One factor consisted of features emphasizing intimacy, such as trust, caring, honesty, supportiveness, understanding, and openness. A second factor consisted of features emphasizing commitment, such as loyalty, devotion, being long lasting, needing each other, putting the other first, and sacrifice. And the third factor consisted of features emphasizing passion, such as butterflies in the stomach, heart rate increases, wonderful feelings, sexual passion, and excitement. What this means is that while people tend to agree overall on what love means, there are differences in emphasis which are characterized by the extent to which people rate features in one or more of these three factors as particularly central. We did not find, however, that women and men differed on which factors they emphasized.

Another consideration is the relation of the three factors to the centrality of the features they comprise. The intimacy factor included mainly central features; the commitment factor included both central and peripheral features; and the passion factor, mainly peripheral features. This suggests that intimacy is generally seen as particularly central to love and passion as least central.

It is also interesting that this three-factor pattern corresponds to an influential way of thinking about love developed by Robert Sternberg in 1986, which he called the triangular theory of love. Sternberg's theory was based not so much on what people believe about love as on an integration of scientific theories of love (several of which are described below). This integrative theory identified three components of love also, which Sternberg labeled intimacy, commitment, and passion.

In sum, one way in which people appear to differ in their prototype of love is in how much they emphasize each of these three aspects. Most of us especially think of love in terms of closeness and intimacy. But some of us give relatively higher weight than others to commitment—to the security of "I'll love you always." And some think more than others about the excitement and moments of union that passion seems to offer.

Love Styles

In 1977, a decade before Fehr applied prototype theory to love, John Alan Lee published results of a comprehensive study he had done to understand love, using a very different approach. Lee began by pouring over everything he could find that had been written about love, "from Plato and Ovid to Augustine and Capellanus to Burton and Stendhal to modern authors" (p. 175). Using the conclusions from his readings as a guide to what aspects of people's experiences to focus upon, he collected extensive, structured accounts of people's own love experiences. Taking all of this information together, Lee identified six different love styles which characterize the way people think about and experience love. Lee gave each of his styles a Latin or Greek name, corresponding as much as possible to types of love described in classical literature. The six types are:

1. Eros—romantic, passionate love.
2. Ludus—flirtatious, game-playing love.
3. Storge—friendship love.
4. Pragma—practical love.
5. Mania—possessive, dependent love.
6. Agape—all-giving, selfless love.

Working with Lee's original list, Clyde and Susan Hendrick (1986) developed a scale that measures people's tendency to endorse one or more of these six styles. Using this scale in studies of college students, the Hendricks have found a fairly consistent pattern—most people rate Eros, Agape, and Storge highest; Mania and Pragma next highest; and Ludus lowest. Differences between the genders are generally small, though women tend to be slightly more likely than men to emphasize Storge, Mania, and Pragma; and men tend to be slightly more likely than women to emphasize Ludus. The Hendricks did find, however, that people who were in love at the time of filling out the questionnaire were considerably more likely (compared to those who were not in love at the time), to emphasize Eros and Agape and somewhat less likely to emphasize Ludus.

Another interesting finding in the Hendricks' research was that the pattern of emphasis was fairly similar among students of the different ethnic groups included in their study (mainly Blacks, Hispanics, Asians, and Anglos). The only substantial exception was that Asian students were generally a bit less likely than other groups to emphasize Eros, and a bit more likely to emphasize Pragma and Storge—perhaps representing a tendency of many Asian cultures to stress community and family values over the more Western accent on individuality.

It is also worth considering the links between the love styles and the prototypical features of love. The most endorsed love styles in the Hendricks' study were Eros, Agape, and Storge, and the love prototype features rated most central in the Fehr study were in the intimacy factor. This apparent link is reasonable, since what these three love styles have in common, especially when compared to the other three, is that they all encompass intimacy-type themes. Mania on the other hand (perhaps along with Eros) would seem to be linked with the passion factor (and results of a 1989 study by the Hendricks support a connection of this kind). On the other hand, Pragma does not have any obvious link to the three factors, and Ludus would seem to function primarily in terms of a negative link with both commitment and intimacy.

Loving versus Liking

Another way of looking at the issue of differences in the meaning of love is in terms of loving versus liking. It certainly seems possible to like someone but not love them—and perhaps even to love someone you do not like. Indeed, in one of the first major developments in the scientific study of love, in 1970 Zick Rubin constructed and tested questionnaires that attempted to measure the liking and loving one feels for a particular individual. Rubin's Liking Scale includes questions about similarity and respect for the other person, while his Love Scale includes items about need for, willingness to help, and exclusiveness and absorption in the other person. Rubin found that people love their romantic partners a lot more than they love their friends, but they like their romantic partners only a little more than they like their friends. In another study he found that couples with high scores on the love scale spent more time looking at each other—gazing in each other's eyes—when reading a paragraph about a couple contemplating marriage.

Love versus In Love

Even granting that one feels love, there may be quite a difference between love in general and being in love. If Terry tells Chris, "I love you." Terry will probably not be pleased if Chris replies, "I love you, but I am not *in* love with you."

Looking at this distinction, Victoria Luby and Arthur Aron conducted a series of studies in 1990 using Fehr's prototype features approach. This study identified features of being in love and their relative centrality to this concept, and also obtained features and their centrality ratings for love (which, as expected, came out nearly identical to what Fehr had found). In general, love and in love had quite similar features—both emphasized caring, friendship, respect, happiness, intimacy, and so forth. However, desire, affection, sex, satisfaction, positive outlook, and euphoria were rated as considerably more central to in-love than to love. This suggests that in-love is a more passionate, physical, emotionally intense form of love.

Am I Acting and Feeling Like a Person in Love?

Another way of telling whether one is in love is to look at behaviors and feelings. If it walks like a duck and feels like a duck, then maybe it is a duck.

Behaviors of Love

Clifford Swensen, back in 1961, asked a group of students to describe incidents connected with people they loved "which distinguished this relationship from that with people they only liked" (p. 167). Based on the responses to this initial study, Swensen constructed a scale of love expressions and administered this scale to a new group of students, asking them to indicate which of the expressions they had given or received in various love relationships—for each parent, for closest same-sex friend, for fiance or closest friend of the opposite-sex, and for closest sibling.

In most categories, behaviors were similar among both romantic and nonromantic kinds of love relationships: Non-material evidence of love (giving advice, encouragement, etc.) was fairly common in all types of love relationships; shared activities were typical of love relationships other than with parents; self-disclosure (talking about personal matters) and expressions of similarity of outlook were about equally common for friends and romantic partners; and material evidence of love (giving money, doing chores, etc.) was most usual with parents and siblings and less usual for same-sex friends and romantic partners. But all in all, these categories of behaviors seem to be basic to most types of love relationships.

However, there were two categories of behaviors in which relationships with romantic partners stood out: verbal expression of feelings of love (expressions of love, of enjoyment of getting together, of missing the other when gone, etc.) and physical expressions of love (mainly hugging and kissing—this was, remember, 1961).

More recently, in 1988, David Buss reported a study on the same topic—what he called love acts. Buss's results, which focused on romantic love, were similar to Swensen's in that this type of love included physical expressions of love as well as verbal expression of feelings of love. (Buss's results also heavily emphasized behaviors having to do with making or demonstrating a commitment.)

Feelings of Love

What do you feel when you are in love? In 1987 Philip Shaver and his associates reported results of a study in which they gave students 135 index cards, each with an emotion word written on it, and asked them to sort the cards into piles of emotions that seemed to them to go together. The 135 emotion words were selected based on other research in which these words were found to be representative of the major emotions people experience in life.

Shaver et al. then analyzed the sortings students had made using a sophisticated statistical technique that is something like the factor analysis described earlier (the procedure they used is called cluster analysis). They found five main groups of emotions—love, joy, anger, sadness, and fear. This result is typical of what researchers have found using other approaches to categorizing emotions. What is especially interesting for our purposes were the two main subgroupings of emotion words within the general grouping for love. One of these two subgroups of love emotions, which they labeled affection, included adoration, affection, love, fondness, liking, attraction, caring, tenderness, compassion, and sentimentality. The other subgroup, which they labeled lust, included arousal, desire, lust, passion, and infatuation. (There was also a third subgroup that included only a single emotion—longing.)

Will It Last?

Our students often ask us, "what is the difference between infatuation and love?" Based on our informal observations, the answer seems to be that if things work out, people call it love—if they don't, they say "it was just infatuation." In any case, people seem to feel that if what they are experiencing is love, it should last—if not forever, at least for more than a week or two. Thus, in this section we examine the issues of how love changes over time. Also we touch on whether love can last if the lovers come from troubled or unloving homes.

How Love Changes Over Time

In 1978 Ellen Berscheid and Elaine Hatfield (then Walster) distinguished between passionate love and companionate love. They defined the former as involving intensity and absorption in the partner, while the latter is a kind of deep intimacy. In fact, Elaine Hatfield and Susan Sprecher in 1986 developed a Passionate Love Scale, and the items in this scale make it quite clear what they mean by passionate love: For example, "Sometimes I can't control my thoughts; they are obsessively on ___," "I sense my body responding when ___ touches me," and "I possess a powerful attraction for ___." When Berscheid and Hatfield introduced the term passionate love, they also proposed that it is generally short-lived, being part of the initial phase of a relationship of falling in love and romance. (Companionate love, on the other hand, if people are lucky, grows over time; it is a part of a long-term relationship.) But why should passionate love decrease over time? What theories explain this hypothesized change?

One of the earliest theorists to address this issue was Theodore Reik, a clinical psychologist whose thinking was in the general tradition of Sigmund Freud. In 1944 Reik suggested that the passion of initial love is built upon idealizing the other, so that the lover imagines the beloved to have all the characteristics the lover would like to have in her or himself. But if a relationship develops, the beloved becomes known as a real person, with limitations and flaws. At this point, Reik argues, the fire built upon idealization (the passionate love, to use Berscheid and Hatfield's term) inevitably declines. (What remains, according to Reik, is "an afterglow" from which a new kind of companionship arises, based on reality and characterized by "ease and harmony." With time, he says, there can be a "mutual identification and common experience, joy and grief that bind people more intimately together than romance ever did," p. 92.)

Other theorists have suggested that passion declines simply due to habituation, or getting used to the other. For example, we (Aron and Aron 1986) proposed that a person seeks to form relationships in order to expand her or himself by including the partner in the self. The euphoria of falling in love arises from the excitement of the rapid expansion of self that is occurring through, for example, the staying up all night talking, the doing each thing together for the first time, the shared new adventures. But, inevitably, if the relationship develops, one gets to know the partner pretty well. The beloved is always changing and growing, and there are always things not yet discovered—but the dramatic transition from a stranger to an intimate can not be repeated with the same person.

Of course, there are other ways people can feel excitement about their relationship—by making fresh efforts to deepen it, for example, through working on communication skills, or using it as a basis for achieving some goal together, such as raising a family. Charlotte Reissman recently conducted a study (Reissman, Aron, and Bergen 1993) in which she found that married couples could increase their satisfaction with their relationship simply by doing exciting things together. In terms of the self-expansion way of thinking, if they can no longer enjoy rapid expansion through getting to know the other, they can still enjoy rapid expansion by doing expanding activities as a team.

But let us return to the question of what generally happens to love over time, if no unusual efforts are taken to change this course. Several researchers have addressed the question of what happens to passionate love over time among married people, including studies reported by Eugene Mathes and Paula Wise in 1983, Jane Traupmann and Elaine Hatfield in 1981, and Paula Tucker and Arthur Aron in 1993. The results of these studies suggest a surprising pattern: Yes, passionate love declines over time and declines especially over major transitions in the relationship—such as from before to after marriage or from before to after birth of the first child. But the surprise is that the decline in passionate love is not that great. For example, the longest-married group in the Traupmann and Hatfield study were women who had been married for a third of a century or more. The typical woman in this group described herself as experiencing some or a great deal of passionate love for her husband. More generally, the studies show that there are very great variations in the amount that passionate love declines with time.

In sum, the idea that love (especially passionate love) inevitably declines has been widely theorized but only somewhat supported by data. While the decline does typically occur, it is much less precipitous, and much more variable, than has been implied by many of the theorists.

Can Love Last If the Lovers Come from Troubled or Unloving Homes?

Eric Fromm wrote in 1956 that to love someone else you must first love yourself. Sigmund Freud suggested that the sign of a successful analysis was the ability to love well and to work well. But it is also hard not to notice that sometimes the most troubled people are the ones most prone to falling in love. And certain studies seem to verify this. For example, in a 1975 study Karen and Kenneth Dion found that students low in self-esteem reported stronger experiences of romantic love, but saw their feelings as less predictable and controllable. Similarly, other studies have found that those low in self-esteem are likely to be especially needy and to be more ready to feel attracted to and to idealize others (for example, see a study by Elaine Hatfield [then Walster] reported in 1965).

As for how long love lasts, as opposed to how intensely or how often one falls in love, the Dions and others have found that those high in self-esteem are more likely to be in love relationships, and it is more likely that their love relationships will last. (This especially makes sense in light of the material covered in Chapter 6, on attachment style.) More generally, studies have found that mental health plays a central role in the long-term success of relationships. For example, E. Lowell Kelly and James Conley in 1987 reported the results of a major study in which personality questionnaires had been given to 300 engaged couples in the mid 1930s, who were then recontacted yearly for the first few years, and then again in 1955 and 1980. The main finding was that initial level of mental health (absence of neuroticism) in the 1930s predicted whether the marriage lasted over all of these years and, among those who did stay together, it also predicted their level of marital satisfaction.

Kelly and Conley also administered questionnaires in the initial testing that focused on the home environments in which people grew up. These measures did not predict divorce, but they did predict how satisfied people were in the early and middle years of their marriages.

We think of Sigmund Freud as the one who drew our attention to the importance of childhood for healthy relationships in adulthood. But Freud emphasized the importance of the Oedipal period, the stage of about three to six years, when he thought children long to possess their opposite-sexed parent. An offshoot of

Freud's work, called object relations theory, pushes the important period much earlier, to the first two years of life, when the first relationship is formed, between the infant and its primary caretaker. The chapter in this book on attachment theory looks at an attempt to demonstrate experimentally some of the ideas associated with object relations theory.

Does the importance of mental health for a long and satisfying close relationship weight the odds against those with unhappy childhoods? Far from it. It is true that studies, for example, of parenting styles have found that parents who were troubled and abused as children often not only ended up in brief or unhappy marriages, but produced troubled and abused children. In a study of parents reported in 1985, Mary Main and her colleagues found that some parents with histories of rejection or trauma had integrated or come to terms with their childhood, so that their relationship style was secure and satisfying. Likewise Cindy Hazan and Philip Shaver, who in 1987 first applied attachment theory to adult romantic relationships, thought that healing relationships later in life could alter the effects of early childhood relationships—our childhoods or family difficulties are not the final determinant of our ability to love in a healthy, lasting way. (If this were not so, it would be hard to explain why so many people attest to the value of family and individual therapy.)

Is It Just Lust?

Besides Freud's emphasis on early childhood, he is also remembered for his proposal that love (and a lot else) is really just sex in another form. In recent years the notion that love is basically sex has thrived among those social psychologists who emphasize the role of biological evolution in shaping human behavior. Others, especially thinkers influenced by the Judeo-Christian tradition and some humanistically oriented psychologists, argue that love and sex are two different things. Many current love researchers handle the conflict by suggesting that sexuality is especially important to the passionate aspect of love. But even the relationship of sexuality to passionate love is not a simple question, and many of the issues are discussed in some detail in Chapter 11 on sexuality. (We have also written a fuller discussion of the specific relation of love and sex—see Aron and Aron 1991a.)

We will comment here, however, on just one line of work that bears on this issue. In 1957 Vernon Grant was among the first to point out that there are many accounts of children experiencing what seems like romantic love, and that this is probably quite common. In 1988 Elaine Hatfield and her associates reported a study in which they administered a children's version of the Passionate Love Scale to a large group of boys and girls, ranging from four to eighteen years old. (The younger children had the test read aloud to them.) As shown in Figure 7-1, the average degree of passionate love was about the same for four year olds as for eighteen year olds. For girls, in fact, the level was about the same at every age in

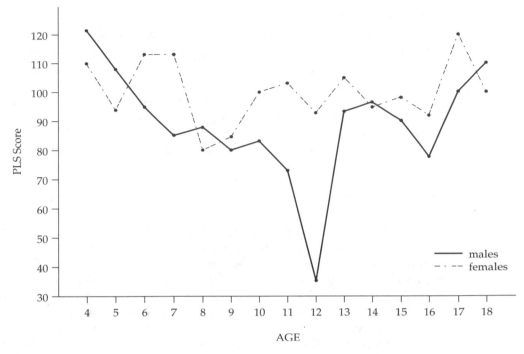

FIGURE 7–1   The Relationship Between Sex, Age, and PLS Score

between. For boys, however, there was a dip around age twelve—that period when boys are heard to say "girls are yucky." If children fall in love well before the onset of puberty and adult sexuality, it could be that they are imitating adult behaviors, but the strength of these attachments are probably not fired very much by a desire for sexual contact.

Do I Love This Person for Her or Himself and Not for What She or He Can Do for Me?

The Judeo-Christian ideal of love is that it is selfless, all-giving—saintly. Recall John Alan Lee (1977), who developed the six styles of love discussed earlier. When describing this ideal of love, which in Greek is called agape, Lee referred to Paul's use of this word for love in the Christian Bible. For example,

> *Love is patient and kind; love is not jealous or boastful; it is not arrogant or rude. Love does not insist on its own way; it is not irritable or resentful; it does not rejoice at wrong, but rejoices in the right. Love bears all things, believes all things, hopes all things, endures all things. (1 Corinthians 13:4–7)*

Maslow and B-Love

Abraham Maslow, writing in 1962, expanded on this theme by differentiating between D-Love and B-Love. D, or deficiency-motivated love, is love out of need. Terry loves Chris because Terry needs Chris's good qualities. This kind of love is okay, and inevitable at times, but can give rise to anxiety, possessiveness, and the limiting of the other's growth. B, or Being-motivated love, appreciates the other for themselves, is nonpossessive, never sated, autonomous rather than merged, and always good for the other. It only gets stronger with time.

Although Maslow's image of B-Love is much like Paul's description of agape, one important difference is that Paul saw love as a duty that everyone should practice. Maslow, on the other hand, saw B-Love as an ideal achieved by people who are self-actualizing—those who have attained a very high level of psychological functioning as Maslow defined it. And tests of self-actualization and of B-love, used by James Dietch in 1978, and also by Karen and Kenneth Dion in 1985, have found a moderate association between the two measures.

Also, for everyone, even for those whose desire for love is out of need, the experience of love may be more like Maslow's B-Love. In 1980, Dan McAdams conducted a study in which he analyzed stories subjects had made up about a drawing they were shown, and he compared the content of stories written by people who were currently in love versus people who were not currently in love. McAdams found that the stories written by people in love were substantially more likely to include themes of union and harmony, and of intimacy as a kind of sanctuary, a retreat from the demands of ordinary life.

Love as Valuing

This traditional ideal of love as selflessness has also been studied by Edward Rousar. Writing in 1990, Rousar took issue with Fehr and the prototype approach to love (described at the start of the chapter), suggesting that there may in fact be a classical definition of love and that it is this classical definition which really determines what people mean by love. Just as the key to recognizing a figure as a triangle is to know it has three sides, Rousar says the key to recognizing something as love is that one values the other for themselves, for their intrinsic worth as a person, independent of what they can do for me. Obviously Rousar was influenced by Maslow.

To demonstrate this idea, Rousar added some items to the Fehr list of love features. The added items emphasized valuing the beloved. Rousar then asked people to rate the centrality of the various features. He found that the items he added were generally rated as only slightly less central than the most central features on Fehr's original list. Of course, Rousar had expected the valuing features to be most central. Nevertheless, he took their relatively high centrality as some support for his theory. He also noted that those features from Fehr's original list that were rated as most central (such as caring, trusting, accepting) may in fact be especially direct indicators of valuing—perhaps even better indicators of valuing than the features he created. Also, in two other studies, Rousar showed that when presented with scenarios about love relationships, people do not really consider a claim of love to be valid if the person ceases to love when she or he discovers the beloved has lost their beauty or wealth.

Self Love—of Ourselves

From the perspective of the self-expansion model, we (Aron and Aron 1986) have argued that as people love more, they become more selfless and more selfish, both at once. This is because when one is in love, the other becomes to some extent part of one's self, so that whatever Chris does to benefit Terry also benefits Chris; if Terry feels good, Chris feels good.

To demonstrate this idea, we conducted a study (Aron et al. 1991) in which we asked students to make a series of decisions about allocating money to themselves and to another person. For example, in one decision, Option A is that I gain 80¢ and other gains 20¢; Option B is I gain 30¢, other loses 50¢. In another decision, Option A is I lose 40¢ and other gains 30¢; Option B is I gain 50¢, other loses 10¢. And so on. Each decision is presented on a computer screen (see Figure 7–2). In our experiment each subject made a series of decisions in which the other was their best friend, and another series of decisions in which the other was a stranger (the best friend of someone else in the experiment). Real money was involved—participants in our study took home several dollars, and the amount allocated to their best friend was also sent to the best friend along with additional money allocated by other subjects (in this way it was impossible for the best friends to know how much was allocated to them by our participants, so that what the friend would think of them did not enter into the subject's motivation).

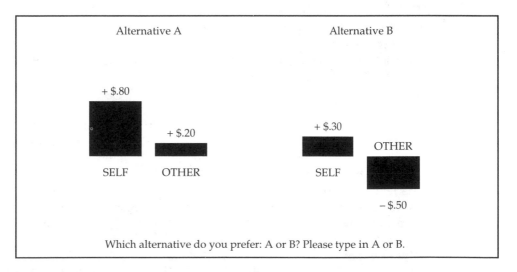

FIGURE 7–2

The point of all this was to test our prediction that in a close relationship, doing something for the other is like doing something for yourself. And indeed, that is what we found (at least in the case of money). When the other was a stranger, people allocated an average of about $19 more to themselves than to the other. But when the other was their best friend, the difference was less than a dollar.

We have to add some qualifications to this idea of course. These were small amounts of money, and so often in relationships the issues are equally small—shall we go out for Chinese food or Italian? Usually we are as willing to make the other happy as ourselves. Sometimes conflicts arise that have to do with our core sense of identity—my career demands we live in the city, you cannot survive except in the wide open spaces. To give in without a thought for one's own future would seem strange indeed. Sometimes we do see couples in which one person does that for another—usually these days it is called co-dependency. This is not what we mean by self-expansion, because, in a sense, in these cases there was very little self to expand. Yet we would argue that even in these situations such people are trying to find a shortcut to developing a strong self, by borrowing on the other's strength, and we suspect that in some cases it is a helpful step, as long as self-expansion does not stop there.

As Erik Erikson explained in 1950, one first must have a firm sense of identity before real love and intimacy can develop, and research has borne this out (for example, a study by Orlofsky, Marcia, and Lester 1973). Otherwise one may take on another person's needs and desires as a substitute for having discovered one's own needs.

Is This the Passion Immortalized in Song and Story?

In the study of love, when all the data are in and analyzed, one can still feel that the essence of love has slipped away like the wind through this iron gate of science which was supposed to capture and define it. Is love selfless and all-giving or passionate and ecstatic? Is it long-lasting, or fleeting as the sharp word that kills it?

The Extreme of Love

In search of these ultimate answers, some researchers have looked at the extremes of love to try to understand its essence. Dorothy Tennov, in 1979, wrote about certain people's actual experiences with very, very intense, desperate love—what she called limerence. While many of those she questioned had never had this experience even once in their lives (yet felt they had certainly been in love), those who had had it found it had changed their lives—and also the lives of those they had felt this feeling towards, usually for the worse. In the end Tennov could not explain the phenomenon, except that it might be some inherited tendency in certain people.

Similarly, James Averill and Phyllis Boothroyd reported a study in 1977 of a group of single individuals ranging in age from eighteen to fifty-four, about 40 percent of whom reported intensely romantic falling-in-love experiences (Romeo and Juliet was one of the examples to which subjects were to compare themselves). Age and gender made no difference in whether or not a person's experience conformed to the extreme of the romantic ideal.

Unrequited Love

Another kind of falling in love that allows us to look at the phenomenon freshly is unrequited love, that odd situation when there is no relationship, and one suffers willingly without the other loving back. This seemingly miserable and unrewarding situation happens fairly often. In a study we reported in 1991 (Aron and Aron 1991b), we found that about three-fourths of college students had at some time experienced loving someone who did not love them back. In about 40 percent of these cases, the beloved did not even know about it (the love was secret).

The self-expansion model of love (Aron and Aron 1986) mentioned earlier in the chapter is that we love others who offer the potential to expand ourselves. According to this view, the potential expansion arises, usually, from the benefits of a relationship with the other. Coming to love someone, is based on seeing a relationship with this person as being really wonderful (very expanding)—and also likely to occur. We think that often in the case of unrequited love, even if the chance of relationship is seen as very small, a person may still fall in love if having a relationship with this person is seen as being extraordinarily wonderful. It is like betting on a lottery in which your chances of winning are slim but the prize is huge.

It also seemed possible that unrequited love might promote expansion in another way: Just being in love, enacting the role of the romantic hero, offers a new and exciting perspective on life—"better to have loved and lost then never to have loved at all."

Thus, in the 1991 Aron and Aron study, we also tested these ideas about how self-expansion might explain the intensity of unrequited love, and the results of our study were quite consistent with this viewpoint. For most people experiencing unrequited love, the intensity of love was directly related to how much the lover thought a relationship with the beloved would be really wonderful. For many others, however, the intensity of the love was related mainly to the extent that they considered it a desirable thing to be in love. (We called this latter group the Don Quixotes, after the Spanish character of Cervantes's novel, the old man so taken with romantic tales of knighthood that he set out on his broken down horse to become a knight errant, tilting at windmills and vowing his eternal, steadfast love and devotion to a serving woman at a wayside inn, a lady of very doubtful repute.)

Love That Has Made History

In 1988 Sharon Brehm wrote about passionate love, analyzing the detailed writings on love of two great lovers: first, an eighteenth century thinker, Marie-Henri

Beyle, better known as Stendahl, who wrote the famous treatise, *De l'amour,* and second, the sixteenth century nun, Teresa of Avila, who elaborated in great detail her intense experiences arising from her love of God.

Interestingly, both described seven stages—from admiration, or the initial decision to love, to the final state, in which everything in the person's life is focused on the other, or in the case of the love of God, one is received in a permanent union or spiritual marriage. Stendhal's examples, all of human love, were always maximized by uncertainty—there is hope, but no actual possession of the other. That is, unrequited love can increase the feelings—after all, one cannot grow tired of the other if one is never with the other. Likewise, in Teresa's case, God is not exactly an individual one gets used to.

Brehm concluded that this sort of intense love requires "the capacity to construct in one's imagination an elaborated vision of a future state of perfect happiness" (p. 253). To her, the effect of such love is not necessarily negative, and indeed the imagination and strength of emotion that are required may suggest all sorts of capacities for creativity and happiness. For example, Brehm believes this endowment may help humans to construct a vision of a better world and to work to bring that vision about.

The Effect of Falling in Love

So is falling in love a good or a bad thing? Some theorists, including Tennov, think that at least intense love is often disturbing and troubling to people. In fact, Stanton Peele, who, with A. Brodsky, in 1976 wrote a book called *Love and Addiction,* saw this kind of intense love as basically a social and psychological illness. Ralph Linton, in 1936, wrote that

> *All societies recognize that there are occasional violent emotional attachments between persons of opposite sex, but our present American culture is practically the only one which has attempted to capitalize on these and make them the basis for marriage. Most groups regard them as unfortunate and point out the victims of such attachments as horrible examples. Their rarity in most societies suggests that they are psychological abnormalities to which our own culture has attached extraordinary value just as other cultures have attached extreme values to other abnormalities The hero of the modern American movie is always a romantic lover just as the hero of the old Arab epic was always an epileptic. (p. 175)*

In our view, all love, whether intense or not, unrequited or not, is at least an attempt to expand the self. No one lacks a self entirely, and no matter how dependent and seemingly unhealthy the bond, the lover is trying to expand, or at least to protect the expansion already acquired, all in the best way he or she knows how. (Not that people do not go through phases of expansion, then of rest and recovery—we will discuss that in the next section.) There is at least some data to suggest that love does expand the self, in certain senses.

For example, in a 1990 study by Meg Paris, students completed a question-naire every two weeks over a ten-week period. Included were measures of sense of self-efficacy (feeling capable of accomplishing what one desires) and of self-concept (they were asked "who are you"—list all the words or phrases you can in answer to this question). In addition, the students were asked at each testing whether they had fallen in love during the preceding two weeks.

The study was done in the fall, and half the participants were brand new first-year students. Thus, perhaps it was not surprising that about a third of all the participants fell in love during the ten weeks of the study. The important results of the study, however, were two. First, falling in love was associated with a substantial change in the self-concept—many more new and different words appeared. Second, falling in love was associated with a clear increase in self-effi-cacy. (For both findings, the changes from before to after falling in love were significantly greater than the same individuals' changes from before to after other testings, and significantly greater than for changes for people who did not fall in love.)

Thus, Paris's findings support the notions that falling in love does change the self, and that this change is at least in part a positive one. This does not mean that the participants were better off in every way being in love—falling in love may have been a quick fix that solved nothing. Nor does it mean that in the long run the relationship will be good for them. It does suggest that love changes us—and no one grows without changing.

Conclusion and Summary

So what is love? We have seen that there is pretty widespread agreement (at least in the mainstream North American culture) about what features characterize love, and that there are also considerable differences of emphasis about the different aspects of love that are considered important for different people and different theorists. In this section we attempt to build on many of the various findings and theories we have considered and propose an integrated scheme for under-standing just what this core meaning is and the ways in which it differs.

The core meaning of love, we think, is about the connection of selves. That is, to some extent, you becoming part of me and me becoming part of you. We have illustrated this in Figure 7–3 as the overlap of two circles, one representing self and one representing other.

In terms of Fehr's (1988) prototypical features of love, this overlap of selves describes the features her subjects rated as most central—trust, caring, honesty, friendship, respect, and so forth. In terms of Aron and Westbay's (1992) factor analysis of Fehr's prototype features of love, and of Sternberg's (1986) triangular theory of love, this overlap of selves describes intimacy. (In a 1988 overview of research and theory on intimacy, Dan McAdams noted that most definitions of intimacy "converge on the central idea of sharing that which is inmost with

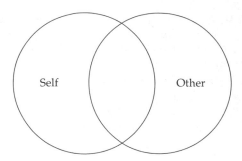

Self   Other

FIGURE 7–3

others," p. 18.) This notion of overlap of selves is also behind most of the behaviors identified in Swensen's (1961) study as common to many kinds of love relationships—shared activities, self-disclosure, expressions of similarity, along with mutual giving (of material and nonmaterial support).

The ideals of love we considered can also be understood as having this core of connectedness or overlap of selves. As we noted earlier, to the extent the Judeo-Christian ideal of selfless love is actually achieved, it is as a result of an interconnectedness of self and other in which benefiting other is benefiting self. And the extremes of love, such as intense unrequited love, Tennov's (1979) limerence, and the ecstatic love of religion and literature described by Brehm (1988), are all examples of seeking for unity with a seemingly unattainable ideal.

Also, the distinction between the seeking of such a connectedness on the one hand, and the living of such a connectedness on the other hand, can help us understand the differences in emphasis on the aspects of love we have seen. The seeking of such a connectedness—indeed the intense yearning for it—is Aron and Westbay's (1992) Passion factor (and Sternberg's 1986 passion component). It is included in Lee's (1977) and Hendrick and Hendrick's (1986) Eros love style—and when it is particularly intense, it is their Mania love style. In terms of Luby and Aron's (1990) work, it is being in-love (versus just love). The behaviors which this seeking emphasizes are especially those that Swensen (1961) found to be specific to romantic love: They are the things we try in order to become very close, the verbal expression of feelings of love and the physical expressions of love (such as hugging and kissing). It is also here, in this seeking, that feelings of all kinds are most involved, including both of Shaver et al.'s (1987) main subgroups of love feelings, affection and lust.

Most obviously, perhaps, this deep desire for connectedness is associated with the early stages of love, with Berscheid and Hatfield's (1978) passionate love. On the other hand, the living of the connectedness, after it is achieved, or the gradual development of even more deeply connected selves as each partner grows as an individual—this is what, at its best, is meant by companionate love.

In sum, we see love as basically about selves connecting. The achievement of that connection is the core of love. The intense desire for that connection with a specific other person is also called love, but in this case in-love or passionate love or mania love or limerence.

So Chris and Terry can be deeply connected, or only strongly desire to be—either way, it seems to be love that they feel. Whether their love is enough to satisfy them, whether it will last—those may be the questions they really wish to ask. The answers to those lie only within themselves.

References

Aron, A., and E. Aron. 1986. *Love and the expansion of self: Understanding attraction and satisfaction.* New York: Hemisphere.

Aron, A., and E. Aron. 1991a. Love and sexuality. In *Sexuality in close relationships,* ed. K. McKinney and S. Sprecher, 25–48. Hillsdale, NJ: Lawrence Erlbaum Associates.

Aron, A., and E. Aron. 1991b. *Motivational structures of types of unrequited Love.* Paper presented at the Third International Network Conference on Personal Relationships, Normal/Bloomington, IL.

Aron, A., E. Aron, M. Tudor, and G. Nelson. 1991. Close Relationships as including other in the self. *Journal of Personality and Social Psychology,* 60:241–53.

Aron, A., and L. Westbay. 1992. *Latent structure of love-prototype feature and the Love Prototype Scale.* Manuscript submitted for publication.

Averill, J., and P. Boothroyd. 1977. On falling in love in conformance with the romantic ideal. *Motivation and Emotion,* 1:235–47.

Berscheid, E., and E. H. Walster. 1978. *Interpersonal attraction,* 2nd ed. Reading, MA: Addison-Wesley.

Brehm, S. 1988. Passionate love. In *The psychology of love,* ed. R. Sternberg and M. Barnes, 232–263. New Haven, CT: Yale University Press.

Buss, D. 1988. Love acts: The evolutionary biology of love. In *The psychology of love,* ed. R. Sternberg and M. Barnes, 100–18. New Haven, CT: Yale University Press.

Dietch, J. 1978. Love, sex roles, and psychological health. *Journal of Personality Assessment,* 42:626–34.

Dion, K. K., and K. L. Dion. 1975. Self-esteem and romantic love. *Journal of Personality,* 43:39–57.

Dion, K. K., and K. L. Dion. 1985. Personality, gender, and the phenomenology of romantic love. In *Self, situations and behavior: Review of personality and social psychology,* ed. P. R. Shaver, vol. 6, 209–39. Beverly Hills, CA: Sage.

Erikson, E. 1950. *Childhood and society.* New York: Norton.

Fehr, B. 1988. Prototype analysis of the concepts of love and commitment. *Journal of Personality and Social Psychology,* 55:557–79.

Fromm, E. 1956. *The art of loving.* New York: Harper and Row.

Grant, V. W. 1957. *The psychology of sexual emotion: The basis of selective attraction.* New York: Longmans, Green.

Hatfield, E., E. Schmitz, J. Cornelius, and R. L. Rapson. 1988. Passionate love: How early does it begin? *Journal of Psychology and Human Sexuality,* 1:35–51.

Hatfield (Walster), E., and S. Sprecher. 1986. Measuring passionate love in intimate relationships. *Journal of Adolescence,* 9:383–410.

Hazan, C., and P. Shaver. 1987. Romantic love conceptualized as an attachment process. *Journal of Personality and Social Psychology,* 52:511–24.

Hendrick, C., and S. Hendrick. 1986. A theory and method of love. *Journal of Personality and Social Psychology,* 50:392–402.

Hendrick, C., and S. Hendrick. 1989. Research on love: Does it measure up? *Journal of Personality and Social Psychology,* 56:784–94.

Kelly, E. L., and J. J. Conley. 1987. Personality and compatibility: A prospective analysis of marital stability and marital satisfaction. *Journal of Personality and Social Psychology,* 52:27–40.

Lee, J. A. 1977. A typology of styles of loving. *Personality and Social Psychology Bulletin,* 3:173–82.

Linton, R. 1936. *The study of man: An introduction.* New York: Appleton-Century.

Luby, V., and A. Aron. 1990. *A prototype structuring of love, like, and being in-love.* Paper presented at the International Conference on Personal Relationships, Oxford, England.

Main, M., N. Kaplan, and J. Cassidy. 1985. Security in infancy, childhood, and adulthood: A move to the level of representation. In *Growing points of attachment: Theory and research,* ed. I. Bretherton and E. Waters, 66–104. Chicago: University of Chicago Press.

Maslow, A. H. 1962. *Toward a psychology of being.* Princeton, NJ: Van Nostrand.

Mathes, E., and P. Wise. 1983. Romantic love and the ravages of time. *Psychological Reports,* 53:839–46.

McAdams, D. P. 1980. A thematic coding system for the intimacy motive. *Journal of Research in Personality,* 14:413–32.

McAdams, D. P. 1988. Personal needs and personal relationships. In *Handbook of Personal Relationships,* ed. S. W. Duck, 7–22. New York: John Wiley and Sons.

Orlofsky, J. L., J. E. Marcia, and I. M. Lester. 1973. Ego identity status and the intimacy versus isolation crisis of young adulthood. *Journal of Personality and Social Psychology,* 27:211–19.

Paris, M. 1990. *Falling in love and the transformation of self-concept.* Unpublished doctoral dissertation, California Graduate School of Family Psychology, San Francisco.

Peele, S., and A. Brodsky. 1976. Love and addiction. New York: NAL.

Reik, T. 1944. *A psychologist looks at love.* New York: Farrar and Rinehart.

Reissman, C., A. Aron, and M. Bergen. 1993. Shared activities and marital satisfaction: Causal direction and self-expansion versus boredom. *Journal of Social and Personal Relationships,* 10:243–54.

Rosch, E. 1973. Natural categories. *Cognitive Psychology,* 4:328–50.

Rousar, E. 1990. *Valuing's role in romantic love.* Unpublished doctoral dissertation, Pacific Graduate School of Psychology, Palo Alto, CA.

Rubin, Z. 1970. Measurement of romantic love. *Journal of Personality and Social Psychology,* 16:265–73.

Shaver, P., J. Schwartz, D. Kirson, and C. O'Connor. 1987. Emotion knowledge: Further exploration of a prototype approach. *Journal of Personality and Social Psychology,* 52:1061–86.

Sternberg, R. J. 1986. A triangular theory of love. *Psychological Review,* 93:119–35.

Swensen, C. H., Jr. 1961. Love: A self report analysis with college students. *Journal of Individual Psychology,* 17:167–71.

Tennov, D. 1979. *Love and limerence: The experience of being in love.* New York: Stein and Day.

Traupmann, J., and E. Hatfield. 1981. Love and its effect on mental and physical health. In *Aging: Stability and change in the family,* ed. J. March, S. Kiesler, R. Fogel, E. Hatfield, and E. Shana, 253–74. New York: Academic Press.

Tucker, P., and A. Aron. 1993. Passionate love and marital satisfaction at key transition points in the family life cycle. *Journal of Social and Clinical Psychology,* 12:135–47.

Walster, E. 1965. The effect of self-esteem on romantic liking. *Journal of Experimental Social Psychology,* 1:184–97.

C h a p

Commitment and Its Communication in Romantic Relationships

MARK L. KNAPP
University of Texas at Austin

ERIC H. TAYLOR
Office of the Governor
State of Texas

Outline

Don't underestimate the importance of this topic. Perceptions of commitment are crucial in determining whether relationships get started or not; whether they become close or not; whether they are satisfying or not; whether they last a long time or not; and whether a failing relationship can be saved or not (Acker and Davis 1992; Schlesinger 1982; Dindia and Baxter 1987; Becker 1960; Brickman 1987; Davis 1973; Swenson and Trahaug 1985). Commitment may even affect your physical and emotional health (Kessler and Essex 1982; Kobasa 1982).

Even though you may not have read any books or articles about commitment, your experiences with relationships probably gives you a good sense of the critical nature of relationship commitment—whether it is romantic, friendly, whether to a family, an organization, or a community. Commitment is a frequent, familiar, and sometimes puzzling topic when people talk about their relationships.

In the first part of this chapter we will explore the nature of this complex and sometimes confusing concept that has been referred to by some couples as the "C word. We believe it is important to first understand the many ways commitment can be experienced. Therefore we identify different types of commitment and different dimensions of the construct which can affect the ways you experience commitment. The second part of the chapter focuses entirely on the role of communication in creating your experiences with commitment. This includes the explicitness of your talk, the topics you discuss, and stylistic factors which affect the intensity of your commitment talk. The chapter concludes with a discussion of how commitment talk can be affected by the nature and stage of your relationship and by the way each individual perceives, understands, and reports on the discourse associated with commitment.

Commitment: What Is It?

Types of Commitment

You may have observed a hesitancy on the part of some people to commit themselves to a relationship. They fear it won't work out and they want to avoid the potential pain and entanglements. Paradoxically, though, the process of committing oneself to a relationship may go a long way toward increasing the chances that the relationship will work. On the other hand, there are also situations where someone tenaciously clings to a relationship that does not work (e.g., a destructive relationship involving physical and/or mental abuse) which makes his or her life increasingly miserable. Committing oneself to an idea, a course of action, or a relationship has the effect of creating resistance to other alternatives and of guiding future behavior (Kiesler 1968). In popular usage, commitment is a term we use when we refer to a kind of love, and a term we use when we refer to something that holds people together in the absence of love (Brickman 1987). In view of the preceding, it should be clear that the phenomenon we know as commitment is a complex and multi-faceted one. To define it we need to dissect it.

In an effort to better understand the nature of commitment, we need to recognize that there are several different types of commitment (Johnson, 1973, 1982, 1991; Kanter, 1972). Consider the following:

1. "Want To" Commitment. This type of commitment is based on one's own personal choice and desire. It is the kind of commitment to a relationship which is rooted in positive feelings for one's partner. The feelings may vary from weak to strong.

2. "Ought To" Commitment. This type of commitment stems from a sense of obligation. It may be a perceived obligation to the other person ("I said I'd stay with him and I am a person who keeps her promises"). Or a perceived obligation to the relationship ("Marriage is a once in a lifetime deal"). Sometimes the motivation for this type of commitment is associated with anticipated guilt which would accompany a break-up. A person who is tempted to leave a relationship may not want to hurt his or her partner or believe their partner would not be able to make it without me. In actual practice, of course, some of these perceived obligations may be quite strong (e.g., keeping your promises or believing in the inviability of marriage) while others may be quite weak (e.g., suffering in order to save your partner the grief of living without you).

3. "Have To" Commitment. This type of commitment is based on one's perception that there is no good alternative to maintaining membership in the relationship. Due to constraints such as financial needs, perceived inability to find another suitable partner, disinclination to let go of investments already made in the current relationship, or social pressure from friends and family, the person perceives greater costs in terminating the relationship than in keeping it—even though he or she may not particularly want it. "Have to" perceptions, like those associated with other types of commitment, may range from weak to strong.

To distinguish the preceding types of commitment, we discussed each one separately. During relationship life, though, these types blend together in different ways at different times. Notice how all three types of commitment are interwoven in the following response from one of the people we interviewed about commitment:

> *This is my third marriage. I'm bound and determined to make it in this one so I don't want to get a divorce. And mostly I don't ever think about it because we have a really good relationship. I think we really love each other, but there are those times when you do wonder if its worth sticking it out—whether the love is really as strong as you thought. But I can't stand the thought of starting all over again . . .*

We also know that the overriding type of commitment may change during the life of the relationship. This ability to maintain a mixture of different types of commitment and to emphasize one or the other at different times may, indeed, be quite functional. A study of couples who had been married for more than fifteen years points out the utility of beliefs such as "marriage is a long-term commitment" and "marriage is forever" in sustaining a relationship during periods when "want to" commitment wanes (Lauer and Lauer 1985). Of course, one does not always know the strength of one's "ought to" and "have to" commitment until something happens that creates a test. This could happen when one's "want to" commitment is no longer a major force in holding the relationship together and other types of commitment seem strong until an attraction to another person develops. In this culture which tends to idealize intimacy, there is a tendency to consider "ought to" and "want to" types of commitment as somehow inadequate for a satisfying relationship. This view, however, overlooks our ability to effectively meld different types of commitment as Huey Lewis' song, "Happy To Be Stuck With You" so succinctly captures.

Understanding that there are different types of commitment and that they blend together in different ways at different times should make us appreciate the important role communication plays as we try to gauge our partner's commitment and our own. As communication scholars, our interests lie primarily in identifying the nature of the messages couples exchange (e.g., the content, structure, style) and in understanding the processes through which partners co-construct meanings (e.g., through reciprocal or complementary acts). In order to understand how we interact on this subject of commitment, we need to know more about the basic building blocks of the construct. What are the central dimensions of commitment which enable us to better understand and describe the many faces of commitment?

Dimensions of Commitment

In our studies (Knapp 1989; Taylor 1991) and those of other scholars (Buchanan 1974; Davis 1973; Levinger 1991; Lund 1985; Kelley 1983; Michaels, Acock, and Edwards 1986; Rusbult 1983; Rusbult, Johnson, and Morrow 1986; Sheldon 1971; Sprecher 1988; Stanley 1986; Strube and Barbour 1983), six dimensions of commitment stand out. These six include: the perception of future rewards; the identification with the relationship; the desirability of alternatives to the relationship; the effort expended for the relationship; the investments made in the relationship; and the personal responsibility assumed for the commitment. Now we examine these in more detail:

1. Future Rewards. To commit oneself to a relationship is to commit to its future. The extent to which we see that future as rewarding is influential in determining how much of that future we want and how intensely we want it. Sometimes we base our expectations for future rewards on past experiences; sometimes future rewards are forecast during discussions between the partners; and sometimes the anticipation of future rewards is merely wish-based fantasy. For example, the commitment you feel toward someone who is currently a student may involve

the expectation that this person will someday provide the relationship with the benefits of a lucrative profession.

2. Identification With The Relationship. Another gauge for commitment is the extent to which we identify with the relationship. We are more likely to identify with those relationships whose goals and values we share and believe in. The process of identification is one of moving from a primary focus on oneself as an individual ("I") to one where you think of yourself as part of a couple or team ("We"). An increasing commitment to a joint identity does not necessitate the loss of one's individual identity. In fact, in some cases, the appeal of the "we" is a shared belief that the "I" has to have plenty of opportunities to develop.

3. Alternatives To The Relationship. We cannot commit ourselves to the same extent to all the attractive choices we face. Thus, the way we deal with alternatives to our relationship can tell a lot about the strength of commitment we have for our relationship. The underlying assumption is that increasing commitment to a relationship means there will be a corresponding decrease in the likelihood that desirable relationship alternatives will be actively sought. Alternatives to the relationship are usually relationships with other people, but it is not uncommon for a person to gradually redirect his or her commitment from a relationship to a hobby or to a career. When the desired level of commitment is associated with the elimination of any alternatives to the relationship, the issue becomes one of exclusivity. Exclusivity was the primary factor college students used to assess the strength of commitment in their dating relationships (Taylor 1991). The possibility of contracting AIDS is an important factor in the sexual exclusivity of some couples. A video dating service we are familiar with has a process called "going on hold" which means the subscribers are not open to dates from other members because they have found a person they want to date exclusively. Since they have not completely removed their names from the service, however, they are allowing for the possibility that alternative relationships may be desirable in the future.

4. Effort Expended. When someone says, "I don't have time to do that," this usually means, "I am not willing to take the time to do that." When we devote our time and energy to something, it is a measure of what is important to us. Stated another way, we show our commitment to various aspects of our life by the effort we expend toward them. Effort can take many forms. It may involve helping your partner with a problem, listening to your partner, working on a project of mutual concern, or simply spending time together. If, instead of going to a party you remain with your partner to help him or her study for an exam or discuss a family problem, you show your commitment by giving the relationship priority in your time.

5. Investments in the Relationship. We tend to invest in things we value, things we expect to gain benefits from. Investments need not be tangible resources. The expenditure of effort for the relationship can become an investment in it. Sometimes people consider the amount of time spent in a relationship as an investment. Thus, increasing investments normally means increasing commitment. When a person feels like his or her investments in a relationship are substantial enough to maintain the relationship in the face of minimal investment returns, the conditions may dictate an increasing "have to" orientation toward commitment. For instance, you may stick it out through an unhappy time with someone because you have put in so many years already that you don't want to lose it all by walking out on your investments.

   6. Personal Responsibility for Commitment. To the extent that you take personal responsibility for your commitment, you have increased your involvement in the relationship. Even if you express a relatively low commitment to a relationship, it is more involving if it is perceived as your free choice than if your connection is attributed to factors outside your control. The "have to" type of commitment may, in certain circumstances, be very effective in holding a relationship together. However, the perceptions associated with this out of my control accountability relegate it to commitment with little strength. The cultural emphasis on the concept of freedom of choice in the United States may give this factor a stature in this society it does not have in others. Consider whether you feel special ties to people who do not put chains on you or expect loyalty from you, compared to those you do not feel free to leave.

   The preceding dimensions can be useful for understanding the nature of one's commitment even though we still have much to learn about how these dimensions interrelate and how much they contribute in certain situations. For example, a couple who has been together for twenty years may be more influenced by the investment dimension than the future rewards dimension. It should also be noted that a strong relational commitment may reveal the participants are low on one or more dimensions for an extended period of time, but high during a period critical to the relationship. For example, during a given period of time, a person may expend little effort on behalf of a relationship he or she feels strongly committed to. This, in turn, precipitates the need for a relationship talk. It is during this talk and subsequent to it that highly committed individuals should show a dramatic rise in the effort directed at the relationship and relationship partner. There will also be some patterns experienced by couples when the issue of commitment is at a low level of awareness. One couple we spoke to put it this way:

> *Commitment wasn't an issue we were particularly aware of; we just kept doing things and seeing each other and one day . . . there we were.*

   The "How Committed Are You?" test in Box 8–1 helps to summarize the various dimensions of the commitment construct. It contains statements representing each of the dimensions we've outlined plus one general item. It is designed to help you reflect on various issues associated with commitment in your relationship. It may help readers find answers to familiar questions about commitment—e.g., "How did they come to terms with their relationship after the affair was revealed?" "Why do guys keep thinking I want a more serious relationship when I don't?" or "Why does she keep asking for so much more than I can give?" In this sense, then, your response to a particular item may be more impor-

---

BOX 8–1   How Committed Are You?*

Answer the following questions while thinking about a current romantic relationship. It can be a serious, long term relationship, a casual dating relationship, or anywhere in between. Answer each question with a number from 1 to 7, with 1 being "Absolutely" and 7 being "Absolutely Not."

1. _____ I am likely to pursue another relationship or a single lifestyle.
2. _____ I believe there will be a lot of future rewards associated with the relationship.
3. _____ I feel a strong sense of "we" when thinking of my partner and me.
4. _____ I am willing to exert a great deal of effort on behalf of this relationship.
5. _____ I have a lot invested in this relationship.
6. _____ I can imagine having an affair with another person and not having it affect my relationship with _____.
7. _____ I expect to be with _____ for the rest of my life.
8. _____ There is nothing holding me in this relationship except my own free choice.

Scoring: Add your scores from questions 2, 3, 4, 5, 7, and 8. Now add your scores from items 1 and 6 and subtract the sum of these two items from 16. Add your two totals together. Lower scores are associated with greater commitment. Scores range from 8 to 56.

*Source: E. H. Taylor, *Communicating commitment in romantic relationships.* Unpublished Master's Thesis, University of Texas, 1991. Items six and eight are new.

---

tant than your overall score. This test has not been validated as a way to measure the complexity of one's commitment to a romantic relationship, however. Scores should therefore only be viewed as good or bad in the context of a particular relationship.

The Social Construction of Commitment Through Communication

Up to this point we have discussed the nature of the commitment experience—how it is perceived and what it means to the individuals involved in a relationship. These meanings and perceptions, though, are constantly in process, constantly subject to modification through interaction between the partners. The kind of changes created by the dynamics of two interacting perspectives on commitment can be illustrated in the following example. Petunia exerts a great deal of effort on behalf of her relationship with Porky. Porky, on the other hand, appears to exert very little effort on behalf of the relationship. When you talk to Porky, he says he is extremely committed to their relationship. It isn't that he would not or could not exert a lot of effort in this relationship, but he says Petunia seems to be doing enough for both of them right now. Perhaps he thinks Petunia is unnecessarily displaying feelings and ideas that should be understood. In time, the lack of effort on Porky's part becomes critical to Petunia. She feels something has to be done. Should she increase her displays of effort—assuming that intensified efforts will elicit more effort from Porky? Or should she decrease her effort displays to communicate the idea that she cannot keep on as the only partner who is working hard for this relationship's success? No matter what course Petunia follows, there is a strong chance that she and Porky will soon be discussing the course of their relationship and what needs to be done in order to get it back on track. Effort, for example, may or may not be discussed, but negotiations about future behavior will be aired. There are at least two important points contained within this example: Individual thoughts and feelings about commitment are best understood as social constructions, and the structured acts of initiation and reciprocation can be as important for understanding commitment as the content itself.[1]

In an effort to find out more about how couples communicate on this subject of commitment, we conducted in-depth interviews with fifty individuals and/or couples. In addition, we supervised over a hundred additional interviews conducted by student interviewers. The interviews were not highly scripted, but the interviewees were encouraged to tell stories about commitment in their relationship; to reflect on the meaning of commitment to them; and to talk specifically about how commitment manifests itself in their interactions with their partner. We also tape recorded fifteen couples who interacted with each other about times in their relationship when commitment increased or decreased. Data from these sources helped us answer the following questions: Are there different kinds of commitment talk? What do committed partners talk about? How is commitment communicated?

Types of Commitment Talk

Are there different types of commitment talk? Yes. Commitment talk seems to occur in three primary forms which include both indirect and direct interaction. Perhaps the most common form of commitment talk is *indirect* and focuses on things other than the relationship itself even though it usually interfaces with one of the six dimensions we discussed earlier. For example, one woman told us about how her husband had made sacrifices for his fellow employees at work and how he had also taken time off work to help his sister when she was in trouble. This information became mentally dispersed so that she increased her view of her husband as a person capable of strong commitment in their relationship (even though their relationship was never discussed). Because of her husband's increasing stature in her eyes, she felt her own commitment to their relationship strengthen.

---

[1]Another familiar example of the influence of initiator-reciprocator roles concerns the use of the phrase, "I love you." If one partner is always the initiator, this partner may eventually wonder why the other is never the initiator. The partner who always echoes the "I love you" may get used to this role and when the initiator stops initiating, the reciprocator may perceive a decrease in affection—exactly the same perception which led the initiator to stop initiating!

Another common type of commitment talk is also indirect in nature. In this case, one partner overhears the other partner telling a story about some aspect of their relationship to a third party. Again, these stories are not likely to use the word "commitment," but they deal with issues which can readily be transposed into a commitment theme. They may not even have a primary focus on the storyteller's relationship with his or her partner. Consider this example: Leon overhears Carla telling a story about how she quickly lost interest in a physically attractive guy after she realized he only talked about himself and never listened to others. Carla has told Leon repeatedly that one of his behaviors she truly values is his ability to focus on what she is saying. As Leon listens to Carla tell her story, he interprets it as commentary on exclusiveness and Carla's commitment to their relationship. For Carla, the act of telling the story to a third party may serve, in and of itself, to strengthen Carla's commitment.

Another type of commitment talk is both indirect and direct. Our couples did not report this type of talk with nearly the same frequency as the preceding indirect types. In this type, the subject of commitment is clearly the focus of the discourse, but the frame of reference is another person or couple. For example, Pat talks to Chris about the subject of how Ben treats his partner and the persistent rumor of his affairs. The way Pat and Chris talk about Ben's behavior and the nature of commitment in his relationship may be quite informative about their views of commitment to their own relationship.

What about direct, face-to-face talk about commitment between the partners to a relationship? It does happen, but not as often as we might suppose given the importance of such discourse when it does happen. In long term relationships, the knowledge of the investments made along the way and previous commitment talk may go far in sustaining commitment without any direct talk about it for long periods of time. Usually, direct talk about "your," "my," or "our" commitment occurs at relationship junctures when there is the likelihood of a sharp increase or decrease in commitment—e.g., dating exclusively, deciding to live together or get engaged, after the revelation of an affair or some other event which throws one's commitment into question, during the period following a fight, or during any relationship talk with overtones of repair or rejuvenation.

Topics Associated With Commitment Talk

When we examined the actual conversations about commitment and the reports of commitment conversations recalled by our interviewees, we identified five topic areas—many of which correspond with the dimensions of commitment mentioned earlier.

Affection/Caring

For our couples, interactions on the subject of affection and caring provided a most useful context for making inferences about commitment. Several mentioned the immensely powerful affect the words "I love you" can have when used for the first time. The expression not only signals the degree of affection one partner feels but simultaneously demands that the recipient identify his or her level of commitment to the relationship. Notice how the concern and care expressed at a particular time in this relationship served to increase perceptions of commitment:

M: You came over and your face was so worried. I thought you were going to pass out, you were so pale. I know it was because you thought I was pregnant. Hahahha.

D: Hahahah.

M: It was really funny because I was really sick, but I wasn't pregnant, and I wasn't about to die. You were so concerned about me, and that really touched me. Even though you thought I was pregnant you were really concerned about me. And I guess that made me realize if I did get pregnant you wouldn't desert me, and that was important for me to realize. Not that I doubted you before then, but it made it more concrete.

The perceived absence of caring and affection at a time it is expected and/or needed has the potential to decrease commitment as well. The dialogue that follows comes from a couple who reported this incident as a time when commitment decreased. Notice how each partner blames the other for not caring.

K: We were driving around in my car and I thought you hadn't gotten me a birthday present. And I totally freaked out and got angry and just kind of lost it. It made me feel like you didn't care about me when you didn't get me a present.

M: I know, because you didn't have a present the first thing when you woke up in the morning.

K: I know, but you never did get me one.

M: Well yeah, I wasn't going to get you one after that. After the scene you caused, I mean hell, I was going to, but I didn't have any money, and after that I didn't want to.

K: Yeah, well did that change the way you felt about me?

M: Yeah, of course it did. It pissed me off.

K: What did you start thinking?

M: That you really didn't care who was giving you the gift as long as you got the present. It seemed to be all you really cared about. You could have cared less that I only had four bucks to my name.

Relationship Alternatives
Whenever couples have state of the relationship talks, the question of alternatives is often an inherent part of the discussion. The accepted practice for most romantic couples in this culture is to maintain only one such relationship at a time. As a result, most of the dialogue our couples engaged in or reported about relation-

ship alternatives dealt with matters of exclusivity and the threat of another relationship replacing the current one. In a few cases, the relationship alternative under discussion was a job opportunity. The question was literally, "Should we give up the relationship so we can accept certain job opportunities?"

When the focus is on other relationships, the discussion is often difficult and tense. Some people expressed this by saying they were very much in love and not at all hesitant about agreeing to have an exclusive relationship with their partner, but at the same time they knew there were other people who interested them, and they knew there was a possibility that a time might come when another relationship would be attractive. They also felt that if they admitted this to their partner it would ruin the potential they had for having a lifelong exclusive relationship.

Other couples who agreed to an exclusive relationship only considered the possibility of other relationships being attractive after they had had an exclusive relationship for an extended period of time. They, too, were reluctant to discuss their thoughts for fear it would be misinterpreted or detract from their current relationship. Those couples who did discuss such issues told us they had established a norm of discussing difficult topics early on in their relationship and had experienced the benefits of working through problems together. This process was not always without its heartaches.

The nature of the discourse on relationship alternatives changes as the relationship develops. The couple in the following dialogue are at an early stage of their relationship and are beginning to negotiate the issue of exclusivity:

J: So. Where are we?

B: I still want to see you.

J: But? . . .

B: But . . . I'm not ready for a really serious relationship.

J: It's not like I want to get married or anything. I just don't want to be one of several playthings.

No matter what is said, there will be tests which will either substantiate the agreement or not. Notice the irony involved in the following account in which the woman's boyfriend is charged with having too much contact with an ex-girlfriend, and in order to demonstrate his willingness never to contact her again, he has to contact her.

L: I got upset when you got in contact with that old girlfriend I don't get along with very well. And you didn't understand what that had to do with your commitment to me. Finally when you saw how upset I was you said if it was that big a deal to me then you wouldn't ever talk to her again. "It's not worth it." When you saw that it made me doubt your commitment you said "this isn't going to be an issue, I'll just call her and tell her I'm never going to talk to her again."

Even after various tests have been passed, there may still be conversations which review past experiences in order to determine what the future may hold.

B: You were kind of drunk and you said that you were tired of not having your freedom and not being able to go out with your friends. You were feeling too tied down.

C: I was.

B: So you told me.

C: I'm thinking I'm remembering the same situation, but at that point we weren't that serious as I am now, obviously, but when I don't see my friends and go out with them. . .

B: It makes you mad.

C: . . . No. Then when I do go out with them. . .

B: They rag on you.

C: Kind of. I can't be a flirt like I used to be able to, but . . .

B: But?

C: I'm OK now.

B: You're OK it doesn't bother you, or you're OK, you don't flirt? Hahahah.

For some couples, the issue of relationship alternatives continues for many years; for others, it is an assumed state of the relationship unless a specific event causes one partner to believe otherwise. Our research has focused entirely on heterosexual romantic couples, but the commitment involving a same-sex best friend may also spawn dialogue about alternative relationships and their effects.

Family and Friends

The subject of whether and how the social network of each partner will be integrated with the couple's relationship is another source of rich commitment talk. Sometimes it is the talk between the relationship partners and those in the social network which is salient; sometimes it is talk between the partners about members of their social networks which impacts on commitment.

Positive evaluations of a relationship from one's family may have a beneficial effect on a couple's commitment, but negative evaluations may too. In some cases, negative evaluations polarize and push a couple together in an "us against them" mentality. In some cases, a positive evaluation can negatively affect commitment. Consider the example of the mother who talks to her daughter about what a nice husband her boyfriend would make when the daughter's commitment is still very weak. The positive evaluation may be perceived as a threat to her own free choice and lead to unproductive commitment talk with her boyfriend. The two interactions which follow illustrate how both positive and negative experiences with family affected the relationship of the couple.

T: When we came back from eating at your grandparents' house in Austin this summer, we talked about how your grandfather felt about me and how. . .

D: At Marmie and Poppie's?

T: Yeah, and they really enjoyed me. I think that as your family has progressively gotten to know and like me it has increased the value of our relationship.

D: That's a good assessment. I believe that.

T: I know it's true for you because they didn't approve of the last person you were with, and it had a direct effect on everything else.

D: Yeah, I'm very very close to my family, I mean you can see that. I always get kind of a warm feeling in my heart when they have something nice to say about you. It makes me feel good that Mom wants to include you, because she doesn't have to do that, and that has definitely increased the level of commitment and the way you and I feel about each other.

V: Nancy and your Dad had done something. I don't remember what it was, and I was all mad. I had really had it with her because she had just been really ugly, and she and your Dad weren't telling us about the budget and stuff like that, and I remember you coming in and talking to me about it and . . . we talked about it a long time and I was crying and all upset and just real mad and yelling, remember that?

J: Yeah, we've had a few of those about my parents.

V: Yeah, but this is the one I really remember because I finally said, "that's it." I'd finally had it with her. I finally had to blow her off. She must have been saying insulting things about you again.

J: I guess, but um, I remember that day you came over my place, and I came in and you were upset.

V: And then at the end I was laughing again, we must've made jokes or something about them, just kind of teasing around type stuff.

The interaction about friends has an important difference about it. A person's friends are voluntary and freely chosen—not like family. When, as one person told us, he said: "I don't want Paula to go with us. She's such a goose," his partner was greatly offended and worried that the response signaled incompatibility since Paula had been her friend for some time. It is true that the kind of friends a couple will select and attract may not be similar to those each individual selected and attracted. The role of these old friends in the newly developing relationship must be negotiated, and that negotiation may have a great deal to say about the commitment perceived and experienced by the couple.

Sacrifice

Conversations involving sacrifices made for the relationship were much like the dimension we earlier called effort. Interviewees used phrases like: "He's there when it isn't convenient for him"; "She was willing to change her plans"; "She puts up with a lot"; "We had to endure long separations." The following conversations focused on the effort involved in keeping a long distance relationship going and how it affected commitment to the relationship.

S: Right before you left, after we had spent the week together.

L: And then I moved back to Dallas.

S: And we said we should try to keep the relationship going and you said it would be hard and Ma Bell would love us, haha, and she has.

L: Yeah.

S: It made me realize how much I love you and how much I wanted to keep it going.

In the preceding dialogue, a specific event called for extra effort and sacrifices for the relationship. Commitment is impacted by situations where sacrifices and extra effort are called for, but going out of your way when it is not expected or needed may also pay important dividends for commitment. Our couples also observed that sacrifices can also boomerang in the sense that one person's sacrifice may create an obligation for the other. It can be particularly difficult when guilt is invoked. Sometimes, the act of sacrificing made the person doing it feel more committed to the relationship. One person told of cancelling an important trip so she could be with her husband on his birthday. Her account identified this as an important event associated with increasing her commitment to the relationship. A subsequent interview with the husband found that this event was a pleasant surprise for him, but he didn't think it had much impact on his commitment to the relationship.

The Future

Talking about the future need not involve any explicit mention of expected rewards. Rewards are an inherent part of talking about the future when the talk is focused on the couple and not the individual and when costs to the relationship are not the driving force of the interaction. Not talking about the future of the relationship when it is expected is likely to be interpreted as a sign of decreased or absent commitment. Musing about sitting on the front porch in two rocking chairs when you are seventy years old is not only a statement about expecting to be together a long time, but testimony to the enjoyable nature of the other's company. Discussions about a future that might be play an important role in perceptions of commitment, but specific plans about a future that is can be very powerful, as this conversation demonstrates:

S: We were at your mom's house and were talking about when we were actually going to get married. We talked about this a lot, but this was the time we were sitting there and really making plans.

J: Was this the first time we talked about it or something?

S: No, but this is the first time we sat down and said "let's make plans." Because you had all your books, your law school books, and you're like, "let's see what schools have your major," Speech Path, which we could go to both. That was one of the times you seemed more committed. I mean we always talked like "let's get married," but that was more the first time we started making plans. Like concrete plans. That made it seem committed.

The people we talked to agreed that investments and relationship identification were important parts of commitment, but these were less likely to be conversational topics and more likely to be feelings derived from discussing other topics or engaging in some behavior together. Investments, for example, were often reportedly related to sharing secrets and personal information, going through difficult times together, and the accumulation of experiences and interactions which come from spending a lot of time together. Relationship identification was said to emanate from positive conversations which made both partners feel good; engaging in a difficult conversation about the "I-want-to-go-my-own-way vs. I-want-to-be-with-you" tension in a mutually satisfying way; and the accumulation of time together.

The content alone may not be sufficient to fully understand the communication of commitment. Also important are a number of factors which have to do with the way commitment messages are communicated.

How Commitment Is Communicated

Two people can say the same thing, but one person's message lacks the effectiveness of the other's. The following behaviors were reported to us as crucial for understanding why a message intended to show commitment may or may not be understood that way. Of course, any methods for increasing the strength and/or clarity of commitment messages may boomerang if they are employed at an inappropriate time in the relationship or with an unreceptive partner.

Intensity

Intensity may take many forms, but the underlying message is: "I care enough about this message to try extra hard." One woman told us about a time when she was walking down a busy street in an urban area with her boyfriend. After declaring his love to her as they walked, he suddenly started yelling to anyone within hearing range, "I LOVE LINDA! I LOVE LINDA!" She said, "It was embarrassing, but it meant a lot to me." Intensity can also be communicated by using language extremes and unqualified absolute statements like, "I could never stop loving you even if I tried" or through the rapt attention and focus usually achieved by long mutual gazes and close proximity.

Repetition

In order to firmly establish one's resolve and credibility, it is necessary to repeat one's commitment message. Exact repetitions may eventually lose their force ("Can't you say anything other than you want me?") so variations on the same theme will be the most effective in sustaining perceptions of commitment.

Explicitness

When you leave little doubt about what you are saying, you may be rewarded for making yourself vulnerable and making it easier for your partner to respond in kind. You may also get burned, but that may be a blessing in disguise. If your partner punishes you for being clear about your commitment, you may not be in the right relationship. Obviously, there are times when ambiguity about commitment is called for, but our couples felt most people were not explicit enough when they did try to communicate the nature of their commitment—particularly in situations when the partner wanted to know.

Permanence

When commitment messages are codified, it has the effect of making them more permanent—giving them the potential to be lasting relationship symbols. Writing it down was the most common method described. One couple had saved two large notebooks of letters and cards they had exchanged during a time when they were engaged but living in two cities separated by hundreds of miles.

Reliving these times by reading and talking about information in these documents on their anniversaries was an important way for them to annually re-commit themselves to the relationship. When partners tell commitment-related stories to friends and family, this is also a way of adding to the longevity of the messages.

Timing

When commitment messages are communicated also seems to have an important effect on their impact. Finding the appropriate and/or expected time for a discussion of commitment added greatly to its effectiveness, just as unexpected and inappropriate timing tended to detract from it.

The preceding sections have addressed the nature of commitment messages. To further understand the process of constructing commitment through communication, it is necessary to identify some of the influential variables affecting these messages.

The Influence of Relational Factors

The content and delivery of commitment messages are influenced by both relational and individual factors.

Developmental Point in the Relationship

Sometimes the nature of commitment messages and the way they are communicated is similar during different stages of relationship development—i.e., establishing a relationship, maintaining a relationship, or rejuvenating a relationship. Sometimes they differ radically because the relationship goals are so different for these different stages.

In the early stages when neither person is sure about the commitment of the other, we may observe a hesitancy or caution in communicating—or, as one of our interviewees put it, "do it so as not to scare them off." Once it is clear that this is a relationship where expressing commitment is most appropriate, prolonged and intense communication of commitment may be necessary to firmly establish the relationship. Once it is established, occasional reminders may be all that is needed—unless the relationship is threatened. Then the reminders may not be enough to rejuvenate it.

As we noted earlier, direct talk about commitment is most likely to occur at junctures where sharp turns (up or down) in the relationship are anticipated.[2] Let's assume one partner in a dating couple proposes to the other that they have an exclusive relationship—that they do not date others. The ensuing interactions may be charged with the expectation that, depending on how the two interactants negotiate this issue, the relationship may change dramatically (for better or worse). The pressure for direct talk about each partner's commitment should be high during this time. There may be a lot of concern for the exclusivity dimension until it is assumed to be a firmly established norm of the relationship; then there may only be occasional indirect verifications needed to sustain the relationship. If there is an apparent challenge to the exclusivity norm, we would expect a resumption of more direct commitment talk. Perhaps, after agreeing to an exclusive dating relationship, one partner begins spending an unusual amount of time with an attractive member of the opposite sex from his or her work. This may trigger interactions in which both partners seek unambiguous declarations of the other's commitment. In long term relationships, the knowledge of the investments that have been made along the way and previous commitment talk may go far in sustaining commitment without any direct talk about it for long periods of time.

The Influence of Individual Factors

The preceding examples show how commitment talk can be influenced by the relationship, but other factors associated with individual behavior may also exert a powerful influence on how we experience and understand commitment. Each individual involved in the process of communicating commitment will be engaged in three important acts: perceiving the discourse, understanding the discourse, and reporting on the discourse.

---

[2]Developmental sequences, patterns, trajectories, and phases associated with actual or imagined relationship changes in romantic relationships have been examined from several different perspectives. See, for example: Huston et al. 1981; Knapp and Vangelisti 1992; Baxter and Bullis 1986.

Perceiving the Discourse

Both interactants enter commitment conversations with a set of perceptions. These include perceptions about themselves, their partner, the relationship, and those things which have a bearing on the relationship. These perceptions can be slightly or greatly modified as the result of any given interaction or series of interactions. This makes the issue of how one perceives the discourse a crucial one. Too many times we mistakenly believe that what is said (or written) is what the intended audience perceives. What this means—and it is an important point to remember—is that the mere presence of a commitment message does not ensure that it is perceived nor that it will be subsequently incorporated in the partner's view of the world. There are times when perceptual awareness for commitment on the part of both interactants is high; at other times one will be particularly alert; and still other times when neither will be particularly mindful of commitment messages. Sometimes perceptions are affected by needs. When one partner is trying to cope with the revelation of the other partner's affair, he or she is likely to have a strong need for frequent, sincere, and intense commitment talk from his or her partner. In fact, the need may be so great that it will be difficult to satisfy. The partner who had the affair may be truly repentant and tell his or her partner over and over again in no uncertain terms of his or her commitment, but the recipient may perceive these efforts as far less frequent, far less sincere, and far less intense than the other partner—or a third party observer for that matter.

The person communicating a commitment message is, of course, a perceiver of his or her own messages as well. As such, a communicator can come to know his or her attitudes and feelings about commitment by making inferences from his or her own behavior and the circumstances surrounding it. Bem's (1972, p. 2) theory of self-perception goes on to suggest that if a person's "internal cues are weak, ambiguous, or uninterpretable, the individual is functionally in the same position as an outside observer who must necessarily rely upon those same external cues to infer the individual's inner states." Some of our interviewees seemed to grasp the self-reflexive nature of commitment communication and commitment cognitions. As we listen to our own accounts of effort expended in the name of the relationship, our cognitions are likely to reflect such accounts. It is also possible to increase our relationship identification talk about a relationship we perceive somewhat negatively, and find ourselves perceiving fewer negatives in the future. In any case, one's communication about commitment can affect commitment just like one's commitment affects the choice of communicative strategies.

Understanding the Discourse

This is the process of making sense out of what was said. It involves attributing meanings and making inferences. Even if some form of commitment talk takes place and is perceived clearly by both partners, each may interpret it differently or fit it into the total relationship in a different way. For example, each partner may tell the other "I love you," but to one partner it means, "I feel a great deal of sexual attraction for you and I want to spend more time with you if it means we will have sex." To the other partner the phrase means, "I am making the ultimate commitment to a lifelong relationship." In addition to these differences in intended meanings, each partner may also attribute very different meanings to the "I love you" expressed by their partner.

And, not surprisingly, the way we understand something at one point in time is not necessarily the way we will understand it later. The passage of time in a relationship offers great opportunity for the partners to do some rewriting of history. One couple who had been together for many years told us about a lifelong trail of commitments which may or may not have occurred, but which formed their current relational reality: "Bill and I have always given each other 110 percent." Couples' inferences stemming from their perceptions are sprinkled with large doses of the couple's unique history and idiosyncratic patterns. For an outsider (or researcher) this can make the job of understanding the communication of commitment for any given couple akin to deciphering hieroglyphics. One woman told us she had needed to be alone with her grief after her mother's death. Therefore, she asked her boyfriend to leave her and return to school in a distant city. He said he understood, and he left. She told us this was the greatest demonstration of commitment to their relationship she could ever have received. In another instance, a male interviewee, who had never discussed this ground rule with his dating partner, said her failure to back him during an argument with another couple was a clear sign she wanted out of the relationship. In fact, he said, it was not just a demonstrated lack of commitment, it was anti-commitment. This last example not only highlights the issue of how commitment is understood, but how these understandings are reported to others—e.g., the use of the term anti-commitment.

Reporting on the Discourse

In order to make a point, let's assume both partners in a close relationship interact about commitment. Their perceptions of the dialogue are the same; the meanings and inferences each associates with the dialogue are the same. Even if this scenario were possible, each partner could still express his or her experience in very different ways. These differences in the way each partner discusses his or her experiences can, in turn, lead each to suppose there were differences in their perceptions and/or understandings. It is also the case that differences in perceptions and/or interpretations of commitment dialogue may be reported on in such a way that the partners assume there were hardly any differences at all. Up to this point we have been talking about what can happen when people are trying to report their experiences accurately. If we consider all the instances where one or both partners may want to deliberately distort their account of what happened, it should be clear that the act of communicating about one's commitment talk plays a major role in structuring future commitment talk.

Part of the process of reporting on one's commitment requires selectivity. When asked, for example, what are the reasons for the strength or weakness of your commitment to your partner, you know you cannot recount all the complex and varied factors involved. So you try to focus on something that others can understand and something that addresses a major category of influence. For example, researchers who have asked this question (Surra 1987; Surra et al. 1988) find respondents report four major categories of factors:

1. statements about luck, fate, God, the calendar, job hirings/firings and other circumstances which brought or kept people together;
2. statements about how actions and evaluations by members of the social network (friends, family) were influential;
3. statements about various interpersonal transactions including the revelation of important information, their ability to express affection, or their skill in managing conflict;
4. statements comparing some aspect of self, other, or the relationship to what ought to occur—e.g., "I was twenty-six and it was time to settle down."

Each of these statements is like a single headline in a newspaper full of commitment stories. None of these capsulized statements can capture the intricate web of subtle and direct communications used to construct and deconstruct relationship commitment. However, they can be useful for initiating discussion that will.

Conclusion and Summary

This chapter had two goals: to help you understand the complex nature of commitment in romantic relationships; and to help you understand how communication processes may create, sustain, and destroy commitment. Implicitly, we have also had an applied goal as well. We hope the information in this chapter will assist you as you reflect and analyze the nature of your commitment and the interactions affecting it.

Even though the most socially desirable type of commitment is "want to" motivated, it is important to remember that we may also have "ought to" and "have to feelings and that these can serve the relationship well. The strength and substance of our commitment varies during the course of the relationship, and an examination of the six dimensions of commitment may give insights about those fluctuations. To what extent do you and your partner see yourselves getting future rewards in this relationship? How much extra effort have you and your partner put into this relationship when it was needed? To what extent do you and your partner perceive this relationship as part of your identity? How attractive do relationship alternatives seem to you and your partner? How much investment have you and your partner made in this relationship? To what extent do you and your partner accept responsibility for the commitment in your relationship?

The foregoing questions are targeted at diagnosing the nature of commitment. They do not address the important questions relating to the communication of commitment which comprised the last half of this chapter. Commitment is not something we conjure up in our own mind by ourself; instead, it is co-constructed through interactions with our partner and with others.

Communication can be viewed from three perspectives: structure, content, and style. The structural aspects of communication processes are not readily recognized as influential to the overall impact of the message, but they certainly can be. Two important structural features of commitment messages were mentioned: direct vs. indirect interaction and initiator vs. reciprocator roles. When couples face important junctures in their relationship, we would expect to find more direct talk with each other about commitment. The majority of commitment talk is indirect—overhearing your partner talk to someone else about commitment-related issues; talking to your partner about commitment in someone else's relationship; or interacting with your partner on a topic other than commitment—yet drawing inferences about commitment from it. If one person always assumes the role of the initiator of commitment talk (in whatever form), this act, in and of itself, is likely to be perceived as representative of greater commitment and the partner's reciprocator role as less.

The content of commitment talk was viewed through an examination of the topics people most frequently associated with commitment information. These included: affection/caring; relationship alternatives/exclusivity; family/friends; sacrifices; and the future.

The stylistic devices we use to communicate our messages may play an important role in commitment talk. Several methods that have been effectively employed were reported, but without a full knowledge of the context it is difficult to predict the effectiveness of any method. Language intensity, repetition, explicitness, permanence, and appropriate timing are methods which have been used to ensure the effectiveness of a commitment message. An important point to remember about these or any other communication practices is that, given the right situation, an effective technique can become an ineffective one. For example, the repetition of commitment messages may be most effective in establishing a close relationship and irritating if it persists when only occasional reminders are called for. The important principle here is that one must first be able to assess when it is important to communicate commitment messages which show strength and clarity. Then, a knowledge of specific techniques for doing so can be employed.

We concluded the chapter by observing that there are relational and individual factors which will exert influence on the nature of commitment talk. Commitment talk, for example, used to establish, sustain, and rejuvenate a relationship is responding to different goals and a relationship with different histories. We would expect it to be different at these broad stages of development; there may be other phases during the progress of the relationship which call for commitment talk of a particular nature. Finally, we cautioned that what is said may not be what is perceived or what is understood or what is reported to have been said. Partners interested in commitment talk, like any interactants interested in effective communication, must consider and deal with the possible sources of distortion—because these help to forge the foundation for subsequent interactions.

This chapter focused specifically on commitment in romantic relationships, but the concept of committing ourselves to all aspects of our everyday lives—our friends, our family, our studies in school, the groups we belong to, and our work—is central to our success in these arenas and endeavors. To understand and learn how to effectively communicate that commitment is knowledge we can all profit from.

References

Acker, M. and M. H. Davis. 1992. Intimacy, passion and commitment in adult romantic relationships: A test of the triangular theory of love. *Journal of Social and Personal Relationships,* 9:21–50.

Baxter, L. A. and C. Bullis. 1986. Turning points in developing romantic relationships. *Human Communication Research,* 12:469–93.

Becker, H. S. 1960. Notes on the concept of commitment. *American Journal of Sociology,* 66:32–40.

Bem, D. J. 1972. Self-perception theory. In *Advances in experimental social psychology,* ed. L. Berkowitz, vol. 6, 1–62. New York: Academic Press.

Brickman, P. 1987. *Commitment, conflict, and caring.* Englewood Cliffs, NJ: Prentice-Hall.

Buchanan, B. 1974. Building organizational commitment: The socialization of managers in work organizations. *Administrative Science Quarterly,* 19:533–46.

Davis, M. S. 1973. *Intimate relations.* New York: The Free Press.

Dindia, K., and L. A. Baxter. 1987. Strategies for maintaining and repairing marital relationships. *Journal of Social and Personal Relationships,* 4:143–158.

Huston, T. L., C. A. Surra, N. M. Fitzgerald, and R. M. Cate, 1981. From courtship to marriage: Mate selection as an interpersonal process. In *Personal relationships: 2. Developing personal relationships,* ed. S. W. Duck, and R. Gilmour, 53–88. New York: Academic Press.

Johnson, M. P. 1973. Commitment: A conceptual structure and empirical application. *Sociological Quarterly,* 14:395–406.

———. 1982. Social and cognitive features of the dissolution of commitment to relationships. In *Personal relationships 4: Dissolving personal relationships,* ed. S. Duck, 51–73. New York: Academic.

———. 1991. Commitment to personal relationships. In *Advances in personal relationships,* ed. W. H. Jones and D. Perlman, vol. 3, 117–43. London: Jessica Kingsley.

Kanter, R. M. 1972. *Commitment and community.* Cambridge, Massachusetts: Harvard University Press.

Kelley, H. H. 1983. Love and commitment. In *Close relationships,* ed. H. H. Kelley, E. Berscheid, A. Christensen, J. H. Harvey, T. L. Huston, G. Levinger, E. McClintock, L. A. Peplau, and D. R. Peterson, 256–314. New York: W. H. Freeman.

Kessler, R. C. and M. Essex. 1982. Marital status and depression: The importance of coping resources. *Social Forces,* 61:484–505.

Kiesler, C. A. 1968. Commitment. In *Theories of cognitive consistency: A sourcebook,* R. P. Abelson, E. Aronson, W. J. McGruire, T. M. Newcomb, M. J. Rosenberg, and P. H. Tannenbaum, 448–455. Chicago: Rand McNally.

Knapp, M. L. 1989. *Communicating relationship commitment: Some initial thoughts.* Manuscript presented at the Second Annual Iowa Network on Personal Relationships Conference, Iowa City, Iowa.

Knapp, M. L. and A. L. Vangelisti, 1992. *Interpersonal communication and human relationships,* 2nd ed. Boston: Allyn and Bacon.

Kobasa, S. C. 1982. Commitment and coping in stress resistance among lawyers. *Journal of Personality and Social Psychology,* 42 4:707–17.

Lauer, J. and R. Lauer. 1985. Marriages made to last. *Psychology Today,* 19:6, 22–6.

Levinger, G. 1991. Commitment versus cohesiveness: Two complementary perspectives. In

Advances in personal relationships, ed. W. H. Jones, and D. Perlman, vol. 3. 145–150. London: Jessica Kingsley.

Lund, M. 1985. The development of investment and commitment scales for predicting continuity of personal relationships. *Journal of Social and Personal Relationships,* 2(1):3–24.

Michaels, J. W., A. C. Acock, and J. N. Edwards. 1986. Social exchange and equity determinants of relationship commitment. *Journal of Social and Personal Relationships,* 3(2):161–76.

Rusbult, C. E. 1983. A longitudinal test of the investment model: The development (and deterioration) of satisfaction and commitment in heterosexual involvements. *Journal of Personality and Social Psychology,* 45(1):101–17.

Rusbult, C. E., D. J. Johnson, and G. D. Morrow. 1986. Predicting satisfaction and commitment in adult romantic involvements: An assessment of the generalizability of the investment model. *Social Psychology Quarterly,* 49:1, 81–9.

Schlesinger, B. 1982. Lasting marriages in the 1980s. *Conciliation-Courts-Review,* 20(1):43–9.

Sheldon, M. E. 1971. Investments and involvements as mechanisms producing commitment to the organization. *Administrative Science Quarterly,* 16:143–50.

Sprecher, S. 1988. Investment model, social support determinants of relationship commitment. *Social Psychology Quarterly* 51:4, 318–28.

Stanley, S. M. 1986. *Commitment and the maintenance and enhancement of relationships.* Unpublished doctoral dissertation, University of Denver.

Strube, M. and L. S. Barbour. 1983. The decision to leave the abusive relationship: Economic dependence and psychological commitment. *Journal of Marriage and the Family,* 45:785–93.

Surra, C. A. 1987. Reasons for changes in commitment: Variations by courtship type. *Journal of Social and Personal Relationships,* 4:17–33.

Surra, C. A., Arizzi, P., and Asmussen, L. 1988. The association between reasons for commitment and the development and outcome of marital relationships. *Journal of Social and Personal Relationships,* 5:47–63.

Swenson, C. H., and G. Trahaug. 1985. Commitment and the long-term marriage relationship. *Journal of Marriage and the Family,* 47:939–45.

Taylor, E. H. 1991. *Communicating commitment in romantic relationships.* Unpublished master's thesis, University of Texas.

Chapter 9

Resource Allocation in Intimate Relationships

MARGARET S. CLARK
Carnegie Mellon University

KATHLEEN CHRISMAN
Carnegie Mellon University

Outline

Imagine going to lunch with a friend. You each order what you feel like eating. You enjoy your meal together while discussing issues of interest to both of you. When the bill comes, your friend looks it over and says, "I ordered more than you did." He pauses for awhile at this point while continuing to look at the bill. What will you do? Offer to split the bill equally? Figure out what you ordered and pay just for that? Offer to pay the entire bill because your friend has no job right now?

Imagine a different situation. Your friend has a birthday coming up next week. You are thinking about what you to do in honor of her birthday. What factors will go into your decision? Will you think back to what she did for you on your birthday and attempt to do something comparable? Will you think about her tastes and preferences and try to find something just right for her—something that will suit her needs perfectly? How much money will you spend? How much time will you devote to this project? What factors will go into your decisions?

The types of questions just posed are ones that arise frequently in just about everyone's lives. When social psychologists discuss questions such as these, they refer to them as questions about distributive justice. Distributive justice in intimate relationships is the topic that will be discussed in this chapter. This topic falls into a larger category of questions social psychologists have asked about relationships—questions of social exchange. That is, what factors determine the pattern which the giving and receiving of benefits in relationships will take? There is a vast amount of research on exchange processes in relationships. We cannot hope to cover it all here—hence our decision to break off just a little piece of such work to discuss: the work on distributive justice in intimate relationships.

Current State of the Literature

What Distributive Justice Rules Might People Use in their Intimate Relationships?

Much work exists dealing with the rules or norms by which people supposedly distribute resources in relationships such as friendships, family relationships and romantic relationships. Many researchers in this area have taken the approach that a single rule is the only rule that ought to govern the giving and receiving of benefits in such intimate relationships. People will be happy when they (and their partners) follow this rule and unhappy when they (and their partners) fail to follow it. These researchers have examined both adherence to various rules and satisfaction in relationships given apparent adherence (or failure to adhere) to such rules.

Unfortunately, with different researchers making different claims and providing different sorts of evidence with regard to this issue, no clear picture has emerged regarding what the correct rule is. Some say the rule is equity. Equity refers to benefits being allocated in such a manner that the ratio of each person's inputs into the relationship relative to his or her outcomes is equal to the ratio of the other person's inputs into the relationship relative to the other person's outcomes. Some claim the rule is equality—benefits should just be divided equally. Some argue that resources in intimate relationships are best divided according to each member's needs. Still others say that adherence to none of these rules best predicts satisfaction in intimate relationships. Instead, the only thing that matters is how many rewards each person receives from the other in a given relationship. The more rewards received, the happier the person will be.

In this chapter, we review the literature in this area, identify some key positions researchers have taken, state our own position, and discuss how we, personally, would interpret the existing literature. We start our discussion by considering the types of evidence that researchers with each of the different points of view just mentioned have accumulated.

Do People Use an Equity Rule?

The most commonly advocated rule as the rule governing all relationships, including intimate ones, has been equity. Following an equity rule requires striving to keep the ratio of one's inputs into the relationship relative to one's outcomes equal to the ratio of the other person's inputs relative to his or her outcomes. Presumably, the closer members of relationships, including intimate ones, come to this ideal, the happier they will be and the more stable their relationship will be (Walster, Walster, and Berscheid 1978).

In terms of the first scenario set forth at the beginning of this chapter—the one involving paying a check at a restaurant after dining with a friend—equity theorists would predict that you and your friend would get along best if you equitably divided the check. That is, your relationship would be best served if you each paid for your own meal—unless, of course, you had a specific previous debt to your friend to repay. In connection with the second scenario—the one involving selecting a way to honor your friend on her birthday—equity proponents would expect you to spend time tallying factors such as how much money, time and effort your friend had expended on your birthday (partner inputs, your outcomes) as well as other benefits (outcomes) you have received from your friend (e.g., favors, meals, rides to work, etc.). You should also tally up your inputs into the relationship and your friend's other inputs and his or her outcomes from the relationship. Only after having given these factors thought and assessing how equitable the relationship is would you select a way to celebrate your friend's birthday. You would do so with an eye toward restoring or maintaining equity.

Do people follow an equity rule in their intimate relationships? If so, does following such a rule predict satisfaction and commitment in the relationship as well as stability of the relationship? There is, in fact, not much work aimed at documenting that people actually do follow an equity norm more often than other possible norms in their intimate relationships. However, many studies have yielded results consistent with the idea that following norms of equity is associated with satisfaction, commitment and stability in intimate relationships (e.g. Lloyd, Cate and Henton 1982; Sabatelli and Cecil-Pigo 1985; Utne et al. 1984).

Sprecher (1986), for example, asked 185 male and 317 female college students currently involved in intimate relationships to complete two measures of equity/inequity. The first was the Hatfield Global Measure of Equity (as cited in Walster, Walster and Berscheid 1978). This measure poses the following question to respondents:

> *Considering what you put into your relationship, compared to what you get out of it . . . and what your partner puts in compared to what he or she gets out of it, how does your relationship stack up?*

1. *I am getting a much better deal than my partner.*
2. *I am getting a somewhat better deal.*
3. *I am getting a slightly better deal.*
4. *We are both getting an equally good . . . or bad . . . deal.*
5. *My partner is getting a slightly better deal.*
6. *My partner is getting a somewhat better deal.*
7. *My partner is getting a much better deal than I.*

In the second measure of equity, specifically designed for Sprecher's study, respondents were told:

> *Sometimes things get out of balance in a relationship and one partner contributes more to the relationship than the other. Consider all the times when the exchange in your relationship has become unbalanced and one partner contributed more than the other for a time. When your relationship becomes unbalanced, which of you is more likely to be the one who contributes more?*

1. *My partner is much more likely to be the one to contribute more.*
2. *My partner is somewhat more likely to be the one to contribute more.*
3. *My partner is slightly more likely to be the one to contribute more.*
4. *We are equally likely to be the one to contribute more.*
5. *I am slightly more likely to be the one to contribute more.*
6. *I am somewhat more likely to be the one to contribute more.*
7. *I am much more likely to be the one to contribute more.*

On a scale of 1 (never) to 9 (extremely often), Sprecher also asked her subjects to " . . . indicate the degree to which they experienced" a number of positive emotions (e.g., passionate love, sexual excitement, trust, and liking) and negative emotions (e.g., anger, hate, depression, and sadness) in their relationships during the previous month. Finally, subjects completed measures of self-esteem and relationship dependency (interpreted as a measure of commitment to the relationship).

Analyses revealed that among male and female college students in intimate relationships, those holding global impressions that their relationships were equitable also reported experiencing more positive and less negative emotions than did those who perceived their relationships to be inequitable. Sprecher (1988) also found that, among college students, perceptions of global equity were positively and significantly associated with reports of commitment to the relationship.

Providing additional support for equity theory is a study by Utne et al. (1984). Utne and her colleagues surveyed couples who had applied for marriage licenses. Husbands and wives were interviewed separately. Perceived equity was assessed via two measures: the 1977 Walster Global Measure and the 1977 Traupmann-Utne-Walster Scale (both as described by Walster, Walster, and Berscheid 1978). Results showed that people classified as following an equity rule scored slightly, but significantly, higher on measures of marital contentment and stability than did people who rated themselves as being under- or over-benefited.

Lending still more support to the equity rule applying in intimate relationships, Sabatelli and Cecil-Pigo (1985) found that among married subjects, high overall self-reports of equity were associated with more favorable evaluations of outcomes derived from marriage and with more commitment to marriage than were lower overall self-reports of equity. Lloyd, Cate, and Henton (1982) found that self-reports of equity were associated with greater relationship satisfaction among both casually and more seriously dating couples; and Desmarais and Lerner (1989) reported similar results among married as well as dating couples.

Not all researchers have found support for equity theory, however. Clark and Mills (1979), for example, have found that among persons led to desire a communal relationship (such as a friendship or romantic relationship) with another person, liking actually decreases when that other specifically repays the person for a favor or when that other requests repayment for a benefit given to the person—things that would seemingly maintain equity. Moreover, these researchers have also observed that when people desire communal relationships or when they actually are involved in ongoing friendships, they do not attempt to keep track of individual inputs into joint tasks for which there will be a reward. In contrast, members of pairs of people who are strangers to one another do keep track (Clark 1984; Clark, Mills, and Corcoran 1989). It would certainly seem as though keeping track of such inputs would facilitate efforts to maintain equity in the relationship if that was, in fact, what people wished to do.

In addition, consider some research results reported by Lujansky and Mikula (1983). They asked male students to answer some questions about their girlfriends. Rather than assessing equity globally, these researchers asked their subjects to answer questions about twenty-eight different relationship inputs and outcomes along with questions about the perceived positivity and negativity of these inputs and outcomes. From subjects' answers, Lujansky and Mikula calculated a measure of overall equity in the relationships. This measure was not useful in predicting members' perceptions of the quality of their relationship. Neither did it predict whether or not the relationship was intact five months later. Similarly Cate, Lloyd and Henton (1985) have done research in which measures of global equity were not useful predictors of the future stability of relationships.

Finally, some equity theorists have predicted that, given the assumptions that people seek equity in relationships and leave relationships that prove to be inequitable, relationships should become more equitable over time (Hatfield,

Utne, and Traupmann 1979; Hatfield et al. 1985). Why? They should become more equitable because people continually striving to achieve equity should come closer and closer to meeting that ideal. Moreover, those who are not achieving it ought to leave relationships. Thus, in general, relationships which have lasted for three years ought to be more equitable than, say, those which have lasted just six months. Although there is a bit of evidence for this notion (Schafer and Keith 1981), more often researchers have been unable to obtain support for this idea (Berg and McQuinn 1986; Traupmann, Hatfield, and Sprecher 1981). Indeed, Berg (1984) has actually observed equity to decrease over time among college roommate relationships.

Do People Use an Equality Rule?

Other researchers have suggested that it is an equality rule that, ideally, governs the giving and receiving of benefits in intimate relationships—or at least in some intimate relationships. Deutsch (1975; 1985) suggests that use of an equality norm ought to promote a sense of solidarity in friendships. Lerner, Miller, and Holmes (1976) suggest that parity (equality) is what people who perceive themselves to be in a unit relationship with another will feel they deserve. That is, people should be most satisfied when benefits are divided as equally as possible in the relationship.

So, if you find yourself in a restaurant with a friend, equality theorists presumably would predict you would suggest splitting the check evenly (and presumably you would be more likely to do so than if you were eating with a business acquaintance). Likewise, if you need to buy a birthday gift for your friend, theorists who believe in the equality norm probably would predict you would give one as equal as possible in value to what your friend gave you on your birthday—all other things in your relationship being equal.

There is research consistent with the claim that equality is the norm people use in their intimate relationships. For instance, Greenberg (1983) asked undergraduates to read one of three stories about two people having a luncheon meeting at a restaurant. In all three stories, Person A ordered a complete meal costing four times as much as Person B's small snack. Then, in the first experimental condition (the equity condition), subjects learned the diners had agreed to pay the exact amount of their own meals. In the second experimental condition (the equality condition), the diners had agreed to split the check equally. In the third (control) condition, no mention was made of the manner in which persons A and B divided the check.

After reading the stories, subjects gave their impressions of the relationship between A and B in terms of how much the diners liked each other, how well they knew each other, how close their relationship was, the type of relationship they had, and how likely it was they would see one another again in the future. In this study, Greenberg (1983) found that the observers believed that people who had eaten lunch together liked each other more, had a closer relationship, were better friends, and were more likely to see one another in the future if they divided the check evenly than if they divided it according to who had eaten what.

In another study, Austin (1980) found that college roommates (who presumably are fairly likely to have become friends) tend to divide resources equally regardless of whether they have contributed more or less to the task than the other. Strangers, on the other hand, tend to follow a merit (equity) rule if they have contributed more than the other and an equality rule only if they have contributed less than the other.

Finally, Pataki, Shapiro and Clark (1992) have reported a study in which first and third graders worked with a partner on a joint task, performed more work than their partner, and received a joint reward which they were asked to divide between themselves and their partner. Overall, children tended to divide the reward equally. Most importantly for the present point, though, both first and third graders showed a greater preference for an equality relative to an equity rule when working with a friend than when working with another classmate. This effect was marginal among first graders but larger and statistically significant among third graders.

Do People Use a Need-Based Rule?

Still other theorists, ourselves included, have argued that members of intimate relationships, as contrasted with members of other relationships, believe a need-based rule should be used to allocate benefits in relationships such as friendships, romantic relationships and family relationships. That is, benefits should be given in response to needs as those needs arise on each person's part (e.g., Deutsch 1975, 1985 for family relationships; Lamm and Schwinger 1983; Mills and Clark 1982; Clark 1985).

With regard to the situation of dividing a restaurant check with a friend, if you were following a need-based rule you would probably take into consideration the fact that she is out of a job, quickly take the check and pay it. (Although, in recognition of her pride, you might suggest she pay the tip.) Alternatively, you might have avoided the issue altogether by asking her to dinner at your house to avoid her having to spend any money. If you are buying a birthday gift for your friend, you should take a relatively long time choosing just the right one to suit your friend. You would think about what your friend really needs or what would make your friend especially happy. That is, you would spend the time to select the perfect gift.

Is there evidence for this view? The answer is yes. Some of the supporting research comes from a program of studies conducted by the first author in collaboration with Mills and others. In particular, Clark and Mills have differentiated communal and exchange relationships from one another (Clark and Mills 1979). Communal relationships, they say, are often exemplified by relationships between family members, friends and romantic partners. Exchange relationships are often exemplified by relationships between strangers (who anticipate remaining strangers), acquaintances, and people who do business with one another.

In several studies, Clark and her colleagues have observed that subjects desiring or having existing communal relationships with one another are more responsive to one another's needs than are subjects desiring or having existing exchange relationships with one other. For instance, subjects desiring a communal relationship (as opposed to those led to desire an exchange relationship) have been observed to more carefully keep track of the other person's needs when that other is working on a task, even when there was no clear opportunity for the other to keep track of the subject's needs in return (Clark, Mills, and Powell 1986).

You may wonder how it was possible to lead subjects to desire a communal (or an exchange) relationship with another person. Briefly, in this study, under the pretense that they were participating in a problem-solving experiment, subjects were first led to believe an attractive woman seen on a television monitor was another subject in an adjacent room. They read a questionnaire the woman had supposedly filled out indicating either that she was single and interested in meeting people (communal condition) or married (exchange condition). In the communal condition, subjects also learned the woman was a transfer student, new to the campus that semester, and thought the experiment might be a good way to meet people. In the exchange condition, the questionnaire revealed the woman had been at the university for two years and signed up for the study because it was scheduled conveniently, such that her husband could pick her up afterwards. Clark (1986) examined the effectiveness of this procedure. She confirmed that subjects exposed to the communal manipulation later indicated a preference for a communal (relative to an exchange) relationship; while those exposed to the exchange manipulation later expressed a preference for an exchange (relative to a communal) relationship.

Returning to evidence supporting a need-based rule of social exchange, Clark, Mills and Corcoran (1989) have found that greater attention to the other's needs also characterizes ongoing friendships relative to relationships with strangers. In addition, subjects desiring a communal relationship have been observed to help the other more and to be more responsive to the other's sadness than have subjects led to desire an exchange relationship (Clark et al. 1987). Finally, members of communal relationships show larger improvements in mood after having helped the other than do members of exchange relationships (Williamson and Clark 1989; 1992) and they also react more positively to the other's expressions of emotions (Clark and Taraban 1991).

What About Simple Reinforcement? Do People Only Care About Receiving Rewards?

The confusion regarding what resource allocation rule best characterizes intimate relationships does not end with those advocating a need-based rule. Still others have argued that the only thing that really matters to people is the absolute amount of rewards they receive. The more rewards they get, the happier they are, argue these researchers.

In terms of our examples at the beginning of this chapter, reinforcement theory would have to predict that you would be most satisfied in relationships when you receive the most benefits and incur the lowest costs. Hence, in the case of picking up the restaurant check you should be happiest when your friend picks up the entire check at the restaurant and does not seem to resent it—meaning your costs literally and psychologically would be low. In the case of the birthday gift you presumably would spend the least amount you could get away with without having to endure costs, such as your friend being angry with you. Of course, if one assumes that your friend's satisfaction with the relationship is also dependent upon receiving high benefits and incurring low costs, it is clear that your friend probably would not be similarly happy if you were to follow these principles.

What is the evidence for a simple reinforcement view? Cate, Lloyd and Henton (1985) administered questionnaires to a large group of students regarding their dating relationships. Perceptions of global equity were measured as were perceptions of the respondent's and the partner's outcomes. Reward levels were assessed by simply counting the rewards participants felt they had received from the relationship in the categories of love, status, services, goods, money and information. Three and then again seven months later, the researchers re-contacted their respondents and found out which relationships had broken up and which had not. Neither measures of equity nor equality collected at the first point in time predicted break-ups. However, absolute levels of rewards received did predict break-ups. The more rewards respondents had reported receiving, the more likely they were to still be together.

Quite a few other researchers have reported similar results (Cate et al. 1982; Martin 1985; Desmarais and Lerner 1989, Michaels, Edwards, and Acock 1984, and Hansen 1987). For instance, Hansen (1987) asked 220 married students at a southern university to complete questionnaires, indicating how rewarding or unrewarding they viewed the resources received from their marriages (e.g., love, status, information, sexuality) to be. Following statistical analyses, Hansen concluded that reward level was a "powerful predictor of marital adjustment."

Finally, a study by Hays (1985) supports the idea that the absolute level of rewards received in a relationship is a good predictor of success in intimate relationships—this time success in same-sex friendships. He had new college students think about two persons of the same sex whom they had met and whom they thought might become friends. Then at several different points in time during the following semester, these students indicated what benefits they received from these relationships. They also rated the intensity and intimacy of these relationships. At all times the number of benefits received from the relationships was highly, positively correlated with friendship intensity.

Interestingly, though, and contrary to the simple reinforcement view advocated by Cate et al. (1982) and others, in the Hays (1985) study perceived relationship costs were either unrelated or significantly positively related (depending upon the particular measurement session) to rated relationship intensity. Indeed, a measure of benefits plus costs scores was more highly correlated with friendship intensity than was a measure of benefits-minus-costs. While this may seem like a mystery from a reinforcement perspective, we can explain it simply and we will do so shortly.

So, Where Do We Stand? What is the Rule That Governs the Giving and Receiving of Benefits in Intimate Relationships?

By now the reader is probably confused. We have cited evidence to support a variety of rules that may govern the giving and receiving of benefits in intimate relationships. Who is right? Which rule is the rule? Are any of these rules right? Perhaps some other rule governs benefit allocation. Perhaps the person who has more power in an intimate relationship can insist on receiving more benefits, and the relationship will work best when the person lower in power provides such benefits.

While the existing literature is confusing, we actually believe it can be integrated in a meaningful way. We will attempt to do so in the remainder of the chapter. We must begin with an admission, though. We have a clear bias regarding which is the rule most people believe ought to apply to intimate relationships. We believe it is a need-based rule. That is, we suspect most people believe that ideally members of relationships such as friendships, romantic relationships and family relationships ought to be concerned about the welfare of the other member and ought to act upon that concern to the best of their ability. Given this bias, our job is to make a case for this being the ideal rule while at the same time adequately explaining other literature in the field which seemingly does not fit with this view.

A Case for the Ideal Rule for Distributing Benefits in Intimate Relationships Being a Need-Based Rule

Our Position

As just mentioned, our own a priori view is that a communal rule, (feeling a responsibility for and responsiveness to the other's needs without expecting repayments), is the ideal that most people hold for their intimate relationships. To the best of their ability, each person should benefit the other in response to that other's needs. In most cases (given mutual communal relationships), each person should also reasonably expect the other to be responsive to his or her needs if and when those needs arise and if the other person has the ability to do so.

Before making our case that the evidence accumulated to date on the giving and receiving of benefits in intimate relationships can all be viewed as at least consistent with this rule, we need to elaborate on our views somewhat. First, while to this point we have described various distributive justice rules in qualitative terms, we believe there is a quantitative aspect to communal relationships which must be understood if one is to fully understand the application of a needs-based rule to relationships such as friendships, romantic relationships and family relationships (Mills and Clark 1982; Mills, Clark, and Ford 1992). What do we mean? We believe that communal relationships differ in strength and that this fact has important implications for the applicability of need-based rules for distributing benefits. When we postulate quantitative variations in the strength of communal relationships we mean we feel a greater obligation to meet the other's needs in some intimate relationships than in others. For instance, people are likely to feel a stronger obligation to meet the needs of their children (typically very strong communal relationships) than to meet the needs of their friends (typically less strong communal relationships).

How is this stronger obligation evidenced in behaviors and feelings in relationships? It is evidenced in a variety of ways. One way is that the stronger the communal relationship, the greater the costs we are willing to incur to meet the needs of the other (without expecting specific repayment). For instance, parents might be quite willing to pay college tuition as well as room and board costs for their children. However they usually are unwilling to do the same for their friends—even though both relationships can be thought of as primarily communal in nature. Another way the strength of communal relationships may be evidenced is that we will place meeting the needs of people with whom we have strong communal relationships above meeting the needs of people with whom we have weaker communal relationships (in situations in which meeting both person's needs would be impossible.) For example, if one's child needed to be taken to the physician at the same time one's friend needed to be taken to a different physician, one would be likely to take care of the child's needs and to make excuses (legitimate ones) to the friend. (This, of course, assumes approximately equal needs to go to the respective physicians.) Still another way differences in strength will be reflected is that we will feel greater guilt if we fail to meet the needs of someone with whom we have a strong communal relationship than we will if we fail to meet the needs of someone with whom we have a weaker communal relationship.

Pointing out this dimension of strength in communal relationships is, we believe, important to understanding the use of communal rules in intimate relationships. It suggests that although communal norms may be used for distributing benefits in intimate relationships, there are boundary conditions regarding their application. One important one is that we will follow this rule up to a certain cost level of giving benefits, and beyond that we will not follow it. For example, we will meet our friend's needs up to a certain cost level without expecting anything in return. However, we will be reluctant to do so beyond that. To be specific, we might comfort our friend when she is feeling down, we might drive her to the airport when she needs a ride, we might help her with her statistics homework, and we might take her out to lunch on her birthday; but we would not give her a car when she needs one. That would exceed our implicit cost limit. So what does happen when that cost limit is exceeded? Most often, we suspect, benefits simply will not be given and accepted. (For instance, the issue of giving her a car will simply not be discussed or even considered). Alternatively, and more rarely, we suspect, benefits will be given on what we call an exchange basis. (That is, we might sell our car to her). Clearly, this implies we believe more than one rule can govern the giving and receiving of benefits in relationships that are primally communal—a communal rule when benefits fall below a certain cost level and, on occasion, an exchange rule when they fall above that limit.

In addition to pointing out that communal relationships can vary in strength and that this has implications for understanding distributive justice in intimate relationships, we need to make another point. That is, we believe this norm to be an ideal for close relationships. We believe people wish to apply this rule within their intimate relationships (at least within implicit cost limits). However, this is not the same as saying that people always do apply the rule. Due to other concerns and demands, people sometimes do neglect the needs of their friends, family members and romantic partners. Moreover, their friends, family members and romantic partners sometimes neglect their needs. This is a simple point but an important one, and one that has been ignored in much of the existing literature. It means that just because one can sometimes find people behaving in ways that are inconsistent with communal norms—even within cost boundaries—does not necessarily mean that the people in those relationships do not believe that a communal, need-based norm for giving and receiving benefits is the ideal they ought to be following.

We have made our points about variations in the strength of communal relationships (and the attendant boundaries on following a need-based rule) and that the need-based rule must be viewed as an ideal. We turn now to making a case that our view of a communal rule being most people's ideal for their intimate relationships need not be seen as inconsistent with the existing literature.

Integrating the Existing Literature

How can we fit together the diverse sorts of findings reviewed at the beginning of this chapter? Are equity, equality, need-based, and reinforcement findings really as inconsistent with one another as they seem on the surface? We think not. Two reasons why one may observe inconsistent findings with regard to the apparent use of distributive justice rules in intimate relationships have already been pointed out: different rules may apply on different sides of an implicit cost boundary; and although people may hold a need-based rule as their ideal, other factors will influence their behavior as well, and they will sometimes violate that rule and follow other rules or simply act in a self-interested manner. However, we actually do not believe these two things are the primary reasons for the apparent inconsistencies which have appeared in the literature. Rather, we think that the literature itself may not be nearly as inconsistent with need-based rules being applied to most intimate relationships as it might seem.

Let us begin to explain this by showing how some equity findings may be seen as consistent with a need-based rule. Specifically, how can we account for the fact that people who report a sense of global equity in their relationships also report being more satisfied with those relationships? We acknowledge it is possible that believing in the correctness of an equity rule and carefully following it could account for these findings. However, since such a view cannot account for findings, such as people having existing communal relationships not keeping track of individual inputs into joint tasks (Clark, Mills, and Powell 1986) and reacting negatively to repayments for favors given and to requests for repayments for favors received (Clark and Mills 1979), we are skeptical and suspect that the correct explanation for these equity findings lies elsewhere.

Several alternative explanations exist. All rest at least partially on the fact that all the studies we could locate supporting the applicability of an equity rule to intimate relationships were cross- sectional, retrospective surveys. This, of course, means two things: one cannot safely make any assumptions about one variable which has been measured (equity, in this case) having causally influenced other variables measured at the same time (e.g., variables such as satisfaction in the relationship or desire to break-up) and one must worry about the real possibility that people's recollections of past events (e.g., inputs into the relationship, benefits derived from the relationships) may be inaccurate. In this regard one must worry both about respondents' abilities to accurately recall past inputs into and outcomes from their relationships, and one must worry about respondents' current moods or evaluations of their relationships biasing what is recalled and reported. Keeping these things in mind, consider the following alternative explanations for observations that perceptions of global equity are associated with reports of relationship satisfaction and indices of relationship stability.

One explanation for such observations is that there are two simultaneous consequences of following a need-based rule. First, following a need-based rule may increase satisfaction in the relationship. Second, following such a rule may usually (though not always) result in more objectively equitable than inequitable relationships over the long run (assuming roughly equal needs of most pairs of partners). This could be why an overall sense of equity is associated with satisfaction. Yet, this explanation does not assume the operation of an equity rule day-to-day. Another explanation is that it is possible that feeling satisfied (for whatever reason) leads one to feel the relationship is fine and that this feeling, in turn, leads one to report good things about the relationship when asked. If one is asked if the relationship is equitable, one probably will say yes accounting for the equity results. (If one were, instead, to have been asked if the other responded to one's needs, one probably also would have said yes.) One last possibility worth mentioning is that feeling dissatisfied may lead one to report one's relationship is inequitable and/or actually to begin to calculate exactly who contributes what to a relationship and who gets what benefits. Given that one's own contributions are likely to be more salient than the other's contributions (Ross and Sicoly 1979), such calculating often may lead to a sense of inequity and may produce the observed relationship between lack of equity and dissatisfaction.

It is important to note that none of these three explanations for the equity findings is contrary to the idea we are arguing for—that most people hold a need-based norm as the ideal for their intimate relationships (within cost limitations), and they would like to do their best to live up to this ideal. We cannot tell which explanation for the equity results is correct. However, we can argue that the fact that reports of a global sense of equity are associated with satisfaction in relationships does not necessarily contradict our own view.

What of the equality findings? Can we explain those? We think so. Recall that Austin (1980) found that roommates are more likely than others to divide rewards equally and that Pataki, Shapiro and Clark (1992) found that friends were more likely than non-friends to divide rewards equally. In addition, Greenberg (1983) found that if diners divide the cost of a meal equally, they are perceived to be better friends than if they divide checks equitably. We would note, however, that in none of these studies were subjects given any information which might have led them to believe that one potential recipient of a benefit was needier than another. Assuming that we are right about a need-based rule being the ideal in intimate relationships and assuming people in an intimate relationship have equal needs, what should they do when they must divide a reward or a restaurant check? If needs are equal, it seems clear they should divide things equally. Given this, results such as those reported by Austin (1980), Greenberg (1983) and Pataki, Shapiro and Clark (1992) also can be viewed as consistent with the view that a need-based distributive justice rule is most people's ideal for their intimate relationships.

Finally, can we deal with the data that have been taken to indicate that the only thing members of intimate relationships really care about is the absolute number of rewards they receive? We think so. First, it is important to note that advocates of a need-based rule would expect the number of rewards received to predict satisfaction and stability. After all, the extent to which another gives you benefits seems to be a reasonable measure of the extent to which that other is responding to your needs. So, the results of the Cate et al. (1982), Cate, Lloyd and Henton (1985) and Martin (1985) studies can be viewed as entirely consistent with a need based rule applying to intimate relationship. Moreover, it should be noted that in the research supporting the view that rewards are the best predictors of satisfaction in and stability of intimate relationships, only measures of equity, equality or rewards were included. In none of the studies we located were measures of mutual responsiveness to needs collected. Had a good measure of mutual responsiveness to needs also been collected, it might well have been an even better predictor of relationship satisfaction and stability.

In connection with this last point, it is noteworthy that the norm of mutual responsivity to needs suggests that a measure which takes into account not only what a respondent receives from his or her partner but also what that person gives to his or her partner should be an even better indicator of relationship success than should a measure of rewards alone. This implies that a measure of rewards plus costs ought to be an even better predictor of relationship satisfaction than a measure of rewards minus costs. Given this, it is intriguing that, as already pointed out, Hays (1985) has found that an index of rewards plus costs is a better predictor of relationship success than is an index of rewards minus costs. This too supports our view that mutual responsivity to needs is the ideal most people hold for their intimate relationships. It also provides some evidence it a simple reinforcement view from which one would have expected the rewards-minus-costs index to be the best predictor.

In sum, we believe that none of the evidence reviewed earlier in this chapter supporting the applicability of an equity rule, an equality rule or a simple rewards rule in intimate relationships necessarily need be considered contradictory to our own viewpoint that a rule of mutual responsiveness to one another's needs is the ideal most people hold for their intimate relationships. In contrast, we would argue, it is difficult to explain findings such as members of communal relationships not keeping track of inputs into joint tasks (Clark 1984; Clark, Mills, and Powell 1986) and reacting negatively to receiving repayments for benefits given and to requests for repayments of benefits received (Clark and Mills 1979) in terms of rules such as equity, equality or the notion that people simply like others who provide the most rewards to them.

Conclusion and Summary

In this chapter we have reviewed some literature on distributive justice—how people allocate goods, service, and other sorts of benefits in their intimate relationships and how those allocations influence satisfaction in and stability of those relationships. There is considerable literature in this area and, at least at first, it seems quite confusing. Parts of it seem to contradict other parts of it.

Once a sizeable literature accumulates in an area such as this, and seemingly discrepant results have been reported, a job for researchers in that area emerges. They must try to integrate the literature. We have tried to do that in this chapter in the context of arguing that the ideal distributive justice norm most people hold for their intimate relationships is a need-based one. We have claimed that much of the literature supports this rule and that even literature which might appear to contradict this rule can be seen as consistent with it.

In choosing to address a constrained question in the area of social exchange, we have left out large amounts of other literature regarding social exchange processes in relationships in general and in intimate relationships in particular. We urge you to explore this area more fully. We suggest reading some of Harold Kelley's work on exchange processes as described in Kelley (1979; 1983) and some of Caryl Rusbult's closely related work, particularly on concepts such as commmitment and accommodation processes in intimate relationships (e.g., Rusbult 1980; 1983; Rusbult and Verette 1991; Rusbult et al. 1991). You might also be interested in some research examining how individual differences between people influence their application of justice rules in relationships (e.g., Major and Deaux 1982) and how the perceived attributes of people who are the potential recipients of benefits (e.g., whether or not they are directly responsible for being in need of benefits) influence application of justice rules (e.g., Skitka and Tetlock 1992). There is certainly no shortage of literature in this area for the interested reader to pursue.

References

Austin, W. 1980. Friendship and fairness: Effects of type of relationship and task performance on choice of distribution rules. *Personality and Social Psychology Bulletin*, 6:402–08.

Berg, J. H. 1984. Development of friendship between roommates. *Journal of Personality and Social Psychology*, 46:346–56.

Berg, J. H. and R. D. McQuinn. 1986. Attraction and exchange in continuing and noncontinuing dating relationships. *Journal of Personality and Social Psychology*, 50:942–52.

Cate, R. M., S. A. Lloyd, and J. M. Henton. 1985. The effect of equity, equality, and reward level on the stability of students' premarital relationships. *Journal of Social Psychology*, 125:715–21.

Cate, R. M., S. A. Lloyd, J. M. Henton, and J. H. Larson. 1982. Fairness and reward level as predictors of relationship satisfaction. *Social Psychology Quarterly*, 45:177–81.

Clark, M. S. 1984. Record keeping in two types of relationships. *Journal of Personality and Social Psychology*, 47:549–57.

———. 1985. Implications of relationship type for understanding compatibility. In *Compatible and Incompatible Relationships*, ed. W. Ickes. New York: Springer-Verlag.

———. 1986. Evidence for the effectiveness of manipulations of communal and exchange relationships. *Personality and Social Psychology Bulletin*, 12:414–25.

Clark, M. S. and J. Mills. 1979. Interpersonal attraction in exchange and communal relationships. *Journal of Personality and Social Psychology*, 37, 12–24.

Clark, M. S., J. R. Mills, and D. M. Corcoran. 1989. *Personality and Social Psychology Bulletin*, 15:533–42.

Clark, M. S., J. Mills, and M. C. Powell. 1986. Keeping track of needs in communal and exchange relationships. *Journal of Personality and Social Psychology*, 51:333–38.

Clark, M. S., R. Ouellette, M. C. Powell, and S. Milberg. 1987. Recipient's mood, relationship type, and helping. *Journal of Personality and Social Psychology*, 53:94–103.

Clark, M. S. and C. Taraban. 1991. Reactions to and willingness to express emotion in communal and exchange relationships. *Journal of Experimental Social Psychology*, 27:324–36.

Desmarais, S. and M. J. Lerner. 1989. A new look at equity and outcomes as determinants of satisfaction in close personal relationships. *Social Justice Research*, 3:105–19.

Deutsch, M. 1975. Equity, equality and need: What determines which value will be used as a basis of distributive justice? *Journal of Social Issues*, 31:137–49.

———. 1985. *Distributive justice: A socio-psychological perspective*. New Haven: Yale University Press.

Greenberg, J. 1983. Equity and equality as clues to the relationship between exchange participants. *European Journal of Social Psychology*, 13:195–96.

Hansen, G. L. 1987. Reward level and marital adjustment: The effect of weighing rewards. *Journal of Social Psychology*, 127:549–51.

Hatfield, E., J. Traupmann, S. Sprecher, M. Utne, and J. Hay. 1985. Equity and intimate relations: Recent research. In *Compatible and Incompatible Relationships*, ed. W. Ickes. New York: Springer-Verlag.

Hatfield, E., M. K. Utne, and J. Traupmann. 1979. Social exchange in developing relationships. In *Equity theory and intimate relationships*, ed. R. L. Burgess and T. L. Huston. New York: Academic Press.

Hays, R. B. 1985. A longitudinal study of friendship development. *Journal of Personality and Social Psychology*, 48:909–24.

Kelley, H.H. 1979. *Personal relationships: Their structures and processes*. Hillsdale, NJ: Erlbaum.

———. 1983. Love and commitment. In *Close relationships*, ed. H. H. Kelley, E. Berscheid, A. Christensen, J. H. Harvey, T. L. Huston, G. Levinger, E. McClintock, L. A. Peplau, and D. R. Peterson, 265–314. New York: W. H. Freeman.

Lamm, H., and Schwinger, T. 1983. Need consideration in allocation decisions: Is it just? *Journal of Social Psychology*, 119:205–09.

Lerner, M. J., D. T. Miller, and J. G. Holmes. 1976. Deserving and the emergence of forms of justice. In *Advances in Experimental Social Psychology*, ed. L. Berkowitz and E. Walster, Vol. 9. New York: Academic Press.

Lloyd, S., R. M. Cate, and J. Henton. 1982. Equity and rewards as predictors of satisfaction in casual and intimate relationships. *The Journal of Psychology*, 110:43–8.

Lujansky, H. and G. Mikula. 1983. Can equity theory explain the quality and stability of romantic relationships? *British Journal of Social Psychology*, 22:101–12.

Major, B., and K. Deaux. 1982. Individual differences in justice behavior. In *Equity and justice in Social Behavior*, ed. J. Greenberg and R.L. Cohen. New York: Academic Press.

Martin, M. W. 1985. Satisfaction with intimate exchange: Gender-role differences and the impact of equity, equality, and rewards. *Sex Roles*, 13:597–605.

Michaels, J. W., J. N. Edwards, and A. C. Acock. 1984. Satisfaction in intimate relationships as a function of inequality, inequity, and outcomes. *Social Psychology Quarterly*, 47:347–57.

Mills, J. and M. S. Clark. 1982. Communal and exchange relationships. In *Review of Personality and Social Psychology*, ed. L. Wheeler. Beverly Hills: Sage.

Mills, J., M. S. Clark, and T. Ford. 1992. Development of a measure of strength of communal relationships. Unpublished manuscript, University of Maryland.

Pataki, S., C. Shapiro, and M. S. Clark. 1992. Acquisition of a distinction between communal and exchange relationships. Unpublished manuscript, Carnegie Mellon University.

Ross, M., and F. Sicoly. 1979. Egocentric biases in availability and attribution. *Journal of Personality and Social Psychology*, 37:322–36.

Rusbult, C. E. 1980. Commitment and satisfaction in romantic associations: A test of the investment model. *Journal of Experimental Social Psychology*, 16:172–86.

———. 1983. A longitudinal test of the investment model: The development and deterioration of satisfaction and commitment in heterosexual involvements. *Journal of Personality and Social Psychology*, 45:101–17.

Rusbult, C. E., and J. Verette. 1991. An interdependent analysis of accommodation processes in close relationships. *Representative Research in Social Psychology*, 19:3–33.

Rusbult, C. E., J. Verette, G. A. Whitney, L. F. Slovik, and I. Lipkus. 1991. Accommodation processes in close relationships: Theory and preliminary empirical evidence. *Journal of Personality and Social Psychology*, 60:53–78.

Sabatelli, R. M., and E. F. Cecil-Pigo. 1985. Relational interdependence and commitment in marriage. *Journal of Marriage and the Family*, 47:931–37.

Schafer, R. B. and P. M. Keith. 1981. Equity in marital roles across the family cycle. *Journal of Marriage and the Family*, 43:359–67.

Skitka, L. J. and P. E. Tetlock. 1992. Allocating scarce resources: A contingency model of distributive justice. *Journal of Experimental Social Psychology*, 28:491–522.

Sprecher, S. 1986. The relation between inequity and emotions in close relationships. *Social Psychology Quarterly*, 49:309–21.

———. 1988. Investment model, equity and social support determinants of relationship commitment. *Social Psychology Quarterly*, 51:318–28.

Traupmann, J., E. Hatfield, and S. Sprecher. 1981. The importance of "fairness" for marital satisfaction of older women. Unpublished manuscript.

Utne, M. K., E. Hatfield, J. Traupmann, and D. Greenberger. 1984. Equity, marital satisfaction, and stability. *Journal of Social and Personal Relationships*, 1:323–32.

Walster, E., G. W. Walster, and E. Berscheid. 1978. *Equity: Theory and Research*. Boston: Allyn and Bacon.

Williamson, G. M. and M. S. Clark. 1989. Providing help and desired relationship type as determinants of changes in moods and self-evaluations. *Journal of Personality and Social Psychology*, 56:722–34.

———. 1992. Impact of desired relationship type on affective reactions to choosing and being required to help. *Personality and Social Psychology Bulletin*, 18:10–18.

Sexuality in Close Relationships

SUSAN SPRECHER
Illinois State University

KATHLEEN MCKINNEY
Illinois State University

The Relationship Diary of a Couple: Sex and Intimacy

On their first date, they engage in heavy necking but don't progress to more intimate sexual contact.

After several dates, one partner wants more intimate sexual activity and exerts verbal pressure on the other partner. The other partner has more traditional standards and resists . . . for now.

They reveal their respective sexual histories; that is, they share information about past sexual partners and experiences (although one of them lies slightly about the number of previous partners), and they bring up the topic of protection against STDs.

They have their first intimate sexual encounter. It's a positive experience for both of them, but only one of them has an orgasm. Their love and commitment for each other increase as they feel a heightened sense of passion.

They move in together and initially have sex almost every day of the week. They like it in the dark and they sometimes watch an X-rated movie to get in the mood. Sexual initiation is rarely mutual. One partner usually takes the role of initiator.

Years go by, and they get busy with jobs, the community, and family. Sex is now once a week, at best. They both complain about being tired and not having enough time for sex.

One of them has a sexual affair outside the relationship, and jealousy, rage, and a threat of a breakup follow.

After the relationship is repaired, a sexual problem develops. They see a sex therapist and are helped by the therapy.

Many more years go by. As they face their last few years, they experience a resurgence of love for each other. Although they are no longer able to engage in vigorous lovemaking, they touch and caress each other more than they did at a younger age.

Introduction

In this chapter, we discuss the role of sexuality in close relationships. Although this book summarizes information on friendship and family relations, the main focus is on the type of relationship that is called romantic, spouse/lover, or sexual. Some sociologists (Scanzoni et al., 1989) state that the underlying feature of this type of relationship, and what distinguishes it from other close relationships, is sexual interdependence. John Scanzoni and his colleagues (1989) have called these relationships sexually based primary relationships and define them as relationships in which "the persons define sexual exchanges or interdependence as a legitimate element/expectation for their type of relationship (whether or not they are currently engaging in sexual activities)" (p. 47).

There are two major sections to this chapter. In the first section we review the theoretical contribution of sociology to the study of sexuality in close relationships. In the second and the larger section, we review the empirical research on sexuality in close relationships. Occasionally, we will refer back to our hypothetical pair above, who could be either a homosexual or a heterosexual couple. (We want to note that this couple should not be considered to be typical in their sexual history because there is a range of variation in sexuality and intimacy.)

The Theoretical Contributions of Sociology to the Study of Sexuality in Close Relationships

Sexuality in close relationships has been studied by scholars working in all of the following fields: sociology, social psychology, psychology, communication, family studies, anthropology, and history. We are both sociologists who have conducted research in the interdisciplinary fields of close relationships and sexuality and in the interface between these two areas. In this section, we define sexuality from a sociological perspective and then provide a brief overview to perspectives or theories in sociology (including social psychology) that have been or could be applied to the study of sexuality in close relationships. Sociology differs from psychology and some other disciplinary approaches to sexuality by its focus on groups and societies.

A Sociological Definition of Sexuality

What do we mean by sexuality? To answer this question, we turn to a sociological definition provided by Ira Reiss (1989): "the erotic arousal and genital responses resulting from following the shared sexual scripts of that society" (p. 6). Sexual scripts refer to the how, when, with whom, why and where arousal and response should occur according to the norms of a given culture, subculture or group (Gagnon and Simon 1973; Reiss 1989). For example, cultural scripts may contain norms that dictate that males should initiate sexual activity or that sexual behavior should occur in private. Thus, according to this definition, very little of sexual behavior is truly spontaneous. Couples also develop their own idiosyncratic, couple-specific sexual scripts. For example, our hypothetical couple's initial script included frequent sex, in the dark, and sometimes with a movie. Couples establish their own patterns of sexual activity early in the relationship, and these patterns typically continue.

Sociological and Social Psychological Theories Applied to Sexuality

Below we show how some commonly used sociological and social psychological theories can be applied to sexuality in close relationships. Sociological theories of sexuality take a macro perspective. This means the focus is on how societal (e.g., social institutions such as the political system or the family), cultural (e.g., values), and subcultural (e.g., religion, ethnicity) factors affect sexual expression.

Social psychological theories emphasize interpersonal (e.g., communication) and group (e.g., the influence of friends) processes. These views are in contrast to a micro perspective which focuses on individual and intrapersonal processes.

Functionalism

Some sociologists have asked why sex is important, what function it has for society, for institutions within society, for the couple, and for the individual. One primary function of sexuality, of course, is reproduction. Although this function of sex may be particularly important at the time heterosexual couples who desire children are trying to conceive, most acts of intercourse in heterosexual couples and all sexual activity in homosexual couples are not oriented toward reproduction. Reiss (1989) argues that there are other factors more important than reproduction in the explanation for why sex is important. He writes: "I have no doubt that sexuality would be of vital importance in human societies even if all babies were produced in artificial wombs" (p. 7). He states that the two reasons that sexuality is important in society are: it has the potential for physical pleasure, and it is a form of self-disclosure.

Thus, sexuality is important because it makes us feel good and because it is a way to reach out to another and disclose a very special part of ourselves that is generally not revealed to most people, even others who are considered close.

Conflict Theory

Conflict theory (e.g., Collins 1974) focuses on society as consisting of numerous subgroups, varying in power, each with its own values and interests. Groups come into conflict, with social change a likely outcome, as they compete for limited resources in society and try to have their own interests and values dominate. For example, conflict theorists would argue that their ideas help explain the laws and law enforcement emphasis in the area of sexuality. Because men have more political and economic power than women, some laws, such as the marital exemption to rape (which says a man cannot be prosecuted for raping his wife), favor men's interests over women's.

Some of the ideas of conflict theory can also be applied to the couple. Within a relationship, individuals may differ in their attitudes toward sexuality and in their power relative to their partner. Conflict theory would predict that the more powerful partner will usually be able to control the couple's progression to sexual involvement. Take, for example, our hypothetical couple: one partner used verbal pressure to try to change the willingness of the other to engage in sexual activity.

Symbolic Interactionism

This perspective emphasizes that all human reality and meaning, including the meaning of sexual standards, values, relationships, and behaviors, are negotiated among people in interaction with each other through language and symbols (e.g., Blumer 1969; Goffman 1959). For example, symbolic interactionism theorists might study how members of couples use verbal and nonverbal communication (e.g., key words, clothing, and touching) to negotiate the roles each will play in their sexual relationship (e.g., initiator), how or when they will engage in sexual activity, as well as what the sexual activity means for the relationship (e.g., "we a∝ sexually intimate so we must be in love").

Social Exchange

From the social exchange perspective, relationships are seen as involving a series of somewhat reciprocal exchanges (Gouldner 1960). Individuals may exchange a variety of resources, and within this exchange, one person's sexual favors may be exchanged for the other's sexual favors and/or for other types of rewards in the relationship (e.g., love, gifts). The exchange value of sex is illustrated in the following quote from a woman who was interviewed by sociologist Lillian Rubin in 1976 for *Worlds of Pain: Life in the Working Class Family*: "He gets different treats at different times, depending on what he deserves. Sometimes I let him do that oral stuff you're talking about to me. Sometimes when he's very good, I do it to him." (p. 207)

In sum, each discipline brings certain concepts and theoretical perspectives to the interdisciplinary topic of sexuality. We have emphasized the contributions of our own discipline, sociology. Next, we turn to empirical studies conducted on sexuality in close relationships.

Empirical Research on Sex in Close Relationships

Most research on sexuality in close relationships has had a social psychological emphasis; that is, it has focused on interpersonal factors. In our review of this literature, we will follow loosely the events of the hypothetical couple whose diary was introduced at the beginning of the chapter.

The Sexual Attitudes and Behaviors the Partners Bring to the Relationship

Individuals bring with them to a new relationship their sexual standards and history of sexual behaviors. These attitudes and past behaviors can affect what sexual activity occurs, how soon it occurs within the current relationship and its meaning to the partners. These attitudes and behaviors can also affect the attraction process.

Sexual Standards

The four standards in Box 10–1 were identified about twenty-five years ago by Reiss (1964; 1967), in a model of premarital sexual permissiveness. Of the standards identified, permissiveness with affection is probably the most common standard today (e.g., DeLamater and MacCorquodale 1979; Robinson and Jedlicka 1982; Sherwin and Corbett 1985). Fifty years ago, however, the abstinence standard and the double standard were most common.

Not surprising, women express less permissiveness for themselves than men do for themselves, particularly for early stages of the relationship (Sprecher 1989).

BOX 10–1   Which Sexual Standard is Yours?

What are your standards about sex in a dating context? Check which of the following best describes your attitudes.

_____ *Abstinence:* You believe that a couple should wait until marriage to have sex.
_____ *Permissiveness with affection:* You believe that sex before marriage is acceptable as long as the two people experience love or affection for each other.
_____ *Permissiveness without affection:* You believe that it is acceptable for two people to have sex in a very early stage of the relationship (e.g., first date), and in the absence of strong affection, as long as they both desire it.
_____ *Double standard:* You have more permissive standards for men than for women.

Women are also less permissive than men for others (e.g., Sprecher et al. 1988) and in sexual attitudes more generally (Hendrick and Hendrick, 1987a and b). Furthermore, a young female is judged more negatively than a young male for having sex early in a relationship (Sprecher, McKinney, and Orbuch 1987).

Prior Sexual Behaviors

It is likely that the partners in our hypothetical couple were sexually active with other people prior to their involvement with each other. Melvin Zelnick and Farida Shah (1983) report an average age at first intercourse for females in the United States of 16.2 and for males of 15.7. By age 19, approximately 80 percent of females and 86 percent of males have had intercourse (e.g., London et al. 1989). A male is likely to have more prior sexual experience than a female (DeLamater 1987), and gay males are likely to have more prior sexual experience than heterosexuals and lesbians (Bell and Weinberg 1978; Symons 1979).

Effects of Sexual Standards and
Prior Sexual Behavior on the Relationship

The sexual standards and experiences an individual brings to the relationship may affect how much he or she is liked and desired as a partner. Recent research suggests that college students are more attracted to someone as a marital partner if he or she is low to moderate rather than high in sexual permissiveness and previous sexual experience, particularly if the students who make the attraction ratings aren't very permissive themselves (e.g., Istvan and Griffitt 1980; Jacoby and Williams 1985; Oliver and Sedikides 1992; Sprecher, McKinney, and Orbuch 1991; Williams and Jacoby 1989). A gender difference has been found, however, in how much sexual permissiveness is desired in a dating partner. A man is perceived as more attractive as a dating partner when he is low or moderate rather than high in sexual permissiveness, whereas a woman receives higher attractiveness ratings if she is more permissive (Oliver and Sedikides 1992; Sprecher, McKinney and Orbuch 1991). Another finding from the literature is that an individual who has had any previous homosexual experience is rated as undesirable for a heterosexual dating or marital relationship (Williams and Jacoby 1989).

The partner's sexual attitudes and past sexual behavior are also likely to affect the stage at which a newly formed couple has sex. If two partners come to the relationship with extensive sexual experience and/or liberal sexual attitudes, they are likely to have sex relatively soon in the development of the relationship. The woman's previous experiences have a greater impact than a man's in heterosexual relationships. For example, Anne Peplau, Zick Rubin, and Charles Hill in 1977 described the influence of the previous sexual behaviors of the dating partners from their *Boston Dating Couples* study in the following way: "If the woman was sexually experienced, the couple had intercourse within an average of two months, regardless of the man's experience. If the woman was a virgin, the average was over eight months, depending on whether the man was experienced (mean of six months) or the man was a virgin (mean of twelve months)" (p. 95).

When one has a sexual history in today's AIDS (Acquired Immune Deficiency Syndrome)-conscious society, there may be an ethical obligation to tell a potential sexual partner about one's previous sexual experiences. Do young adults share their sexual pasts? In one recent study, a majority of a sample of sexually active men and women were not confident that they knew the number of their partner's previous sexual relationships (Edgar et al. 1992) and in another study young adults reported that they would be more likely to "try to guess" if a new partner had been exposed to AIDS than to ask directly (Gray and Saracino 1991). Susan Sprecher (1991) found that only about one-half of a sample of dating individuals were at all likely to ask their partner about previous sexual contacts because of the threat of AIDS. If young adults ask, do they get accurate information? As depicted in our hypothetical couple, maybe not. In one study, Susan Cochran and Vickie Mays (1990) surveyed college students from southern California and found that 47 percent of the men and 42 percent of the women would underestimate the number of their previous partners, and 20 percent of the men and 4 percent of the women would lie about the results of an HIV-antibody test. Research conducted among gay couples suggests that they are more likely than heterosexual couples to talk about their behaviors in relation to AIDS and, more generally, are more likely to use cautious behaviors (e.g., Juran 1989).

The First Time for the Couple

Most couples give special significance to the first time they have sex together. They can often remember it in vivid detail months and years later, as a "flashbulb memory" (e.g., Harvey, Flanary, and Morgan 1986). The first time a couple has sex is also often considered a significant *turning point* that has a positive effect on the relationship and results in an increase in commitment (Baxter and Bullis 1986).

Couples decide when they are ready to have sex for the first time, and they may weigh several factors in their decision. F. Scott Christopher and Rodney Cate (1984, 1985a) developed a scale, called the *Inventory of Sexual Decision-Making Factors*, to measure the factors that might be considered in the decision to have sex for the first time in a relationship. They found four general reasons underlying young adults' decisions to have sex for the first time. The four dimensions and an example item used to measure each dimension are as follows:

1. Positive Affection/Communication (Love for partner)
2. Arousal/Receptivity (Partner's [or own] physical arousal immediately prior to intercourse)
3. Obligation and Pressure (Partners' pressure on participant to have intercourse)
4. Circumstantial (Amount of alcohol/drugs consumed by partner).

Women rated Positive Affect/Communication to be more important than did men, whereas Obligation/Pressure was rated more important by men than by women. Sexually inexperienced subjects rated Positive Affect/Communication as more salient than did the sexually experienced subjects, whereas Arousal/Receptivity was judged to be more important by the highly experienced subjects.

Dating couples vary a great deal in how soon in their relationship they begin sexual involvement. Based on data collected from fifty-four serious dating couples, Christopher and Cate (1985b) identified four premarital sexual pathways. Each partner of the couples completed the Bentler (1968a and b) Sexual Involvement scale (which asks about twenty-one sexual behaviors ranging from "one minute continuous lip kissing" to "mutual oral manipulation of genitals to mutual orgasm") at four times in their relationship: first date, casually dating, considering becoming a couple, and perceiving themselves as a couple. Through an analysis of the retrospective data, Christopher and Cate identified the following sexual pathways:

> *Rapid-involvement couples* (7 percent): These couples had sex very early in the relationship, often on the first date.
> *Gradual-involvement couples* (31 percent): These couples reported a gradual increase in sexual behavior over the four stages of dating.
> *Delayed-involvement couples* (44 percent): These couples tended to delay sexual involvement until they considered themselves a couple.
> *Low-involvement couples* (17 percent): These couples were still not very sexually intimate at the time they felt like a couple.

These couple types differed not only in their level of sexual involvement at each of the stages of dating, but also in the development of relationship dimensions, such as love and conflict. For example, rapid-involvement individuals reported more love early in the relationship than did the individuals from the other sexual pathway types. The researchers wrote: "Such a trend may suggest that rapid-involvement individuals report high levels of love to justify their high levels of sexual interaction on their first date. Alternatively, it may be that only individuals in this pathway who experience high levels of love accompanying high levels of sexual activity on first dates go on to form into couples" (p. 282).

Interestingly, the rapid-involvement couples also reported a higher level of conflict during early dating than did the other couple types. Other researchers have also developed typologies of sexual pathways. For example, Peplau, Rubin, and Hill (1977) delineated three groups based on the timing and occurrence of sex among the participants of the Boston Dating Couples study: early-sex couples (41 percent of their sample) who had sex within the first month of dating, later-sex couples (41 percent of the sample) who did not have sex until they had been dating at least one month, and abstaining couples (18 percent of the sample) who had not had sex at the time of the investigation.

Patterns of Sexual Behavior and Sexual Satisfaction

Now, imagine that our hypothetical couple introduced at the beginning of this chapter has advanced far beyond having sex for the first time. They have now been together for years and have had sex together hundreds of times. In this section, we consider the sexual behaviors and sexual satisfaction of developed couples.

Sexual Behaviors

How often do couples have sex, on the average? Several studies, including the early famous sexuality studies conducted by Alfred Kinsey and his colleagues (1948; 1953) and by Morton Hunt (1974), demonstrate that young married couples have sex, on the average, about two or three times per week. Other studies, conducted with national probability samples of women who are questioned about their childbearing decisions, have found slightly lower rates—around two times per week for women under the age of forty-five (e.g., Udry 1980; Westoff 1974).

Note that for our couple, the frequency of sex declined after several years to once a week at best. What has been clearly documented, in a number of studies using different types of methods, is that sex declines with number of years married and with age, two variables that are highly associated in the general population (e.g., Blumstein and Schwartz 1983; Greenblat 1983; James 1981; Udry 1980). Why does sex decline over time? Novelty wears off, familiarity grows, and couples get busy with other life commitments (Greenblat 1983). Not surprising, a decline in sex is also associated more specifically with pregnancy, having small children, and having demanding jobs (Call, Sprecher, and Schwartz 1992). Later in life, one or both partners may also experience illness and/or a decline in physical abilities (Riportella-Muller 1989), but some couples experience an increase in nongenital caressing, as was the case for our hypothetical couple.

Although most of the research on sexual frequency has been conducted with married couples, a few studies have considered sexual frequency in other types of couples. Cohabiting couples report having sex more frequently than do married couples, even when other factors are controlled (Blumstein and Schwartz 1983; Call, Sprecher, and Schwartz 1992; Newcomb 1983), which suggests that cohabitation might be a sexier living arrangement than marriage (Blumstein and

Schwartz 1983). Cohabiting couples also have sex more frequently than dating couples. For example, results of the Boston Dating Couples study indicate that of the forty couples who were living together, approximately 40 percent reported having sex six times per week or more. Among the dating couples, however, the percentage was 12 percent (Risman et al. 1981).

Very few studies have examined sexual frequency in dating couples. In the Boston Dating Couples Study, a difference was found between how often the early-sex dating couples and the later-sex dating couples had sex. Peplau, Rubin, and Hill (1977) reported that early-sex couples, those who had sex relatively early in the relationship (e.g., within one month), had sex at a median frequency of four to five times per week, whereas the later-sex couples, those who began sex after about six months, had sex two to three times per week. Jeffry Simpson (personal communication; February 1992) reports a slightly lower rate of sex for the dating couples who participated in one of his studies (Simpson and Gangestad 1991). In his sample of ninety-four sexually active dating couples, the frequency of sex per month was slightly over seven times a month (or less than twice a week).

Homosexual couples have also been compared to heterosexual couples on frequency of sexual activity. Lesbian couples have genital sex less frequently than either gay (male homosexuals) or heterosexual couples, but they tend to engage in more nongenital physical contact, such as cuddling, touching, and hugging. Gay couples have sex more frequently than lesbian and heterosexual couples, but only during the first few years of the relationship. After ten years or more in the relationship, many gays seek outside sexual involvements and reduce the amount of sex in their primary relationship (Blumstein and Schwartz 1983).

Some sex researchers have studied not only how often couples have sex but what, more specifically, couples do while they have sex. Most couples engage in foreplay for several minutes (Hunt [1974] found foreplay lasted an average of twelve minutes), kiss and caress while they have sex, and frequently engage in oral-genital sex (Blumstein and Schwartz 1983). Recent research suggests that anal intercourse is practiced by approximately 10 percent of heterosexual couples (Voeller 1991), and by a majority of gay couples at least some of the time although it is not the predominant form of sexual outlet among homosexuals (e.g., Bell and Weinberg 1978; Blumstein and Schwartz 1983). In heterosexual couples, the missionary position (male on top of female) may be the most commonly used position, but other positions (e.g., woman on top, rear-entry) are at least occasionally used by many couples (Hunt 1974). Finally, many couples report that they engage in some sexual experimentation. For example, Andrew Greeley (1991) reported that one-half of a national sample of married couples reported that they had experimented with new ways of lovemaking at least some of the time. What are some of the activities they engage in? The percent who said that they either "a lot" or "sometimes" engage in the following behaviors were: abandon all of your sexual inhibitions (32 percent), swim nude together (19 percent), watch X-rated videos (21 percent), buy erotic underclothes (20 percent), make love outdoors (22 percent), go to a hotel or motel to spend time alone with each other (34 percent), and take showers or baths together (39 percent).

Sexual Satisfaction

Sexual satisfaction or sexual adjustment is an important goal for most married couples and those in other sexually bonded relationships. This has not always been the case, however. Wrote John DeLamater in 1991: "Concern about satisfaction or adjustment is a recent phenomenon. Prior to 1960, sexual partners were rarely concerned about the quality of their sexual relationship" (p. 62).

Research conducted on sexual satisfaction suggests that couples have a relatively high level of sexual satisfaction. For example, in a recent telephone survey conducted by the Gallup organization in the winter of 1989/1990, Greeley (1991) found that about two-thirds of husbands and wives reported either "a very great deal" or "a great deal" of satisfaction. Couples in other studies have also been found to be highly satisfied with the sexual aspect of their relationship (e.g., Blumstein and Schwartz 1983; Brown and Auerback 1981).

Several factors have been found to be associated with sexual satisfaction in close couples. For example, all of the behaviors or conditions listed in Box 10–1 below have been found to be related to greater sexual satisfaction. Whether they cause sexual satisfaction or are the result of sexual satisfaction, however, is unknown. Both causal directions are probably operating.

Sexuality and Other Dimensions of the Relationship

Although sexuality is an important part of a sexually bonded relationship, there are many other important aspects of the relationship. In this section, we will show how sexuality is related to three other relationship dimensions that are covered in this volume: love, exchange and equity, and communication. We begin, however, by discussing the relationship between sexuality and general relationship satisfaction.

BOX 10–2   Behaviors or Conditions Associated with Greater Sexual Satisfaction

Having sex frequently (Blumstein and Schwartz 1983; Greeley 1991)

Engaging in oral-genital sex, for heterosexual men and homosexual men and women, although not for heterosexual women (Blumstein and Schwartz 1983)

Having orgasms (Perlman and Abramson 1982; Pinney, Gerrard, and Denney 1987)

Having orgasms before or around the time one's partner does (rather than after), for women (Darling, Davidson, and Cox 1991)

Being experimental in sex, for example, bathing or showering together, swimming in the nude, using erotic underwear, making love outdoors (Greeley 1991)

Sexually initiating and sexually refusing about as often as one's partner (Blumstein and Schwartz 1983)

Perceiving one's partner to be good looking (Greeley 1991), although this has been found to be less important for lesbian couples (Blumstein and Schwartz 1983)

Communicating effectively with the partner about sex (Cupach and Comstock 1990)

Being sexually assertive, for women (Hurlbert 1991)

General Relationship Satisfaction

One of the most frequently examined variables in the literature on close relationships, particularly marriage, is relationship satisfaction. How important is the sexual aspect of the relationship for determining how satisfied the partners are with their overall relationship? The research examining the relationship between sexual activity and relationship satisfaction among dating couples has focused on whether premarital couples who have sex are more satisfied overall than premarital couples who have not had sex. Peplau, Rubin, and Hill (1977) did not find any difference in overall relationship satisfaction among the three types of couples identified in their study: couples who have sex early in the relationship (within the first month), couples who have sex later (sex around the sixth month), and couples who abstain from sex.

Research on more committed couples (e.g., married couples) has focused on the relationship both between sexual frequency and relationship satisfaction and between sexual satisfaction and relationship satisfaction. In several studies, both sexual frequency and sexual satisfaction have been found to be positively related to relationship satisfaction (e.g., Blumstein and Schwartz 1983; Hunt 1974; Tavris and Sadd 1977).

Does sex contribute to relationship satisfaction (or dissatisfaction) or does the reverse occur? That is, does relationship satisfaction affect the sexual interaction? Philip Blumstein and Pepper Schwartz (1983), who conducted a landmark survey study of thousands of couples, address the issue of the causal direction between frequency of sex and relationship satisfaction:

> It is hard to know whether an unsatisfactory relationship leads to less frequent sexual activity and reduced sexual pleasure or whether the problems begin in the bedroom and eventually corrode the entire relationship. From our vantage point it looks as if other problems come into the bedroom and make it less likely that the couple will want to have sex together. The low frequency then becomes a source of dissatisfaction in and of itself (p. 201).

Love

Sexuality and love are tightly connected in our society. We have already discussed that many young adults hold a permissiveness-with-affection standard—that is, they believe that sex is not acceptable until there is affection or love (DeLamater and MacCorquodale 1979). Many young adults also rate a reason such as "love for partner" as the major factor affecting their decision to have sex for the first time with a particular partner (e.g., Christopher and Cate 1984). Furthermore, the degree of love between two romantic partners is a good predictor of how sexually intimate they are, particularly in the dating stages of the relationship (Christopher and Cate 1988; DeLamater and MacCorquodale 1979).

Although love and sexuality may go together, some types of love may be more associated with sexuality than other types. Does the type of love one experiences for a partner affect the degree to which and how sexuality is expressed? Very little research has been conducted to address this question. One exception is the empirical work of Susan and Clyde Hendrick (1987a and b), who have worked with the lovestyle scales originally identified by John Lee (1973). Commenting on their own work linking love and sexuality, Hendrick and Hendrick (1987b) write: "The study of love and sexuality as companion variables is one of our goals in close relationship research, because it is apparent to us that trying to separate love from sexuality is like trying to separate fraternal twins: they are certainly not identical, but, nevertheless, they are strongly bonded" (p. 282).

Hendrick and Hendrick (1987a and b) looked at the relationship between their Love Attitudes scale and their Sexual Attitudes scale. The Love Attitudes scale measures six lovestyles: Eros (romantic, passionate love), ludus (game-playing love), storge (friendship love), mania (possessive, dependent love), pragma (logical, shopping-list love), and agape (selfless love). The major subscale in the Sexual Attitudes scale is Permissiveness (e.g., casual sex is acceptable), but three other types of sexual attitudes are also measured: Sexual practices (responsible sex; e.g., birth control is part of responsible sex); Communion (emotional sex; e.g., at its best, sex seems to be the merging of two souls), and Instrumentality (egocentric sex; e.g., the main purpose of sex is to enjoy oneself). Hendrick and Hendrick (1987 a and b) report that a ludus lovestyle is associated with a permissive attitude and with instrumentality (egocentric sex). The eros lovestyle is associated with communion. Furthermore, there was a tendency for agape, storge, and pragma to be negatively correlated with permissiveness.

Exchange and Equity

According to equity theory (e.g., Walster, Walster, and Berscheid 1978), which is a specific theory within the general exchange framework, individuals are happiest in their relationships when the benefits received from and the contributions made to the relationship are perceived to be balanced with the partner's benefits and contributions. (If one partner receives more benefit than the other, the relationship can still be equitable if this partner also contributes more). Individuals who believe that they are underbenefited or overbenefited in their close relationships are likely to feel distressed (Sprecher 1986). Elaine Hatfield[1] and her colleagues have argued and found that distress experienced by inequitably treated partners, particularly those who are underbenefited, will interfere with pleasurable sexual encounters. For example, Walster, Traupmann, and Walster (1978) found that undergraduate students who described their dating relationships as equitable reported going further sexually than the students in inequitable dating relationships. In later studies, Hatfield and her colleagues also found that dating and married individuals experienced less sexual satisfaction in their relationship when they were underbenefited (Hatfield et al. 1982; Traupmann, Hatfield, and Wexler 1983).

Equity and extramarital relationships has also been examined. Walster, Traupmann, and Walster (1978) found evidence in a sample of cohabiting and married couples who responded to a *Psychology Today* survey that individuals who were

[1]Work by Dr. Hatfield published before 1979 appears under the name E. Walster.

underbenefited in their relationship were more likely to report that they had an extramarital affair. In a more recent study, Prins, Buunk, and VanYperen (1993) found that, for women, inequity was associated with both actual extramarital behavior and the desire to engage in extramarital sex, controlling for other predictors (e.g., marital dissatisfaction). Engaging in an extramarital affair may provide women with a means to increase their benefits and/or reduce their inputs into the relationship, hence, reducing feelings of inequity. The same relationship was not found for men, however. Extramarital and extradyadic relationships will be discussed further in a later section.

Communication

Not only is sex an act of communication or self-disclosure, but verbal and non-verbal communication is essential for the accomplishment of rewarding sexual episodes. To receive full sexual satisfaction, it is often necessary for partners to tell each other what feels good ("to the left and up a little, please"). Furthermore, erotic talk may be used to increase sexual arousal (Wells 1990). In this section, we will discuss how communication is used to initiate sex and to resist sexual advances.

Initiation of Sex. Men are more likely than women to initiate sex. This is true in dating, cohabiting, and marital relationships (Brown and Auerback 1981; Byers and Heinlein 1989; DeLamater and MacCorquodale 1979; Grauerholz and Serpe 1985; McCormick and Jesser 1983; Rubin 1976), although there is some evidence to suggest that over time in a relationship, women become more comfortable initiating sex (Brown and Auerback 1981). In lesbian and gay couples, the more emotionally expressive partner more often initiates sex. Being an emotionally expressive partner is also associated with initiating sex in heterosexual couples (Blumstein and Schwartz 1983).

Men and women tend to use nonverbal, indirect strategies, such as body movement, kissing, and touching to initiate sex (Brown and Auerback 1981; McCormick 1979; Perper and Weis 1987), particularly early in the relationship. Indirectness allows a person to try to initiate sexual activity but at the same time avoid rejection. Couples, especially more established ones, are also likely to use verbal initiation. In one study (Brown and Auerback 1981), five types of verbal initiations were identified: Let's statements ("Let's make love"); I statements ("I want to make love to you"); comments on the partner's appearance ("You look sexy to me"); demands ("Do it to me"); and questions ("Are you in the mood?"). Mildred Brown and Alfred Auerback (1981) found that men were more likely to use let's statements, whereas women were more likely to use I statements.

Resistance to Sex. Not surprisingly, women are more likely than men to resist sex. For example, females feel more comfortable than males saying no to a partner who wants sex (e.g., Grauerholz and Serpe 1985; Zimmerman et al. 1992) and are actually more likely to say no (Clark 1990; Clark and Hatfield 1989) in casual and dating contexts. In more committed relationships, women are also more likely to resist sexual advances. Blumstein and Schwartz (1983) found that 13 percent of the husbands and 22 percent of the male cohabitors in their study said that they themselves were more likely to refuse sex, compared to 53 percent of wives and 43 percent of female cohabitors. Byers and Heinlein (1989) found that women in their sample gave more negative responses than men to sexual initiation; however, women also reported a greater number of positive responses. When the researchers controlled for the number of sexual initiations, there was not a significant difference in men's and women's responses to sexual initiation. Other individual factors, in addition to gender, have also been found to be associated with a greater likelihood of refusing sex. These include being less emotional and being more powerful (Blumstein and Schwartz 1983).

How do individuals tell their partners that they don't want to have sex? As part of a larger study, Perper and Weis (1987) asked women from both the U.S. and Canada to write essays on how they would try to influence a man to avoid having sex. The authors identified two general categories of rejection strategies: Avoid Proceptivity and Incomplete Rejection. In the first strategy, the woman attempts to avoid or ignores the man's advances. In the second strategy, she may indicate that she needs to be in love first and is not ready yet. These kinds of strategies, however, can lead to misinterpretation. Elizabeth Allgeier and Betty Royster (1991) discuss how the Incomplete Rejection strategy can be interpreted in at least three different ways: "I'm resisting, but please persist"; "Give me a little more time"; or "Back off, Buster! Can't you take the hint that I'm not interested?" (p. 140).

In long-term relationships, after sex has already become an integral part of the relationship, refusal is most likely to be direct (Byers and Heinlein 1989). Individuals in well-established couples always know that if tonight is not a good night, there is always tomorrow night. Direct refusal is probably not as threatening to developed relationships as it is to developing relationships, because, as stated by William Cupach and Sandra Metts (1991), "Directness seems to fulfill simultaneously the goals of averting unwanted persistence of initiation by the partner and of maintaining the face of the rejected individual by offering an account" (p. 103). In other words, being direct is both the clearest and most considerate strategy for refusing sex.

When Sex Goes Awry

Although sex in close relationships can be wonderful, blissful, and orgasmic, problems can also develop in this aspect of the close relationship.

Sexual Incompatibility or Disagreements

Most couples occasionally have disagreements about when or how to have sex. Some couples, however, disagree more than others. For example, one partner may want sex frequently (and with the lights on, while tied up . . .) whereas the other partner may want sex only occasionally and in a more conventional fashion. To what degree do couples disagree about sex and what are the consequences?

In one study, college students recorded information about their dates over a four-week period. Forty-seven percent of the students reported disagreeing with their dating partner about sex at least once during this period, although disagreement occurred on only 7 percent of the total number of dates. It was always the case that the man wanted to engage in a particular behavior and the woman did not (Byers and Lewis 1988). David Buss (1989) looked at disagreement and conflict with samples of university students and married couples. Although men and women were bothered by many of the same things in the relationship, some gender differences were found. Sexual demands by the partner bothered a woman about a man (more than the reverse) whereas sexual rejection bothered a man about a woman (more than the reverse).

Can these sexual problems and incompatibilities break up the relationship? It seems that they can—at least people who have experienced a recent breakup say that sexual incompatibility was a contributing factor in the dissolution of their relationship. This has been found in married couples (e.g., Cleek and Pearson 1985), dating couples (e.g., Hill, Rubin, and Peplau 1976), and homosexual couples (e.g., Kurdek 1991).

Extradyadic Relationships

Most people in our society disapprove of extradyadic relationships (sexual relationships outside of the primary relationship), particularly of extramarital affairs (e.g., Sponaugle 1989). Yet, as with our hypothetical couple, extradyadic relationships do occur. Kinsey and his colleagues (1948, 1953) found that 50 percent of the men and 26 percent of the women in their study had an extramarital affair by the age of forty-five. Although a few other studies have found rates as high or higher (e.g., Wyatt, Peters, and Guthrie 1988), other recent studies have found that American couples are more monogamous than we may have originally thought. For example, Blumstein and Schwartz (1983) found the rates to be 26 percent for married males and 21 percent for married females. They found higher rates, however, among other couple types: male cohabitors (33 percent), female cohabitors (30 percent), gay men (82 percent), and lesbians (28 percent). Greeley (1991) reported that only 9 percent of women and 11 percent of men in his recent national probability sample of married couples said that they have had sex with someone other than their current spouse for the duration of their marriage.

Opportunity seems to play an important role in the development of extradyadic involvement, but many other factors, including sexual boredom in one's present relationship, dissatisfaction with or a lack of commitment to one's relationship, and a general liberal sexual attitude, play a role as well (e.g., Atwater 1979; Blumstein and Schwartz 1983; Buunk 1980). Not surprising, an extradyadic relationship committed by one or both partners can have a negative influence on the primary relationship, although the effect may depend on a number of factors, including whether it is consensual or nonconsensual (i.e., whether the partner knows about it and approves of it) and whether it is love-centered vs. pleasure-centered (Reiss and Lee 1988). Nonconsensual and pleasure-centered affairs are probably the most common type of extradyadic involvement, particularly among men.

As shown for the couple we introduced at the beginning of the chapter, one emotional reaction a person will have to the knowledge or suspicion that his or her partner is engaging (or has engaged) in an outside sexual involvement is jealousy. Jealousy is most likely to be experienced when it is believed that the extradyadic relationship threatens the primary relationship. Some individuals, particularly those low in self-esteem and dependent on their relationship, may experience suspicious jealousy. For example, researchers find that they may engage in any of the following: "worrying, vigilance, suspiciousness, mistrust, snooping, testing the relationship, and attempting to control the partner's behavior" (Bringle and Buunk 1991; p. 137).

Sexual Dysfunctions

Our couple introduced at the beginning of the chapter developed a sexual problem. William Masters and Virginia Johnson (1970), well-known sex therapists, have estimated that about 50 percent of American married couples currently have or will have some type of sexual problem, such as premature ejaculation, inhibited sexual excitement (e.g., lack of vaginal lubrication), inhibited orgasms, or painful intercourse. Although there are many possible causes of sexual problems, including physiological ones, relationship factors may be particularly important. Partners fall out of love with each other, and in some cases, even come to abhor each other. This can have profound effects on sexual desire and sexual performance. Other relationship problems that may contribute to sexual problems in one or both partners include struggles over power in the relationship, insufficient trust of the partner, and boredom that is associated with a long-term relationship. Of course, these relationship problems can also develop as a consequence of sexual dysfunctions. Based on a review of several studies, however, Kathryn Kelley and Donn Byrne (1992) conclude that "unhappy marriages lead to sexual dysfunctions more commonly than sexual dysfunctions lead to unhappy marriages" (p. 455). Many of the therapies for sexual dysfunctions take a relationship approach involving improving communication, dealing with nonsexual problems in the relationship, and having couples do behavioral or emotional homework assignments together (e.g., Heiman and Verhulst 1990; Masters and Johnson 1970).

Sexual Coercion

Coercive sex is not something that occurs only between strangers. Women in dating, cohabiting, and marital relationships are sometimes forced or pressured to have sex by their partners. Coercive sex also occurs in homosexual relationships, and occasionally (see, for example, Struckman-Johnson 1988), men report that they were forced to have sex with a woman, mostly through psychological pressure (for a review, see Muehlenhard et al. 1991). It is difficult to know in how many close relationships coercive sex is experienced. However, consider the statistics from the studies summarized in Box 10–3.

BOX 10–3   Statistics on the Prevalence of Coercive Sex in Close Relationships

About 20 percent of college women report that a date attempted to force sexual intercourse on them during the previous year (Kanin 1957; Kanin and Parcell 1977).

In a survey of over 3,000 female college students, about 54 percent reported some form of forced sexual contact, and of these cases, about one-half occurred on dates (Koss, Gidycz, and Wisniewski 1987).

In a recent study of a national, probability sample of married couples, Andrew Greeley (1991) found that 10 percent of married women in his sample reported being forced to have sex against their wishes. Of these, 25 percent were raped by their husband, 22 percent by a friend, 16 percent by a date or relative, and 6 percent by a stranger (16 percent did not or could not identify the person).

Why would coercive sex, particularly of the more violent type, ever occur in a close or potentially close relationship? R. Lance Shotland (1989) argues that the processes that lead to rape in close, dating relationships depend on the stage of the relationship.

The first type of date rape he identified as beginning date rape, which occurs during a couple's first few dates. If rape occurs during the first few dates, it is probably because a male began dating a female with the intent to rape her if she was not willing to put out. This type of date rapist is likely to be a sexually aggressive male. A female increases her risk for this type of rape if she has a reputation for sleeping around and thus is targeted by a sexually aggressive male.

The second type of date rape is early date rape, which occurs after several dates and while the couple is still getting to know one another. Shotland proposes that early date rape, in contrast to beginning date rape, can be explained primarily in terms of "normal courtship processes that affect men and women of college age" (p. 252). The explanation for rape at this stage of the relationship is centered around misunderstandings about sex between the partners, due to such factors as a man's greater tendency to perceive sexual intent in others, the belief of some men that women engage in token resistance to sex (i.e., say no when they mean yes), and the lack of communication between the partners about their sexual intentions. Furthermore, the men who rape at this stage in the relationship may place higher value on sexuality and have a more difficult time coping with sexual frustrations than other men.

Relational date rape, the third type of date rape, occurs after the couple has been dating for a while. After several weeks or months of dating, a man may begin to expect that sex should occur if the relationship is really a close one and moving toward greater commitment. If sex has not occurred, he may sense inequity or feel cheated in comparison to other men in his social network, who he assumes are getting it. The woman who is a victim of this type of rape is likely to hold conservative sexual standards.

Why would husbands rape their wives? Charlene Muehlenhard and her colleagues (1991) discuss several beliefs about close relationships that may lead to sexual coercion in marriage and other committed relationships. One belief is, "Close relationships should be sexual." Husbands who force sex on their wives often believe that sex is a wife's marital duty. A second belief is, "The man should be the head of the household" and thus have the control to obtain anything he wants from the relationship, including sex. As several feminists have declared over the years, marital rape is more often an act of power than an act of sex.

Coercive sex in developing or close relationships can have many negative outcomes, both for the victim and for the relationship. If the relationship does not end, it is likely to be strained by the distrust and resentment that develops. In addition, sexual problems in the relationship may occur as the result of coercion.

Conclusions and Summary

Sex seems to be a very important part of what has been called the sexually based primary relationship. Although it has been estimated (e.g., Ford 1980) that couples spend only about fifteen minutes a week engaged in actual genital-genital contact (or genital-other orifice contact), they spend considerable time thinking and fantasizing about those fifteen minutes, preparing and primping for those fifteen minutes, and engaging in other physical touching. Furthermore, those fifteen minutes affect many other aspects of the relationship.

We began this chapter by describing the sexual developments occurring throughout the life of one hypothetical couple. The reader should not assume that this couple is representative of typical couples. In fact, today probably only a small proportion of couples advancing to at least one intimate sexual encounter go on to spend the rest of their lives together. Furthermore, the events that happen to this couple may not happen to all couples who remain together for a lifetime. The major message of the sexual diary, however, is that the quality, quantity, and meaning of sex changes over the life of a relationship.

In this chapter, we began by summarizing our own discipline's (sociology) theoretical contribution to the area of sexuality in close relationships, which includes a focus on cultural, subcultural, and group influences on sexuality. In the second and major section of the chapter, we summarized empirical research on sexuality in close relationships. We discussed all of the following topics:

1. the sexual attitudes and experiences each partner brings to the relationship and their possible influences on the relationship;
2. the significance, timing, and decision-making process behind the couple's first time for sex;
3. the frequency with which couples have sex and the kinds of sexual activities in which they engage;

4. satisfaction with the sex in the relationship and factors associated with this satisfaction;

5. how the sex in the relationship is related to other dimensions of the relation-ship—general relationship satisfaction, love, equity, and communication; and

6. a discussion of four ways that sex in the relationship can go awry—sexual disagreements and incompatibilities, extradyadic relationships, sexual dys-functions, and sexual coercion.

In the context of this text, we have discussed each of the above topics only very briefly. We encourage you to explore some of the references cited in this chapter. If you are seeking a topic for a research project, we encourage you to consider addressing a research question in this area of sexuality in close relation-ships. For example, more research is needed on the following questions:

How is the sexuality in the relationship related to other dimensions of the relationship (e.g., love, power, satisfaction)?

How does sexuality change over the course of the relationship and why do these changes occur?

How do couples communicate (and miscommunicate) about sex?

What have been the effects of AIDS on intimate relationships?

How do cross-gender platonic relationships (e.g., the film "When Harry met Sally") handle possible sexual tensions?

When, why, and with whom does sexual coercion occur within the context of a close relationship and what are the effects on the close relationship?

If your interest in sexuality in close relationships does prompt you to explore the literature and conduct research on these or other questions, the next genera-tion of students may turn to you someday for the answers.

References

Allgeier, E. R., and B. J. T. Royster 1991. New approaches to dating and sexuality. In *Sexual coercion: Its nature, causes and prevention,* ed. E. Grauerholz and M. Koralewski, 133–47. Lex-ington, MA: Lexington Books.

Atwater, L. 1979. Getting involved: Women's transition to first extramarital sex. *Alternative Lifestyles,* 2: 33–68.

Baxter, L. A., and C. Bullis. 1986. Turning points in developing romantic relationships. *Human Communication Research,* 12: 469–93.

Bell, A. P., and M. S. Weinberg. 1978. *Homosexuali-ties: A study of diversity among men and women.* New York: Simon and Schuster.

Bentler, P. M. 1968a. Heterosexual behavior as-sessment-I, males. *Behavior Research and Ther-apy,* 6: 21–25.

———. 1968b. Heterosexual behavior assess-ment-II, females. *Behavior Research and Ther-apy,* 6: 27–30.

Blumer, H. 1969. *Symbolic interactionism.* Engle-wood Cliffs, NJ: Prentice-Hall.

Blumstein, P., and P. Schwartz. 1983. *American couples.* New York: Morrow.

Bringle, R. G. and B. P. Buunk. 1991. Extradyadic relationships and sexual jealousy. In *Sexuality in close relationships,* ed. K. McKinney and S. Sprecher, 135–153. Hillsdale, NJ: Erlbaum.

Brown, M., and A. Auerback. 1981. Communication patterns in initiation of marital sex. *Medical Aspects of Human Sexuality*, 15: 105–17.

Buss, D. M. 1989. Conflict between the sexes: Strategic interference and the evocation of anger and upset. *Journal of Personality and Social Psychology*, 56: 735–47.

Buunk, B. 1980. Extramarital sex in the Netherlands: Motivations in social and marital context. *Alternative Lifestyles*, 3: 11–39.

Byers, E. S., and L. Heinlein. 1989. Predicting initiations and refusals of sexual activities in married and cohabiting heterosexual couples. *Journal of Sex Research*, 26: 210–31.

Byers, E. S., and K. Lewis. 1988. Dating couples' disagreements over the desired level of sexual intimacy. *The Journal of Sex Research*, 24: 15–29.

Call, V., S. Sprecher, and P. Schwartz. 1992. The frequency of sexual intercourse in American couples: Results from a national sample. Paper presented at the National Council on Family Relations; Orlando, Florida.

Christopher, F. S., and R. M. Cate. 1984. Factors involved in premarital sexual decision-making. *The Journal of Sex Research*, 20: 363–76.

———. 1985a. Anticipated influences on sexual decision-making for first intercourse. *Family Relations*, 34: 265–70.

———. 1985b. Premarital sexual pathways and relationship development. *Journal of Social and Personal Relationships*, 2: 271–88.

———. 1988. Premarital sexual involvement: A developmental investigation of relational correlates. *Adolescence*, 23: 793–803.

Clark, R. D. 1990. The impact of AIDS on gender differences in willingness to engage in casual sex. *Journal of Applied Social Psychology*, 20: 771–82.

Clark, R. D., and E. Hatfield. 1989. Gender differences in receptivity to sexual offers. *Journal of Psychology and Human Sexuality*, 2: 39–55.

Cleek, M. G., and T. A. Pearson. 1985. Perceived causes of divorce: An analysis of interrelationships. *Journal of Marriage and the Family*, 47: 179–83.

Cochran, S. D., and V. M. Mays. 1990. Sex, lies, and HIV. *New England Journal of Medicine*, 322: 774–75.

Collins, R. 1974. *Conflict sociology: Toward an explanatory science.* New York: Academic Press.

Cupach, W. R., and J. Comstock. 1990. Satisfaction with sexual communication in marriage: Links to sexual satisfaction and dyadic adjustment. *Journal of Social and Personal Relationships*, 7: 179–86.

Cupach, W. R., and S. Metts. 1991. Sexuality and communication in close relationships. In *Sexuality in close relationships*, ed. K. McKinney and S. Sprecher, 93–110. Hillsdale, NJ: Erlbaum.

Darling, C. A., J. K. Davidson, and R. P. Cox. 1991. Female sexual response and the timing of partner orgasm. *Journal of Sex and Marital Therapy*, 17: 3–21.

DeLamater, J. D. 1987. Gender differences in sexual scenarios. In *Females, males, and sexuality: Theories and research*, ed. K. Kelley, 127–139. Albany, NY: State University of New York Press.

———. 1991. Emotions and sexuality. In *Sexuality in close relationships*, ed. K. McKinney and S. Sprecher, 49–70. Hillsdale, NJ: Erlbaum.

DeLamater, J. D., and P. MacCorquodale. 1979. *Premarital sexuality: Attitudes, relationships, behaviors.* Madison, WI: University of Wisconsin Press.

Ford, B. 1980. *Patterns of sex.* New York: St. Martin's Press.

Edgar, T., V. S. Freimuth, S. L. Hammond, D. A. McDonald, and E. L. Fink. 1992. Strategic sexual communication: Condom use resistance and response. *Health Communication*, 4: 83–104.

Gagnon, J. H., and W. Simon. 1973. *Sexual conduct: The social sources of human sexuality.* Chicago: Aldine.

Goffman, E. 1959. *The presentation of self in everyday life.* Garden City, NY: Double-Day.

Gouldner, A. W. 1960. The norm of reciprocity: A preliminary statement. *American Sociological Review*, 25: 161–78.

Grauerholz, E., and R. T. Serpe. 1985. Initiation and response: The dynamics of sexual interaction. *Sex Roles*, 12: 1041–59.

Gray, L. A., and M. Saracino. 1991. College students' attitudes, beliefs, and behaviors about

AIDS: Implications for family life educators. *Family Relations*, 40: 258–63.

Greeley, A. M. 1991. *Faithful attraction: Discovering intimacy, love, and fidelity in American marriage.* New York; Doherty.

Greenblat, C. S. 1983. The salience of sexuality in the early years of marriage. *Journal of Marriage and the Family*, 45: 289–99.

Harvey, J. H., R. Flanary, and M. Morgan. 1986. Vivid memories of vivid loves gone by. *Journal of Social and Personal Relationships*, 3: 359–73.

Hatfield, E., E. Greenberger, J. Traupmann, and P. Lambert. 1982. Equity and sexual satisfaction in recently married couples. *The Journal of Sex Research*, 18: 18–32.

Heiman, J. R., and J. Verhulst. 1990. Sexual dysfunction and marriage. In *The psychology of marriage: Basic issues and applications*, ed. F. D. Fincham and T. N. Bradbury, 299–322. New York: Guilford Press.

Hendrick, S. S., and C. Hendrick. 1987a. Love and sex attitudes: A close relationship. In *Advances in Personal Relationships*, ed. W. H. Jones and D. Perlman, 141–169. London: JAI Press.

———. 1987b. Love and sexual attitudes, self-disclosure, and sensation seeking. *Journal of Social and Personal Relationships*, 4: 281–97.

Hill, C. T., Z. Rubin, and L. A. Peplau. 1976. Break-ups before marriage. The end of 103 affairs. *Journal of Social Issues*, 32: 147–68.

Hunt, M. 1974. *Sexual behavior in the 1970s.* Chicago: Playboy Press.

Hurlbert, D. F. 1991. The role of assertiveness in female sexuality: A comparative study between sexually assertive and sexually nonassertive women. *Journal of Sex and Marital Therapy*, 17: 183–90.

Istvan, J., and W. Griffitt. 1980. Effects of sexual experience on dating desirability and marriage desirability: An experimental study. *Journal of Marriage and the Family*, 42: 377–85.

Jacoby, A., and J. D. Williams. 1985. Effects of premarital sexual standards and behavior on dating and marriage desirability. *Journal of Marriage and the Family*, 47: 1059–65.

James, W. H. 1981. The honeymoon effect on marital coitus. *The Journal of Sex Research*, 17: 114–23.

Juran, S. 1989. Sexual behavior changes as a result of concern about AIDS: Gays, straights, females, and males. *Journal of Psychology and Human Sexuality*, 2: 61–77.

Kanin, E. 1957. Male aggression in dating-courtship relations. *American Journal of Sociology*, 63: 197–204.

Kanin, E., and S. R. Parcell. 1977. Sexual aggression: A second look at the offended female. *Archives of Sexual Behavior*, 6: 67–76.

Kelley, K., and D. Byrne. 1992. *Exploring human sexuality.* Englewood Cliffs, New Jersey: Prentice Hall.

Kinsey, A. C., W. B. Pomeroy, and C. E. Martin. 1948. *Sexual behavior in the human male.* Philadelphia: Saunders.

Kinsey, A. C., W. B. Pomeroy, C. E. Martin, P. H. Gebhard. 1953. *Sexual behavior in the human female.* Philadelphia: Saunders.

Koss, M. P., C. A. Gidycz, and N. Wisniewski. 1987. The scope of rape: Incidence and prevalence of sexual aggression and victimization in a national sample of higher education students. *Journal of Consulting and Clinical Psychology*, 55: 162–70.

Kurdek, L. A. 1991. The dissolution of gay and lesbian couples. *Journal of Social and Personal Relationships*, 8: 265–78.

Lee, J. A. 1973. *The colors of love: An exploration of the ways of loving.* Don Mills, Ontario: New Press.

London, K. A., W. Masher, F. Pratt, and L. Williams. 1989. Preliminary findings from the National Survey of Family Growth, Cycle IV. Paper presented at the Annual Meeting of the Population Association of America. Baltimore, March.

Masters, W. H., and V. E. Johnson. 1970. *Human sexual inadequacy.* Boston: Little, Brown.

McCormick, N. B. 1979. Come-ons and put-offs: Unmarried students' strategies for having and avoiding sexual intercourse. *Psychology of Women Quarterly*, 4: 194–211.

McCormick, N. B., and C. J. Jesser. 1983. The courtship game: Power in the sexual encounter. In *Changing boundaries: Gender role and sexual behavior*, ed. E. R. Allgeier and N. B. McCormick, 64–86. Palo Alto, CA: Mayfield.

Muehlenhard, C. L., M. F. Goggins, J. M. Jones, and A. T. Satterfield. 1991. Sexual violence and coercion in close relationships. In *Sexuality in close relationships*, ed. K. McKinney and S. Sprecher, 155–175. Hillsdale, NJ: Erlbaum.

Newcomb, M. D. 1983. Relationship qualities of those who live together. *Alternative Lifestyles*, 6: 78–102.

Oliver, M. B., and C. Sedikides. 1992. Effects of sexual permissiveness on desirability of partner as a function of low and high commitment to relationship. *Social Psychology Quarterly*, 55: 321–33.

Peplau, L. A., Z. Rubin, and C. T. Hill. 1977. Sexual intimacy in dating relationships. *Journal of Social Issues*, 33: 86–109.

Perlman, S. D., and P. R. Abramson. 1982. Sexual satisfaction among married and cohabiting individuals. *Journal of Consulting and Clinical Psychology*, 50: 458–60.

Perper, T., and D. L. Weis. 1987. Proceptive and rejective strategies of U.S. and Canadian college women. *Journal of Sex Research*, 23: 455–80.

Pinney, E. M., M. Gerrard, and N. W. Denney. 1987. The Pinney sexual satisfaction inventory. *The Journal of Sex Research*, 23: 233–51.

Prins, K. S., B. P. Buunk, and N. W. VanYperen. 1993. Equity, normative disapproval and extramarital relationships. *Journal of Social and Personal Relationships*, 10: 39–53.

Reiss, I. L. 1964. The scaling of premarital sexual permissiveness. *Journal of Marriage and the Family*, 26: 188–98.

———. 1967. *The social context of premarital sexual permissiveness*. New York: Holt, Rinehart, and Winston.

———. 1989. Society and sexuality: A sociological explanation. In *Human sexuality: The societal and interpersonal context*, ed. K. McKinney and S. Sprecher, 3–29. Norwood, NJ: Ablex.

Reiss, I. L., and G. R. Lee. 1988. *Family systems in America*, 4th ed. New York: Holt, Rinehart, & Winston.

Riportella-Muller, R. 1989. Sexuality in the elderly: A review. In *Human sexuality: The societal and interpersonal context*, ed. K. McKinney and S. Sprecher, 210–36. Norwood, New Jersey: Ablex.

Risman, B. J., C. Hill, Z. Rubin, and L. A. Peplau. 1981. Living together in college: Implications for courtship. *Journal of Marriage and the Family*, 43: 77–83.

Robinson, I. E., and D. Jedlicka. 1982. Change in sexual attitudes and behavior of college students from 1965 to 1980: A research note. *Journal of Marriage and the Family*, 44: 237–40.

Rubin, L. B. 1976. *Worlds of pain: Life in the working class family*. New York: Basic Books.

Scanzoni, J., K. Polonko, J. Teachman, and L. Thompson. 1989. *The sexual bond: Rethinking families and close relationships*. Newbury Park, CA: Sage.

Sherwin, R., and S. Corbett. 1985. Campus sexual norms and dating relationships: A trend analysis. *The Journal of Sex Research*, 21: 258–74.

Shotland, R. L. 1989. A model of the causes of date rape in developing and close relationships. In *Close relationships*, ed. C. Hendrick, 247–270. Newbury Park, CA: Sage.

Simpson, J. A., and S. W. Gangestad. 1991. Individual differences in sociosexuality: Evidence for convergent and discriminant validity. *Journal of Personality and Social Psychology*, 60: 870–83.

Sponaugle, G. C. 1989. Attitudes toward extramarital relations. In *Human sexuality: The societal and interpersonal context*, ed. K. McKinney and S. Sprecher, 187–209. Norwood, NJ: Ablex.

Sprecher, S. 1986. The relation between inequity and emotions in close relationships. *Social Psychology Quarterly*, 49: 309–21.

———. 1989. Premarital sexual standards for different categories of individuals. *The Journal of Sex Research*, 26: 232–48.

———. 1991. The impact of the threat of AIDS on heterosexual dating relationships. *Journal of Psychology and Human Sexuality*, 3: 3–23.

Sprecher, S., K. McKinney, and T. L. Orbuch. 1987. Has the double standard disappeared? An experimental test. *Social Psychology Quarterly*, 50: 24–31.

———. 1991. The effect of current sexual behavior on friendship, dating, and marriage desirability. *The Journal of Sex Research*, 28: 387–408.

Sprecher, S., K. McKinney, R. Walsh, and C. Anderson. 1988. A revision of the Reiss premarital sexual permissiveness scale. *Journal of Marriage and the Family*, 50: 821–28.

Struckman-Johnson, C. 1988. Forced sex on dates: It happens to men, too. *The Journal of Sex Research*, 24: 234–41.

Symons, D. 1979. *The evolution of human sexuality*. New York: Oxford University Press.

Tavris, C., and S. Sadd. 1977. *The Redbook report of female sexuality*. New York: Dell.

Traupmann, J., E. Hatfield, and P. Wexler. 1983. Equity and sexual satisfaction in dating couples. *British Journal of Social Psychology*, 22: 33–40.

Udry, J. R. 1980. Changes in the frequency of marital intercourse from panel data. *Archives of Sexual Behavior*, 9: 319–25.

Voeller, B. 1991. AIDS and heterosexual anal intercourse. *Archives of Sexual Behavior*, 20: 233–76.

Walster (Hatfield), E., J. Traupmann, and G. W. Walster. 1978. Equity and extramarital sexuality. *Archives of Sexual Behavior*, 7: 127–41.

Walster (Hatfield), E., G. W. Walster, and E. Berscheid. 1978. *Equity: Theory and research*. Boston: Allyn and Bacon.

Wells, J. W. 1990. The sexual vocabularies of heterosexual and homosexual males and females for communicating erotically with a sexual partner. *Archives of Sexual Behavior*, 19: 139–47.

Westoff, C. F. 1974. Coital frequency and contraception. *Family Planning Perspectives*, 6: 136–141.

Williams, J. D., and A. P. Jacoby. 1989. The effects of premarital heterosexual and homosexual experience on dating and marriage desirability. *Journal of Marriage and the Family*, 51: 489–97.

Wyatt, G., S. Peters, and D. Guthrie. 1988. Kinsey revisited, Part I: Comparisons of the sexual socialization and sexual behavior of white women over 33 years. *Archives of Sexual Behavior*, 17: 201–39.

Zelnick, M., and F. K. Shah. 1983. First intercourse among young Americans. *Family Planning Perspectives*, 15: 64–72.

Zimmerman, R, S. Sprecher, L. M. Langer, and C. D. Holloway. 1992. Which adolescents can't say "No" to unwanted sex in a dating relationship? Manuscript submitted for publication.

Chapter 11

Jealousy in Close Relationships: Multiple Perspectives on the Green-ey'd Monster

DAVID A. DeSTENO
Yale University

PETER SALOVEY
Yale University

Outline

Introduction

> *O, beware, my lord, of jealousy!*
> *It is the green-ey'd monster which doth mock*
> *The meat it feeds on. That cuckold lives in bliss*
> *Who, certain of his fate, loves not his wronger;*
> *But O, what damned minutes tells he o'er*
> *Who dotes, yet doubts; suspects, yet strongly loves!*
> —Iago to Othello in Shakespeare's Othello.

The literature of the world is replete with tales recounting the trials and tribulations of the jealous. From classical Athens, to Elizabethan England, to American daytime television, our interest and empathy are peaked by the examination and expression of jealousy. Not surprisingly, throughout history this inquiry into the causes and phenomenology of jealousy was the domain of the playwright and philosopher. Although jealousy and the related emotion of envy have not received the extensive research attention given to other prominent psychological areas, they have recently emerged as legitimate topics of scientific inquiry (Salovey 1991a). The psychological research of the past two decades has provided some intriguing findings and insights regarding jealousy, and, in its own way, has begun exposing the mysteries of the "green-ey'd monster."

Structure of Chapter

In this chapter, it is our intention to review some of the major psychological theories of jealousy and their respective research support in order to provide a broad perspective from which to examine this complex experience. As one might imagine, the actual number of theories is vast. Therefore, in order to provide a thorough yet balanced overview, we have divided the various theoretical stances into five broad perspectives: the evolutionary perspective, the personality perspective, the basic emotion perspective, the social psychological perspective, and the socio-cultural perspective. Discussions of each perspective will be followed by an illustrative example and critique. For purposes of comparison among the perspectives, we will use Dante's famous romantic triad of Francesca, Paolo, and Gianciotto from *The Divine Comedy* as our illustrative example. Dante subtly alludes to the tragic events of this romantic triangle in *The Inferno*, but, while the subtleties may not be apparent to most of us at first glance, the references were clear to his intended audience. Francesca and Gianciotto were married. Paolo was Gianciotto's younger brother, who, over time, engaged in a romantic relationship with Francesca. One fateful day, Gianciotto found them in an amorous embrace, and slew them in a fit of jealousy. Although this example may not represent the most common result of jealousy, the scenario will allow us to examine each of the perspectives' theoretical suppositions and predictions for the same situation. However, it is important to keep in mind that, as discussed later, jealousy may occur in many different types of relationships, not only those between a heterosexual couple in a romantic relationship.

We, as social psychologists, study jealousy in the context of the self-system and social processes (e.g., self-esteem maintenance, social comparison, etc.). It is our belief that jealousy is a phenomenon that acts to prevent a decrease in self-evaluation by motivating an individual to behave in ways that may prevent the loss of an important relationship. Therefore, like many social psychologists, we examine variables such as level of self-esteem, domain of self-definition, and type of social comparison processes in our research on jealousy. However, there are many different theories that attempt to explain the causes and phenomenology of jealousy, and each of these different theories, or perspectives, makes an important contribution to the investigation of it.

The term perspective is used to denote a particular frame of reference from which to examine jealousy. Perspectivism, the approach that guides our review of jealousy, was characterized by William J. McGuire as a method of investigation proposing that " . . . any hypothesized relationship should be embedded in multiple theoretical explanations, any one of which can be pertinent, depending on the perspective from which one views the phenomena and the contextual limitations within which one is thinking" (McGuire, 1989, p. 217). The five different perspectives that we will discuss represent divergent ways of understanding the phenomenon of jealousy; they each highlight distinct causes and models that aim to describe the nature of this complex emotion. These five perspectives should be viewed as complementary, for it is a principle of perspectivism that "[a]lternative theoretical explanations are seen as supplementary rather than antagonistic" (McGuire 1989, p. 217). When taken together, these perspectives may provide a more comprehensive method for investigating jealousy than any one would by itself.

Definition of Jealousy

Before delving into an exposition of each perspective, we feel it is important to start at a common point, a definition of jealousy. Most researchers agree that jealousy is an aversive emotional experience characterized by feelings of anger, sadness, and fear, induced by the threat or actual loss of a relationship with another person to a real or imagined rival (Parrott 1991; Salovey 1991; Sharpsteen 1991). The element of loss is a defining feature of jealousy; it differentiates jealousy from the kindred emotional experience of envy. These two terms have become so interchangeable in modern language that they are in danger of losing their distinctive meanings. Envy is the term reserved for the begrudging of another's possession of an attribute or relationship that one would like to have for oneself (Salovey 1991a). There is no threat of loss, only a desire to possess what another has and thereby deprive him or her of it. For example, employing our literary example, Paolo experienced envy, while Gianciotto experienced jealousy. Both men desired a relationship with Francesca. However, Gianciotto initially was involved with her. Envy is basically the aversive emotional state caused by the desire for what another possesses. Consequently, Paolo would have been envious of Gianciotto because of the latter's relationship with Francesca. Gianciotto, by virtue of the fact that he was already in the relationship, must have necessarily been jealous, not envious—he realized that his relationship with Francesca had changed. It is the threat to or loss of a close relationship which is characteristic of jealousy. To be jealous, one must have a relationship to lose and a rival to whom to lose it. This fact, more than any other, is what ties together inextricably the study of close relationships and the study of jealousy.

Evolutionary Perspectives on Jealousy

Evolutionary perspectives on jealousy, unlike the other four perspectives to be reviewed, rely on biology for their theoretical suppositions; they attempt to explain behavior with reference to genetic predispositions of one type or another. The presuppositions and theoretical bases of evolutionary theories of behavior are both too numerous and complex to delineate fully in the scope of this chapter. Therefore, we will briefly summarize some of the basic tenets of evolutionary theory, and the allied field of sociobiology, that we believe to be relevant for our discussion of jealousy. Readers who wish a more comprehensive understanding of these fields are encouraged to consult texts such as *Sex, Evolution, and Behavior* (Daly and Wilson 1983), *Sociobiology* (Wilson 1980), and *The Selfish Gene* (Dawkins 1989).

Evolutionary Theories of Jealousy

It is a basic principle of evolutionary theories that the behaviors of organisms should be viewed with reference to their adaptive significance. In other words, any behavior that increases the probability of progeny should be a behavior that is passed on from parent to child. This is not to say that an organism's genotype (e. g., an organism's unique combination of genetic material) fully determines its behavior, but rather that it predisposes organisms to act and react in certain ways. Genes are the carriers of these behavioral tendencies and sexual reproduction allows for the passage of these tendencies to offspring. However, the level of behavior specificity that a gene carries is open to debate, especially in humans. It may be, as many sociobiological theorists suggest, that specific social behaviors may be genetically programmed to a high degree, or, as other evolutionary theorists suggest, that an organism's genotype may provide it with abilities that predispose it toward certain ranges of behavior other than cause it to enact specific behaviors. In this case, the genetic predispositions interact with environmental influences to determine behavior.

No two people, with the exception of identical twins, share the same genotype. Sexual reproduction combines information from the genotypes of two individuals (e.g., the parents) into a new and unique genotype (e.g., the child). Because we all have different genetic compositions, it follows that some of our behavioral predispositions may vary. Some of these different behavioral tendencies will enhance an individual's chances for reproduction, but others will not. Genes that predispose individuals to act in adaptive (e.g., reproduction enhancing) ways, will be inherited by more offspring than genes that do not promote adaptive behaviors because, by definition, individuals who possess these adaptive genes are more likely to mate and bear children (Wilson 1980). It is not an individual organism's survival that drives the genetic selection process, but rather its ability to reproduce and thereby pass on its genetic material; this is what is meant by fitness. An organism's fitness is determined by the number of offspring it raises to the age of sexual maturity; note that this age requirement is necessary because propagation of an organism's genes is not enhanced by progeny that are never given the opportunity to reproduce. Daly and Wilson (1983, p. 21) aptly summarize the situation as follows: "Long-lived celibates are evolutionary failures whose genes die with them. The important criterion of success is reproduction."

Evolutionary theorists, following this line of reasoning, view an individual's various behaviors as comprising a strategy whose aim is to produce progeny. Daly and Wilson (1983) note that this theory does not imply that individuals are involved in creating a conscious strategy, but rather that adaptive genes lead to fitness promoting behaviors. Again, it is important to remember that fitness refers to reproductive success. The question now becomes how does jealousy in close relationships fit into the evolutionary perspective? How is it related to reproductive success? However, before examining these questions, we feel it important to discuss briefly the concepts of parental investment, paternity confidence, and female mate selection.

Trivers (1972, p. 139) defined parental investment as "any investment by the parent in an individual offspring that increases the offspring's chance of surviving (and hence reproductive success) at the cost of the parent's ability to invest in other offspring." Nurturing young is an example of parental investment; it is necessary for the child's survival, but limits the number of future children by demanding the parent's resources and time. Therefore, a balance is struck between the number of offspring and parental investment demands. Fitness would not be increased by many matings when the survival of the offspring is unlikely because of a lack of nurturance.

For humans, like all other mammals, there is a disparity between male and female parental investment. Females, in general, invest much more time and resources in children than do men. Consequently, fitness pressures should dictate that males, being less burdened by parental investment, will most likely adopt a polygynous mating strategy (e.g., where each male mates with several females) (Daly and Wilson 1983; Wilson 1980). Three pressures balance this philanderous tendency: necessary paternal investment, paternity confidence, and female mate selection. The first pressure, necessary paternal investment, is dictated by the species and environment. Simply put, in some situations the male must provide a certain level of investment that could preclude his taking advantage of opportunities for other matings. It is better to attempt to guarantee the survival of a few offspring than to have many offspring with little chance of survival. The final two pressures, paternity confidence and female mate selection, are what give rise to jealousy in humans according to the evolutionary perspective.

Paternity confidence is the degree to which a male of a species that reproduces by internal fertilization is confident that a given child is his; obviously, there is never any doubt that the child shares genetic information with the mother. A male wishes to avoid the possibility that he will invest time and energy toward the nurturing of another male's child, thereby increasing another's fitness at the expense of his own. Therefore, males in a biparental species like our own should evolve behavioral tendencies whose primary purpose is to prevent the mating of one's partner with another male, called cuckoldry (Daly and Wilson 1983, Wilson 1980). In human males, according to the evolutionary view, jealousy is the psychological predisposition which acts to prevent cuckoldry.

Female mate selection, the third check on polygyny, is characterized by the selectivity shown by females in choosing a mate. For females, as previously mentioned, paternity confidence is not an issue; it is the future investment of the male which is paramount. If the male simply copulates and leaves, the female may not be able to provide sufficiently for the young. "The world is full of suitors and promises are cheap. How is a female to ensure that the male of her choice will provide for her rather than absconding?" wrote Daly and Wilson (1983, p. 169) in characterizing this situation. The female must seek to select a male who is willing to invest; courtship rituals usually serve as the proving ground. Human females, like males, should also experience jealousy according to the evolutionary perspective, but centered on a different elicitor. Women should be more jealous of the diversion of resources and attention to a rival female than of an actual sexual union of their mate with another; male jealousy, as mentioned before, should focus primarily on the sexual act itself.

The notion that jealousy has a different focus for men and women has been supported by empirical research. For example, David Buss (1989) conducted a study investigating mate selection; his sample was drawn from 33 different countries. Participants were asked to complete questionnaires concerning many aspects of mate choice. Buss found evidence suggesting that women primarily valued information concerning the ability of their potential mate to provide resources, but men primarily valued information concerning a woman's capacity for reproduction. Another study by Buss and his colleagues (Buss, Larsen, Westen, and Semmelroth 1992) asked undergraduate men and women to rate the intensity of their jealous responses to imagined jealousy-evoking events. Men reported significantly more distress in response to imagined instances of sexual infidelity than to imagined scenarios of their girlfriends expressing emotional feelings toward a rival. Women, conversely, reported more distress in response to imagined scenarios of their boyfriends falling in love with someone else than to imagined instances of infidelity. Daly, Wilson, and Weghorst (1982) postulate that male jealousy may also be manifested in numerous social constraints imposed on women, in biased adultery laws, and in high percentages of homicides involving jealousy-evoking situations as motives.

Jealousy, according to the evolutionary perspective, is thus an inherited psychological tendency. An individual is jealous when the possibility of the loss of his or her mate to a rival is salient. Those individuals who experience and act on jealousy have a better chance of preventing the dissolution of their relationship or cuckoldry/philandery (e.g., fitness decreasing events). As mentioned previously, genes fostering fitness enhancing behavioral tendencies tend to be selected for and passed on to more progeny. Therefore, the jealous response, or a predisposition to exhibit jealousy, should, in most cases, be passed on to each new generation.

How would the evolutionary perspective explain Gianciotto's jealousy at discovering a romantic relationship between Francesca and Paolo? His jealousy, according to the model, is an inherited behavioral predisposition. He not only had reason to believe that Francesca and Paolo may be involved sexually, but actually caught them in the act. Since the sexual act is hypothesized to be the primary focus of male jealousy, Gianciotto's jealousy at discovering them is expected. A jealous response—although perhaps not a homicidal one—increases Gianciotto's chances for successful matings and reduces the probability that he will invest energy and resources in raising another man's child. If he were not jealous, Francesca and Paolo would, in all probability, continue their relationship. Gianciotto would not know for certain if he was the father of Francesca's children. Consequently, the odds of his passing on his genetic material would be decreased. Jealousy acts to increase Gianciotto's fitness and, according to the evolutionary perspective, is a selected for behavioral predisposition.

Critique

A criticism of evolutionary theories concerns their vagaries and disconfirmability. It is not clear what types of behavioral tendencies in humans are the result of inheritance. For sociobiology in particular, it is difficult, if not impossible, to prove that genetic factors, as opposed to other social or psychological variables, actually represent the source of ultimate causation. The idea that specific adaptive behaviors argue for a genetic cause is provocative, but not unassailable. Even the studies conducted by the psychologist David Buss are open to this criticism. Buss (1989) concedes that his work, while suggesting genetic influences, provides no disconfirmable conclusions about the exact mechanisms that influenced mate selection. Linda Caporael (1989, p. 17) in her critique of this study pointed out that "[w]ithout a clue to the mechanism, there is no way to distinguish sex differences from the multitude of gender differences that have no basis in biological evolutionary processes." Consequently, although intriguing, the evolutionary perspective leaves nagging questions concerning causation. Is the source of jealousy, or even a predisposition toward it, rooted in the genotype of an organism, or is jealousy solely the result of learned behavior and social influences?

Personality Perspectives on Jealousy

The investigation of jealousy by personality theorists and researchers is relatively sparse. Of the principal personality theories, only the psychoanalytic model explicitly discusses the causes and experiences of jealousy. However, recent research from alterative theoretical perspectives in personality psychology has suggested that certain people may be more prone to jealousy than others, and that this predisposition may be due, in part, to a stable, inherent personality trait. We will first discuss the psychoanalytic theory of jealousy and then turn to the more recent personality research and examine the evidence for jealousy as a personality trait.

Psychoanalytic Theory of Jealousy

Freud (1922/1955) regarded jealousy as a normal emotional state. He believed it to be so common that he felt comfortable asserting, "If anyone appears to be without it [jealousy], the inference is justified that it has undergone severe repression . . . " (Freud 1922/1955, p. 223). His use of the term *normal* in this context implies a sense of commonality rather than triviality. In other words, jealousy is an emotion experienced by a majority of individuals, but, this universality does not preclude the fact that for some, it may become pathological.

Freud divided jealous experiences into three levels: normal or competitive, projected, and delusional. For him, normal jealousy required little explanation. He characterized it as a compound of "grief, the pain caused by the thought of losing the loved object, and of the narcissistic wound, in so far as this is distinguishable from the other wound . . . [and] further, of feelings of enmity against the successful rival, and of a greater or lesser amount of self-criticism which tries to hold the subject's own ego accountable for his loss" (Freud 1922/1955, p.223). Freud went on to point out that even though he regarded this experience as normal jealousy, the psychic reactions and pain experienced were usually not completely rational, controlled, or in proportion to the actual eliciting situation.

Rather, nominal jealousy, like the other two levels, has its origins in the early childhood emotional experiences of the Oedipal complex. The Oedipal complex, according to Freud, is caused by the young child's desire for the parent of the opposite sex and the resulting fear of and anger toward the same sex parent. This desire is obviously thwarted, and therefore, the child comes to identify with the same sex parent in order to end the fear/anger and to be similar to his or her superior competitor. The jealousy that a person feels, Freud believed, carries with it remnants from this emotional life of early childhood that consequently influences both one's interpretations and reactions in a jealousy-provoking situation. Melanie Klein (1955, p. 326), another prominent psychoanalyst, described more explicitly this Oedipal conflict as the infant's desire for his mother's breast, which " . . . someone else, above all the father, has taken . . . away from him and is enjoying. . . . " What this theory implies about feminine jealousy remains open to debate.

Projected jealousy, the second level of jealousy postulated by Freud, derives, as its name suggests, from the use of the psychological defense mechanism, projection. Freud viewed fidelity as a constant struggle against a multitude of temptations. Everyone, he believed, experienced these temptations and, regardless of whether they were acted upon or only entertained mentally, welcomed a method for eliminating the psychic pressure they caused. Projection is the route to alleviation. "[Anyone] can obtain this alleviation—and, indeed, acquittal by his conscience—if he projects his own impulses to faithlessness on to the partner to whom he owes faith," Freud (1922/1955, p. 224) wrote in describing the use of projection. Such a mechanism allows one to vindicate oneself by assuming that one's partner also possesses the same desires.

Freud referred to the third type of jealousy as delusional. Delusional jealousy is similar to projected jealousy, except that it is much more intense and lacks any type of basis in reality. Freud believed that it originated from repressed homosexual desires; for Freud, homosexuality was an aberration. Today, delusional jealousy is viewed as an exhibition of intense jealousy and related paranoia that has no basis in reality. The origins of delusional jealousy are not based on sexual orientation. Jealousy can occur in both homosexual and heterosexual relationships.

Transactional Theory of Jealousy

Robert Bringle (1981, 1991) has developed what he terms a transactional model of jealousy suggesting that individuals may vary with regard to both the types of situations they find jealousy-evoking and the types of jealous behaviors they manifest. The transactional model implies an interplay between interpersonal events and intrapersonal interpretations in eliciting jealousy. It is Bringle's view that "[a]n individual's beliefs, value system, expectancies, past history, and personality characteristics relevant to social relationships and jealousy define where interpersonal events are perceived to be located on a continuum from 'benign' to 'catastrophic' " (Bringle 1991, p. 103–104). This perspective aptly meets the challenge of explaining why certain events may be seen as jealousy-provoking by some individuals and not by others. Each individual in a close relationship interprets relationship-relevant events through a lens shaded by individual uniqueness; such individual differences in interpretation may lead to misunderstandings between the couple if they are not taken into account.

Bringle (1991) defines the transactional model of jealousy as composed of three constructs: commitment, insecurity, and arousability. Commitment refers to one's level of involvement in a relationship. Insecurity concerns an individual's appraisal of the level of commitment of his or her partner to the relationship; a partner's lower commitment level provides good reason for feelings of insecurity. Arousability refers to both an individual's chronic and momentary states of arousal. Physiological arousal, Bringle believes, increases the emotional intensity of a jealous experience. These three constructs are necessary for evoking a jealous response, and the exact nature of that response is determined by the levels of each and the interactions among them.

Each of the three constructs, Bringle (1991, p. 105) notes, is "a function of variables from three different loci." He terms the loci person, relationship, and situation. In other words, the constructs commitment, insecurity, and arousability are each determined by intrapersonal factors (e.g., person locus), interpersonal factors (e.g., relationship locus), and environmental factors (e.g., situation locus). The intrapersonal factors, the elements of the person locus, are what we will focus on here because they represent the individual traits and tendencies that color an individual's interpretations of relationship-relevant events.

Bringle and his colleagues (Bringle 1991; Bringle, Roach, Andler, and Evenbeck 1979) hypothesized that some people should tend to experience jealousy more intensely and in response to a wider range of eliciting events than should others. Bringle termed this characteristic dispositional jealousy. By using the term dispositional he was invoking the view of personality traits as dispositions to react in specific ways (Argyle and Little 1976). The specific reaction depends upon characteristics of both the situation and the person. "However, the rank order of a number of persons should remain the same . . . " (Argyle and Little 1976, p. 33) across different jealousy-evoking situations. Persons high in dispositional jealousy should experience more intense jealousy over a variety of situations as compared to persons lower in dispositional jealousy. If dispositional jealousy is an aspect of an individual's personality, then it should be both distinct from other personality traits and measurable; we turn our discussion to an examination of both of these issues.

An individual's level of dispositional jealousy is measured by the Self-Report Jealousy Scale (SRJS), developed by Bringle and his colleagues (1979). What characterizes a person high in dispositional jealousy? Bringle found through correlational studies employing the SRJS and other standard personality scales that a person high in dispositional jealousy was "more likely to have less positive self-esteem, to have a less benevolent attitude toward the world, to report lower life satisfaction, to have a more external locus of control, to be more dogmatic, to be more easily aroused, and to be more sensitive to threatening stimuli . . . " (Bringle 1991, p. 114, Bringle 1981).

To chart the effects of disposition on behavior across situations, Bringle and his colleagues (1983) asked a diverse group of subjects to rate a wide-range of jealousy-evoking situations for the type of responses that they would elicit. Both the effects of dispositional jealousy and of the specific situations, as well as the interaction between these two effects, were found to contribute substantially to subjects' ratings. If jealousy is a dispositional trait, then persons high in dispositional jealousy should experience more intense jealousy over a variety of situations as compared to persons lower in dispositional jealousy; this is precisely what Bringle's data showed. These findings confirmed Bringle's belief that jealous responses are indeed controlled to some degree by stable personality characteristics. However, differences in jealousy were also associated with differences in the jealousy-provoking situations, suggesting that although dispositional jealousy may be one determining factor of jealousy, it is not the only one.

The personality perspective can predict Gianciotto's jealousy in one of two ways. Although history is unclear on this matter, it seems probable that Gianciotto may have suspected some type of relationship was developing between Francesca and Paolo before he actually discovered them. This suspicion lead to what Freud termed normal jealousy characterized by all the negative feelings mentioned above, as well as enmity toward Paolo, the rival. According to Freud, these feelings stemmed from Gianciotto's Oedipal conflicts and his desirous feelings toward his mother and consequent disdain for his rival, his father. These unresolved Oedipal conflicts were imposed on his present situation. On the other hand, Bringle and his colleagues would say that Gianciotto's jealousy both prior to and at his discovery of Francesca and Paolo may have been due to a personality trait, namely dispositional jealousy. If he were a person high in dispositional jealousy, he would tend to react more intensely jealous in many, different situations. This trait is the result of individual expectancies about jealousy developed in Gianciotto's upbringing, not necessarily the specific result of early sexual feelings and conflicts with his parents.

Critique

The personality perspective presents two divergent but interesting models of jealousy. The psychoanalytic model is open to all the usual criticisms raised against Freud and his followers. It is not based on empirical research, and, consequently, is difficult to test. Without an objective method for collecting information about unconscious Oedipal conflicts, we can neither prove nor disprove the causal influences of these conflicts. Bringle's dispositional model of jealousy is open to other criticisms. For years, the debate in personality psychology has waged between those who believe traits cause behaviors and those who find causation in the immediate demands of the situation (Epstein 1983; Mischel and Peake 1982). Bringle attempts to walk the line between these two camps with his dispositional model that incorporates both traits and situational effects; however, as he himself has mentioned (Bringle 1991), other researchers have had a difficult time replicating his findings. Also, with the great variability in interpersonal interactions and situations from relationship to relationship, is dispositional jealousy a meaningful concept? Some would argue it is not.

Basic Emotion Perspectives on Jealousy

Emotion researchers are concerned primarily with the phenomenological experience of jealousy as an emotional event, as opposed to its biological or childhood origins. Most of their research aims both to describe and to delineate the actual experience of jealousy as a feeling. The views we will present in this section are variants of cognitive appraisal theories of emotion (Lazarus 1991; Roseman 1984; Smith and Ellsworth 1985). Such theories share the belief that mental, or cognitive, processes aimed at categorizing the situation in which one finds oneself must take place in order for an emotion to be felt. The hypothesized types of categorizations and processes by which they occur serve to differentiate these theories of emotion.

Cognitive Appraisal Theories of Jealousy

W. Gerrod Parrott (1991) offers the observation that individuals usually provide a narrative account when describing a jealous experience. What they describe, according to Parrott, is an emotional episode. Consisting of more than the simple feelings one experiences, an emotional episode "includes the circumstances that lead up to an emotion or sequence of emotions, the emotions themselves, any attempts at self-regulation or coping that occur, subsequent events and actions, and the resolution or present status quo" (Parrott 1991, p. 4). "In short," Parrott (1991, p. 4) continues, "an emotional episode is the story of an emotional event." John Harvey and Ann Weber (see chapter 15, Harvey, Agostinelli, and Weber 1989) also suggest that a narrative, or account, is an important component of emotional experiences within close relationships; such accounts help individuals to make sense of events that occur in the relationship and lead them to hold expectations about future occurrences.

In order to comprehend completely the functioning of an emotion, Parrott suggests, we must be aware of its antecedents and behavioral consequences. Accordingly, in the study of jealousy, the exact situation and beliefs of the couple play an important role in determining the nature of the emotional event. This point is characteristic of cognitive appraisal theories of jealousy; a situation is not a priori jealousy- evoking, but rather requires a cognitive appraisal to classify it as one in which jealousy would be the resultant emotion. Once that decision is made, the individual experiences jealousy and usually engages in specific types of coping behaviors. However, before turning to a discussion of Parrott's findings regarding the experience of jealousy, we will briefly describe his view of the cognitive appraisal mechanism. As discussed later, appraisals are important because some researchers have suggested that they may lead to different types of jealous experiences (Sharpsteen 1991).

Jealousy results from the fear of loss of a relationship to a real or imagined rival. The rival is a defining factor. If one loses a relationship, but no rival is waiting in the wings, many negative emotions may be experienced, but jealousy will probably not be among them (Parrott 1991). Parrott also points out that the rival need not be a romantic rival, or even a human one. For example, an individual may become jealous of his or her best friend's newly developed friendship, or a man may feel jealous toward his wife's new time-consuming job. The integral factors, Parrott asserts, are the existence of a triangular relationship and the loss of formative attention. The term formative attention was coined by Tov-Rauch (1980) to refer to a type of attention that sustains part of an individual's self-concept. Tov-Rauch believes that specific facets of the self-concept are interpersonal in nature (see Markus and Cross 1990 for a discussion of the interpersonal nature of the self-concept), and therefore, require formative attention to exist. An individual's idea of him/herself as attractive or as a good racquetball player requires someone to find him or her attractive or to be a racquetball partner. People who fulfill these roles provide formative attention. An appraisal of a threat to this formative attention, Parrott believes, is what leads to jealousy. We will discuss in greater detail threats to self-evaluation in our review of jealousy from the social psychological perspective.

Narrowly defined, jealousy refers to feelings of anxiety and insecurity concerning the loss of a relationship to a rival. A broader definition would characterize jealousy as a constellation of emotional experiences that could allow for some internal variation (Parrott 1991). In other words, the exact experience of jealousy may vary depending upon the type of situation individuals find themselves in and the cognitive appraisals that they make. Parrott believes that two types of jealousy may result: suspicious jealousy and *fait accompli* jealousy. Suspicious jealousy occurs when individuals suspect that their partners are providing formative attention to others at their expense. It is characterized by intense feelings of anxiety and insecurity, and is surely what Iago is speaking of when he asserts, "But O, what damned minutes tells he o'er / Who dotes, yet doubts; suspects, yet strongly loves!" (Shakespeare, *Othello*).

Fait accompli jealousy, Parrott's other type, flares when there is no doubt that the relationship is lost, and the rival has won. This type of jealousy is usually free, as would be expected, of anxiety concerning the relationship status. *Fait accompli* jealousy is characterized by a variety of other negative emotions. For example, if individuals focus on the loss of the relationship, sadness is the salient feeling. If they focus on the perceived betrayal, anger will result. And if they focus on their new status of being alone, anxiety may predominate (Parrott 1991). This view that different foci of attention, leading to differently focused appraisals, influence emotional experience is echoed by other cognitive appraisal emotion theorists (Ellsworth 1991), and in particular regard to jealousy by Sharpsteen (1991), to whose model we turn shortly.

Prototype Theory of Jealousy

Philip Shaver and his colleagues (Shaver, Schwartz, Kirson, and O'Connor 1987) have proposed that the majority of emotions can be categorized with reference to five or six basic emotions (love, joy, anger, sadness, fear, and possibly surprise).

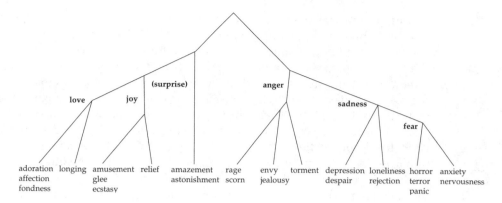

FIGURE 11–1   **Example of Prototype Model of Emotions. (Reprinted/adapted with permission from Shaver, et al. (1987)).**

Other emotions, such as jealousy, are subtypes of one of the basic emotions; in Shaver et al.'s analysis, jealousy is a subtype of anger. These subordinate level emotion terms (e.g., the subtypes of the basic emotions) are used to delineate fine distinctions between emotions; according to Shaver's model, envy and jealousy represent slightly different experiences of anger.

Figure 11–1 is a simplified illustration of Shaver's prototype model of emotions. The six basic emotions (if surprise is included) represent mid-level categories. Each of the basic emotions may be additionally subdivided into more fine-grained, distinct emotions. The basic emotion anger is a parent of rage, jealousy, and torment; each of these emotions shares elements with what Shaver calls the anger prototype.

Every emotion, according to Shaver (Shaver et al. 1987), has a prototype. As reviewed in Chapter 8 of this volume, a prototype is a specific collection of attributes that characterizes the most common occurrence of an event or object (Rosch 1975). Emotion prototypes are composed of distinct components. Each of the five basic emotion prototypes contain antecedent and response components, and the negative basic emotion prototypes (fear, sadness, anger) also contain a self-control component. The anger prototype contains notions of what causes anger (the antecedent component), of how anger is emotionally and behaviorally experienced (the response component), and of how to control this negative emotion (the self-control component). The information contained in these prototypes is abstracted from the numerous experiences each of us has had with these different emotions. The prototypes of the subordinate level emotions will be more similar to those of their parent emotions than to those of any of the other basic emotions (Shaver et al. 1987). This relation can be seen from Figure 11–1. For example, the subordinate emotion panic, is most similar (as seen by the lines indicative of descent) to its parent prototype fear.

Emotional Blend Theory of Jealousy

Don Sharpsteen (1991) proposes that jealousy be viewed as a blended emotion. Emotional blends, also suggested by Shaver (Shaver et al. 1987), are manifested as subordinate level prototypes that share elements with more than one basic level emotion prototype. Jealousy, according to Sharpsteen, is a blend of anger, sadness, and fear. In this view of emotions, subordinate prototypes may not only serve to make finer distinctions between emotions, but also allow some combinations of the basic emotions. Figure 11–2 shows how jealousy may be viewed as an emotional blend. Here, even though it is most prominently associated with anger, it also shares elements with the prototypes of sadness and fear (denoted by the dotted lines). Blends allow the subordinate emotions to be related to more than one parent basic emotion. It has also been suggested that instead of representing a unique mixture of components of different basic emotions, blends may be composed of a sequence of reappraisals and the resulting emotions one would experience as each different appraisal is made (Sharpsteen 1991). As individuals focus on different aspects of a jealousy-evoking situation, fear, sadness, or anger may momentarily become the salient emotion, and together this sequence may form a blend. Hupka (1984) provides supporting evidence for this hypothesis. He presented subjects with different aspects of a jealousy-evoking situation and asked them to indicate what the jealous person was feeling toward his or her partner. The emotion attributions varied depending upon which aspect of the jealousy-evoking situation was salient; when different aspects of the situation were focused upon, participants believed that the person was either sad, angry, or fearful.

In Sharpsteen's model of jealousy, as in Parrott's, the phenomenology of jealousy seems to center around feelings of anxiety, anger, and sadness. Whether jealousy is viewed as a unique, complex emotion or as a blend, the cognitive

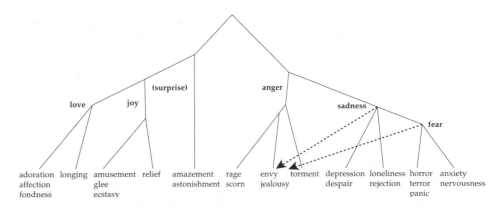

FIGURE 11–2   **Example of Prototype Model of Emotions Showing Blends. (Reprinted/adapted with permission from Shaver, et al. (1987)).**

appraisals one makes concerning the jealousy-evoking event play an important role in the resulting emotional experience.

Gianciotto's discovery of Francesca and Paolo led him, as it would most anyone else, to appraise the situation as one in which jealousy would be the proper emotion; the situation clearly involved a threat to the continuance of his relationship with her. Once this cognitive appraisal had been made, he experienced the aversive phenomenological manifestation of jealousy. At that moment, he was a victim of fait accompli jealousy. There was no doubt that his relationship with Francesca had been seriously altered. He, who desired formative attention from her, had discovered that she was offering it to another. According to Parrott's theory, this loss of formative attention led to Gianciotto's jealousy. Consequently, Gianciotto most likely felt betrayal, anger, sadness, and anxiety.

The question that Sharpsteen raises concerns the structure of jealousy. Is it a unique emotional experience, or can it be reduced to some combination or sequence of the basic emotions anger, fear, and sadness? Sharpsteen's model predicts that Gianciotto's experience of jealousy was characterized by the nearly simultaneous occurrences of elements common to experiences of fear, anger, and sadness. This sequence of emotions was produced as Gianciotto focused on different aspects of the situation.

Critique

The basic emotion perspective characterizes jealousy as either a distinct emotion in its own right, or as a blend of basic emotions. Parrott and colleagues argue that jealousy is a distinct emotional experience; however, others have not been able to isolate jealousy in this way. For example, Salovey and Rodin (1986) found it to differ from envy only in intensity. Smith, Kim, and Parrott (1988) have suggested that this lack of discriminability may be due to poor experimental stimuli. The notion of basic emotion and emotional blends also has its critics. Andrew Ortony and Terence Turner (1990) question the validity of research that claims basic emotions exist and act as building blocks for other types of emotional experiences. Phoebe Ellsworth (1991, p.146), another emotions theorist, has commented, "While various versions of the blend idea may be more or less satisfactory on a metaphorical level, they all beg the question of what is actually happening." Are emotional states being combined, or do individuals simply pass from one to another, the entire sequence representing a non-basic emotion, such as jealousy (Hupka 1984)? So far, emotion researchers have no definitive answers to these questions.

Social Psychological Perspectives on Jealousy

Social psychological models of jealousy are constructed with reference to two of this discipline's most traditional topics: the self-system and interpersonal processes. We will discuss two theories of jealousy that specifically emphasize threats to self-esteem and relationship dynamics as central motivating processes in the experience of this emotion (Salovey and Rodin 1989; White 1991). Each of these theories assumes that the phenomenological emotional experience of jealousy is similar to the description provided in the previous section; however, these social psychological models include many other types of cognitive processes and behavioral tendencies in their views of jealousy. As will be seen, cognitive comparisons and resulting motivational tendencies are as important to social psychological models of jealousy as the phenomenological experience itself.

Self-Evaluation Maintenance Theory of Jealousy

In our research, we have found that jealousy most often occurs when specific types of comparisons are made (Salovey 1991; Salovey and Rodin 1984, 1991). An individual is not invariably jealous when his or her lover flirts with someone. Rather, it is when a comparison with this potential rival focuses on a dimension central to one's self-definition that jealousy results. We each have specific domains that are important to how we define ourselves (Tesser 1981). For example, a person might feel that attractiveness and athleticism are important to her self-concept, but that her musical ability is not. Also, in a close relationship, the relationship itself, along with one's partner's view of oneself, typically represent domains important to one's self-definition. Consequently, threats to one's status on these dimensions should induce aversive emotional states. More specifically, jealousy is most likely to be experienced when the termination of an important relationship with another person is threatened by a rival whose characteristics in especially important domains—that is, domains relevant to self-definition—appear to be better than our own (Salovey and Rothman 1991).

This view is grounded in Tesser's Self-Evaluation Maintenance (SEM) model of motivation (Tesser 1986, 1988). According to the SEM model, individuals are motivated to increase or maintain high self-esteem; this motivation is manifested in behaviors that promote positive views of oneself. The situations that allow an individual to receive positive feedback from his or her behaviors are usually of a social nature. These interpersonal situations may lead to two distinct types of social interactions that Tesser (1986) refers to as the reflective process, and the comparison process.

The reflective process is characterized by an individual's attempts to maintain or increase self-evaluation through association with superior others (e.g., persons who possess some superior attribute or ability). Simply put, this process, initially described by Cialdini and his colleagues (Cialdini et al. 1976) as basking in reflected glory, allows one to increase self-esteem by knowing a superior other. For example, a person might feel good about himself if a friend of his is offered a professional sports contract or a promotion to vice-president. The comparison process, however, is quite a different story. It is characterized by a threat to an individual's self-evaluation from knowing superior others. Here, instead of bolstering one's self-esteem, a comparison occurs that decreases an individual's self-evaluation by making him or her feel inferior. In this case, having a friend who is offered a professional sports contract may lower self-evaluation. The integral question becomes, what factor determines whether the social interaction will result in a reflective or comparison process?

According to Tesser (1981), people only care about their attributes or performances in a specific set of domains; this set defines the domains relevant to self-definition. When others are superior to us in non-relevant domains, our self-evaluation is not threatened, and social interactions may result in the reflective process. However, when we interact socially with others who possess superior attributes or abilities in domains we consider relevant to self-definition, comparison processes are invoked. Thus, whether or not a person's self-evaluation is increased or threatened by his friend being offered a professional sports contract hinges on the relevance of athleticism to his self-definition.

In jealousy-evoking situations, both the relationship itself and one's belief of how one's partner views oneself are important to self-definition. Therefore, comparisons in these domains should cause a comparison process. Jealousy is this comparison process—the rival must possess something that the jealous individual is lacking—and motivates behaviors that attempt to restore or maintain positive self-evaluation (Salovey and Rothman 1991). This motivation is due in part, no doubt, to the aversive emotional experience of jealousy described in the previous section.

Salovey and Rodin (1991) found empirical support for the domain-relevance model of jealousy in a large scale study of jealousy and envy (only the results pertinent to jealousy will be discussed here). It was hypothesized that jealousy was most likely to be experienced in situations relevant to a person's self- definition. In 1985, a survey was published in *Psychology Today* magazine and 25,000 individuals responded. From these, 6,482 surveys were randomly selected for analysis (Salovey and Rodin 1985). Participants rated four domains (wealth, fame, popularity, and physical attractiveness) for their importance to self-definition. They then indicated how they actually viewed their accomplishments in these domains as well as how they ideally would like to be with respect to these domains. Respondents next indicated the frequency with which they had previously engaged in acts that might reflect jealousy and rated different hypothetical jealousy-invoking situations for the intensity of jealousy that they would engender. These two variables served as a measure of an individual's jealousy. For analytical purposes, the behavioral and situational data were subsequently grouped according to which life domain was made salient, wealth, fame, popularity, or attractiveness.

Jealousy in a specific domain was associated with the relevance of that domain to self-definition, with the degree individuals felt that they were not meeting their expectations in that domain, and with global self-esteem. Moreover, the strongest relations were found between domain importance and jealousy experienced in that domain. Because these results were obtained using a self-selected sample (e.g., people who read *Psychology Today* and decided to complete the survey), a second study was conducted with a set of 220 randomly selected subjects, and the results were replicated (Salovey and Rodin 1991).

Our model indicates the important role self-evaluation plays in the experience of jealousy and parsimoniously explains why individuals may react jealously in some situations but not in others. Gregory White (1991) and his colleagues propose another social psychological model of jealousy that also acknowledges the importance of self-esteem and incorporates relationship factors. White defines romantic jealousy as "a complex of thoughts, emotions, and actions that follows loss of or threat to self-esteem and/or to the existence or quality of the romantic relationship" (White 1991, p. 232). The loss, or threat thereof, is caused by a real or imaginary rival. White (1981) believes that jealousy is best conceived of as a label given to specific configurations of thoughts, feelings, and behaviors. These configurations may vary from person to person, and as will be discussed later, from culture to culture, but should remain relatively stable over time with respect to the specific individual, relationship, and/or culture. In other words, one individual may experience a certain configuration of thoughts, feelings, and behaviors when jealous that differs from another person's configuration; however, each is recognizable as a jealous reaction (at least by people of the same culture). Viewing jealousy in this manner allows a researcher to probe more intricately its causes and functioning.

White (1981) conducted a study aimed at charting the effects of self-esteem and relationship variables on the experience of jealousy. Specifically, he hypothesized that a person's desire for sexual exclusivity, feelings of inadequacy, dependence on the relationship for self-esteem, general dependence on the relationship, and perceived amount of involvement relative to one's partner would show a positive association with self-reported romantic jealousy, and that global self-esteem would show a negative association. Results of the study showed that individuals' feelings of inadequacy and desires for sexual exclusivity were positively related to ratings of jealousy for both women and men. Dependence on the relationship for self-esteem was positively related to jealousy for men, but not for women, and general dependence on the relationship was positively related to jealousy for women, but not for men. Also, for both sexes, the stronger a person's belief that he or she was investing more effort into the relationship relative to his or her partner, the more likely it was that the person would describe himself or herself as jealous. Interestingly, White (1981) found no association between global self-esteem and jealousy.

Relationship Power and Jealousy

White (1980) also suggests that a power perspective may be useful in understanding the function of jealousy in a close relationship. Sometimes, one partner in a relationship may intentionally act to induce jealousy in the other; such behavior may be viewed as a power tactic. The term power is introduced to emphasize the different levels of control in a relationship. According to this perspective, the person who is less involved or dependent on the relationship is powerful because he or she may leave the relationship with less harm to himself or herself than to the more involved or dependent person (White 1980). So, why would someone (usually the weaker partner) attempt to induce jealousy in his or her partner? According to White, the individual "relatively more involved in a romantic relationship (more dependent) may be able to gain greater outcomes (or control) by leading his or her partner to believe that an attractive alternative relationship is available. . . . [however] this ploy may backfire if the threatened partner's outcomes [e.g., self-esteem, rewards from the relationship] drop below what he or she may want to stay in the relationship" (White, 1980, p. 222). In other words, jealousy may sometimes be used as a "power play." White (1980) found some support for this theory in a study examining jealousy in 150 heterosexual couples. Women were more likely to induce intentional jealousy in their mates if they were in the weaker power position in the relationship; no similar effects were found for men.

Our model of jealousy predicts that Gianciotto's feelings of jealousy stemmed from a comparison with Paolo. Gianciotto's relationship with Francesca and her view of him represented important self-definitional domains for him. By Francesca's acceptance of Paolo, Gianciotto was left to assume that he came up short on these dimensions in comparison with Paolo. Gianciotto's self-perceived inferiority caused an aversive emotional state, jealousy in this case, and motivated him to act to end this comparison situation. Gianciotto's desire for sexual exclusivity may also have played a role in his jealousy. As White reported, besides threats to self-esteem, an individual's desire for sexual exclusivity is associated with his or her jealousy levels. Assuming that Gianciotto placed a high value on Francesca's fidelity, his jealousy at discovering her rendezvous with Paolo would be intense.

Critique

The criticisms of the social psychological models of jealousy revolve around their primary emphasis on self-evaluation and correlational data. Tesser's SEM model applies to any type of situation that causes a threat to self-esteem; it is not primarily a model of jealousy. Consequently, although it provides a reasonable way of understanding jealousy, it does not separate jealousy from other negative emotions; it provides no unique and discriminating information about jealousy per se. The same argument may be raised against the studies reported by White. His correlational studies show many associations between jealousy and self or relationship variables, but no direct causal relations can be definitively stated. White's predictions of power dynamics may not hold in all situations. For example, a jealous person may give up power in a relationship by acting in a dependent way, rather than trying to evoke jealousy in his or her partner. Showing one's devotion, instead of bluffing, may also be an effective method for strengthening a faltering relationship.

Socio-Cultural Perspectives on Jealousy

Theorists representing the socio-cultural perspective view jealousy as a socially constructed phenomenon (Hupka 1991). The word constructed is used to emphasize that jealousy is not a biological given, but rather is built according to one's experiences with the surrounding social environment. Every society contains social norms, and these norms become psychologically represented in memory (Averill 1980). According to Averill (1980, p. 306), "[t]hese structures—like the grammar of a language—provide the basis for the appraisal of stimuli, the organization of responses, and the monitoring of behavior. . . . " Therefore, the emotion of jealousy is theorized to be a learned phenomenon, and precisely because it is learned, it may vary from culture to culture.

Socio-Cultural Theory of Jealousy

Ralph Hupka (1991) has developed a model of jealousy as a social construction. Hupka believes that humans' genetic endowment enables them to experience the phenomenological aspects of jealousy, but that all else is learned. Our physiology allows us to feel jealous, but is not a sufficient condition in and of itself for the experience of jealousy. Hupka (1991, p. 254) characterizes the situation as follows:

> *Before jealousy can be elicited, we must learn to value romantic relationships, the motive for being jealous, the target of the jealousy, the events that trigger the jealousy, who expresses it, when to express it, the manner of expressing it, who is to blame for the predicament, and so forth (Hupka, 1981). The biological heritage provides the physiological fire of jealousy, but it is ignited by a psychological spark.*

Knowledge of these determinants is necessary for an individual to be jealous; they dictate the correct antecedents and responses that a person should experience in a jealousy-evoking situation. Moreover, these determinants come from a society's social norms and are defined and configured differently in various cultures, the result of which is different causes, different expressions, and possibly different phenomenological experiences of jealousy.

The social structures are "elements of the social organization that maintain orderly relationships among individuals, regulate the production and distribution of wealth, and provide a setting for the breeding and socialization of new members of the society" (Hupka 1991, p. 261). With regard to jealousy, we are primarily interested in the social structures that set guidelines for behavior with respect to interpersonal relationships and sexuality. Hupka suggests that living in a society, as opposed to a less social environment, requires the regulation of many issues, sexual behavior among them. The rules a society sets for interpersonal and sexual behavior determine when and how jealousy should be felt. These rules also have psychological consequences, Hupka maintains; they determine the value of men and women to each other. An example from Hupka (1991) illustrates this point quite well.

Suppose two societies existed, A and B. In society A, marriage provides the opportunity to be considered mature and opens the doors to positions of power and influence. Children are expected to provide for their parents in old age, and the nuclear family is the preferred familial unit. As Hupka (1991, p. 262) points out, " . . . husbands and wives [in society A] need each other—not only to enjoy that which is held dear in society, but also to ensure survival and companionship." Society B is constructed quite differently. Here, the clan is the preferred familial unit, and cooperation ensures survival. Companionship comes from any-one in the clan, and there are no sexual proscriptions; consequently, lineage cannot be assuredly determined. Also, age, rather than marriage, is the determi-nant of maturity. Hupka's (1991, p. 206) analysis of society B is that "[m]en and women play less of a role in each other's lives; that is to say, they are less dependent upon each other as individuals than in society A." Jealousy is much more likely to be experienced in society A, where it serves a definite functional purpose—members of this society must guard against rivals if they are to have a prosperous life. In society B, social structures probably do not exist for jealousy, or possibly frown on jealous-type behaviors; jealousy would serve no necessary function. Admittedly, this is an oversimplified example, but it shows the under-lying mechanisms that might account for societal norms of jealousy.

To investigate the validity of this model of jealousy, Hupka and Ryan (in press) conducted a study using subjects from 92 preindustrial societies. They examined the correlation between specific social norms (importance of being married, regulations concerning premarital and extra-marital sex, importance of private ownership of property) and the severity of aggression expressed by males in jealousy-evoking situations. Each of the social norms mentioned above showed a significant positive relation with intensity of jealousy. Although far from con-clusive, these results suggest that social norms may indeed play some role in determining both how and if jealousy is experienced in different cultures.

Cross-Cultural Examples of Jealousy

Jeff Bryson and his colleagues (1984) also investigated the possibility that jealousy may be experienced differently among people of various cultures. Subjects for the study were drawn from the United States, France, Germany, Italy, and the Neth-erlands. Each participant completed a battery of questionnaires measuring such things as current relationship status, beliefs about relationships, levels of jealousy, demographic information, and the like. Members of each culture showed distinc-tive patterns of responses to these measures. For example, the French generally were more sensitive to relationship betrayal, but the Germans were less likely to react aggressively in jealousy evoking situations. Bryson offered the observation that each group might be characterized by its most distinctive reaction to jealousy: "It appears that, when jealous, the French get mad, the Dutch get sad, the Ger-mans would rather not fight about it, the Italians don't want to talk about it, and the Americans are concerned about what their friends think" (Bryson 1991, p. 191).

The socio-cultural perspective would suggest that Gianciotto's jealous re-sponse was due to his socialization in 13th century Italy. As is the case with most Western European societies, marriage is an important socially-defining and eco-nomic institution. Therefore, jealousy most probably acted as a behavioral re-sponse to protect this institution. It may also be the case that Gianciotto's society placed a high value on marital or familial loyalty which encouraged, or at least did not frown upon, retribution. Such a situation would place Gianciotto's jealous and violent response in an appropriate context. The phenomenology and behavioral manifestations of jealousy, as suggested by Bryson, may vary, like indigenous languages, from culture to culture.

Critique

The primary criticism of the socio-cultural perspective is the seeming universality of jealousy. For the most part, it does appear that the people of the majority of cultures do experience some type of jealousy (Daly, Wilson, and Weghorst 1982). Although on the surface some cultures may not seem to show jealousy very much, further examination often reveals the existence of this emotion, although expressed in subtle or different ways (Daly, Wilson, and Weghorst 1982). Such arguments raise the possibility that the source of jealousy may lie in personality dispositions or biological mechanisms, from whence it is modified by the social environment. In such a case, the ultimate causes of jealousy could not be attributed solely to a society's social structures. As psychologists delve more deeply into cross-cultural research, answers to these questions may become clearer.

Conclusion and Summary

Review of Theories

As we have seen, many different theories, or perspectives, may be used to explain jealousy. While each of these theories posits different causes for jealousy, they all agree that its phenomenology is experienced as an aversive emotional state characterized by feelings of anger, sadness, and fear, induced by the threat or actual loss of a relationship with another person to a real or imagined rival. The evolutionary perspective conceives of jealousy as a behavioral tendency that has been passed on because of its functional value in increasing an individual's fitness. The personality perspective offers both a psychoanalytic view of jealousy, whereby its origins may be found in Oedipal conflicts, and a dispositional view that suggests jealousy may be understood much as any other personality trait. The basic emotion perspective seeks both to characterize the phenomenological experience of jealousy and to understand the cognitive appraisals that lead to it. The social psychological perspective views jealousy as a consequence of threats to self-evaluation or of power dynamics in a relationship. Finally, the socio-cultural perspective proposes that the emotion of jealousy may be a culturally learned phenomenon; it also provides some evidence that suggests jealousy may be experienced differently by people of various cultures.

Conclusions

What exactly is jealousy, and how does it work? Is it biologically driven? Are some people inherently jealous? Does a person from India experience jealousy in the same way as a person from the United States, or even at all? It seems we may have raised more questions than we answered by presenting so many different theories. However, if we view these theories as complementary, instead of as antagonistic, we may begin to glimpse a part of what is actually occurring. For example, many different factors may have simultaneously influenced Gianciotto's jealousy. A genetic predisposition to guard against cuckoldry, as well as a socially prescribed value for monogamy may have functioned synergistically. His negative affective state may have been due both to unfavorable comparisons with Paolo in important domains and to a high level of dispositional jealousy. No single theory needs to provide the complete answer. Rather, incorporating the aspects of each that appear valid after repeated investigation into a larger model should prove enlightening. There may in fact be biological motivations for jealousy that are subjected to a learning process determined by one's culture. It seems plausible that people react jealously because of threats to self-evaluation, and that some individuals also seem more prone to jealousy than do others.

Although all the research discussed in this chapter seems provocative, the possible interactions among the various perspectives may allow even greater accuracy in modeling jealousy. As the study of close relationships moves forward, we will continue to refine the study of jealousy. It may be the case that one or two models may provide a very parsimonious account of it, but, it is more likely the case that a more complex theory, incorporating views from many perspectives, may be needed to understand the intricacies of this emotion. In any case, while science continues its objective investigation into the experience of jealousy, no one captures its throes more aptly than Shakespeare's Othello when he avows, "I had rather be a toad and live upon the vapor of a dungeon than keep a corner in the thing I love for others' uses" (Shakespeare, *Othello*).

References

Argyle, M. and B. R. Little. 1976. Do personality traits apply to social behavior? In *Interactional psychology and personality*, ed. N. S. Endler and D. Magnusson, 30–57. New York: John Wiley and Sons.

Averill, J. R. 1980. A constructivist view of emotion. In *Emotion: Theory, research, and experience. vol. 1. Theories of emotion*, ed. R. Plutchik and H. Kellerman, 305–339. New York: Academic Press.

Bringle, R. G. 1981. Conceptualizing jealousy as a disposition. *Alternative Lifestyles*, 4:274–90.

Bringle, R. G. 1991. Psychosocial aspects of jealousy: A transactional model. In *The psychology of jealousy and envy*, ed. P. Salovey, 103–31. New York: Guilford Press.

Bringle, R. G., P. Renner, R. Terry, and S. Davis. 1983. An analysis of situational and person components of jealousy. *Journal of Research in Personality*, 17:354–68.

Bringle, R. G., S. Roach, C. Andler, and S. Evenbeck. 1979. Measuring the intensity of jealous reactions. *JSAS: Catalog of selected documents in psychology*, 9:23–24.

Bryson, J. B. 1991. Modes of response to jealousy-evoking situations. In *The psychology of jealousy and envy*, ed. P. Salovey, 178–207. New York: Guilford Press.

Bryson, J. B., P. Alcini, B. Buunk, L. Marquez, F. Ribey, M. Rosch, F. Strack, and D. van den Hove. 1984. *A cross-cultural survey of jealousy behaviors in France, Germany, Italy, the Nether-*

lands, and the United States. Paper presented at the International Congress of Psychology, Acapulco, Mexico.

Buss, D. M. 1989. Sex differences in human mate preferences: Evolutionary hypotheses tested in 37 cultures. *Behavioral and Brain Sciences,* 12:1–49.

Buss, D. M., R. J. Larsen, D. Westen, and J. Semmelroth. 1992. Sex differences in jealousy: Evolution, physiology, and psychology. *Psychological Science,* 3:251–55.

Caporael, L. R. 1989. Mechanisms matter: The difference between sociobiology and evolutionary psychology. *Behavioral and Brain Sciences,* 12:17–18.

Cialdini, R. B., R. J. Borden, A. Thorne, M. R. Walker, S. Freeman, and L. R. Sloan. 1976. Basking in reflected glory: Three (football) field studies. *Journal of Personality and Social Psychology,* 34:366–375.

Daly, M. and M. Wilson. 1983. *Sex, evolution, and behavior.* Second edition. Belmont, California: Wadsworth Publishing Company.

Daly, M., M. Wilson, and S. J. Weghorst. 1982. Male sexual jealousy. *Ethology and Sociobiology,* 3:11–27.

Dawkins, R. 1989. *The Selfish Gene.* New York: Oxford University Press.

Ellsworth, P. C. 1991. Some implications of cognitive appraisal theories of emotion. *International Review of Studies on Emotion,* 1:143–61.

Epstein, S. 1983. The stability of confusion: A reply to Mischel and Peake. *Psychological Review,* 90:179–84.

Freud, S. 1922/1955. Some neurotic mechanisms in jealousy, paranoia, and homosexuality. In *The standard edition of the complete psychological works of Sigmund Freud* (Vol. 18, pp. 221–232), ed. and trans. J. Strachey. London: Hogarth Press.

Harvey, J. H., G. Agostinelli, and A. L. Weber. 1989. Account-making and the formation of expectations about close relationships. In *Close relationships: Review of Personality and Social Psychology,* ed. C. Hendrick, 10:39–62. Newbury Park, CA: Sage Publications.

Hupka, R. B. 1981. Cultural determinants of jealousy. *Alternative Lifestyles,* 4:310–56.

Hupka, R. B. 1984. Jealousy: compound emotion or label for a particular situation? *Motivation and Emotion,* 8:141–55.

Hupka, R. B. 1991. The motive for the arousal of romantic jealousy: Its cultural origin. In *The psychology of jealousy and envy,* ed. P. Salovey, 252–70. New York: Guilford Press.

Hupka, R. B. and J. M. Ryan (in press). The cultural contribution to jealousy: Cross-cultural aggression in sexual jealousy situations. *Behavior Science Research.*

Klein, M. 1955. On identification. In *New directions in psyco-analysis,* ed. M. Klein, P. Heimann, and R. E. Money-Kyrle. New York: Basic Books, Inc.

Lazarus, R. S. 1991. *Emotion and adaptation.* New York: Oxford University Press.

Markus H. and S. Cross. 1990. The interpersonal self. In *Handbook of personality: Theory and research,* ed. L. A. Pervin. 576–608. New York: Guilford Press.

McGuire, W. J. 1989. A perspectivist approach to the strategic planning, of programmatic scientific research. In *The psychology of science: Contributions to metascience,* ed. B. Gholson, W. R. Shadish, Jr., R. A. Neimeyer, and A. C. Houts, 214–245. New York: Cambridge University Press.

Mischel, W. and P. K. Peake. 1982. Beyond déjà vu in the search for cross-situational consistency. *Psychological Review,* 89:730–55.

Ortony, A. and T. J. Turner. 1990. What's basic about basic emotions? *Psychological Review,* 97:315–31.

Parrott, W. G. 1991. The emotional experiences of envy and jealousy. In *The psychology of jealousy and envy,* ed. P. Salovey, 3–30. New York: Guilford Press.

Rosch, E. 1975. Cognitive representations of semantic categories. *Journal of Experimental Psychology: General,* 104:192–233.

Roseman, I. 1984. Cognitive determinants of emotion: A structural theory. In *Review of personality and social psychology: vol. 5. Emotions, relationships, and health,* ed. P. Shaver, 11–36. Beverly Hills, CA: Sage.

Salovey, P. 1991a. Preface. In *The psychology of jealousy and envy,* ed. P. Salovey, xi–xiii. New York: Guilford Press.

————. 1991. Social comparison processes in envy and jealousy. In *Social comparison: Contemporary theory and research*, ed. J. Suls and T. A. Wills, 261–85. Hillsdale, NJ: Erlbaum Associates.

Salovey, P. and J. Rodin. 1984. Some antecedents and consequences of social-comparison jealousy. *Journal of Personality and Social Psychology*, 47:780–92.

————. 1985. The heart of jealousy. *Psychology Today*, 22–25, 28–29.

————. 1986. Differentiation of social-comparison jealousy and romantic jealousy. *Journal of Personality and Social Psychology*, 50:1100–12.

————. 1989. Envy and jealousy in close relationships. *Review of Personality and Social Psychology*, 10:221–46.

————. 1991. Provoking Jealousy and envy: Domain relevance and self-esteem threat. *Journal of Social and Clinical Psychology*, 10:395–413.

Salovey, P. and A. J. Rothman. 1991. Envy and jealousy: Self and society. In *The psychology of jealousy and envy*, ed. P. Salovey, 271–286. New York: Guilford Press.

Shakespeare, W. 1974. *Othello*. In *The Riverside Shakespeare*, ed. G. B. Evans, 1198–1248. Boston: Houghton Mifflin Company.

Sharpsteen, D. J. 1991. The organization of jealousy knowledge: Romantic jealousy as a blended emotion. In *The psychology of jealousy and envy*, ed. P. Salovey, 31–51. New York: Guilford Press.

Shaver, P., J. Schwartz, D. Kirson, and C. O'Connor. 1987. Emotion knowledge: Further exploration of a prototype approach. *Journal of Personality and Social Psychology*, 52:1061–86.

Smith, C. A. and P. C. Ellsworth. 1985. Patterns of cognitive appraisal in emotion. *Journal of Personality and Social Psychology*, 48:813–38.

Smith, R. H., S. H. Kim, and W. G. Parrott. 1988. Envy and jealousy: Semantic problems and experiential distinctions. *Personality and Social Psychology Bulletin*, 14:401–09.

Tesser, A. 1981. *Self-evaluation maintenance processes: Implications for relationships and development*. Paper presented at the Nashville Conference on Boundary Areas in Psychology: Developmental and Social, Nashville, Tennessee.

Tesser, A. 1986. Some effects of self-evaluation maintenance on cognition and action. In *Handbook of motivation and cognition: Foundations of social behavior*, ed. R. M. Sorrentino and E. T. Higgins, vol. 1, 435–64. New York: Guilford Press.

Tesser, A. 1988. Toward a self-evaluation maintenance model of social behavior. In *Advances in experimental social psychology*, ed. L. Berkowitz, vol. 21, pp. 181–227. New York: Academic Press.

Tov-Ruach, L. 1980. Jealousy, attention, and loss. In *Explaining emotions*, ed. A. O. Rorty, 465–88. Berkeley: University of California Press.

Trivers, R. L. 1972. Parental investment and sexual selection. In *Sexual selection and the descent of man 1871–1971*, ed. B. Campbell, 136–179. Chicago: Aldine Publishing Company.

White, G. L. 1980. Inducing jealousy: A power perspective. *Personality and Social Psychology Bulletin*, 6:222–27.

————. 1981. A model of romantic jealousy. *Motivation and Emotion*, 5:295–310.

————. 1991. Self, relationship, friends, and family: Some applications of systems theory to romantic jealousy. In *The psychology of jealousy and envy*, ed. P. Salovey, 231–51. New York: Guilford Press.

Wilson, E. 0. 1980. *Sociobiology*. Cambridge, MA: Harvard University Press.

Authors' Notes

We would like to thank our editors, Ann Weber and John Harvey, for their helpful comments on an earlier draft of this chapter. We would also like to thank Amy Vitale and Anne McGuire for the insights and contributions to this chapter. Preparation of this manuscript was facilitated by an NSF Graduate Fellowship to David DeSteno and an NSF Presidential Young Investigator Award to Peter Salovey BNS-9058020. Please address correspondence concerning this manuscript to Peter Salovey, Department of Psychology, Yale University, P.O. Box 208205, New Haven, CT 06520–8205.

C h a p t

Betrayal in Relationships

WARREN H. JONES

University of Tennessee

MARSHA PARSONS BURDETTE

University of Tennessee

Outline

Introduction

A married woman (age 37) realizes that her best female friend is having an affair with her husband when she finds her friend's wedding ring in her own bed. Rather than confronting either her husband or her friend, the woman seeks her revenge by wearing her friend's ring rather than her own until her friend notices that she is doing so, whereupon she hocks the ring to a pawn broker.

Two salesmen who had known each other and had been friends since childhood decided to go into business for themselves by pooling their savings and starting a small partnership. Events unfold as expected until the day on which one of the partners fails to show up for work without notifying the other. Subsequent investigation establishes that the partner in question has disappeared by skipping town after having withdrawn the partnership's working capital from the bank.

A young woman often engages in heated quarrels with her mother, who she believes continues to meddle in her life. On one particular occasion, the young woman attempts to retaliate against her mother by telling her that her other daughter is a lesbian, a secret the woman's sister shared on the condition that their mother never be told.

By her own admission a flirtatious teenage girl seduces her older sister's fiance into a sexual relationship which results in the termination of the engagement. A few years later, the now adult woman divorces her first husband after discovering that he is having an affair with the same older sister. When asked why in her opinion, her sister betrayed her, she replies, "I have no idea."

When asked to report his worst betrayal of a relational partner, one elderly man describes his attempt, years earlier, to break-up the engagement between his daughter and her fiance whom he did not like. As it turned out, he was successful in preventing the marriage, but in a way he had not anticipated. Because of his interference, his daughter killed herself!

There is virtually no aspect of human experience that is not profoundly influenced by the quality and quantity of one's close personal relationships. For this reason, psychologists and other investigators of human behavior have begun to examine in great detail the health and adjustment implications of being with or without close relationships as well as the origins, development, consequences, and dissolution of interpersonal ties. In general, these investigations suggest that at least some minimal number of close relationships and some minimal degree of intimacy are associated with and may be necessary in order to maintain individual health, to ameliorate the effects of stress, and to avoid at least some forms of psychological disturbance (cf. Duck 1988; Sarason and Sarason 1984). Indeed, some theorists have even suggested that the human propensity for close relationships played an important role in human evolution and survival of humans as a species (e.g., Hogan 1982). On the other hand, although this emphasis on the beneficial aspects of relationships is important and appropriate it tends to obscure an equally important but negative truth regarding personal relationships; specifically, the very same people who are one's most important relationship partners (e.g., friends, family members, companions, lovers) also seem to cause most of the pain, disappointment, stress, and grief that one experiences (cf. Fischer 1982; Metts 1989; Miller, Mongeau, and Sleight 1986; Rook 1984; Rook and Pietromonaco 1987). Similarly, research on troubled relationships and relationship problems such as abuse, adultery, and divorce suggests that sometimes intimacy and companionship are pursued at great personal risk and cost (cf. Lawson 1988; Hotaling et al. 1988; Nunnally, Chilman, and Cox 1988). In this chapter we focus on interpersonal betrayal, one of the potentially negative features of close relationships.

In a sense our focus on betrayal is not new among psychologists and social scientists. However, previous work on this topic is scattered across various disciplines, such as sociology, marriage and family studies, psychology, and under various categories, such as research on adultery, lying, detection of deception, relationship violence, and so forth. Research on each of these topics is interesting and useful but also limited because each treats on only one type of potential betrayal, typically in only one type of relationship. By contrast, our approach to betrayal attempts to subsume a broader array of betrayal in all types of close relationships. Also, as social psychologists we have attempted to understand betrayal in its social context rather than exclusively as an individual phenomenon (i.e., something one person does to another). In this regard, we have studied betrayal from the perspective of the victim and that of the instigator. Furthermore, we have examined betrayal in relation to other social psychological phenomena such as attitudes, expectations, and social structure.

We begin with a definition of betrayal as contrasted with interpersonal rejections and an explanation of the relationship characteristics associated with betrayal. Next, we present an overview of our research on betrayal beginning with a brief examination of our methods and their implications. We then present a summary of our research on the Interpersonal Betrayal Scale followed by a brief description of our own research examining betrayal as a feature of the social support network. The central focus of our discussion will be on what we call betrayal narratives or accounts, in which participants describe in their own words their experiences with betrayal. In this section we present data and analyses from one specific set of betrayal accounts obtained in a survey of a large sample of non-college adults. Finally, we conclude this chapter with a summary of the findings that have emerged across the different methods of surveying betrayal with a brief discussion of the implication of each of these findings.

Conceptualizing Betrayal

All betrayals have a common element; specifically, they are violations of the trust or expectations on which a relationship is based. In a sense, to betray means to be a traitor to the relationship. The treachery is not just in the actual harm done to another, but also in the fact that betrayals threaten a major source of one's feelings of identity and well-being. Basically, betrayal is one of the two major psychological dangers of becoming intimately involved with another person. One negative aspect of interpersonal life is the potential for rejection. For example, one person may have strong feelings of friendship, attraction, love, or sexual arousal toward another and those feelings may not be shared. Not every interpersonal approach toward another person is welcomed, and this is part of what makes being with strangers, introductions, first dates, "blind" dates, and certain social occasions so anxiety provoking (Russell, Cutrona, and Jones 1986). Thus, the advantages of taking the initiative in trying to develop a relationship with another person are offset by the risk that such overtures will not be reciprocated. By definition rejection occurs fairly early in the acquaintanceship process. Even so, rejection appears to be associated with a wide array of unpleasant emotional experiences (e.g., anxiety, anger, shame), self-denigrating thought processes, and self-defeating or self-destructive behaviors (e.g., withdrawal, drug and alcohol consumption; Jones 1990).

By contrast, betrayal is a potential consequence of becoming or being involved with another person which can occur at any point in the development of a personal relationship. As such, betrayal has a greater potential for psychological damage than rejection because as relationships progress, typically each participant has an increasing commitment to and dependence on the relationship. This is so not only in the sense that one may, for example, alter one's behavior and lifestyle extensively in order to accommodate the relationship, but also because relationships are important determinants of identity and self-esteem (e.g., Rubin 1985). To have interpersonal overtures rejected is painful but means that a potential relationship will not be realized, that is, something potentially valuable will not be gained; but to be betrayed by one's partner in an important relationship implies that something of realized value has been lost. Specifically, for example, betrayal often means one has lost the time, effort, caring, and trust that have been invested in the relationship. Moreover, to the extent that one's identity and self-esteem derive from or are connected to the relationship in question, betrayal constitutes a serious threat to the self and one's sense of well-being.

Given that it is highly likely any relationship of almost any duration will involve some disappointments and negative experiences the question remains: How is betrayal distinguished from the ordinary ups and downs of an ongoing relationship? We believe that perceptions of betrayal follow when problems arise within any of three characteristic domains of relationship experience: expectations, commitment, and trust.

Relationship Expectations

Perhaps the most basic aspect of any relationship is expectations (Bar-Tal et al. 1991). With the presumed exception of children who are born into their relationships with parents and other family members, an individual generally enters a relationship with an ideal or model regarding what the relationship will and should be like, how he or she wishes to be treated, and so on. Additional expectations develop out of the relationship itself. Thus, we assume that there are two types of relationship expectations. First, there are general or global expectations that one would apply to any relationship or any interaction for that matter. For example, one typically expects the partner in a relationship to be attentive, responsive, supportive, and generally pleasant, and one does not expect to be subjected to undue criticism, abuse, or harm. Such expectations are not necessarily overtly expressed to one's relationship partner. Instead, they may derive from each participant's personality and experience, and specifically, their beliefs about relationships and human nature.

The second type of expectations may develop out of the specific pattern of experiences in the relationship itself. For example, a spouse may return home from work every evening at six o'clock creating the expectation that he or she will always arrive home at that hour. Or again, a wife may expect that her husband will not make fun of her mother—at least in public—because she has told him that it hurts her feelings or because it has caused arguments and difficulties between them in the past.

The violation of any of these expectations by one partner will not necessarily be perceived by the other partner as a betrayal. This is partly because the expectation that one's partner is not perfect and will at least occasionally make a mistake is presumably a common part of a mature concept of relationships. In addition, the partner may not consider the expectation to be a sufficiently important feature of the relationship. On the other hand, the violation of any expectation may result in a feeling of betrayal on the part of the non-offending partner, which may, in turn, result in serious damage to or the termination of the relationship.

Commitment

Commitment is an additional characteristic of on-going relationships (Johnson 1991; Rusbult 1980; Knapp and Taylor, this volume). Specifically, although the degree of commitment need not be the same for both partners and although the sense of commitment even of one partner can and does change over the developmental course of a relationship, in most cases each participant in a personal relationship would prefer that the relationship continue (at least in some form) and each participant assumes at least some degree of responsibility for the partner's welfare. Therefore, behaviors on the part of one partner that may be interpreted as actually or symbolically lessening that partner's degree of commitment toward the relationship will often lead to feelings of having been betrayed on the part of the other partner. Typically, we put effort and energy into the various parts of our lives that we are committed to, and at times a person may change the focus of his or her commitment to include more time for a hobby or in pursuit of a career goal and consequently less time will be spent in their relationship with a significant other (Knapp and Taylor, this volume). For example, wives may feel betrayed by their husbands, not for any specific overt act, but rather because the husbands fail to demonstrate sufficient caring, or because of a perceived unwillingness to work on the relationship. Obviously, a sense of betrayal also describes the thoughts and feelings that arise when one's partner seeks to terminate (e.g., by divorce, breaking-up, abandonment, etc.) any relationship to which one is committed.

Trust

Finally, research suggests one's most important and most satisfying relationships are characterized by trust (Holmes and Rempel 1989). Trust involves the ability to rely on the relationship partner to do what he or she promises and to be faithful to the relationship. Trust also implies having a sense of freedom to say whatever is on one's mind or to be oneself without fear that one's secrets will be betrayed or that one will be rejected. For example, what psychologists call self-disclosure (e.g., Cozby 1973; Derlega 1984; Montgomery, this volume) involves revealing private feelings, thoughts, and attitudes to one's relational partner. Part of what it means to develop a close friendship, or for an initial attraction to grow into a deeper love is that each participant reveals at least a portion of his or her inner self to his or her partner, and that each participant increasingly believes and feels that his or her partner may be trusted to hold in confidence and without rejection or ridicule the various disclosures and intimacies which are exchanged. Thus, when you perceive that your relational partner has failed to be trustworthy you are likely to feel betrayed.

We should emphasize that expectations, commitment, and trust are abstractions used to characterize relationships that may be exemplified by numerous specific behaviors, thoughts, feelings, and tendencies. These concepts are also related to one another and overlap in meaning and importance. For example, if you feel betrayed because of your partner's sexual infidelity, this experience could be construed a violation of the expectation that your partner will be faithful, a weakening of a sexual commitment, as well as a violation of trust that your sexual partner will not seek alternative sexual outlets. For our purposes in this chapter, the important point is that a betrayal may be perceived as resulting from the violation of any of these normative relational processes—expectations, commitment and trust—precisely because they are the necessary components in mutually satisfying, mature personal relationships.

As is the case with any feature of a relationship, betrayal may be either mutually or individually experienced and defined. For example, if a husband is detected cheating on his wife, he may admit to his indiscretion and even agree with his wife's negative characterizations of his behavior. It is even possible that he will seek her forgiveness and understanding as further evidence of their fundamental (albeit subsequent) agreement regarding the meaning and importance of his betrayal. On the other hand, a husband who withholds from his wife information regarding his sexual behavior prior to marriage may feel he has done nothing wrong. Indeed, he may believe that his behavior is in the very best interests of both the relationship and his wife. And yet the wife, upon learning the withheld information, may genuinely feel betrayed depending on various factors such as her moral values, sex role orientation, and relationship expectations. However, even if only one partner concludes that a betrayal has taken place while the other partner disagrees, perceiving that a betrayal has taken place is likely to influence both partners' satisfaction with the relationship.

Research on Betrayal

Methodological Considerations

Before we summarize our research we should discuss the methods we have used to measure and study betrayal, and how these methods might influence our findings. We have defined betrayal in three separate ways. Initially, we collected respondent-generated accounts of betrayal (cf. Baumeister, Stillwell, and Wotman 1990); that is, we simply interviewed or asked people to write essays about their relevant experiences. Our goal was to learn the kinds of events and actions that are seen as acts of betrayal. In addition, these accounts contained information regarding the types of relationships in which betrayal occurs, how people explain their own and others' betrayals, and how betrayal influences their relationships.

Next, we examined betrayal as an individual difference variable by creating a behavioral self-report test called the Interpersonal Betrayal Scale (IBS, Box 12–1). The IBS was designed to measure a general tendency toward betraying one's relational partners in everyday experience. Our purpose was to generate a "tendency to betray score" for each participant. We could then compare these scores to measures of various personality, demographic, and attitudinal characteristics. This allowed us to explore the kinds of people who are more likely to betray their relational partners and the circumstances—such as, occupation, income, or religious practices—of their lives. Also, we used the IBS as a means of exploring the impressions formed of persons who are more or less likely to betray their partners.

Third, we have examined the issue of betrayal in the context of what is called the social network. The social network consists of one's friends, family, co-workers, and neighbors—that is, the people from whom one obtains information, support, companionship, and many other benefits of relationships, typically called social support (Sarason and Sarason 1984; Gottlieb, this volume). We asked participants to identify persons they had betrayed or who had betrayed them from a list of their current social network. We hoped to explore, for example, whether betrayers say they have smaller social networks, and how people feel about persons they have betrayed or who have betrayed them.

All three of these approaches to studying betrayal are examples of self-report methodology, meaning that the data consist of participants' descriptions of their experiences or answers to questions about their betrayal experiences. As with all research methods these techniques have both advantages and disadvantages. The primary disadvantage is that sometimes participants may not be willing or able to honestly describe their behavior, thoughts, or feelings, particularly with respect to an experience which is socially undesirable and devalued. On the other hand, this approach has the advantage of focusing on actual relationships and experiences rather than contrived laboratory situations. It also avoids the ethical problems of attempting to directly manipulate betrayals which might have harmful effects on actual relationships.

Individual Differences in Betrayal

As a first step in developing the IBS, we examined people's open-ended accounts of betrayal (described further in a later section), looking for common examples of betrayal that might be relevant to almost any type of relationship. We limited the betrayal themes in the scale to general events (applicable to most types of relationships) and eliminated those pertinent only to specific relationships (e.g., marital infidelity). Next, we converted the basic idea of each theme to a brief, statement about a broad relationship category (e.g., friendship or family) such as the following: "snubbing a friend when with people I want to impress," and "gossiping about a close friend behind his or her back." We presented these items to a large group of college students and had them rate each item on the frequency with which they had engaged in that behavior. Thus, the lowest level of frequency was described as "I have never done this," and the highest level of frequency was listed as "I have done this many times."

We retained the most reliable items for the final version of the scale. The final version of the IBS contained betrayal items such as "lying to a family member", "complaining to others about your friends or family members", "making a promise to a family member with no intention of keeping it", and "failing to stand-up for a friend when criticized or belittled by others." In addition, our analysis retained a few items about ingratiation and false expressions of acceptance, such as "agreeing with people so that they will accept you," and "pretending to like someone you detest." Ultimately we developed an IBS consisting of the 15 items shown in Box 12–1.

In assessing the validity of the scale, we found that IBS scores were inversely correlated with measures of respondent's moral standards, which would be expected if the IBS is measuring a tendency to betray relationships. Unfortunately, we found that the scale was modestly contaminated with social desirability which means that some people may not fully admit the extent to which they are likely to betray their relationships. On the other hand, we have discovered some evidence that IBS scores reflect a unique personal concept; for example, IBS scores are not simply the same as delinquency or antisocial personality.

Biographical Characteristics

The IBS has been administered to hundreds of respondents along with a variety of questionnaires and psychological instruments in order to determine what variables best characterize people who admit to a tendency to betray others. Samples of elderly people, college students, adult men and women, children and adolescents have been investigated. We have also gathered information about betrayal from a psychiatric population. In these various samples, we have found that IBS scores (meaning greater self-reported betrayal) are higher among people who are younger and less well educated. Divorced persons tend to score higher than married persons. Although some analyses should be viewed with caution because of small and possibly non-representative samples, it is interesting to note that betrayal scores were higher among persons with occupations that bring them into greater contact and perhaps conflict with many other people, such as school administrators, psychotherapists, salespersons, and attorneys. In contrast, occupations with the lowest scores included computer operators, carpenters, and nurses. Among college students, scores were higher for students in the social sciences, education, and the humanities and lower among the physical sciences, engineering, and technical fields of study. IBS scores for white respondents were significantly higher than those for minority respondents, and scores for U.S.

BOX 12–1   Interpersonal Betrayal Scale

Read each item and respond to it using the scale below:

> 1 = I have never done this
> 2 = I have done this once
> 3 = I have done this a few times
> 4 = I have done this several times
> 5 = I have done this many times

_____ 1. Snubbing a friend when with a group you want to impress.
_____ 2. Breaking a promise without a good reason.
_____ 3. Agreeing with people you really disagree with so that they will accept you.
_____ 4. Pretending to like someone you detest.
_____ 5. Gossiping about a friend behind his/her back.
_____ 6. Making a promise to a friend with no intention of keeping it.
_____ 7. Failing to stand up for what you believe in because you want to be accepted by the "in crowd".
_____ 8. Complaining to others about your friends or family members.
_____ 9. Telling others information given to you in confidence.
_____ 10. Lying to a friend.
_____ 11. Making a promise to a family member with no intention of keeping it.
_____ 12. Failing to stand up for a friend when criticized or belittled by others.
_____ 13. Taking family members for granted.
_____ 14. Lying to parents/spouse about activities.
_____ 15. Wishing that something bad would happen to someone you dislike.

Scoring the IBS: Scores range from 15–75 points, sum your answers to arrive at your score.

(In a sample of college students (n = 109), the average score was 35.91. Noncollege adult males (n = 496) scored 35.04 on average, while females (n = 523) had an average score of 34.96. In a sample of elderly people age 65 or older, the average score was 27.57.)

---

college students were higher than those for foreign students studying in the United States. Persons claiming no religious affiliation scored higher on the IBS than persons who subscribe to a particular faith and who actively attended religious services (Jones 1988).

Not surprisingly, we found particularly strong connections between self-reported betrayal and indices of both personal and relational problems. Alcoholics and psychiatric patients scored especially high, as did those who reported having been either the victim or instigator of physical and/or sexual abuse. Other groups with higher than average scores on the IBS included children of divorced parents, adult children of alcoholics, psychiatric patients, adjudicated delinquents, and adolescents permanently expelled from the public schools. On the other hand, analyses of several biographic variables were not related to scores on the IBS; the most notable of these was gender, with males and females reporting comparable levels of engaging in the kinds of everyday betrayals reflected in the items of the IBS (Carver 1990). In summary, IBS scores tend to be higher among respondents who are: young, less well educated, divorced, white, person's who were not religiously affiliated, children of divorce, adult children of alcoholics, and psychiatric patients.

Psychological Characteristics

We have also examined the statistical relationships between IBS scores and measures of various psychological characteristics, in particular, measures of personality and self-description. To summarize, we have found that people who score higher on the IBS are more likely to describe themselves using personality traits such as sullen, vengeful, jealous, and suspicious. In one study, college students completed the IBS and selected self-descriptive adjectives from a list that we provided. Results indicated that the self-portraits of betrayal were more likely to include terms such as contemptuous, blaming, sulky, envious, cynical, doubting, solitary, aloof, morose, regretful, guilty, exploitive, gossipy, pompous, jealous, and suspicious; conversely, these portraits were less likely to include terms like truthful, pleased, relaxed, involved, trusting and courageous (Jones 1988).

These results were consistent with analyses involving comparisons between IBS scores and standardized measures of personality. For example, IBS scores were significantly correlated with measures of self-reported shame, guilt, suspiciousness, resentment, and resistance to authority. Similarly, using a measure of what are called personality disorders, we found that higher scores on the IBS were also associated with higher scores for histrionic persons, those who use emotional display or exaggerated emotions in order to influence other people; and the dependent personality dimension, such as persons who are so desperate in their relationships that they will do anything or tolerate anything to maintain the relationship (Carver 1990). In a separate study, it was found that higher IBS scores were related to lower scores on the following normal personality dimensions: responsibility, well-being, self-control, and tolerance (Montgomery and Brown 1988).

Relationship Characteristics

We have also compared scores from the IBS to measures of relationships. Among a sample of adults these scores were inversely related to satisfaction with one's family of origin and, for men only, marital commitment (Carver and Jones 1992; Monroe 1990). Also, married betrayers reported experiencing more marital problems; in particular, loss of interest in the marriage, extramarital affairs, dissatisfying sexual relations, lying, negative emotions, and being impatient. They were more likely to blame their spouses for these and other problems rather than themselves or the couple jointly. By contrast, self-reported betrayal was unrelated to marital satisfaction for either men or women (Monroe 1990).

For a subset of one sample, data were also available from respondents' spouses. We analyzed these data by first comparing husband's betrayal scores with wives' marital satisfaction, commitment and so on, and then the comparable analyses between husband's marital ratings and wives' betrayal scores. Neither marital satisfaction nor commitment were significantly related to the spouses' betrayal scores for either husbands or wives. However, wives' betrayal scores were positively correlated with the husbands' view of total marital problems. Furthermore, wives' IBS scores were correlated with husbands' attributions of blame to the spouse (rather than to oneself). On the other hand, wives' ratings of various marital problems were less extensively related to the betrayal scores of husbands. Most remarkably, however, wives' attributions of blame were related to husbands' betrayal scores such that the higher the husband's level of self-reported betrayal, the more the wife tended to blame herself for the problem in question! Finally, the intracouple correlation for betrayal was not significant, thus, betrayers apparently do not necessarily marry other betrayers. In short, although self-reported betrayal defined by scores on the IBS does not appear to be a factor in choosing a husband or wife, husbands whose wives were self-confessed betrayers reported more problems in their marriage and blamed their wives for those problems. By contrast, wives whose husbands were betrayers tended to blame themselves for their extensive marital problems.

Social Network Analyses

As introduced above, one approach we took examined betrayal from the perspective of the social support network. Specifically, we used an instrument called the Social Network List (cf. Jones and Moore 1987), for which respondents were asked to identify persons who are important to them, who provide social support, and with whom they have relatively frequent contact. Respondents were then asked to complete a series of questions regarding each person on the list. From these responses we were able to calculate network characteristics such as size, composition and quality. Thus, we asked each respondent to identify the age, gender, type of relationship, and length of acquaintance of each member of his or her social network. Respondents also rated how much they could confide in, were satisfied with, and felt equally important to each person listed. Finally we focused this general procedure by having respondents also rate how much they had betrayed and been betrayed by each network member.

In one study of non-college adults we found that almost half (45.2 percent) of the respondents indicated that they had betrayed at least one member of their current social network and a somewhat higher percentage (52.4 percent) indicated that they had been betrayed by at least one network member. A few persons indicated that they had betrayed or been betrayed by every member of the network. By contrast, according to our respondents, the average proportion of the social network who had betrayed the respondent was 18.8 percent and the average proportion of network members who had been betrayed by the respondent was 20.3 percent. Unfortunately, with this specific methodology it is not possible to determine whether or not each betrayal referred to was serious or trivial;, instead, this approach only indicates whether the respondent believes he or she has betrayed or been betrayed by a particular relational partner. There was a tendency for network members identified as targets of betrayal to be cited as instigators as well. In addition, and consistent with our earlier results, the difference between men and women in terms of the proportion of relationships involving betrayal was not significant.

There were other analyses from this study as well, such as correlations between the indices of betrayal (which also included the IBS) and overall network characteristics. We found that IBS scores were related to the proportion of persons in the network betrayed by the respondent, supporting the validity of the IBS, and also the proportion the respondent indicated had betrayed him or her. Also, with the exception of gender and network size, betrayal—viewed either from the perspective of IBS scores or the network definition—was unrelated to network composition, that is, the relative proportions of friends, family and so-on, who comprise the network.

Our analyses also revealed an interesting gender difference. For men, ratings of various interpersonal dimensions (e.g., satisfied with, jealous of, can depend on, etc.) were correlated with both measures of having betrayed and having been betrayed in a similar manner. For example, ratings of being satisfied with a particular person were inversely correlated both with the extent of having betrayed that person and with the extent of having been betrayed by that person. By contrast, for women ratings were generally related only to indications of having been betrayed by the person in question, whereas the comparisons between betraying and the ratings were generally unreliable. In other words, men indicated that they disliked both persons who had betrayed them (as would be expected) as well as persons they had betrayed. Women, on the other hand, indicated that they did not like persons who had betrayed them, but there were no significant correlations between having betrayed a person and ratings of that person.

Accounts of Betrayal

Another approach to defining betrayal involved participant generated descriptions. We asked several samples of respondents to answer questions (in writing or sometimes interviews) about betrayal from each of two perspectives: the most significant experience in which each had betrayed someone else; and the most significant incident in which each had been the victim of betrayal. We asked them to provide certain details of each incident, such as the relationship to the other person, when the betrayal occurred, whether the victim was aware of the betrayal, the respondent's motives for betraying or guess about why he or she was betrayed, and any effect on the relationship. We have presented these questions to participants of various backgrounds including, for example, college students, non-college adults, elderly people, normal children and adolescents, juvenile delinquents, and psychiatric patients (Carver 1990; Carver and Jones 1992; Cohn,

Miller, and Jones 1990; Hansson, Jones, and Fletcher 1990; Hogan and Jones, in press; Jones 1988; Jones, Cohn, and Miller 1991; Jones, Sanchez, and Merrell 1989; Monroe 1990). For purpose of illustration, data from one sample of over 200 adults will be used.

Type of Betrayal

One of the first questions we attempted to answer was what are the common acts of betrayal. In other words, among the many occurrences which take place in the context of relationships everyday, which will be seen as instances of betrayal in the lives of most people? Table 12–1 presents a summary of the types of betrayal contained in the responses of this sample of adults. For both men and women and consistent in all subsequent tables, the columns labeled "OF" refer to narratives in which the respondent was describing having betrayed (been the betrayer of) an important relationship partner, whereas the columns headed with "BY" refer to the descriptions of the instances in which they had been betrayed by the partner.

As suggested in Table 12–1, although a variety of types of betrayals were described by participants, as expected, the majority concerned violations of trust, commitment, and generalized relationship expectations. For example, among adult men, respondents reported having betrayed or having been betrayed by an extramarital sexual affair more commonly than any other type of betrayal, followed by betrayals involving telling lies, jilting a girlfriend, revealing secrets and confidences, two-timing girlfriends, and lack of emotional support. For women, extramarital affairs and lies were more-or-less equally common, followed by betrayals of confidence. Two-timing boyfriends, excessive criticism, ignoring and avoiding relationship partners, lack of emotional support and jilting boyfriends were comparable in frequency.

In similar studies among college students, two-timing one's steady dating partner and rejection or jilting replaced extramarital affairs as the most common way in which participants indicated they had betrayed or been betrayed in an

TABLE 12–1 Percent Types of Betrayal

Type	Men		Women	
	OF	BY	OF	BY
Extramarital Affair	38.6	36.2	21.2	16.4
Lies	20.4	15.2	18.2	20.6
Betrayed Confidence	9.1	6.2	21.2	5.5
Two-timing	9.1	4.2	7.6	5.5
Jilting	4.5	14.6	3.0	4.1
Lack of Support	2.3	6.2	3.0	4.1
Ignoring/Avoiding	0.0	4.2	0.0	8.2
Criticism	0.0	0.0	4.5	4.1
Gossip	2.3	0.0	4.5	0.0
Miscellaneous	13.7	13.2	16.8	31.5

important relationship partner (Jones 1988). Otherwise, the types of betrayal were very similar for both college students and adults. Among the elderly, similar types of betrayal were cited, with the difference being that most of the events described had taken place, on average, thirty or forty years earlier, when the respondents were young adults (Hansson, Jones, and Fletcher 1990). As might be expected, adjudicated delinquents and psychiatric patients tended to describe either severe forms of betrayal such as being physically abused or abandoned by one's parents, or they claimed that they had never betrayed or been betrayed in a close relationship because they had never been in a close relationship (Carver 1990; Jones, Cohn, and Miller 1991)!

Type of Relationship

The types of relationships involved in betrayal, not surprisingly, tended to be the most important relationships in the lives of our respondents. Among adults (see Table 12–2), for example, spouses were most frequently cited as both the victims and perpetrators of betrayal, although betrayals of and by same-sex friends, work relationships, parents, siblings, and one's own children were also mentioned with some frequency. Table 12–2 suggests some interesting differences in the pattern of betrayal. For example, note that men were almost four times more likely to say that they had betrayed their wives, than their wives had betrayed them, whereas for women the reported rates of betraying and having been betrayed by the spouse were roughly the same. This finding is consistent with research on specific types of betrayal such as adultery (e.g. Lawson 1988). Also note that betrayals of and by same-sex friends were considerably more common among women than men, and men were more likely to cite betrayals involving work relationships than were women. These patterns are likely due, in part, to gender differences in both employment rates as well as what men vs. women are likely to consider as important dimensions of self-definition.

TABLE 12–2 Percent Types of Relationships Involved in Betrayals

| | Men | | Women | |
Type	OF	BY	OF	BY
Spouse	45.0	14.3	31.7	28.1
Same-sex friend	7.5	9.7	25.0	26.5
Boy/girlfriend	20.0	12.7	8.4	15.6
Co-worker	10.0	18.8	0.0	4.7
Mother	5.0	9.7	5.0	3.2
Father	4.0	10.2	0.0	1.6
Opposite-sex friend	2.5	5.1	5.0	3.1
Daughter	2.5	3.5	1.7	4.7
Boss	0.0	6.6	1.7	4.7
Sister	0.0	0.0	6.7	1.6
Brother	1.5	1.5	1.7	3.1
Son	1.5	2.0	1.7	0.0
Others	2.5	3.9	9.4	3.1

Results for the elderly were again similar to those for younger adults (Hansson, Jones, and Fletcher 1990). College students were most likely to describe betrayals involving their romantic relationships and their college friends, followed by betrayals involving their parents (Jones 1988), whereas children and adolescents most often cited parents and siblings (Cohn, Miller, and Jones 1990). Delinquents and psychiatric patients most often cited betrayals involving their parents (Carver 1990; Jones, Cohn, and Miller 1991).

Betrayal and Gender

Another issue examined was whether males or females are more likely to betray their relational partners. As may be seen in Table 12–3, using the gender of the other in these open-ended accounts as the criterion, both men and women seem to agree that men are more likely to be the instigators in these most significant incidents of betrayal (Jones 1988). However, we are cautious about generalizing from this particular result for two reasons. First, among children and adolescents, the mother was cited as the most common victim and instigator of betrayals. In addition, as will be recalled, when methods for operationalizing betrayal other than the open-ended accounts were explored such as the IBS, we failed to find gender differences in the rate of betrayal. Thus the gender difference may have less to do with gender than with social status, power, or other factors.

Motives for Betrayal

We have examined the motives that respondents attribute both to themselves for their betrayals and to others when they have been the victims of betrayal (Jones, Sanchez, and Merrell 1989). Here we have found that the motives presumed to underlie betrayals depend largely on one's perspective; specifically, they depend on whether one is describing an experience of being the instigator or the victim of a betrayal. For example, in the study examining the alleged motives for betrayals among the adult sample we have been describing, we classified each response on the basis of three attributional categories (similar to Weiner 1986): internal vs. external motives (e.g., personality vs. peer pressure); stable vs. unstable causes (e.g., enduring personal characteristics vs. transitory mood states); and intentional vs. unintentional motives.

As indicated in Table 12–4, when describing the betrayal of another, most respondents attributed their own motives to intentional but unstable causes, with about two-thirds admitting that the locus of causality was within themselves. Many of their explanations for betraying another concerned intentional acts resulting from temporary emotions such as anger. By contrast, most respondents

TABLE 12–3   Percent Gender of and by Betrayers

Type	Men		Women	
	OF	BY	OF	BY
Males	24.4	51.2	55.8	55.5
Females	75.6	48.8	44.2	44.5

TABLE 12–4   Percent Attributional Categories of Betrayal Accounts

Category	Men		Women	
	OF	BY	OF	BY
Internal Locus	68.1	75.5	65.5	86.0
Stable Causes	8.4	79.1	14.6	68.8
Intentionality	85.8	97.8	74.2	98.8

explained those instances in which they had been betrayed by others in terms of the betrayers' internal, stable, and intentional motives. Here participants were more likely to talk about a person's mean streak, or dispositional weaknesses. Thus, our respondents tended to see their own betrayals as acts they intentionally engaged in because they were angry, or sometimes (about one-third of the time) due to an external cause. Perhaps such explanations reduce one's sense of moral responsibility for undesirable behaviors. When explaining their victimization by others, however, respondents were more likely to assume that the person who had betrayed them did so intentionally and for persistent (i.e, stable) and personal (i.e., internal) reasons, suggesting that others are seen as morally culpable for their betrayals.

One interesting result not shown in the table which we noted was that even when the two accounts of betrayal involved the same person and the same type of interpersonal transgression, there remains a tendency for respondents to explain away their own betrayals but at the same time to hold their partners morally responsible for their betrayals. For example, several of the adults we have surveyed indicated that their most significant betrayal of a relationship was when they had an extramarital affair and that the most significant instance in which they were betrayed was when their spouse had an extramarital affair. Do such similar or identical patterns of betrayal lead respondents to be more insightful and understanding about the philandering behavior of their marital partners? Apparently not. In every such instance we have examined thus far, the respondent has explained his or her own violations by citing extenuating circumstances (e.g., "I was intoxicated at the time"; "I was under a lot of pressure at work"; "My wife never understood or really cared about me or how I felt"), while, at the same time, explaining the betrayal by the spouse in less than flattering terms (e.g., "He had the affair because he's a horny, demented pervert!").

Change in the Relationship

We have also classified into three categories the respondents' descriptions of how the betrayal had changed the relationship, if at all:

1. *worse:* the relationship was described as having ended (e.g., getting a divorce, "breaking-up", never speaking again, etc.), or the relationship continued but was less satisfying because of lingering doubts, unpleasant emotions, and suspicion;
2. *same:* the relationship was described as initially harmed by the betrayal, after which it returned to what it had been before, or the relationship was described as

not changing at all as a function of the betrayal as was common for betrayals in which one's relational partner remains unaware of the betrayal;

   3. *better:* respondents who actually claimed that the relationship had somehow improved because of the betrayal.

As indicated in Table 12–5, when describing their own betrayals of their relational partners, about half of the men and 40 percent of the women indicated that the betrayal had ended or at least made the relationship worse than before. For about another 40 percent of the respondents, the relationship was described as remaining the same, whereas in the remaining 20 percent or so it was described as improving. By contrast, in the descriptions of having been betrayed by another person, over 90 percent of the respondents indicated that the relationship was worse than before with only a handful of participants claiming that it had remained the same or improved. In other words, according to our participants, what happened to the relationship after the betrayal incident seemed to depend largely on whether one was the victim or the perpetrator of the betrayal, and this pattern of findings has remained roughly the same across samples differing in age and other characteristics (Hansson, Jones, and Fletcher 1990; Jones 1988; Jones, Cohn, and Miller 1991).

   Finally, we observed that participants from all samples tended to refer to relatively recent events when describing their own betrayals of others, whereas the incidents of having been betrayed could vary in time from recent occurrences to events that took place years ago. This is related to another finding from this series of studies. We asked a small group of raters to judge the seriousness (in terms of potential harm to the relationship) of a sample of the descriptions, and discovered that betrayals of others were rated as less serious violations of relational expectations than incidents involving having been betrayed. Whether this is due to a reluctance to admit to one's own negative behavior or some other factor cannot be determined on the basis on this methodology.

Conclusion and Summary

Several basic findings have emerged from our studies of betrayal. First, these studies suggest that betrayal is a relatively common feature of the interpersonal lives of our respondents. In our social network surveys, for example, par-

TABLE 12–5 Percent Change in the Relationship Following Betrayal

	Men		Women	
Type	OF	BY	OF	BY
Worse	51.4	93.0	38.2	93.7
Same	39.7	4.6	40.0	5.8
Better	18.9	2.3	21.8	1.5

ticipants indicated that just under 50 percent of the members of their social networks had betrayed them in some way and that they had betrayed a somewhat lower proportion of their social network members. For the narrative accounts over 90 percent of all the participants we sampled described both a betrayal by another person and a betrayal of another person. We might generalize, therefore, that half of one's most important current relationships involve betrayal, while virtually everyone has betrayed and been betrayed at some point in life, and thus it is a relatively common problem which may arise in a close personal relationship.

Second, many of the consequences of betrayal appear to depend on one's perspective; that is, whether one betrays or has been betrayed. To some extent this is hardly surprising as a general tendency toward self-protective attributional processes frequently has been noted in the literature (e.g., Arkin, Appelman, and Burger 1980). What is less obvious, however, is the extent to which one's perspective appears to determine not only judgments regarding the stability of motives but also the likelihood that the relationship will continue. Moreover, it is evident from these studies that complementarity of betrayals within or across relationships does not encourage either insight or forgiveness. In short, participants appear to be far more willing to excuse their own transgressions against others than similar offenses by others against them. Similarly, the belief that a betrayal has taken place appears to be a subjective and perhaps even an idiosyncratic judgment. As a consequence, the phenomenon of betrayal appears to be embedded in the perceptions, beliefs, and expectations of the observer or the unique interpersonal perspective of the person who thinks such an act has occurred.

Third, although we found contradictory evidence regarding whether men or women are more likely to betray, there were consistent gender differences in the patterns of betrayal. For example, women are more likely to betray or be betrayed by their same-sex friends than are men, whereas men are more likely to betray their wives and sweethearts and to experience betrayal in the workplace. Similarly, men indicated more frequently that they had betrayed by being sexually or romantically unfaithful, whereas women were more likely to tell secrets or betray a confidence. The reasons for these differences are not clear as yet, however. They may derive from differences in the socialization of males and females, or perhaps from some more fundamental gender difference in relating to others (e.g., Maccoby 1990).

Fourth, betrayal of course occurs primarily among one's closest relationships, and the most devastating betrayals occur among the most important and most intimate relationships. Even so, betrayal does not always end the relationship entirely. For example, in what might be called nonvoluntary relationships (e.g., parent-child relationships, work relationships) a relationship with the betrayer may continue for reasons beyond the relationship itself such as needing to keep one's job. By contrast, in relationships over which one has a greater degree of choice (e.g., romantic relationships or friendships), betrayals may more frequently result in termination. Even when the relationship continues, however, as would be expected, betrayals do appear to make relationships less satisfying and less intimate.

Fifth, there are consistent personality correlates of betrayal. Likely betrayers appear to be more jealous, suspicious, envious, and resentful of others and to have more personal problems. From these analyses it is not possible to determine whether such personality characteristics lead to a greater likelihood of betraying, or if the act of betrayal leads to the development of a suspicious, resentful, and troubled personality. There is some evidence that betrayal is inversely correlated with age, education, and religious commitment. It is also interesting to note that betrayal appears to be more common among people who hold occupations involving greater contact and involvement with others.

Work on betrayal has only just begun. Although additional research is needed, our studies demonstrate the incidence and importance of betrayal in most people's interpersonal lives, and they suggest clues regarding the underlying motives, causes, and consequences of betrayal. One interesting issue for future research concerns whether betrayal is inevitable in all close relationships because of the role of subjectivity and personal perspective. Close relationships, even the most satisfying ones, are typified by ups and downs, periods of contentment and satisfaction interspersed with disappointments and conflict. This is so because most relationships unfold over relatively long periods of time during which many adjustments must be made and because it would seem psychologically impossible to remain in a constant state of passion or even liking. Thus, it is likely that virtually every relationship partner will sooner or later do or say something untoward that may be perceived by his or her partner as a betrayal. Ultimately, the experience of betrayal may have less to do with how you are treated by your partner than with your own characteristics—your beliefs, expectations, degree of trust and commitment, and personality.

References

Arkin, R. M., A. J. Appelman, and J. M. Burger. 1980. Social anxiety, self-presentation, and the self-serving bias in causal attribution. *Journal of Personality and Social Psychology*, 38:23–35.

Bar-Tal, D., Y. Bar-Tal, N. Geva, and K. Yarkin-Levin. 1991. Planning and performing interpersonal interaction: A cognitive-motivational approach. In *Advances in personal relationships*, ed. W. H. Jones, and D. Perlman, vol. 2. London: Jessica Kingsley.

Baumeister, R. F., A. Stillwell, and S. R. Wotman. 1990. Victim and perpetrator accounts of interpersonal conflict: Autobiographical narratives about anger. *Journal of Personality and Social Psychology*, 59: 994–1005.

Carver, M. D. 1990. *Personality disorder dimensions and relational functioning.* Unpublished dissertation, University of Tulsa, Tulsa, OK.

Carver, M. D., and W. H. Jones. 1992. The Family Satisfaction Scale. *Journal of Social Behavior and Personality*, 20: 71–84.

Cohn, M. G., C. E. Miller, and W. H. Jones. 1990. Betrayal among delinquent and nondelinquent males. Paper presented at the meeting of the Southwestern Psychological Association, Dallas.

Cozby, P. C. 1973. Self-disclosure: A literature review. *Psychological Bulletin*, 79: 73–91.

Derlega, V. J. 1984. Self-disclosure and intimate relationships. In *Communication, intimacy, and close relationships*, ed. V. J. Derlega, 1–8. New York: Academic Press.

Duck, S. ed. 1988. *Handbook of personal relationships.* New York: Wiley.

Fischer, C. S. 1982. *To dwell among friends*. Chicago: University of Chicago Press.

Hansson, R. O., W. H. Jones, and W. L. Fletcher. 1990. Troubled relationships in later life: Implications for support. *Journal of Social and Personal Relationships*, 7: 451–63.

Hogan, R. 1982. A socioanalytic theory of personality. In *Nebraska symposium on motivation: Personality—Current theory and research*, ed. M. M. Page, 55–90. Lincoln: University of Nebraska Press.

Hogan, R., and W. H. Jones. In press. Trust and betrayal: The psychology of trust violation. In *Espionage: Studies in trust and betrayal*, ed. T. R. Sarbin, R. M. Carney, and C. Eoyang. New York: Pergamon.

Holmes, J. G., and J. K. Rempel. 1989. Trust in close relationships. In *Review of personality and social psychology*, ed. C. Hendrick, vol. 10, 187–220. Newbury Park, CA: Sage.

Hotaling, G. T., D. Finkelhor, J. T. Kirkpatrick, and M. A. Straus. eds. 1988. *Family abuse and its consequences: New directions in research*. Newbury Park, CA: Sage.

Johnson, M. P. 1991. Commitment to personal relationships. In *Advances in personal relationships*, ed. W. H. Jones and D. Perlman, vol 3. London: Jessica Kingsley.

Jones, W. H. 1988. Psychological and interpersonal issues in betrayal and treachery. Paper presented at the Fourth International Conference on Personal Relationships, Vancouver, British Columbia, Canada.

———. 1990. Loneliness and social exclusion. *Journal of Social and Clinical Psychology*, 9: 214–20.

Jones, W. H., M. G. Cohn, and C. E. Miller. 1991. Betrayal among children and adults. In *Children's interpersonal trust: Sensitivity to lying, deception, and promise violations*, ed. K. J. Rotenberg, 118–34. New York: Springer-Verlag.

Jones, W. H., and T. L. Moore. 1987. Loneliness and social support. *Journal of Social Behavior and Personality*, 2: 145–56.

Jones, W. H., D. Sanchez, and J. Merrell. 1989. Explanations of betrayal accounts. Paper presented at the meeting of the Southwestern Psychological Association, Houston, TX.

Lawson, A. 1988. *Adultery*. New York: Basic Books.

Maccoby, E. E. 1990. Gender and relationships: A developmental account. *American Psychologist*, 45: 513–20.

Metts, S. 1989. An exploratory investigation of deception in close relationships. *Journal of Social and Personal Relationships*, 6: 159–79.

Miller, G. R., P. A. Mongeau, and C. Sleight. 1986. Fudging with friends and lying to lovers: Deceptive communication in personal relationships. *Journal of Social and Personal Relationships*, 3: 495–512.

Monroe, P. 1990. *A study of marital problems, marital satisfaction, and commitment*. Unpublished doctoral dissertation, University of Tulsa.

Montgomery, R. L., and E. O. Brown. 1988. Betrayal, treachery, the CPI, and the Jenkins Activity Survey. Paper presented at the Fourth International Conference on Personal Relationships. Vancouver, British Columbia, Canada.

Nunnally, E. W., C. S. Chilman, and F. M. Cox. 1988. *Troubled relationships*. Newbury Park, CA: Sage.

Rook, K. S. 1984. The negative side of social interaction: Impact on psychological well-being. *Journal of Personality and Social Psychology*, 46: 1097–1108.

Rook, K. S., and P. Pietromonaco. 1987. Close relationships: Ties that heal or ties that bind? In *Advances in personal relationships*, ed. W. H. Jones and D. Perlman, vol. 1. Greenwich, CT: JAI Press.

Rubin, L. B. 1985. *Just friends: The role of friendship in our lives*. New York: Harper and Row.

Rusbult, C. E. 1980. Commitment and satisfaction in romantic associations: A test of the investment model. *Journal of Experimental Social Psychology*, 16: 172–86.

Russell, D., C. E. Cutrona, and W. H. Jones. 1986. A trait-situational analysis of shyness. In *Shyness: Perspectives on research and treatment*, ed. W. H. Jones, J. M. Cheek, and S. R. Briggs, 239–52). New York: Plenum.

Sarason, I. G., and B. R. Sarason. eds. 1984. *Social support: Theory, research and applications*. Dordrecht, Netherlands; Martinus Nijhof.

Weiner, B. 1986. *An attribution theory of motivation and emotion*. New York: Springer-Verlag.

Chapter 13

Physical Abuse in Close Relationships: Myths and Realities

LINDA L. MARSHALL
University of North Texas

STEPHANIE A. VITANZA*
University of North Texas

Outline

Introduction
Women's Voices
Overview of Chapter
What is Physical Abuse and How is it Measured?

Approaches to Physical Violence

Myths About Physical Violence
Myth 1: Violence in Close Relationships Never Happens to People Like Me
Myth 2: People Never Tell Anyone About Violence in their Relationships
Myth 3: Only Males, Usually Macho Men, Inflict Violence on their Partner
Myth 4: Boys Learn to be Aggressors and Girls Learn to be Victims from
    Observing their Parents
Myth 5: Females Stay in Relationships Where They Are Beaten Repeatedly
    Because They Are Passive

*The personal examples cited in this chapter were provided by participants in a study of psychological abuse funded by the National Institute of Mental Health, Grant Number 1 R29 MH44217, awarded to the first author. References to that study were also made in other sections.

> *Myth 6: In Couples, There Is a Cycle of Violence*
> *Myth 7: Battered Women Are Masochistic, and Batterers Are Mentally Ill*
> *Myth 8: Violence Involves the Use of Alcohol*

Conclusion and Summary

Introduction

Women's Voices

What do these different women have in common?

> *"I've had to call the police sometimes because I was scared. He screams so much, says such nasty things and calls me horrible names."*
>
> *"He just sulks or pouts until I ask him what's wrong. Then it starts."*
>
> *"Sometimes he just walks in the door all tense and quiet. Then I try to walk on eggshells and make it better for him. Sometimes it works and sometimes it doesn't."*
>
> *"I asked him if he'd forgotten we were supposed to get together the night before. I wasn't mad or anything and I tried not to show I was hurt that he must have forgotten about me."*
>
> *"Sometimes he tries to wake me up by putting a pillow over my face and leaning on it. When I wake up scared, he starts tickling me and telling me the day is wasting. He acts like he was teasing, but he's not."*
>
> *"Every time I had to study for a test, he'd try to get me to pay attention to him and not my studies. I tried to understand for a long time, but one time I just got mad and yelled that I had a test so would he please leave and let me study."*
>
> *"We'd been out having a good time. We laughed all the way home. I went into the kitchen to get us another beer. He followed me and when I turned around he just hit me. To this day I never found out why."*
>
> *"Two nights after we got married I woke up with his hands were around my throat. He was choking me. He said it was because he wanted to wake me up."*

Overview of Chapter

These examples were drawn from a study we recently completed with women in stressful relationships. Most of these women had received violence from their partner in the past and, except for the first example, violence accompanied these incidents. The partner of the woman who called the police never physically abused her or threatened her directly with physical violence, but had hit walls and broken objects. Although the other women have sustained acts of violence and been physically hurt, only one ever called the police.

The women who shared their stories with us were different from each other in many ways, yet they had all been abused by their partner. In the final sample, 11 percent of the women were ethnic minorities, almost 70 percent had attended or completed college, and 38 percent had never worked outside the home. Of those who reported their family income, the range was from nothing to $8,200 per month (median = $2,300 per month). Although we had known that abuse can occur in any close relationship, we were surprised that so many women with so many personal resources (e.g., education, income) were seriously abused.

Physical abuse in close relationships has become of increasing interest to both social scientists and the general public since the early 1980s. With this increased awareness, research has addressed many factors which may be related to physical abuse. In this chapter we describe some of what is known. We present evidence that contradicts or qualifies myths about physical abuse. Since this literature is of an interdisciplinary nature, contributed by individuals in a variety of fields, different theoretical approaches are represented which increases understanding of abusive relationships.

Psychological or emotional abuse may be more harmful than physical violence, but very little is known about it. Although a great many factors make trying to understand physical abuse complex, psychological abuse is more subtle and more complex (Marshall, in press). Research on this type of abuse is only beginning, but other bodies of knowledge may be relevant (e.g., the chapters on jealousy and betrayal). The major approaches focus on psychological abuse as dominance (Murphy and Cascardi 1993; Tolman 1989), as verbal aggression (Mason and Blankenship 1987) and as brainwashing, in which subtle influence tactics undermine a partner's healthy sense of self (Marshall, in press; Vitanza, Walker and Marshall 1991). It is clear from the references in parentheses that these approaches are too new to have generated much knowledge. Therefore, this chapter is restricted to physical abuse.

Logically, a discussion of physical abuse should include sexual aggression in close relationships. This would include date rape, incest, and marital rape. For example, a growing body of research on sexual aggression identifies relevant variables which could be examined in close relationships (e.g., Koss et al. 1985; Malamuth 1989; Muehlenhard and Linton 1987). We also know that viewing films which portray sexually violent scenes increases aggression and negative attitudes toward women (Linz, Donnerstein, and Penrod, 1988). Unfortunately, investigators who examine sexual aggression seldom also assess physical violence, and researchers who study violence rarely examine sexual aggression. Further, although we know that rape in marriage is harmful to women, few studies of violence include forced sexual activity in close relationships (Finkelhor and Yllo 1985; Russell 1982).

This chapter focuses on the dominant culture in the research. Most studies have been conducted with heterosexual Anglo-Americans. Research has almost always asked about or assumed a partner of the other sex. When people from minority groups have been included in samples, researchers have seldom reported similarities and differences between the groups.

One problem with research is the tendency to report and pay attention to statistically significant results. On the one hand, it is necessary to learn how groups differ from each other, for example, how students who have experienced violence differ from those who have not. On the other hand, this allows us to overlook similarities and to place more importance on differences than is perhaps warranted. Results are then in danger of being over-generalized, applied to people who differ from the sample studied. Also, a topic such as abuse has social implications. Laypeople hear about results and naturally focus on the differences, sometimes accepting findings without proper qualification of the results. Researchers and laypeople alike are in danger of focusing on certain factors, sometimes to the point of ignoring similarities or missing the obvious. For example, much of the research on violence has in some way addressed the question "Why do women stay with a man who beats them up?". This focus encourages certain kinds of research questions and discourages others which limits the answers which will be found. Overturning the question and instead asking "Why do women leave?" could lead to very different methods and results. For these reasons, this chapter uses the style of stating myths about physical abuse, then presenting research which qualifies these myths.

What is Physical Abuse and How is it Measured?

If you asked everyone you saw in the next day whether she or he had been in a physically abusive relationship, it is unlikely that anyone would say yes, although several may have experienced physical abuse. One reason is because the term abuse has strong negative connotations so people hesitate to say they had committed an abusive act or that someone had abused them. Abuse happens to the other person. I may hit someone under several specific conditions, but I would never abuse another person. The term is also imprecise and subjective. Researchers tend to use the term violence or aggression. We prefer the term violence because it does not imply anything about the purpose for which an act is performed, whereas aggression may imply intent to harm. Specific behaviors are used so researchers do not have to rely on personal opinions of what constitutes abuse or why someone exhibited the behavior.

For similar reasons, we cannot use physical injury to describe physical abuse. One woman we interviewed said "No, I've never been injured. I've never had to go to the hospital or anything like that." Yet, she talked about bruises and headaches which resulted from violence. The term injury automatically meant a need for emergency treatment. In contrast, another woman who had experienced about the same amount of violence talked about how serious her injuries were, even though her partner seldom gave her bruises. These anecdotes underscore the importance of asking very precise questions to learn about violence in close relationships. Although a term like injury would seem to be objective so that everyone could easily agree with what it meant, there is room for too many different interpretations. Therefore, researchers take care to describe what they mean as precisely as possible.

Unlike O'Leary (1988) and others who argue that violence is always preceded by some level of disagreement, we believe that violence is not always a result of an argument or conflict between the individuals. In the examples at the beginning of this chapter, some women were describing their fights or conflicts, but other women were talking about other factors in their relationship. For example, the woman trying to study was talking about her independence, and the woman in the laughing incident was describing a time her partner had taken her out to show he loved and cared about her.

The most commonly used measure of violence is the Conflict Tactics Scale (CTS; Straus 1979). Although subscales can be made for reasoning and verbal aggression, the violence subscale may be used alone. Three items (throw something; push, grab or shove; and slap) are often called minor or ordinary violence. Five items constitute the severe violence subscale (kick, bite or hit with a fist; hit or tried to hit with something; beat up; threatened with a gun or knife; and used a gun or knife), and recently choked was added (Straus and Gelles 1986). However, there are many problems with this measure. The CTS is usually introduced as describing behaviors which might happen during a conflict, argument or disagreement. Researchers decided which acts are minor or severe, not the people who inflicted or sustained the behaviors; threats of violence are considered to have the same impact as acts of violence; acts with differing potential for harm are included within one item. With several acts in one item, it is impossible to determine which act was actually performed; and although men are usually larger and stronger than women, the CTS has an implied assumption that acts would have the same effect regardless of whether performed by a man or woman. A primary strength of the CTS is its ability to determine whether or not violence has occurred in a relationship. However, to address more sophisticated issues, more sensitive multidimensional scales are needed like the Severity of Violence Scales (Marshall 1992a; 1992b). Some personal reflections on the development of these scales appear in Box 13-1.

On Marshall's scales, forty-six behaviors represent symbolic violence (e.g., hitting or kicking a wall, door or furniture), threats of violence (e.g., threaten to kill), acts of violence (e.g., twisted your arm) and sexual aggression (e.g., using physical force to have sex). To develop the scales, men rated the severity of the behaviors thinking about a woman inflicting each act on a man. Women made the same ratings, but considered a man inflicting each act on a woman. The seriousness of the acts for both males and females was built into the scales, because people could take the usual size and strength difference into account in making their ratings. Factor analysis was performed separately for men's and women's responses. These statistical procedures showed the underlying structure by identifying sets formed by various items in which items are more closely related to each other than to other sets. For females, male-to-female acts are represented by nine severity dimensions, but for males, female-to-male acts are represented by eight dimensions. On the Severity of Violence Against Women Scales (SVAWS), total threats of violence are comprised of four dimensions; symbolic violence and threats of mild, moderate and serious violence. Actual violence is represented by four dimensions; acts which are mild, minor, moderate and serious in their severity. Sexual aggression forms a different dimension. On the Severity of Violence Against Men Scales (SVAMS), the items are ordered differently, and symbolic

BOX 13–1   Scale Development

How I happened to develop the SVAWS and SVAMS illustrates how sometimes an advance is made simply because someone has to do it. First, the CTS kept frustrating me. I was trained that more items usually yield a more accurate account of a phenomenon than do fewer items and that a major error is to include more than one factor in a particular item. Second, since I teach about gender differences, it was apparent that women were probably more likely to perform certain acts and less likely to perform other acts. The differences were not being identified because the CTS was not sensitive enough. Third, research on gender differences shows that males and females may attach different meanings to events. Finally, I was ready to begin a project to describe psychological abuse, but there was no way to determine different levels of violence. Differentiating violence by its level of severity was a first step. In addition to the potential for physical harm, violence has a clear potential for emotional harm. Violence is psychologically abusive as well as physically abusive. For these reasons, it was necessary to create the SVAWS and SVAMS.

My experience also shows that research is not perfect. Although use of my scales will allow studies to address more complex questions (e.g., At what level of severity does violence affect other aspects of relationships? Are fewer, but more severe acts of violence more harmful or less harmful than more frequent acts of mild or minor violence?), the scales are not perfect. In research, progress is incremental.

I made every effort to be as inclusive as possible. I wanted to include all likely behaviors and assess as many aspects of severity as possible. These considerations led to a very long questionnaire which resulted in disappointingly low response rates from community people. Despite my overinclusiveness, I omitted an obvious behavior (hit with a fist). It cannot be added because there is no way to determine where it would fit in terms of its severity. Having people at this time make the same ratings for a partner hitting them with a fist would tell us nothing about how this act relates to the other acts. Another unresolved problem is that more females than males report beating up a partner, even though this is physically unlikely. Future research will have to determine whether this difference is a function of differing perceptions about what is meant by the item.

violence is not a separate dimension. Individual scores can be weighted for the potential for physical and emotional harm, and there are different orderings of items depending upon whether the sample uses students or people from the community. These scales are too new to have been used very often in research. Unless otherwise specified, the research reported in this chapter has used the CTS or a modification of the CTS.

Another way violence has been studied is through descriptions of violent incidents. The examples at the beginning of the chapter are from long interviews we conducted to study psychological abuse and physical violence. Accounts are subjective and relate stories from victims or batterers. This type of information can be helpful in learning about a new area, understanding a particular relationship and in determining interventions for therapy. However, these data are often not systematic because different people may not be asked the same questions or may not give a similar type of information. Coding these descriptions so comparisons can be made is very time consuming and costly. Further, intervening time and events affect retrospective descriptions. Another problem is that personal accounts can be compelling. Sometimes both researchers and laypeople place too much importance on a few accounts so that we do not thoroughly examine alternative possibilities.

An important distinction is whether violence is inflicted (expressed) on the partner or whether it is sustained (received) by the person in the study. Since the mid-eighties, most research has reported both types of acts. Before then, much of the research only examined whether violence had occurred within a relationship, not whether it had been done to the subject or by the subject. This distinction is important when trying to understand individuals and relationships, in part because a violent act is likely to have different meanings depending upon whether a person is the aggressor or the victim.

Approaches to Physical Violence

One of the most exciting things about this topic is the multidisciplinary nature of the specialty. In many areas of research, almost all investigators were trained in the same discipline (e.g., psychology) and often in the same sub-discipline (e.g., social psychology). When this happens, researchers may tend to think alike so that certain variables or statistics are usually included, but others are not. In contrast, violence is examined from many different perspectives. Researchers include social, clinical, counseling and experimental psychologists, physicians trained in different specialties, nurses, social workers, sociologists, criminologists, people trained in communication and in human development, etc.

Since disciplines and sub-disciplines have different assumptions, methods and purposes, and use different terms to talk about these things, communication is sometimes awkward. Also, there is tension between researchers, whose job is to learn as much as possible about violence, and practitioners and advocates, whose job is to end the violence as soon as possible. However, these uncomfortable moments are well worth it because there are many viable ways to gain knowledge. By having so many different kinds of people focusing upon the same issue in so many different ways, the picture that will eventually emerge about violence in close relationships will have considered many more factors than it would have if researchers were trained the same way.

One problem is surprising because we have generally overcome obstacles associated with communication across disciplines. Unfortunately, people who study marital violence rarely study dating violence and vice versa. It sometimes seems as if one group does not even read the work of the other group, even though they often study the same variables. With few exceptions, a study reporting violence among college students does not discuss research on the same factor if it was conducted with married people. This suggests that we are assuming that dating violence is very different from that which occurs in cohabiting or marital relationships. Yet, researchers would agree that it is important to identify the similarities as well as the differences.

Myths About Physical Violence

The popular media, especially talk shows, often paint a certain picture of abusive relationships. This is not always an accurate representation. Self help books in the psychology section of popular bookstores are often more misleading. To help counteract this problem, eight common myths perpetuated by the media and a lack of research based knowledge are presented below.

Myth 1: Violence in Close Relationships Never Happens to People Like Me

People like to think that they would never do anything that might hurt someone they care about and that their partner would never hurt them. Unfortunately, this just isn't true. Violence might occur in any relationship. It is too widespread to have not happened to someone we know.

Prevalence describes whether an incident ever occurred. Incidence describes what happened during a specific time period. O'Leary (1988) reports that at least half of the male and female citizens of the United States will receive at least one act of violence from a partner in their lifetime. Straus, Gelles and Steinmetz (1980) reported a prevalence of about 28 percent from their national sample of married people who were surveyed in 1975. Straus and Gelles (1986) directed a national survey of married or cohabiting people. Incidence had not changed significantly since their previous survey. About 12 percent of the sample reported at least one act of violence during 1985.

Note that these percentages were found with random samples, so people who were satisfied with their relationships were included with those who were not. Marshall (in press) advertised for women in bad or stressful close relationships. Of 620 women who completed the SVAWS, 84 percent said their partner had expressed at least one act of violence during their relationship. About 70 percent reported minor violence and for 60 percent, their partner had inflicted moderate (e.g., slapping) or serious, potentially life threatening acts. These women differed from people in the national surveys because they were volunteering to participate in a study about their unhappy relationships. These prevalence data suggest that women in distressed relationships are likely to have sustained violence. There was no difference by type of relationship, whether women were dating, living with or married to their partner.

Sugarman and Hotaling (1989) summarized the results of twenty studies on violence in dating relationships. Across the studies, prevalence averaged 30 percent. The range was from 9 percent (Roscoe and Callahan 1985) to 66 percent (McKinney 1986) of the samples. More recent studies reported higher violence rates than did earlier studies. This may be because violence is increasing, investigators are conducting better studies, or students feel more at ease admitting violence. In Sugarman and Hotaling's (1989) review, the prevalence for both inflicting and sustaining violence ranged from 10 percent to 59 percent, varying by study.

The variations in rates results from several sources. Almost all the studies used the CTS or modifications of it, but sometimes different acts of violence were added. The samples varied with regard to the characteristics of the subjects. Studies were conducted in different geographic locations. Some studies used the time frame of one or two years (incidence), while others focused on prevalence. In the dating research, participants may have reported on one or even ten different relationships. Variability across the studies makes generalizability a problem. However, regardless of the problems in the research, the incidence and prevalence rates for marital and dating samples show that violence in close relationships is a problem in this country.

There is no consensus on demographic or descriptive characteristics associated with violence. Some studies show that certain racial or ethnic groups are more likely to experience violence in relationships, but others do not. The same is true for income and education. We may find some answers soon because researchers are more often using multivariate statistical techniques. These statistics can uncover expected and unexpected relationships between variables and identify when a relationship is spurious, actually a function of some other variable. For example, early research reported that women who are pregnant women are more likely to receive violence than those who are not. Gelles (1988) recently discovered that this relationship is actually due to women's age, not a factor directly related to their pregnancy.

One reason for sometimes finding racial, income or education differences may result from the type of sample, most often women using public resources (e.g., emergency room, police calls, shelters). It has been argued that these women are the most seriously battered, but the shelter group we used to pilot or pretest our questionnaires and interviews reported much less violence than did our battered group, about the same amount as the group we called moderate in violence. People with fewer resources (e.g., education, income) live more of their lives under the surveillance of others. For example, a neighbor is more likely to call the police when violence occurs on the other side of an apartment wall than when it occurs twenty-five feet away in the next house or 200 feet away in another large house. Unlike poor women, wealthy anglo, black and hispanic women who are beaten do not go to shelters for sanctuary. Similarly, it is much less likely that a male physician or lawyer who beats his wife will be ordered by a court to go to treatment than if a man was unemployed or a blue collar worker. Mild, moderate and even severe violence occurs in relationships regardless of race or ethnicity; among wealthy people as well as poor people; among the highly educated as well as among those with less than a high school education. Unfortunately, the differences in resources allows violence to be hidden for people with middle and upper class incomes. In planning our study, we talked to a vice president of a major corporation who could not divorce her batterer because he kept buying off her lawyers. When he broke one of her bones, a physician came to their ranch and quietly set it.

The family income for students who described violent incidents in Makepeace's (1987) study ranged from under $10,000 (25 percent) to $60,000 (25.5

percent). Thus, half of the students experiencing violence were either from families with a low or high income. Makepeace and others (Lane and Gwartney-Gibbs 1985; Plass and Gessner 1983) have examined a status incongruence hypothesis which suggests that the discrepancy of resources within a couple are related to violence. Victims came from a higher income background, whereas offenders came from a lower income background. These studies show the recent trend to examine relationship characteristics or characteristics of both individuals in relation to each other instead of personal characteristics to understand what happens in couples who experience violence.

When studies use appropriate groups for comparisons, researchers often do not find differences. Caesar (1985) compared men in therapy for battering their partners and a group of non-batterers in therapy. These groups did not differ significantly on age, income, number of children, total number of marriages, number of cohabiting relationships, and months separated from their partner. Similarly, among married men and women, Arias and Beach (1987) found that violence was not related to the length of relationships, income, education, or the number of children.

Myth 2: People Never Tell Anyone About Violence in their Relationships

This myth may stem from people (e.g., doctors or nurses in emergency rooms, therapists) asking women if they had been abused. Because of the lack of specificity in the term and its negative connotations, many (perhaps most) women whose partner had been violent would say no. However, research shows that when asked a direct and specific question (e.g., did your partner do something that gave you those bruises), women will say yes. Moreover, there is increasing evidence that women do tell others about their partner's violence even without being asked a specific question.

Several studies of dating relationships show that students tell others about violence in their relationships (Henton et al. 1983; Olday and Wesley 1988; Pirog-Good and Stets 1989; Roscoe and Benaske 1985). In the recent national survey, Stets and Straus (1990) found that more women than men called a friend or relative (11.4 percent vs. 2.2 percent) or the police (8.5 percent vs .9 percent) when they sustained violence from their partner. In our study we found that women not only tell their friends and family about problems in their relationships, including the violence, but they also actively seek help. Only 19 percent of women in stressful relationships had not sought help from formal sources (e.g., physicians, clergy, police).

Myth 3: Only Males, Usually Macho Men, Inflict Violence on their Partner

A great deal of research shows that people prefer not to admit socially undesirable acts. People do not want to make themselves look bad to someone else. Several studies found that this social desirability bias is related to reports of violence people inflict on their partner, but not to violence they receive (Arias and Beach 1987; Edleson and Brygger 1986). This tendency seems to be somewhat stronger for men than for women. Despite this tendency, O'Leary and Arias (1988) found that reports of violence inflicted were approximately 5 percent higher than reports of sustained violence. Some research suggests that males under-report and females over-report their own acts of violence. This may not be as odd as it first seems. Since men are usually bigger and stronger, they may be aware of ways they hold back and times they refrained from hitting a partner, whereas women, who would be expected to do less damage, have less reason to hold back. Therefore, women would be aware any violent behavior they expressed so they might tend to report more of it.

Both men and women inflict and sustain violence. About 11 percent of the Straus and Gelles (1986) national sample reported at least one act of husband-to-wife violence and 12 percent reported an act of wife-to-husband violence in 1985. In Sugarman and Hotaling's (1989) review of dating violence, the range of expressing violence was from 14 percent of men and 10 percent of women (Makepeace, 1983) to 54 percent of men (Sigelman, Berry, and Wiles 1984) and 59 percent of women (Marshall and Rose 1987). Makepeace's study also found the lowest rates for men (10 percent) and women (11 percent) receiving violence from a partner. Sigelman, Barry and Wiles had the highest proportion of men who had sustained violence (59 percent), and Marshall and Rose reported the highest rate for women (57 percent). In a recent study with students using the SVAWS and SVAMS, Vitanza and Marshall (1992) reported that 77 percent of males and 76 percent of females had threatened their dating partner with violence, and 72 percent of males and 79 percent of females had sustained at least one act of violence.

Although the rates are very similar for male-to-female and female-to-male violence, the average size and strength difference must be considered. Except for lethal violence, act for act, males are likely to cause more harm to females than females cause to males. For example, when the SVAWS and SVAMS were developed, women's ratings of physical and emotional harm were higher than men's ratings. Unfortunately, due to problems previously described for the CTS, we have been unable to determine whether men and women are equally likely to perform the same acts or whether they tend to exhibit different acts of violence. Use of the SVAWS and SVAMS will facilitate determining whether males and females perform different acts. We recently combined data from two of our studies (Marshall, in press) and found that males were more likely to hit or kick a wall, door or furniture; drive dangerously; act like a bully; hold and pin; shake or roughly handle; grab; and twist an arm, and more females reported sustaining these acts. Females were more likely to throw an object; scratch; bite; slap with a palm; slap their partner around his face; kick; and punch, and more men than women sustained these acts.

Logic suggests that men who hit women may have very traditional attitudes about women's place or about how women should act. Logic also suggests that women who receive violence must be traditional or they would not tolerate it. We are surrounded by sources (e.g., parents, peers, school experiences, television, the media) which explicitly and implicitly teach us how men and women should behave. These sources reinforce notions that men and women are supposed to be very different. We even think in terms of the opposite sex. Therefore, researchers have examined gender roles and gender role attitudes. In this research, gender role is usually described as the degree to which men think of themselves as masculine (or the degree to which they think men should be masculine), with instrumental or agenetic traits, and the degree to which females think of themselves as feminine (or think women should be feminine) with expressive traits or those associated with interpersonal caring. Men are often thought of as active and women as passive. Sometimes attitudes about the place of women in society and the family can be thought of as traditional (e.g., women belong in the home) or liberal (e.g., women should receive equal pay for equal work). The results of these studies are mixed, but usually no relationships or only weak relationships are found. One study by Rosenbaum (1988) even found that most physically violent husbands scored low on masculinity compared to men in distressed or satisfied relationships.

The conflicting results and weak relationships are not very surprising. Sometimes investigators have confused gender role attitudes (what participants think about people in general) with gender role orientations (how masculine or feminine the participants themselves are). Much research in basic social psychology shows that attitudes, especially generalized attitudes, are not strongly related to behaviors or beliefs in a specific situation. For example, a man can think women should not receive equal pay for equal work, but think his wife should make as much as the man working next to her. In preparing this chapter, we did not find one study which examined an individual's attitude about his partner or a woman's own attitudes about her position. It may be, however, that an individual's gender role or gender role attitude is related to what occurs in response to violence. Flynn (1990) found that women with liberal attitudes stayed less time in a violent relationship than did traditional women.

(Although we made it clear that both women and men commit and sustain acts of violence, readers may perceive a gender bias in some of the following sections. The bias is the assumption that women receive the violence expressed by men. This is partly a function of the myths themselves which tend to have sexist overtones and partly a function of the research. When serious violence has been closely examined, battered women and male batterers have been the subjects. That is not to say it is impossible for a particular woman to seriously physically batter a particular man. This is possible and it does occur. However, as with other researchers, we want to emphasize that when physical violence is considered, women are much more likely to be more seriously harmed than are men.)

Myth 4: Boys Learn to be Aggressors and Girls Learn to be Victims from Observing their Parents

A weak version of this myth has some accuracy. The belief comes from the intergenerational transmission of violence hypothesis derived from learning theory. This perspective argues that we learn how to behave in relationships from what we experienced and observed in our family of origin. The relationships which have been found are usually statistically significant, but of a magnitude which indicates that most violence in adult close relationships does not result from what occurred in either individual's family. The conclusion that the relationship which does exist is stronger for males than for females, is still tentative.

There are three types of family of origin violence; father-to-mother, mother-to-father and parent-to-child. Until recently these variables have not been separated in research, even though logic suggests that they each may have different effects, some portion of which would depend upon the gender of the persons involved. In studies which have separated the types of family of origin violence and examined effects by gender using multivariate statistics, only a small portion of violence in adult relationships (about 10 percent or less) can be accounted for by what the individual may have experienced or observed in his or her family. For example, Marshall and Rose (1990) reported that family of origin violence became unimportant for women inflicting violence when violence they sustained from a partner was considered. The partner's violence accounted for about 45 percent of the variance. In contrast, sustaining violence from a partner was not related to men's expression of violence, but violence in their family of origin made a small contribution. When we study samples that have been identified as being in a violent relationship (e.g., batterers in treatment, women in an emergency room or shelter, police calls), typically most also report violence in their family of origin. However, when sampling students or using a random technique to interview community people, a much smaller proportion report a history of violence in their childhood.

The current trend in research is to focus less on personality and background characteristics of individuals and pay more attention to characteristics of the relationship. For example, Margolin and her colleagues (Margolin, Burman, and John 1989; Margolin, John, and Gleberman 1988) and Lloyd (1990) have compared couples who are satisfied, distressed with no violence, and a group which was distressed and violent. O'Leary and his associates (Murphy and O'Leary 1989; O'Leary et al. 1989) followed a sample of people from before they were married to thirty months postmarriage. As more researchers plan their studies with appropriate comparisons and use multivariate statistics (rather than percentages and correlations) more accurate results will be reported.

Myth 5: Females Stay in Relationships Where They Are Beaten Repeatedly Because They Are Passive

We know that some women do stay in relationships where they are beaten time after time. However, we also know that some women are able to stop the violence. Unfortunately, there is almost no research on women who end violent relationships or whose partners stop the violence after the first or second time it happens. It is a myth to believe that women get in one violent relationship after another or to believe that once violence occurs it will necessarily happen again. We simply do not yet have enough information to identify strategies women (or men) use to stop violence or to keep from becoming involved in another violent relationship.

Walker (1979) applied learned helplessness theory arguing that battered women become passive because they learn that no matter what they do, they will be unable affect their situation. This hypothesis countered earlier notions that the victim was to blame because battered women were masochistic. Walker's evidence was not compelling. Recently, Campbell (1989) hypothesized that women remain in the relationship because they feel they have no other alternative and may feel powerless. Comparing battered and non-battered women, Campbell found that the learned helplessness model helped explain why battered women stayed in relationships, but did not help to explain why nonbattered women remained in bad relationships. A more effective theory would be able to explain women in both types of relationships.

One reason why battered women appear passive may be due to the context in which observation has occurred. Many people who have argued that battered women have traditional gender roles (showing passivity presumably associated with femininity) have seen these women when they are under a great deal of stress (e.g., in an emergency room, at a shelter in which they have taken sanctuary). The research on traumatic events (e.g., rape, tornadoes, mass killings) shows that in situations when people fear for their lives, they behave in a passive and helpless manner. Women in shelters may appear passive because they have escaped a traumatic, frightening situation, often with their children; are living in an unfamiliar place; and are trying to make decisions that will affect the rest of their life. However, since relatively few battered women go to a shelter, emergency room, etc., we should not assume that most battered women feel or act as if they are passive. For example, in our study, the woman who seemed most passive could be better characterized as numb or traumatized.

Another argument against the learned helplessness model is domestic homicide. When women are killed, they are more often a victim of homicide by their partner or ex-partner, but women also commit homicide. If battered women were passive, they would not kill a physically violent partner. Women report killing their partners for self defense reasons (Saunders and Browne 1991). Jurik and Winn (1990) found that women were living with their victims in 54 percent of the manslaughter cases in Arizona between 1979 and 1984. Over half (52 percent) of women's homicides occurred in situations when the male partner had initiated violence. Goetting (1988) found that 94 percent of the women accused of homicide in her study stated that the act occurred in the context of marital discord. Afterwards they felt shock, disbelief, and a sense of despair at the loss of a loved one. Although Browne (1988) found that battered women who had committed homicide deemed most other alternatives impossible or too costly to risk, the fact that they did take action, even if extreme, argues against the commonly held belief in learned helplessness.

One view applies the Stockholm Syndrome (whereby hostages come to identify with terrorists) to the plight of seriously battered women (e.g., Graham, Rawlings, and Rimini 1989). This view argues that women's defense of and caring about their batterers results from processes related to the violence. The problem with this is the same as that identified by Campbell (1989) for Learned Helplessness Theory. A theory which helps explain women staying in violent relationships should also be able to explain women staying in distressed but nonviolent relationships. When we develop such a theory, we may find that the same processes occur, but that some factors are exacerbated as a result of the violence.

Myth 6: In Couples, There Is a Cycle of Violence

Walker (1984) described this cycle of violence. First there is a gradually escalating period of tension in which the woman withdraws to avoid angering her partner. In the acute battering incident, the batterer unleashes a barrage of physical and verbal aggression. Finally, loving contrition occurs in which the batterer may apologize profusely and may attempt to convince the woman he is truly sorry, show kindness and remorse, and perhaps give gifts and compliments. Most of Walker's evidence for this cycle came from anecdotal accounts of women in her study or who came to her for therapy. Rose, a former student of Marshall, also uses this theory in her clinical work to help women and couples recognize the signs associated with violence. Women, and apparently men, can identify with these phases. However, that does not mean that it is actually what usually occurs. For example, it was much more common for women in our sample to report that violence was generally unpredictable and that their partner's kindnesses were almost always not associated with his violence or other negative behavior toward her. Many of these women in stressful relationships could not think of one example when their partner had shown them love and caring or acted sorry for what he did.

Dutton (1987; 1988; Dutton and Painter 1981) pointed out that the absence of an aversive event can feel positive, which would allow some women to perceive a honeymoon phase even when none exists. His traumatic bonding hypothesis is another perspective on some of the processes associated with violence. Dutton applied principles of negative reinforcement in which the removal of a negative stimulus feels rewarding. (A sick joke illustrates this principle: Why are you hitting your head against the wall? Because it feels so good when I stop.) Even in battering relationships, no man is violent or even hostile all the time. When he is not, the woman would feel relief due to the absence of the negative behaviors. Furthermore, the reinforcement is intermittent and often unpredictable which learning research shows strengthens connections between stimuli and behavior. In this way, a woman becomes strongly attached to her batterer. These same principles could apply to any distressed relationship. People may remain in them because of the good times; those between the bad times or before the bad times became overwhelming. Think about this. In which case would it mean more to receive a flower from your partner if your relationship consisted mostly of bad times or if it consisted mostly of good times? A kind gesture in a good relationship may go essentially unnoticed or be taken for granted, but the same gesture in a distressed relationship may become very important.

Myth 7: Battered Women Are Masochistic, and Batterers Are Mentally Ill

According to McHugh, Frieze and Browne (1990), historically the view was that battered women remained in their relationships because they are masochistic and had self-defeating tendencies. However, the actual reasons battered women give vary widely, including fear of retaliation, economic dependence, love, lack of alternatives, he is a good father, afraid he will take the children, no one else would love her, nowhere to go, hoping for him to change, etc. There is not enough research asking this specific question to definitively describe why women stay in these relationships. That which uses identified samples (e.g., shelter women) often finds that it is simply a lack of resources and alternatives. Many women feel, with a strong measure of accuracy, that they have little choice but to remain.

Just as battered women are not masochistic, they also are not mentally ill. Rosewater (1985) found that women in violent relationships may exhibit symptom patterns similar to women with schizophrenia or borderline personality disorder. They may perceive themselves as lacking internal strength or the ability to cope and do not appear passive on the Minnesota Multiphasic Personality Inventory (Rosewater 1989). Most researchers would agree that any psychological disturbances found in battered women would be the result of the violence, not a contributing cause of the violence.

When research is conducted with battered women who are not seeking or receiving help for the violence, results show emotional disturbances and psychological symptoms, but not of a pathological nature. For example, in the national re-survey, Gelles and Harrop (1989) report more psychological distress among women in violent relationships than among men. These findings are similar to those reported by Follingstad et al. (1991). Unfortunately, we do not know how much of the emotional distress results from the violence. We know that battered women report that the psychological abuse is worse than the physical violence, but this possibility has not been examined until recently. Results from our study suggest that almost all of the distress is more closely related to subtle psychological abuse than to violence (Marshall, in press), including thoughts of suicide. When research examines psychological abuse more closely and differentiates levels of violence, we may find that certain types of distress are associated with some levels of violence but not others. For example, hostility could be associated with frequently occurring minor violence and depression could be associated with relatively rare incidents of serious violence.

Although it would seem that any man who would beat his wife or loved one would have to be mentally ill, this is not the case. Batterers belong to every race, socioeconomic status, religion and background. Although there are many classifications of mental illness, violence toward a loved one is neither a specific disorder nor a specific symptom of any particular mental disorder. Some research has examined the possibility of mental disorder. Hamberger and Hastings (1988; Hastings and Hamberger 1988) described several profiles for batterers. Some appear to be somewhat higher than the norm on aggressiveness, conformity, asocial characteristics, avoidance, submissiveness, paranoia and have alcohol or drug use traits or tendencies. Schuerger and Reigle (1988) reported that the abusive men in their study did not differ from the general population of men. They did find that batterers may tend to be more withdrawn, compulsive, tough-minded and tense. Riggs, O'Leary and Breslin (1990) and Arias and Beach (1987) found that dominance was not related to men's violence toward their partner. Arias and Beach also found that maritally violent men were lower in autonomy and showed less readiness to defend themselves. (Note that this contradicts Myth 3.)

Both men who express serious violence and women who receive serious violence may show elevations on some measures of distress or personality. However, there is not a consensus on what these particular elevations may be. Depression is often associated with violence in the research, but we do not know how much of the depression is actually a result of the violence.

Myth 8: Violence Involves the Use of Alcohol

Like the myth about violence in the family of origin, a more qualified version of this statement is accurate. If the reader focuses on differences between groups, she or he finds that violence is indeed associated with substance abuse. In contrast, if the reader is looking for understanding that may not be related to differences, we see that most violence is probably not associated with substance use or abuse. One woman we interviewed thought we would not believe that her partner committed serious violence against her because he had not been raised in a violent family and he never used alcohol. This woman apparently believed these myths in their strong version. Alcohol is not always involved in violence in close relationships and may not be involved in most incidents. Given what we know about alcohol and aggression, however, we may eventually find that more physical harm results from violence when it is associated with alcohol than when it is not.

Alcohol use has long been believed to contribute to violence in close relationships. For example, police tend to believe that alcohol or substance abuse is usually involved, but it may be that these instances are merely louder so that someone overhears and calls the police. It has been thought that either the wife's drinking or husband's drinking led to increases in marital violence. Some studies have indicated that the incidence of substance abuse does not vary significantly between batterers and non-batterers. Eberle (1982) examined the frequency of alcohol use across four battering incidents, finding that up to 45 percent of the violent men used no alcohol, while up to 38 percent used a lot of alcohol. Among batterers, Fagan, Barnett and Patton (1988) found that 12 percent of the men never, 31 percent seldom, 26 percent occasionally, 17 percent often, and only 14 percent used alcohol very often. Tolman and Bennett's (1990) review concluded that about half of the men receiving treatment for battering abused alcohol. Alcoholic batterers in treatment may show more pathology than nonalcoholic batterers (Hamberger and Hastings 1988). Clearly, not all males who batter use alcohol, not all men who use alcohol batter their partner, and men who use alcohol and do batter their partner are not always using alcohol at the time. The actual relationship between alcohol and violence in close relationships is likely to be complex and not immediately apparent.

Kantor and Straus' (1990) national survey suggested a strong link between alcohol use and physical violence against wives, but alcohol alone was neither a necessary nor a sufficient cause of violence. Although alcohol was involved in about one out of four instances of violence against wives, 80 percent of violent men in high stress and binge drinking groups did not hit their wives during 1985. Leonard and Blane (1992) found that for males low in hostility, alcohol was related to violence if they were not satisfied with their relationship, but for men who were high in hostility, alcohol and violence were related, regardless of men's level of relationship satisfaction. Again, the value of multivariate statistics is clear. They help uncover complex relationships and mitigate against simplistic conclusions that eventually become myths.

Conclusion and Summary

The primary conclusion is that acts of violence in close relationships are not unusual. Unfortunately, these acts are all too common. Despite the increasing number of studies, many questions remain unanswered or only partially answered. As more investigators apply findings from other areas (e.g., date rape, aggression research), integrate results from dating studies into research examining marital violence (and vice versa), improve their methodology and the sophistication of their statistical analyses, more questions will have definitive answers. In the meantime, it is important to be a careful consumer. When everyone knows a certain fact, or when experts who conduct research have proven something, even when it seems logical, a closer examination of the issue is warranted. This may be especially important in an area such as this which touches so many of us and which can be so damaging.

We have shown that violence can occur in anyone's relationship (Myths 1 and 3). It appears to be less likely to result from the personality or background characteristics of specific individuals than from relationship or couple characteristics. Battered women are not passive and helpless (Myth 5), nor are they or their batterers mentally ill (Myth 7). Women in violent relationships may develop serious psychological symptoms, but the symptoms may result from psychological abuse (Marshall, in press). Although batterers in treatment may score higher or lower than the norm on some personality or mental health tests, they generally do not show pathologies.

Methodology may have played an important part in perpetuating myths. From Myth 2 and the discussion of using terms with negative connotations, an underlying message is that we all may know someone whose discussions with us are actually a way to seek help. Our advice may not be immediately taken, but seeking help indicates an effort to cope adaptively with problems. Myth 3 has been perpetuated by research methods which do not include standard attitude and gender role instruments. In part, Myth 6 has been perpetuated because people can readily identify with it. Most of us could describe such a cycle with our own or our partner's anger, but in seriously violent relationships (and probably those which are seriously distressed, but not violent) this cycle may rarely occur.

Myths 4 and 8 seem to have resulted from focusing on differences rather than similarities. When the findings are carefully considered, it becomes clear that most violence is not associated with what the individual experienced or observed in his or her family of origin or with alcohol or drug use or abuse.

In sum, there is a great deal more to learn about violence in close relationships. We hope that by making more people aware of what is (and is not) discovered through research, there will be fewer and fewer women's voices describing events like those in the beginning of this chapter.

References

Arias, I., and S. R. H. Beach, 1987. Validity of self-reports of marital violence. *Journal of Family Violence*, 2:139–49.

Browne, A. 1988. Family homicide: When victimized women kill. In *Handbook of family violence*, ed. V. B. VanHasselt, R. L. Morrison, A. S. Bellack, and M. Hersen, 271–289. New York: Plenum Press.

Caesar, P. L. 1985. Exposure to violence in the families-of-origin among wife-abusers and maritally nonviolent men. *Violence and Victims*, 3:49–63.

Campbell, J. C. 1989. A test of two explanatory models of women's responses to battering. *Nursing Research*, 38:18–24.

Dutton, D. G. 1987. Wife assault: Social psychological contributions to criminal justice policy. *Applied Social Psychology Annual*, 7:238–61.

———. 1988. *The domestic assault of women: Psychological and Criminal Justice Perspectives*. Boston: Allyn and Bacon.

Dutton, D. G., and S. L. Painter. 1981. Traumatic bonding: The development of emotional attachments in battered women and other relationships of intermittent abuse. *Victimology*, 6:139–55.

Eberle, P. A. 1982. Alcohol abusers and non-users: A discriminant analysis of differences between two subgroups of batterers. *Journal of Health and Social Behavior*, 23:260–71.

Edleson, J. L., and M. P. Brygger. 1986. Gender differences in reporting of battering incidences. *Family Relations*, 35:377–82.

Fagan, R. W., O. W. Barnett, and J. B. Patton. 1988. Reasons for alcohol use in maritally violent men. *The American Journal of Drug and Alcohol Abuse*, 14:371–92.

Finkelhor, D. and K. Yllo. 1985. *License to rape: Sexual abuse of wives*. New York: Holt, Rinehart and Winston.

Flynn, C. P. 1990. Sex roles and women's response to courtship violence. *Journal of Family Violence*, 5:83–94.

Follingstad, D. R., A. F. Brennan, E. S. Hause, D. S. Polek, and L. L. Rutledge. 1991. Factors moderating physical and psychological symptoms of battered women. *Journal of Family Violence*, 6:81–95.

Gelles, R. J. 1988. Violence and pregnancy: Are pregnant women at greater risk of abuse? *Journal of Marriage and the Family*, 42:873–85.

Gelles, R. J., and J. W. Harrop. 1989. Violence, battering, and psychological distress among women. *Journal of Interpersonal Violence*, 4:400–20.

Goetting, A. 1988. Patterns of marital homicide: A comparison of husbands and wives. *Journal of Comparative Family Studies*, 20:341–54.

Graham, D. L. R., E. Rawlings, and N. Rimini. 1989. Survivors of terror: Battered women, hostages, and the Stockholm Syndrome. In *Feminist Perspectives on Wife Abuse*, ed. K. Yllo and M. Bograd. Newbury Park, CA: Sage.

Hamberger, L. K., and J. E. Hastings. 1988. Characteristics of male spouse abusers consistent with personality disorders. *Hospital and Community Psychiatry*, 39:763–70.

Hastings, J. E. and L. K. Hamberger. 1988. Personality characteristics of spouse abusers: A controlled comparison. *Violence and Victims*, 3:31–48.

Henton, J., R. Cate, J. Koval, S. Lloyd, and S. Christopher. 1983. Romance and violence in dating relationships. *Journal of Family Issues*, 4:467–82.

Jurik, N. C., and R. Winn. 1990. Gender and homicide: A comparison of men and women who kill. *Violence and Victims*, 5:227–42.

Kantor, G. K., and M. A. Straus. 1990. The "drunken bum" theory of wife beating. In *Physical Violence in American Families: Risk Factors and Adaptations in Violence in 8,145 Families*, ed. M. A. Straus and R. J. Gelles. New Brunswick, NJ: Transaction Publishers.

Koss, M. P., K. E. Leonard, D. A. Beezley, and C. J. Oros. 1985. Nonstranger sexual aggression: A discriminant analysis of the psychological characteristics of undetected offenders. *Sex Roles*, 12:981–992.

Lane, K. E. and P. A. Gwartney-Gibbs. 1985. Violence in the context of dating and sex. *Journal of Family Issues*, 6:45–59.

Leonard, K. E., and K. E. Blane. 1992. Alcohol and marital aggression in a national sample of young men. *Journal of Interpersonal Violence*, 7:19–30.

Linz, D., E. Donnerstein, and S. Penrod. 1988. Effects of long-term exposure to violent and sexually degrading depictions of women. *Journal of Personality and Social Psychology*, 55:758–68.

Lloyd, S. A. 1990. Conflict types and strategies in violent marriages. *Journal of Family Violence*, 5:269–84.

Makepeace, J. M. 1983. Life event stress and courtship violence. *Family Relations*, 32:101–09.

———. 1987. Social factors and victim-offender differences in courtship violence. *Family Relations*, 36:87–91.

Malamuth, N. M. 1989. The attraction of sexual aggression scale: Part two. *Journal of Sex Research*, 26:324–54.

Margolin, G., B. Burman, and R. S. John. 1989. Home observations of married couples reenacting naturalistic conflicts. *Behavioral Assessment*, 11:101–18.

Margolin, G., R. S. John, and L. Gleberman. 1988. Affective responses to conflictual discussions in violent and nonviolent couples. *Journal of Consulting and Clinical Psychology*, 56:24–33.

Marshall, L. L. in press. Psychological abuse and physical violence. In *The dark side of interpersonal communication*, ed. W. R. Cupach and B. H. Spitzberg. Lawrence Erlbaum.

———. 1992a. Development of the severity of violence against women scales. *Journal of Family Violence*, 7:103–21.

———. 1992b. The severity of violence against men scales. *Journal of Family Violence*, 7:189–203.

Marshall, L. L., and P. Rose. 1987. Gender, stress and violence in the adult relationships of a sample of college students. *Journal of Social and Personal Relationships*, 4:299–316.

———. 1990. Premarital violence: The impact of family of origin violence, stress and reciprocity. *Violence and Victims*, 5:51–64.

Mason, A., and V. Blankenship. 1987. Power and affiliation motivation, stress and abuse in intimate relationships. *Journal of Personality and Social Psychology*, 52:203–10.

McHugh, M. C., I. H. Frieze, and A. Browne. 1990. Research on battered women and their assailants. In *Handbook on the Psychology of Women*, ed. M. Paludi and F. Denmark. NY: Greenwood Press.

McKinney, K. 1986. Measures of verbal, physical and sexual dating violence by gender. *Free Inquiry in Creative Sociology*, 14:55–60.

Muehlenhard, C. R., and M. A. Linton. 1987. Date rape and sexual aggression in dating relationships: Incidence and risk factors. *Journal of Counseling Psychology*, 34:186–96.

Murphy, C., and M. Cascardi. 1993. Psychological aggression and abuse in marriage. In *Issues in children's and families' lives: Family violence, Vol. II*, ed. R. L. Hampton, 1–25. Newbury Park, CA: Sage.

Murphy, C. M., and K. D. O'Leary. 1989. Psychological aggression predicts physical aggression in early marriage. *Journal of Consulting and Clinical Psychology,* 57:579–82.

O'Leary, K. D. 1988. Physical aggression between spouses: A social learning approach. In *Handbook of Family Violence*, ed. V. B. Van Hasselt, R. L. Morrison, A. S. Bellack, and M. Hersen, 31–55. NY: Plenum.

O'Leary, K. D., and I. Arias. 1988. Prevalence, correlates and development of spouse abuse. In *Social learning and systems approaches to marriage and the family*, ed. R. dev. Peters and R. J. McMahon, 104–127. NY: Brunner/Mazel.

O'Leary, K. D., J. Barling, I. Arias, A. Rosenbaum, J. Malone, and A. Tyree. 1989. Prevalence and stability of physical aggression between spouses: A longitudinal analysis. *Journal of Consulting and Clinical Psychology,* 57:263–68.

Olday, D., and B. Wesley. 1988. Dating violence: A comparison of high school and college subsamples. *Free Inquiry in Creative Sociology,* 16:183–91.

Pirog-Good, M. A., and J. E. Stets. 1989. The help-seeking behavior of physically and sexually abused college students. In *Violence in dating relationships: Emerging social issues*, ed. M. A. Pirog-Good and J. E. Stets. Praeger.

Plass, M. S., and J. C. Gessner. 1983. Violence in courtship relations: A southern sample. *Free Inquiry in Creative Sociology,* 11:198–202.

Riggs, D. S., K. D. O'Leary, and F. C. Breslin. 1990. Multiple correlates of physical aggression in dating couples. *Journal of Interpersonal Violence,* 5:61–73.

Roscoe, B., and N. Benaske. 1985. Courtship violence experienced by abused wives: Similarities in patterns of abuse. *Family Relations,* 34:419–24.

Roscoe, B., and J. E. Callahan. 1985. Adolescents' self-report of violence in families and dating relations. *Adolescence,* 20:545–553.

Rosenbaum, A. 1988. Of men, macho and family violence. *Journal of Family Violence,* 1:121–29.

Rosewater, L. B. 1985. Schizophrenic, borderline or battered? In *Handbook of Feminist Therapy*, ed. R. B. Rosewater and L. E. A. Walker, 215–25. NY: Springer.

———. 1989. Battered or schizophrenic? Psychological test can't tell. In *Feminist Perspectives on Wife Abuse*, ed. K. Yllo and M. Bograd. Newbury Park, CA: Sage.

Russell, D. E. H. 1982. *Rape in marriage.* New York: MacMillan.

Saunders, D. G. and A. Browne. 1991. Domestic homicide. In *Case studies in family violence*, ed. R. T. Ammerman and M. Hersen, 379–402. NY: Plenum.

Schuerger, J. M., and N. Reigle. 1988. Personality and biographic data that characterize men who abuse their wives. *Journal of Clinical Psychology,* 44:75–81.

Sigelman, C. K., C. J. Berry, and K. A. Wiles. 1984. Violence in college students' dating relationships. *Journal of Applied Social Psychology,* 5:530–48.

Stets, J. E. and M. A. Straus. 1990. Gender differences in reporting marital violence and its medical and psychological consequences. In *Physical violence in American families: Risk factors and adaptations to violence in 8,145 families*, ed. M. A. Straus and R. J. Gelles, 151–65. New Brunswick, NJ: Transaction Press.

Straus, M. A. 1979. Measuring intrafamily conflict and violence: The Conflict Tactics (CT) scales. *Journal of Marriage and the Family,* 41:75–86.

Straus, M. A., and R. J. Gelles. 1986. Societal change and change in family violence from 1975 to 1985 as revealed in two national surveys. *Journal of Marriage and the Family,* 48:465–79.

Straus, M. A., R. J. Gelles, and S. K. Steinmetz 1980. *Behind closed doors: Violence in the American family.* Garden City, NY: Doubleday.

Sugarman, D. B., and G. T. Hotaling, 1989. Dating violence: Prevalence, context and risk markers. In *Violence in dating relationships: Emerging social issues*, ed. M. A. Pirog-Good and J. E. Stets. Praeger.

Tolman, R. M. 1989. Development of a measure of psychological maltreatment of women by their male partners. *Violence and Victims,* 4:159–77.

Tolman, R. M., and L. W. Bennett. 1990. A review of quantitative research on men who batter. *Journal of Interpersonal Violence*, 5:87–118.

Vitanza, S. A., F. A. Walker, and L. L. Marshall. 1991. Psychological abuse and the severity of violence. Presented at American Psychological Association, San Francisco.

Vitanza, S. A., and L. L. Marshall. 1992. *Dating violence, gender and personal characteristics.* Manuscript under review.

Walker, L. E. A. 1979. *The battered woman*. NY: Harper and Row.

———. 1984. *The battered woman syndrome.* NY: Springer.

Accounts in Coping with Relationship Loss

ANN L. WEBER
University of North Carolina at Asheville

JOHN H. HARVEY
University of Iowa

Outline

"Well, everyone can master grief 'cept that he has it."
William Shakespeare

Introduction

Stories

The following two stories are excerpted from readers' reports to Cheryl Lavin's "Tales from the Front" column in the Chicago *Tribune* dated June 3, 1992:

Nina's story: "Jack and I were both seniors, but at different colleges. On Valentine's Day, he sent me a dozen roses, a fancy card and his picture. I said, 'Let's talk about marriage when you come home after graduation.' That was my last contact with him. He stopped writing and ignored messages I left with his roommates.

"A week before his graduation, which I was supposed to attend, I tried to contact his parents. They had moved and changed their phone number. So I called his grandmother. She told me he was getting married the day before graduation. I started to laugh, thinking he was going to surprise me by eloping with me. Then I began to cry. I realized I wasn't going to be the bride.

"He actually got married that day. Apparently he had a girlfriend at college I didn't know about" (p. 3).

Cece's story: "I was dumped by my fiance after a four year relationship. I was miserable. I seriously entertained the thought of doing away with myself. I stayed in bed for a week, not eating, torturing myself with replays of how happy we had been. I don't know what would have happened if reports from friends and family hadn't come back to me about the fun times Steve was having without me.

"I started to get angry. I decided to take up interests that I never pursued because they didn't interest him. I began to look for a more stimulating job and to cultivate new friendships. I subtly made sure that my activities got back to him. And, as I had hoped, he called. He missed me and wanted us to get back together. Oh, what joy! We moved into an apartment together. This was what I wanted, right?

"Wrong. It took me one month of living with him to realize he was a jerk and had been the entire four years we had been together. I had been a doormat for him, but during that summer of pain I woke up. I don't need him to live, nor anyone else. I had become independent. Five months later, I moved out" (p. 3).

Everyone's story is unique, yet common themes seem to emerge, about the fragility of intimacy and the pains of loss. We use these common themes to learn from experience—other people's as well as our own. For example, how realistic is the following exchange, part of a fictitious scenario of marital conflict composed by Crosby (1991)?

Cindy: "I feel that I have given and given and given! And what do I get? I get pain, loneliness, and feelings of guilt and inadequacy. I get the silent treatment from Michael for days at a time . . . "

Michael: "Why should I bother to do things for her? For a long time I did every-thing a person could do. I worked all day, came home and listened to her talk about her day, helped her with her housework, and then did all the routine outside stuff . . . You'd think I was a hired hand" (Crosby 1991, p. 58).

Cindy's complaint of having "given and given and given" is certainly famil-iar, as is her plea of "what do I get?" You do not even need a definition of the silent treatment to be able to imagine how uncomfortable you would feel if your partner used it with you. Similarly, Michael's lament is one we have heard from real people and fictional characters: "I did everything a person could do . . ." Neither of these people—in this case, fictional characters representing common sources of conflict and disillusionment—deserves to be unhappy or disappointed in inti-macy. But for various reasons, relationships become troubled and strained. One person breaks off all contact with another; romantic hopes are spoiled by the realization that one's dream lover "was a jerk"—and had been all along. Why is intimacy so difficult? Are conflicts uncontrollable? Is breaking up inevitable? Whatever happened to "happily ever after"?

The Social Psychological Perspective

This chapter is one of several in this volume that examine the dark side of the fairy tale, the common faults and failings of our human efforts to become close to others. In particular we will look at relationship conflict, breaking up, and the role of accounts or interpretive stories in coping with pain and loss.

In reviewing these interesting but difficult processes, we two chapter authors take the perspective of our particular discipline, social psychology. Specifically, we focus on how the individual's actions, thoughts, and feelings are influenced by social factors. Sometimes, impressed by a vivid story of one person's experi-ence, we leap to the conclusion that people in general react in similar ways. At other times, intrigued by differences in how people respond to the same chal-lenges, we wonder whether more basic processes—such as personality or cogni-tion—might explain distinctions among individuals. As social psychologists, we are fascinated by circumstances, influences, contexts, and meanings that sur-round and captivate individual experience. In this chapter, we consider the com-mon elements and forces involved in experiencing relationship breakdown, termination, and recovery from pain and loss.

"The Story of Our Relationship"

Glance back at the brief story fragments that opened this chapter: Nina's tale, Cece's story, the fictional Cindy and Michael's complaints about each other. Now consider how you reacted when you read them. Are such first-person narratives more engaging than textbook explanations? Could you relate to these narrators, or to parts of their stories? Do you think there is truth to be found in people's personal stories of love or loss? These are the questions and issues that have intrigued us, in our research, for over a decade; thus we begin our discussion of conflict and loss with these ideas.

Accounting and Explaining

The excerpts opening this chapter are fragments of what we refer to as accounts, story-like constructions containing description, interpretation, feelings, beliefs, expectations, and characterization of self and others (Harvey, Orbuch and Weber 1990; Harvey, Orbuch and Weber 1992; Harvey, Weber and Orbuch 1990; Weber, Harvey and Orbuch 1992). People develop accounts, usually in response to experiences, and record them privately or relate them to others. This process—developing and transmitting accounts—we call account-making. In this chapter we will explore the nature of account-making and its significance in close relationship loss, and we will relate account-making to confiding behavior. Confiding refers to the act of telling our inner thoughts, including disclosures about loss, hurt, and very personal secrets, to a close other, whether the confidant is a friend, lover, relative, therapist, or stranger.

In social psychology, the principal progenitor of work on account-making is work on attribution theory, systematic study of how people ask answer "why" questions and explain their experiences (Heider 1958; Kelley 1972). An attribution is a hypothesis or explanation suggesting the basic cause or motivation of an event or action. Basically, work on both account-making and attribution is concerned with people's understandings of events in their own and others' lives. Attribution work tends to focus more on singular attributions, such as blaming/crediting either the individual's personality ("I lost her because I'm a stubborn person") or the situation surrounding the behavior ("We fought a lot then because we were under so much stress when his mother was sick in the hospital"). In contrast, account-making stresses people's inclinations to make and string together multiple attributions and related thoughts and feelings, and, over time, to develop these strings of attributional material into stories about events in their own and others' lives. For example, an account of conflict is more than the sum of its attributional parts, and can include both personal and situational attributions in explaining the same set of events:

> *I was working so hard on that project that I just ignored my wife's needs. I also tend to be pretty single-minded, so I only focus on one thing at a time. The deadline pressure I was under just brought out the worst in me, and I never paid any attention to our relationship. I shouldn't really be surprised that she finally quit trying to get through to me, and walked out.*

In this (fictitious) account, the narrator blames both situational (deadline pressure) and personal (single-mindedness) forces in shaping the demise of his marriage. The story-teller has—and tries to convey—an impression or Gestalt rather than a listing of self-exonerating attributions about his divorce.

Similar to the attributions that make up much of th' accounts may be triggered by events or realizations that tive (Holtzworth-Munroe and Jacobson 1985). For exa' lowing two situations are you more likely to search explanation about why the event has occurred?

A. Your partner has just criticized your work.
B. Your partner has brought you something to drink.

If you are like most people, you will be more baffled by Situation A, and spend more time analyzing and explaining it. According to researchers like Holtzworth-Munroe and Jacobson (1985), negative experiences provoke more attributional concern than positive ones, unexpected events more than predicted outcomes. When actions and events follow a routine, we take them for granted and probe no further. It is the nasty surprise, the painful revelation, the odd or jarring comment that jolts one's explainable world. Why should this be so? The answer may be as simple as the observation that positive and/or expected events do not need an explanation, whereas negative and/or surprising occurrences violate our sense of being prepared or in control, and thus pose a threat to our psychological security. Such threats arouse our need to understand and make sense of things once more.

The Search for Meaning

Gestalt psychologists have long argued that meaning is a motivating goal in human experience. In this sense, therefore, relationship events that are hard to understand or explain trigger new searches for meaning: "Why did he say that to me?" "What did she mean by that?" "How could they let such a thing happen?" These mini-searches may swarm together and contribute to an individual's larger existential excursion: the quest for the meaning of life. In fact, life may involve many meanings—or so Roy Baumeister argues in his 1991 book, *The Meanings of Life*. Baumeister specifically suggests that human beings have four different basic needs for meaning: purpose, value, efficacy, and self-worth. Meaning is derived from purposive, goal-directed action ("By not answering the phone, I meant to discourage Lee from calling me"). Meaning provides value by justifying or at least legitimizing behavior ("When I criticized Joan's lateness I did not mean to hurt her feelings; I only meant to show her that it is important to be considerate of people who are counting on you"). Grasping meaning gives people a sense of control and efficacy in relationships ("Once I realized Marty was terrified of repeating the mistakes of a stifling early marriage, I stopped pressing for proof of commitment—and our relationship has been great ever since"). Finally, people seek meaning in order to discover the positive worth of their lives ("At first, I felt humiliated when Larry threw me over for that teenager, but gradually I realized he was intimidated by my experience and intelligence—and really, I was too good for him"). Meaning is not merely a handy psychological strategy for tying up loose ends; it meets basic human needs for self-acceptance and social approval.

Other theorists have suggested that relationships with others are essential to human fulfillment; in Abraham Maslow's hierarchy of motives, for example, "belongingness" is achieved only by establishing connections to people and places (Maslow 1970). While it is certainly possible to live—perhaps successfully and (it is arguable) happily—without one or more close relationships, modern society deems love important to a meaningful life. Imagine a wealthy recluse, or someone like Charles Dickens' character, Ebenezer Scrooge, before his Christmas conversion, well-fed but friendless: the heart beats, the brain ticks, but there is no life. Beginning with attachment and family bonds (see the chapter by Shaver and Hazan), human beings have an inclination to affiliate with and attract to others, and widely divergent cultures generally agree in enhancing and encouraging these inclinations. We hope for and even expect intimate relationships in our lifetimes. We build our dreams in terms of endearments and commitments, using fairy tales as blueprints; happily ever after—can seem like a birthright instead of a fantasy. After making similar observations, Baumeister (1991) goes on to speculate:

> *Happiness is a state full of meaning. Happy people have meaningful lives that make sense. They have purpose, they feel their actions are right and good and justified, they have a sense of personal efficacy, and they have a firm sense of positive self-worth. . . . Suffering, in contrast, cries out for meaning. A lack or loss of meaning is often central to suffering and unhappiness. The world fails to make sense in some vitally important way. Suffering stimulates the need for meaning (p. 232).*

Well before the ending of a close relationship—and the consequent accounting and story-telling by those involved in the ending—all relationships already generate an unfolding storyline: how we met, how we fell in love, how we decided to make a commitment, how our relationship changed over time (including choices, decisions, and turning points encountered by partners). An interesting finding by social psychologist Daniel Wegner and colleagues is that, in long-lasting couples, partners frequently have the ability to engage in transactive or collaborative remembering (Wegner 1986; Wegner, Erber and Raymond 1991). Wegner suggests that couples may have mutual stories about their relationships, and that in telling their stories, each partner fills in part of the narrative with considerable agreement about how the various parts fit together. For example, in a married couple, the wife may have special expertise in remembering how relations with relatives have progressed over the years, while the husband keeps better track of connections with friends and coworkers. In a well-functioning marriage, these partners complement one another by focusing on different relations and contributing their perspectives to their joint account. Thus in dissolution, such transactional memory is lost, so each ex-partner is bereft of important memories, contacts, and social involvement.

When Accounts Disagree

In short, for each couple there is a "Story of Our Relationship." Among happy couples there may be greater agreement between partners on the story-line—who did what to whom, when, and why—while agreement is less common within distressed couples. As research for conflicted or separated couples has shown, a listener or researcher may discover there are different versions of the Story being distributed (Harvey, Wells and Alvarez 1978). These versions may be so different, especially at the ending of the relationship, that it seems as if the partners had lived totally separate lives in different worlds. Differences may be inevitable, because two people seldom have exactly the same view of an event. In the course of heterosexual relationships, for example, different interpretations may reflect gender differences, with women attending to the story-line from the start while men only attend when trouble begins (Holtzworth-Munroe and Jacobson, 1985).

In one of the first studies of attributional divergence—differences in explanation patterns—in close relationships, Hill, Rubin and Peplau (1976) studied more than 200 heterosexual dating couples attending colleges in the Boston area. They found that in distressed couples who had been seeing each other two years or longer, partners reported seeing the same relationship very differently. Among ex-partners who had broken up, there was disagreement about who had left whom: each respondent claimed it was he or she who wanted to break up, not his or her partner, but data indicated it was generally the women who initiated the breakup more readily than the men. Hill and colleagues interpreted these findings as evidence that, after experiencing conflict or breakup, individuals need to protect their own selfesteem, and one way to do this is to claim having intended to break up rather than having been rejected. If both partners need such self-protection, then why do women initiate breakup more than men? Hill et al. suggest that woman are more sensitive to relationship problems and feel a greater need to move quickly in deciding the relationship should be terminated—especially if a woman wants a family and knows that this man is not the right one with whom to make those plans. In general, Hill et al. found that within weakening relationships, there were fundamental asymmetries in partners' understanding and interpreting. The more differently partners saw things, the more likely they were to have broken up by the time of the follow-up study.

The same fundamental asymmetry shows up in studies by Orvis, Kelley and Butler (1976) and Harvey et al. (1978) of young couples experiencing conflict. These studies found evidence for what has been called the *divergent perspectives hypothesis* (Jones and Nisbett 1972) in interpersonal relations. It was found that an actor in a situation tended to attribute his or her behavior to environmental or situational forces, whereas an observer of the actor's behavior would attribute the same behavior to the actor's personal qualities or disposition. For example, a husband (the actor) who is chronically late in returning home from work might blame his demanding employer, whereas his distressed wife (the observer) more readily blames her husband himself for being insensitive and taking their marriage for granted. Theorists suggest that this difference arises because the actor and observer have divergent perspectives: working late, the husband sees his actions as forced by circumstances; frustrated yet again, his wife sees his pattern of lateness as his deliberate choice.

Divergence and asymmetries in explaining events—especially relationship events—can readily lead to conflict between partners. Orvis and colleagues (1976) offer the fascinating suggestion that couples frequently discuss their different interpretations and thereby try to influence each other to accept more positive attributions. Thus the husband in the above example will seek to persuade his wife to see things from his point of view, so that she will support him and forgive his lateness instead of feeling resentful and angry. If such communication efforts are not successful and partners continue to diverge in their attributions, the couple may have little hope of achieving a happy and satisfying relationship (Bradbury and Fincham 1990, a review of research in this area).

As with so many close relationship phenomena, the pattern of divergence in accounts and attributions shows what seem to be culturally-scripted gender differences. Over time, various studies (e.g., Harvey et al. 1978) have pointed to the different themes of men's and women's perspectives on intimacy. In general, heterosexual women emphasize the desire for more reciprocal, expressive behavior on the part of their male partners. In contrast, men emphasize the desire for more physical relations, including sex. Further, during certain life passages—such as a mid-life crisis (concomitant with Erikson's [1963] generativity crisis)—a common theme for women in distressed marriages is to have her life and career taken more seriously and supported by her husband and family. She may feel it is her time to develop in her work, while her husband and children want her to continue emphasizing their nurturance and development. During this mid-life passage, men may feel unappreciated by their mates and seek self-enhancement or excitement with interests or liaisons outside the marriage.

So divergence in understanding and explaining is common and probably inevitable between couples, at least from time to time in the course of close relationships. But differences do not have to create terminal conflict. Based on the research reviewed in this chapter, the best recommendation for couples who have honest differences in their accounts is to be open about those differences and to work on revisions as seems reasonable. Such openness and hard work take not only good intentions, but commitment, time, and courage.

Deciphering Loss

Inasmuch as achieving intimacy with another may solidify meaning—and thus support happiness—likewise the loss of a close relationship saps and destroys meaning, generates confusion and loss of control, and feeds a gnawing misery. In her work on grieving, Rando (1988) observes that the first response to losing a loved one is avoidance of the truth:

> *The world is shaken; you feel overwhelmed. Just as the human body goes into shock after a large enough physical trauma, so too does the human psyche go into*

shock when confronted with such an important loss. It is the natural reaction to the impact of such a blow (p. 20).

The loss of a personal relationship—whether through death, divorce, or breakup—is often likened to a crushing blow, a jolt, a bolt from the blue, a mortal wound. In its wake one is left numb, shocked, dazed, staggering, bleeding. This may well be the first stage of various models of grief work and recovery (Rando 1988; Staudacher 1987; Leick and Davidsen-Nielsen 1991), but it hardly seems a good time to begin actively healing. Sympathetic friends and onlookers are more likely to respond to one's relationship loss with expressions of disbelief and shared pain ("Oh, no, that's terrible!") than with exhortations to heal ("Get over it. Cheer up! Get out and meet other people"). Ultimately, getting over a loss or breakup will require becoming re-integrated into life without the lost person. But the course of recovery takes time, and can't be rushed. First things first: life in the wake of loss is caught up in a search for meaning, as indicated in these account fragments related by older adult survivors of relationship losses (Harvey, Weber and Orbuch 1990, p. 93):

> *I couldn't believe that this was happening to such a good man. It wasn't fair. . . . I wish to God [that] God would let me in on the purpose because I sure as hell don't see how or why it has happened to him.*
>
> *(66-year-old wife of Alzheimer's victim)*

> *He told others he had never loved me. The years we had spent together, what meaning did they have?*
>
> *(62-year-old divorced librarian)*

The search for meaning moves survivors of loss to express themselves in unaccustomed forms. In remembering and mourning a lost love, you may feel moved to write poetry or compose a song. After the illness and death of his young son, writer David Morrell, author of the popular *Rambo* series of adventure novels, felt compelled to write a very different sort of book, *Fireflies* (1988), a sometimes mystical narrative about his real pain and unreal imaginings and wishes that his son had not in fact died. The novelist C. S. Lewis, whose wife died of cancer after they had been married only a few years, kept random yet intentional journals of his grief, noting in one entry that:

> *Sorrow . . . turns out to be not a state but a process. It needs not a map but a history . . . There is something new to be chronicled every day. (Lewis 1963, pp. 68–69).*

Whether an established writer weaves his account into his latest work or an amateur pens a nostalgic poem, this chronicling process is at the heart of account-making. When you develop your account, recording it or relating it to others is part of the process. You don't necessarily get it right before you write it down or confide in someone; rather, writing and confiding are part of getting it right. As we shall discuss, accounts are a process of discovering and developing meaning, especially after nasty surprises like relationship conflict or loss. Does account-making do any good? We argue that yes, it serves several functions in helping individuals deal with troubled or ended relationships.

Major Functions of Relationship Accounts

Account-making and confiding activities appear to be important ways of dealing with major life events, including disruptions in close relationships. People seem eager to tell their stories of these experiences, as evidenced by the popularity of television talk shows and newspaper columns like the Chicago *Tribune's* "Tales from the Front," quoted in the chapter opening. Apparently, we are just as eager to read and listen to others' stories as we are to tell our own. Before you read on, try this short exercise:

1. Think of a difficult or troublesome experience you have had in a close relationship.
2. If you are recalling a past experience, what do you remember? What happened? What did you do? How did you feel?
3. Why did these events occur in your relationship?
4. Have you ever told anyone about this experience, and your interpretation of what happened?

By calling to mind your own experiences in account-making and confiding, you will find it easier to understand and benefit from the processes described in this chapter.

Elements of Effective Accounts

Most relationships encounter conflict. Because a relationship involves two different individuals, chance alone predicts that partners will occasionally disagree, feel differently about things, or at least be out of synchrony with each other. Most conflict is not terminal or fatal to the relationship, but it must still be acknowledged and worked through. If conflict is so serious that two people part ways, each is left to deal with that loss—despite differences in their roles and feelings (if, for example, the one who leaves feels guilty while the one left behind feels pain and humiliation). Relationship problems are universal: most of us in the course of our lives will need to develop stories for the loss of a lover, spouse, friend, or family member. Why did it happen? Why did it have to happen now, after we've gotten through so much? How could this happen when I know we both love each other? These questions lie at the heart of our accounts. These are the questions behind many sleepless nights, despairing days, hopeless and even suicidal thoughts.

To get through the grief associated with close relationship losses, we may work privately on the story of our relationship, driven sometimes by intense emotions, other times by a palpable need to understand what happened. We may report fragments of the story to close others who can offer insights, critique, or sympathy: "I've pretty much figured out that he must have been seeing somebody else for a long time now. I can hardly believe it. Should I have seen it coming?" Kind and attentive listeners can help us to come to grips with the reality of our loss and our need to resolve our feelings—and move on. This process of *opening up*—a term used by Pennebaker and colleagues (1990) in his similar conception of psychological healing from loss—can be difficult, painful, and protracted. It is also subject to relapse, as when you fear you have said too much to someone, and avoid confiding again. As difficult as it may be, opening up appears to be required work in order for healing to be relatively complete and for psychological and physical health to be restored.

The process of recovery from major loss is not a simple one. It involves a tremendous amount of what we call *working through* one's thoughts and emotions. Consider this excerpt from an Esquire article written by editor Willie Morris. His tale is really an account of his early inability to let go of his ex-wife until he eventually found peace and a new perspective on his divorce. The following refers to the earliest period of this lengthy process:

> *It is a shrill and misty Manhattan dusk: autumn, 1969. A wan sliver of dying sunlight catches the windows of the skyscrapers. I am standing furtively at a street corner. Soon my wife emerges from a door across the way. No—my ex-wife. We have been divorced a fortnight, though I have yet to acknowledge the reality. I have been waiting here for her; I know she is the psychiatrist's last client of the afternoon, and that he himself will sooner or later come out too. . . . My heart literally palpitates with rage and fear and guilt, all of it so horrendously vainglorious, yet it is the man I have come to see, as if merely knowing what he looks like might ease some grievous wrong. . . . For weeks I have harbored the vengeful incubus that he and he alone has razed my marriage. That even had she been an ax murderess he would have counseled her, as surely they all did in that histrionic and debilitating American era: "Do what you must to be happy. If it feels good, do it." (Morris 1990, p. 172).*

Morris's account, related years after the events of his divorce, still preserves the intense emotions and fantasies of his early grief. Recalling and even reliving those feelings is essential to working through, a principle employed by many different approaches to psychotherapy. To cope with real events you must first face them and acknowledge them. Once you are past the pain of this confrontation you can begin the long business of healing and getting on with your life.

Understanding

In his study of marital separation, Robert Weiss (1975) noted that newly separated individuals engaged in obsessive review, a driven, exhaustive review of events leading up to the separation and a search for explanations. Obsessive review can be plagued with doubts and fantasies of "if only," e.g, "If only I hadn't insisted on moving near my parents" or "If only we had talked before she left town." Such review may give survivors of loss a greater feeling of understanding even if it does not directly lead to insights or solutions. More helpfully, reviewing and accounting may give survivors a feeling of being in control, at least of controlling their reactions to the separation. If your story makes sense, at least to you, then you are no longer helpless and in the dark. In this context, you can see how closely connected control is to the search for meaning. Control may also underlie the use of accounts to ventilate emotions, such as unresolved anger, grief, fear, and even guilty relief. By expressing intense feelings, one might experience a catharsis or release of debilitating emotions and anxiety. By getting past these emotional barriers to healing, one reestablishes control of the recovery process.

Completion

Related to understanding is the motive to maintain or enhance self-esteem. Account-making can be pitched to paint the narrator in the best possible light; for example, if your partner has left you, you are free to explain to others that it was he or she all along who was responsible for the conflict and failure of the relationship. Self-esteem motives are closely related to the original use of the term account to describe one's excuse or justification of questionable behavior (Scott and Lyman 1968, Snyder, Higgins and Stucky, 1983, Schönbach 1990). Such rationalizing or apologetic accounts usually conclude with an attribution. This attribution is more likely to be self-serving ("I was so stressed I forgot to return your phone call") than self-indicting ("I was not in the mood to talk to you so I decided not to return you call").

An intriguing recent work exploring self-enhancing accounts is *Breaking Hearts* (1992), by Baumeister and Wotman. The authors have collected respondents' stories of experiencing unrequited love—either from the perspective of the victim (the unwilling recipient of another's love) or that of the perpetrator (the one who proffers unreciprocated attentions). Their work shows that people use their accounts in an excusatory way to try to protect themselves from blame when their negative behavior makes them potentially culpable. Interestingly, Baumeister and colleagues found that, contrary to unrequited lovers' impressions that their beloved would welcome such affection, the recipients of unrequited love were generally very unhappy to be targeted, uncomfortable and even guilty about their inability to return these feelings. Unrequited love, apparently, is a pretty negative experience for all concerned, and it generates a good deal of need for meaning, closure, and freedom.

People have a psychological need for completion, for tying up loose ends (Zeigarnik 1938). Unfinished business—whether or not it is one's own fault that it is not finished—remains a nagging, persistent memory, until one is able to return to the task, finish it off, and file it away. By composing an official version of the breakup story that is much simpler than the reality, we can reassure ourselves that we at last understand what happened, and now it is over. Humans do appear to be often driven to try to finalize a big picture interpretation of major events in their lives, such as divorce. At a certain point, perhaps in later life, no longer is a complete understanding, a better sense of control, or an emotional purging the issue. Rather, the issue is that of tying up loose ends of meaning, and thus feeling that one's life is more complete. Bear in mind the possibility of incorporating later prejudices, discoveries, and hindsight into one's interpretation of remembered events. Today you may remember a past love with kindness or resignation, but at the time of your loss you may well have felt quite differently!

Generativity

Finally, account-making may satisfy a broader human need, especially in adult life, for what developmental theorist Erik Erikson called generativity (1963). In our desire to create or produce something of lasting value in our lives, the account may be a symbol of our efforts to teach or enlighten others. In this use—hear and learn from my story—the account can give others hope and greater will in facing their own dilemmas and, importantly, a model of a real person's experience (the storyteller's) who has dealt with a similar crisis. Frankl's (1959) analysis of people's search for meaning, written while he was a near-hopeless inmate in a Nazi concentration camp, is a quintessential example of such a generative act. Survivors often feel a compelling need to tell their stories in order to inform and possibly save others. As one participant said at a memorial service for survivors of the Holocaust, "Survivors must tell their story over and over and over again so that we may teach of the horror" (Chicago *Tribune*, April 22, 1991).

We turn again to Willie Morris's reflections on his divorce from his first wife for an illustration of how accounts might blend instruction and inspiration:

> *All that was a very long time ago, and I see now that, as with much of life, this really is a little long-ago tale of time passing, and of vanished grief. . . . Close relationships oscillate between tranquility and destruction, between fire and ice. Old fidelities wither, and love dies as the lovers go on living. There are a few small islands of warmth and belonging to sustain us if we are lucky. That is how I wish to think of her now, in the days of our happiness. . . . Finally, I have learned how difficult love is, how hard to achieve and sustain, no matter who the person or how felicitous the circumstance. (p. 175)*

Confiding After Relationship Loss

People differ in their ability to develop and relate articulate accounts. You have no doubt found that some people make even a simple anecdote interesting to hear, while others struggle to express themselves and turn off even a sympathetic audience. Although we agree with Robert Coles (1989) that storytelling is everyone's universal gift, some people are clearly more socialized to engage in effective account-making, story-telling, or narrating. Although confiding might benefit anyone, people differ in their abilities to understand their own experiences, express themselves, and disclose deeply to appropriate confidants.

Confiding is also affected by circumstances beyond personal skill. If you have ever had trouble finding the right time or right place to have a sensitive discussion with someone, you know that good intentions and honesty are not enough to make it happen. Too often people are on the run, or make it clear they have problems of their own and cannot offer to listen. Taken together, the many barriers to confiding probably account for the popularity and growth in recent years of counseling and psychotherapy. At the very least, when you are paying for the services of a therapist, you can expect undistracted interaction and a chance to unburden yourself. Productive confiding is such a precious and delicate event, not to be taken for granted or abused. It requires a strength and generosity of caring by the other, and an openness of self, each requiring a mature perspective, appreciation of the value of social interaction, and personal courage.

Effective Confiding

For all its demanding, exacting nature, how valuable is confiding to the healing process? Our conclusions about the importance of confiding correspond closely to the findings of Pennebaker (1989; 1990; Pennebaker et al. 1990). He and his colleagues provide evidence that people who confide secrets about traumatic experiences (such as having been raped or molested in the past) exhibit less subsequent physical and psychological difficulty than do people who do not confide. These theorists contend that confiding is often best carried out by writing because writing helps the confider to organize and clarify his or her thoughts and feelings. The person who does not confide is assumed to be adversely affected because of resulting guilt and psychological turmoil.

Pennebaker's 1990 book suggests that it is not the number of friends in whom you confide that helps you deal with stressors, but rather the quality of the confiding experience you have with close others. Confiding is more effective when it succeeds in a balancing act of sorts: the discloser must select the right confidant, but not make the listener feel responsible; disclosure must be honest and meaningful, but must not overburden the confidant. Confiding must also be timely. Pennebaker points out that the courses of both romantic love and grief show periods of intensity, plateau, and assimilation. The timeline for grieving after a breakup runs approximately eighteen months, varying by a few months depending on individual factors.

Pennebaker confirms the value and nature of the process of confiding; our own analysis emphasizes more the contents of accounts and confidences. While writing is undoubtedly an enhancing way to relate accounts, we think that private reflection and reciprocal presentation to and feedback from others are vital to successful writing. Finally, Pennebaker may be correct about the eighteen-month timeline for grief after breakups, but we advise caution in interpreting this figure. There are different kinds of losses—marital and nonmarital breakup, sudden death and anticipated death, abrupt abandonment and gradual drifting apart—which precipitate different kinds of grieving. The unfinished business left by a partner's sudden death, for example, surely requires more complex and timeconsuming working through than a death after a protracted illness.

Thus we cannot confidently suggest a time-frame for recovery from loss. The available evidence suggests that grieving is a highly individual phenomenon (Wortman and Silver 1989). Romantic breakups can be so potent as to ripple through eras of a person's life and indirectly affect the course and growth of further relationships. While it may be useful to have a normal time-frame to consider when one suffers a great loss—How long am I going to feel this bad? When will I be able to live normally again?—we must realize that each person must grieve in his or her own way. There are no absolutes and no universal standards when it comes to loss, healing, and the completion of recovery.

The Relevance of Account-Making

Why do we make accounts? Certainly effective story-telling and story-thinking can be an end in itself, as human beings may prefer to think and reason in a narrative way (Vitz 1990). So account-making may be an automatic by-product of our natural ongoing efforts to understand our world and monitor our experiences. In this chapter we further argue that developing, maintaining, and relating accounts is an essentially useful sequence in our experiences of close relationships. Account-making helps one to cope in the wake of loss; it accomplishes some of the tasks of grief work (Leick and Davidsen-Nielsen 1991). By first understanding your account and then confiding it as appropriate, you move to a stage of completion. This readies you to re-enter the world you left when you were hit by loss, and helps you to re-integrate your new status (e.g., suddenly single) into your old self (e.g., accustomed to acting as part of a couple).

For example, joining the world again after a period of bereavement might involve getting ready to date, meeting potential new mates, and expressing interest and availability for a social life. Your account of your recent loss can be quite practical in this endeavor. By remembering what worked—and what you hoped never to repeat—from earlier dating experiences, you can learn the lessons of experience. Harvey, Agostinelli and Weber (1989) asked newly separated romantic partners what they expected of new relationships, and found that respondents made resolutions based on past accounts. For example, a person who feared that the last relationship moved too fast for its own good would express a wish to take the next relationship more slowly.

But recovering from loss is a complicated business, and cannot be summarized in a brief to do list of the tasks of grief. Following is an excerpt from the account of a woman (Neeld 1990) who had recently experienced the unexpected death of her 43-year-old husband. It illustrates the enduring difficulty of trying to move on with one's life. It also may suggest that of all types of losses we could experience, the sudden death of a loved one is among the most daunting to our coping ability:

> *It's chilly this morning here in Texas. Right now I'm listening to Emmylou Harris and thinking of cold rainy winter days when Greg and I were so content and satisfied and dwelled in the sky called love.*
>
> *The stew in the pot, his bringing the wood in from the yard, his bare legs sticking out from under his green trench coat—oh, I miss him so much today. I miss the softness, the lack of trying, the not being constantly under the demand called resolving and adjusting. I am so tired of being brave and getting on with it and learning from my experience and beginning a new life—all those positive things that you're supposed to do after losing. Instead, I'd like to roll in the rug called the world's good, the rug called I love you. (p. 179)*

Recovering

Neither account-making nor confiding can be rushed. For example, after the death of a loved one, the bereaved may not need to confide in others for some period of time. In fact, distraction may be a helpful interim step: keep busy with engrossing tasks, spend time in social activities or passive entertainment like theater and movies. Later, confiding in a professional or a support group setting might be more effective than trying to confide in close friends (Neeld 1990). Close friends may not know how to help one deal with death because they may fear it for themselves or their loved ones, or they may think that avoiding the topic is the best way to help. Friends who are paralyzed by denial will not make effective confidants, and may need time themselves to develop in that role.

Sociologist Robert Weiss (1975) was the first relationships researcher to call our attention to the value of accounts in coping with separation and divorce. He interviewed recently separated men and women and organized support groups of Seminars for the Separated. He found that the account each participant reported appeared to be a vital element in giving them clarity and direction. Also, since these respondents already belonged to a support system, it is likely that their account-making was associated with confiding during their group sessions and interacting with other members. Thus Weiss's groundbreaking research represents an early illustration of the joint effectiveness of account-making and confiding in dealing with the psychological pain of separation and divorce.

In a sense any breakup—whether a marital breakup such as separation or divorce, or a nonmarital breakup without a label—is unfinished business. What was complete—a couple, a partnership, marriage—is now split, torn asunder, broken apart. The Gestalt urge for closure makes it natural for an ex-partner to wish for reunion; by joining the two halves you can once more establish wholeness. But of course this is usually a naive wish, as human relations are not that simple. Weiss (1975) has noted that roughly half of marital separations proceed to the divorce stage; this means that half do not, so perhaps there is realistic hope for reconciliation in many cases. When people part ways, there is always the possibility they will meet again, start over, perhaps reforge the broken connection between them. Arguments and social pressures to get back together may be intense, as when there are children to be co-parented (Wallerstein and Kelly 1980, a review of family issues in divorce). At the very least, as Weiss (1975) observes, ex-partners who do not break off all contact with each other will have some form of continuing relationship to deal with. The survivor of a breakup must deal realistically with accounting for guilt and rejection, dividing custody of mutual friendships, and balancing new liaisons with lingering ties. The breakup will only be complete up to a point, because the ex-partners are lost, not to the world, but only to each other—for now. Even if reconciliation is impossible, and ex-partners maintain only the sparest or more formal of contacts, it is likely they will continue to deal with each other in thinking, remembering, mourning, and dreaming of the past, and the once-possible future. As long as we can remember an experience or an ideal, our close relationships never end.

So most breakups will have a substantial psychological agenda to be dealt with by one or both ex-partners. What a breakup typically need not deal with is the existential anxiety of loss by death. When a spouse or partner has died, the survivor feels the same outcry, denial, anger, fear, and sadness as in a breakup. But loss by death has a finality a breakup lacks. The bereaved survivor has no chance to call back the past and tie up loose ends, say what was unsaid, or fix what was not quite right. He or she cannot try to contact or consult with the departed person. And the survivor is acutely threatened with the reality of his or her own—everyone's—eventual death. This a complex and weighty trauma; recovery will not be short and sweet!

Studies by researchers and therapists have yielded some agreement about the effects of grief and the tasks of grief work. Grief is overwhelmingly sad and negative. Depression—what psychoanalyst Carl Jung once called "being forced downward"—is common among the bereaved, and often accompanies a decline in health. A central relationship—perhaps the central relationship—in the survivor's life has been lost; meaning and value in life are threatened mightily, and there is a void that cannot be filled. One's life pattern and social role is altered; once part of a couple or family, the survivor has been cut loose from moorings and left feeling extraneous, a fifth wheel without a clear place in the social network. Perhaps most staggering, one has lost one's future, in all of its particulars that one has planned with the other. Neeld (1990) poignantly comments on her own loss (when her young husband suddenly died):

> *I had lost my identity. As the weeks passed, it also became clear to me that an equally devastating loss was the loss of the future I had assumed I would have. I had expected to have Greg's children. Katie Rachel Pearl . . . Jeremiah Cade. Now there would be no babies. At night I dreamed of brown-eyed sons and curly-haired daughters. At thirty-seven, I mourned those never-to-be children. (p. 59)*

How does one cope with bereavement? Leick and Nielsen-Davidsen (1991) argue that grief work involves four tasks: (1) the loss has to be recognized; (2) the various emotions of grief must be released; (3) the griever must develop new skills for living and coping; and (4), the survivor must reinvest his or her emotional energy in new directions. Leick and Davidsen-Nielsen are therapists who argue that a task theory of grief makes more sense than the traditional stage theory, because tasks may overlap or be accomplished in different orders—not in discrete, temporally distinct stages. If we accept this theory, it is possible to apply account-making constructively to all four tasks: (1) the account chronicles the loss and confirms its reality; (2) vivid language and powerful memories record the griever's emotions in the account; (3) by formulating and especially confiding the account, the griever actively practices communicating and relating skills; and (4), account-making helps the griever to sort out lessons learned, provides a sense of closure and completion, and readies him or her for the journey ahead.

If you are not grieving but care about someone who is, apply these lessons about mourning and account-making. Be sensitive to the timing of bereavement. Initially, offer distractions, companionship, or busy-ness to your friend. Carl Jung suggested that a bereaved colleague stave off the darkness of depression by seeking out productive and nurturing activities: doing things for others, nurturing animals or plants—anything that would draw rays of light back into one's life. When the time is right, offer (if you can honestly do so) to be the confidant. Invite reminiscences, ask questions about the lost partner—break the silence and bring up his or her name. By communicating your good intentions and friendship, you will make it easy for your friend to protest that it is too soon or that such talk is painful—and even easier for him or her to respond by sharing the stories that remain to be told. Loss is inevitable among the vast possibilities of human intimacy, and in the context of loss, pain, and grief, there can be no greater love than that offered by an accepting, thoughtful confidant.

Conclusion

In our conception of coping with close relationship loss, completion and acceptance are touchstones of successful account-making. These end stages are not easily reached, but when they are attained, they represent psychic healing in a fundamental way. In the daily behaviors that reflect these stages, one truly is moving on with one's life—and may be fostering one's own identity change, a transformation that often follows completion and acceptance.

Consider how an account sounds when the account maker has indeed achieved a fairly complete picture of the event, and has accepted it and its consequences. The following is an excerpt from a letter written by Larkin Warren to her ex-husband, thirty years after their marriage in the 1960s and a few years after their divorce:

You loved me with all your heart, as I loved you. We did the best we could with that love, and the dumb determination that it would be enough for a marriage and a life. Who had time then to grow into friendship, or trust, or compromise, or comfort? Not that young boy, or the girl at his side. It's for them, and for all the emotions pulled around like an old U-Haul, that I write this letter. I am letting you off the hook, and ask you to let me off any hooks hanging around in your memory too. I only regret the losses now, where once I raged at them, but don't want them to be all there was. Remember the touch on the cheek, the child, the Notre Dame game we didn't see. (Warren 1990, p. 212)

Another seemingly resolved account of acceptance is revealed in the following poem, from *How to Survive the Loss of a Love* (Colgrove, Bloomfield and McWilliams 1991). These verses (from p. 147) note the frequent perceived betrayals that may be a part of lost love:

I shall miss loving you

I shall miss the
Comfort
of your embrace.

I shall miss the
Loneliness
of waiting for your
calls that never came.

I shall miss the Joy
of our comings,
and Pain
of your goings.

and,
after a time,
I shall miss

missing
loving
you.

While completion and acceptance are possible for any major loss, we also should note the nature of intense human bonding is such that—psychologically—close relationships never end. They continue to live in our memories and influence our current behavior and future plans, often indirectly and in ways we only vaguely recognize. So in a sense, the account-making career of a person who has bonded strongly with another and then separated probably never really ends until death. We often travel down roads, both literally and figuratively, when images of the departed other catch our eye, beckon to us, lure us to take a moment and try to remember when . . . We often interpret the actions of our new partners in terms of the ideas and experiences we learned with former loves, once upon a time.

Our portrait of account-making pertains mainly to how we deal with losses in our lives. Certainly that is true of the strongest cases of this phenomenon, and those we have emphasized here. However, humans also engage in account-making when they encounter highly positive experiences, such as the unforeseen beginning of a close relationship with someone new, or cataclysmic good fortune like winning a lottery. At present, we have too little knowledge about how account-making may differ for positive versus negative events. Do we, for example, blithely carry on without much reflection or account-making when life's events are expected and generally positive? Many great writers have noted the energizing power of mental suffering and pain; Ralph Waldo Emerson observed that "He has seen but half the universe who has not seen the house of pain." More lyrically yet no less aptly, Emily Dickinson phrased it thus:

Heavenly Hurt, it gives us—
We can find no scar,
But internal difference,
Where the Meanings are.

Summary

As part of our ongoing quest for meaning, we develop and relate stories about our experiences, especially negative or unexpected events such as close relationship losses. Individuals may develop ongoing accounts of relationships from their earliest formation. Partners' versions may not always agree or adopt similar perspectives, and such disagreement between accounts may lead to conflict. Retrospective accounts of relationship loss are influenced by the nature of the loss, whether a breakup or a loss through death.

Account-making is a major strategy for working through the issues and dilemmas of relationship loss. In this sense, account-making serves several functions, such as fostering understanding of relationship events, and helping the bereaved person to achieve a sense of completion and generativity.

Central to our conception of account-making after relationship loss are two processes: private formulation of the account, and public disclosing or confiding in close others. We argue that accounts are useful in relationship maintenance and essential to recovery from loss. They facilitate the tasks of grief, and capture the complex and poignant meaning of love and loss in human existence.

References

Baumeister, R. 1991. *The meanings of life.* New York: Guilford Press.

Baumeister, R. and S. R. Wotman, 1992. *Breaking hearts.* New York: Guilford Press.

Bradbury, T. N. and F. D. Fincham, 1990. Attributions in marriage: Review and critique. *Psychological Bulletin,* 107:3–33.

Coles, R. 1989. *The call of stories.* Boston: Houghton Mifflin.

Colgrove, M., H. H. Bloomfield, and P. McWilliams, 1991. *How to survive the loss of a love.* Los Angeles: Prelude Press.

Crosby, J. F. 1991. *Illusion and disillusion: The self in love and marriage,* 4th edition. Belmont, CA: Wadsworth.

Erikson, E. 1963. *Childhood and society,* 2nd edition. New York: W. W. Norton.

Frankl, V. E. 1959. *Man's search for meaning.* New York: Washington Square.

Harvey, J. H., G. Agostinelli and A. L. Weber, 1989. Account-making and the formation of expectations about close relationships. In *Review of personality and social psychology: Close relationships,* ed. C. Hendrick, 39–62. Newbury Park. CA: Sage.

Harvey, J. H., T. L. Orbuch, and A. L. Weber, 1990. A social psychological model of account-making in response to extreme stress. *Journal of Language and Social Psychology,* 9:191–207.

Harvey, J. H., T. L. Orbuch, and A. L. Weber. (Eds.). 1992. *Attributions, accounts, and close relationships.* New York: Springer-Verlag.

Harvey, J. H., A. L. Weber, and T. L. Orbuch, 1990. *Interpersonal accounts: A social psychological perspective.* Oxford: Basil Blackwell.

Harvey, J. H., G. L. Wells, and M. D. Alvarez. 1978. Attribution in the context of conflict and separation in close relationships. In *New directions in attribution research,* vol. 2, ed. J. H. Harvey, W. Ickes and R. F. Kidd, 235–60. Hillsdale, NJ: Lawrence Erlbaum Associates.

Heider, F. 1958. *The psychology of interpersonal relations.* New York: Wiley.

Hill, C. T., Z. Rubin, and L. A. Peplau, 1976. Breakups before marriage: The end of 103 affairs. *Journal of Social Issues,* 32:147–68.

Holtzworth-Munroe, A. and N. S. Jacobson, 1985. Causal attributions of marital couples: When do they search for causes? What do they conclude when they do? *Journal of Personality and Social Psychology,* 48:1398–1412.

Jones, E. E. and R. E. Nisbett, 1972. *The actor and the observer: Divergent perceptions of the causes of behavior.* Morristown, NJ: General Learning Press.

Kelley, H. H. 1972. *Attribution: Perceiving the causes of behavior.* New York: General Learning Press.

Leick, N. and M. Davidsen-Nielsen, 1991. *Healing pain: Attachment, loss and grief therapy.* New York: Tavistock/Routledge.

Lewis, C. S. 1963. *A grief observed.* New York: Bantam Books.

Maslow, A. H. 1970. *Motivation and personality.* Rev. ed. New York: Harper and Row.

Morrell, D. 1988. *Fireflies.* New York: E. P. Dutton.

Morris, W. 1990, June. Here lies my heart. *Esquire,* 168–75.

Neeld, E. 1990. *Seven choices: Taking the steps to new life after losing someone you love.* New York: Delta Publishing Group.

Orvis, B. R., H. H. Kelley, and D. Butler, 1976. Attributional conflict in young couples. In *New directions in attribution research,* vol. 1, ed. J. H. Harvey, W. J. Ickes and R. F. Kidd, 353–86. Hillsdale, NJ: Lawrence Erlbaum Associates.

Pennebaker, J. W. 1989. Confession, inhibition, and disease. In L. Berkowitz (Ed.), *Advances in experimental social psychology* (Vol. 22, pp. 211–224). Orlando: Academic Press.

Pennebaker, J. W. 1990. *Opening up: The healing power of confiding in others.* New York: Morrow.

Pennebaker, J. W., M. Colder, and L. K. Sharp, 1990. Accelerating the coping process. *Journal of Personality and Social Psychology,* 58:528–37.

Rando, T. A. 1988. *Grieving: How to go on living when someone you love dies.* Lexington, MA: Lexington Books.

Schönbach, P. 1990. *Account episodes: The management or escalation of conflict.* Cambridge: Cambridge University Press.

Scott, M. B. and S. M. Lyman. 1968. Accounts. *American Sociological Review,* 33:46–62.

Snyder, C. R., R. L. Higgins, and R. J. Stucky, 1983. *Excuses: Masquerades in search of grace.* New York: Wiley.

Staudacher, C. 1987. *Beyond grief.* Oakland, CA: New Harbinger Publications.

Vitz, P. 1990. The use of stories in moral development. *American Psychologist,* 45:709–20.

Wallerstein, J. S. and J. B. Kelly, 1980. *Surviving the breakup: How children and parents cope with divorce.* New York: Basic Books.

Warren, L. 1990, June. "P. S., I loved you." *Esquire.* 211–12.

Weber, A. L., J. H. Harvey, and T. L. Orbuch, 1992. What went wrong: Communicating accounts of relationship conflict. In *Explaining one's self to others: Reason-giving in a social context,* ed. M. L. McLaughlin, M. J. Cody and S. J. Read, 261–80. Hillsdale, NJ: Lawrence Erlbaum Associates.

Wegner, D. M. 1986. Transactive memory: A content analysis of the group mind. In *Theories of group behavior,* eds. B. Mullen and G. R. Goethals, 185–202. New York: Springer Verlag.

Wener, D. M., R. Erber, and P. Raymond. 1991. Transactive memory in close relationships. *Journal of Personality and Social Psychology,* 61:923–29.

Weiss, R. S. 1975. *Marital separation.* New York: Basic Books.

Wortman, C. B. and R. C. Silver, 1989. The myths of coping with loss. *Journal of Consulting and Clinical Psychology,* 57:349–57.

Zeigarnik, B. 1938. On finished and unfinished tasks. In *A sourcebook of Gestalt psychology,* ed. W. D. Ellis, London: Routledge and Kegan Paul.

Chapter *15*

Social Support

BENJAMIN H. GOTTLIEB
University of Guelph

Outline

Introduction and Overview

Illustration: Bob Simpson's Breakup

Even though he suspected something, Bob Simpson just couldn't believe his worst fear had come true. After he had spent the entire weekend with the woman he'd been going with for the past two years, she called to say that it was just not going to work anymore and that she wanted to break off their relationship. He had barely gotten in the door of his double room in the residence hall when the phone rang, and there she was feeding him this line about how she'd met someone else and how she had to trust her feelings. The best part was that she hoped she and Bob could still be good friends. Bull! No matter what Adele said to try to smooth it over, the fact was that they were history, and she was starting a new chapter with another guy.

Bob didn't get much sleep that night. His mind was racing, alternating between fantasies about the things he could do or say to get even with Adele or to get the relationship back on the rails, and thoughts about where he had gone wrong and what a loser he was. Alan, his roommate, didn't get much sleep that night either because he was up until four o'clock in the morning, first watching Bob get drunk and then walking it off around town with him. There was Bob, kicking at snow banks and saying all kinds of threatening things about what he was going to do to himself or to the guy who ruined his life. There was Alan, hearing him out and making sure he didn't do anything reckless.

Things only got worse over the next few days. Bob cut most of his classes, missing mid-terms in two courses. He continued to drink too much, lost a lot of sleep, and stopped taking much interest in the way he looked. Two days after the horrible news, one of his buddies on the intramural basketball team happened to stop by. Bob was amazed that this guy never even seemed to notice how crummy he felt. Then when Bob angrily told him what had happened and how bleak and desperate he felt about things, the guy just beat a hasty retreat. Before he disappeared, he dropped a pearl of wisdom on Bob, saying, "Hey, it can't be that bad. Don't forget that there's lots of fish in the sea."

About a week after Bob's breakup, one of the women down the hall who had known Bob ever since his first semester on campus ran into him in the snack bar. Noticing how awful he looked, but not wanting to pry, she told him she was really in the mood for pizza and a movie she had been wanting to see, and did he want to go with her? "Why not?" shrugged Bob. They never did get to the movie but ended up talking about what Bob had been through with Adele and what had gone wrong in relationships that had ended for his dinner partner. They were both struck by what seemed to be the similarities in their experiences and feelings. By the time Bob returned to the residence hall he had lightened up enough to finally be able to break the news about him and Adele to his folks. He even surprised himself when he realized how much more on top of the whole thing he felt.

Defining Social Support

What is going on in this scenario, which is a fictional composite of several people's stories? What sort of issues are at stake for Bob as he tries to absorb the shock of this rejection? What might be going through his mind as he considers other people's reactions to the horrible news? "Can I or should I keep the news from others? Will I feel even worse if I go public or is there a chance it will help me in some way?

What might be going on in the minds of those people who come into contact with Bob? "He's certainly hurting and feeling pretty down, but what can and should I do? Can I figure out what to do or say to make him feel better? I don't want to say the wrong thing, yet I feel for the guy and ought to show him I care. Am I just going to complicate my own life if I get involved with Bob's problems? Would he be there for me if I were struck by some personal tragedy?"

These are some of the questions that have intrigued researchers who have been trying to understand the interpersonal and psychological dynamics of the social support process. The concept of social support can be defined as a process of interaction in relationships which improves coping, esteem, belonging, and competence through actual or predictable exchanges of practical or psychosocial resources. Over the past twenty years, investigators in the fields of social psychology, communications, and community mental health have been delving into the ways people get practical help, emotional support, and certain kinds of information from family members, friends, and other associates with whom they have regular contact in their everyday life. They have also been interested in discovering why people sometimes cannot get the kinds of assistance they might need or want from others. Therefore, some of the research has also focused on the factors that make people more and less capable of offering support to others.

Chapter Overview

This chapter is organized into four sections. In the first section, I use the Bob Simpson scenario to spotlight selected research findings and theoretical perspectives concerning the social support process. I review some of the factors that determine whether and how people signal and recognize that support may be needed, and how social support is subsequently conveyed, miscarried, or withheld. Because social support does not always refer to the help people get when crises or stressful events occur, I also describe what it means in everyday life. In the second section of the chapter, I explain why the topic of social support is important, touching on its role and impact in the stress and coping process, as well as its contribution to our understanding of close relationships. The third section of the chapter presents ideas about how social support might work, spotlighting the psychological processes that are unique to this medium of help. In the final section of the chapter, I address some of the ways social support is being used in programs aimed to help people adjust to stressful events, and I contrast these programs with the help provided by professional therapists.

Social Support as an Interpersonal Process

The first and most important observation about social support in the Bob Simpson scenario is that it is an interpersonal process that unfolds over time. It is an interpersonal process in the sense that Bob's behavior is both influenced by and influences the behavior of people in his immediate social environment. The process unfolds over time because one set of interactions that determines whether the need for support is recognized precedes a second set of interactions that determines whether support is provided, and if so, by whom and how it is expressed.

Initiation of the Support Process

Keeping in mind that behavior includes what people say and do, the way they look, and how they express their feelings, we can identify particular aspects of the interpersonal process that determined how Bob's need for support was recognized. Bob went public about his personal plight in a number of different ways, some more overt and deliberate than others. Although he actually told two people about what had happened, he also nonverbally disclosed to everyone with whom he had contact that something distressful had happened. They could see his disheveled appearance, his depressed mood, his excessive drinking, and his withdrawal from normal routines.

All of these behavioral changes could be detected by those who regularly interacted with and observed Bob. They were in the best position to recognize how different his behavior was from the usual. This is illustrated by the response of the woman down the hall. Noticing that Bob was not himself, she decided to reach out to Bob, and did so in a very graceful manner. In contrast, Bob's basketball buddy appeared to be oblivious to Bob's distress, prompting Bob to disclose his misfortune and his feelings about it more directly. His buddy's response suggests that the disclosure was poorly received because it prompted him to make a hasty departure, and while retreating, to offer a cavalier if not gratuitous expression of support.

These two sets of interactions reveal that there are two ways in which someone's need for support can be communicated to others: either by the distressed party directly disclosing a personal problem or upset feelings, or by the discovery or spontaneous recognition of the problem or upset feelings by members of the affected party's social network. Is one of these routes to problem recognition more desirable than the other? That is, is it better to open up to others or to wait until they take the initiative once they recognize that something is bothering you?

As Eckenrode and Wethington (1990) have pointed out, telling people about your problems or consciously revealing your distress to them is tantamount to requesting support from them, and is therefore psychologically more costly. It can mean that you are not capable of handling your own problems, that you are in a onedown position compared to the person to whom you've opened up, that you will then be indebted to this person, that this person will think less of you, that you have burdened this person with your problem, and that, if you've asked for help, you may have to show gratitude for it even if turns out not to be supportive. In short, by opening up to someone, you take the chance that it will lower your self-esteem and alter your relationship with that person in certain ways (Fisher et al. 1988; Fisher, Nadler, and Whitcher-Alagna 1982).

In contrast, when others initiate the support process, it conveys different information and is less psychologically risky. It lets you know that people are sensitive to your needs without your calling attention to those needs, and it does not presume that you are unable to handle your predicament or feelings (Eckenrode and Wethington 1990). Instead of having to ask people to demonstrate that they care about you, unsolicited expressions of concern confirm to you that they do care. It follows that people would tend to place greater value on the support they receive spontaneously, and that such support would tend to strengthen relationships or communicate the donor's desire for a closer relationship.

For example, in a recent study of women in dual income marriages, my colleague and I asked the participants to evaluate the support they received from their husbands on occasions when their work obligations conflicted with their family responsibilities (Steinberg and Gottlieb 1993). Many of the women reported that they were much more satisfied with their husbands' support when it was provided to them spontaneously than when they had to request it. More generally, research has found that helpseeking is more indirect and support more unsolicited in longer term and more intimate relationships (Clark 1983).

Varied Functions of the Social Network

Another important feature of the support process is that the social network's role changes over time. That is, the people who inhabit our personal community fill different functions at different stages of the support process. From what I have already discussed, you can see that even before they provide or withhold practical or emotional aid, the people with whom we associate are in a strategic position to notice when something is awry and whether it requires attention. As an informal diagnostic system, our social network provides feedback about the performance of our daily social roles, detects the accumulation of signs and symptoms of distress, and acts as a sounding board about whether our reactions to certain events or our general mood poses any threat to our well-being. Through such informal feedback, we can review possible causes of the changes we are experiencing, determine how serious they are and how long they may last, and determine whether to seek help and decide what kind of help is needed (Gottlieb 1982).

In addition to their diagnostic function, network members often make suggestions about where we should go for help with a problem or who would be a good person to talk to. Sometimes they might suggest a professional helper, like a counsellor, but more often than not they will refer us to another person they know who has the experiential knowledge to be of help. When the network sets

BOX 15–1   Mapping Your Support System

Step 1:

On a sheet of paper, draw a large circle, approximately seven inches in diameter, and then draw a second concentric circle within it that is half that diameter. Then draw a small circle around the word "me," at the center or nucleus of both circles.

Step 2:

On a separate sheet of paper list the initials of up to ten people who are important in your life these days. Think of people who are important because they affect the way you feel about yourself, about how things are going for you, and because they have the ability to boost or lower your spirits. You can include people you see on a regular basis, as well as people who you speak to on the telephone or correspond with. Try not to think only of people with whom you have positive interactions, but also of people who may be sources of stress to you.

You do not have to list ten people. There may be just one person who you feel is important in your life these days, two people, or any number up to ten.

Step 3:

Divide your list of significant others into two categories: family members (relatives) and friends. You can either put them in separate columns or simply place an "R" next to relatives and an "F" next to friends.

Step 4:

Now, in order to see how much of your network is composed of friends and how much of it is composed of family members, count up the total number of friends and then divide that number by the total of people on your network list. For example, if you have listed three friends who are important in your life

these days, and four family members, your total network size is seven and the proportion of friends is three divided by seven or about 43 percent.

Using your network map, divide it (like a pie) into two parts that reflect the proportion of family members and the proportion of friends.

Step 5:

Now comes the job of actually mapping your network. Starting with the friendship section of your network, try to show how close you feel to each friend (intimacy of the relationship) by placing him or her closer or farther away from you. Use a small circle to designate each friend, put that friend's initials in the circle, and let the distance of that circle from you reflect how intimate or close that relationship is. Do this for all your friends.

Step 6:

Repeat step 5 for the family section of your network.

Step 7:

The last steps will help you to see how tight-knit or loose-knit your network is. That is, you'll be able to see whether your friends tend to know one another or not and how close their relationships are to one another.

Beginning with the friendship part of your network, draw lines between friends who have a relationship with each other that is more than just a nodding hello. If all your friends have relationships with one another, then you are involved in a tight-knit friendship circle. You may find that there are one or two cliques among your friends, based on certain activities or interests those friends share.

BOX 15–1 *Continued*

Step 8:

Repeat 7 for the people in the family section of your network. Some family members may have close relationships with others and some may have very little to do with one another. For example, when people get divorced and remarried, they may still feel close to relatives from their first marriage, but those relatives may or may not develop relationships with relatives from the second marriage.

Step 9:

The final step will let you see the extent to which your friends and family members have relationships with each other. Draw lines between people in the friendship part of the network who have relationships with your family members.

Some people like to have a network in which everyone know everyone else because it gives them a strong sense of community, while others like to keep their friends separate from their family members, perhaps they find it easier to share certain kinds of information with friends that they prefer not to share with family members.

Questions

Ask yourself these questions about your network, or do this network exercise with someone else, and then use these questions to interview each other:

1. How much has your network changed in the past three years? Why has it changed?
2. How happy are you with the size and the composition of your network?
3. Are there any relationships you would like to make more intimate?
4. What kinds of support do you get from and give to the people in your network? Does the support you exchange with family members differ from the support you exchange with friends?

the trajectory of help-seeking, it therefore also serves as an informal referral system. In short, our family, friends, and other social contacts not only function as an informal support system, but also as an informal diagnostic system and an informal referral system.

Types, Sources, and the Expression of Support

Three different people were in a position to respond to Bob's distress, and a fourth party—his parents—eventually were told once Bob began to feel more on top of things. The ways in which his roommate, his basketball buddy, and the woman down the hall responded to him illustrate three additional aspects of the support process: social support can take a variety of forms; different kinds of support are expected from and provided by different sources; and situational cues determine whether and how social support is expressed.

Types of Support

Bob received several kinds of support. His roommate, Alan, showed solidarity with Bob and protectiveness toward him, all the time giving him an opportunity to vent his anger and hurt in the immediate aftermath of the distressful news. At first, his basketball buddy simply ignored Bob's distress, but when the story and feelings came pouring out, he swiftly departed, offering words that were intended to be supportive. This interaction took place only two days after the break-up, when Bob was still feeling very wounded. The woman down the hall offered companionship to Bob, and their dinner date gave both of them a chance to compare notes about different relationships they had been in. By this time, a week had gone by, Bob had settled down a bit, and was ready to start pulling himself together again. In fact, by the end of his evening out, Bob felt good enough to be able to break the news to his folks.

The literature on social support emphasizes the many forms it can take. They include advice, practical or instrumental assistance, emotional support, socializing and companionship, and appraisal or esteem support (see Tardy [1985] for a recent review of the dimensions of social support). House (1981) distinguishes between three general classes of supportive resources: aid, which consists of practical services and material benefits; affirmation, which has to do with feedback that promotes self-esteem and validates identity; and affect, which has to do with affection, caring, and nurturance. These distinctions are reflected in several measures of social support that have appeared in the past several years, including Sarason et al.'s (1983) Social Support Questionnaire, Procidano and Heller's (1983) measure of perceived social support from family and friends, and Cohen, et al.'s (1985) Interpersonal Support Evaluation List.

Sources of Support

The literature also shows that people expect and obtain different kinds of support for different stressful events from different people at different points in time (Cohen and McKay 1984; Cutrona and Russell 1990; Jacobson 1986). In short, there is a complicated relationship between sources, types, and changing needs for support. There must be a good fit between the kinds of support supplied by particular people and the needs aroused by the stressful demands the recipient faces. For example, the kinds of support that Bob's parents might give him and the kinds that he might seek from them are bound to be very different from the types of support he received from his dinner partner. This goes to show that behavior gains its supportive meaning from the nature of the relationship between the recipient and the provider. And the converse is true as well. The expression of support can alter the meaning of relationships. Consider your own experience for a moment. Have you ever received support from someone from whom you never expected it? Did it make you feel closer to that person? Did you ever feel let down by someone who you had expected to be there for you? Did that disappointment change the way you felt about your relationship with the person? If either of these examples ring a bell for you, then you can see how the expression of support and the meaning of relationships are so closely intertwined.

A number of studies have shown that network members specialize in providing certain kinds of support (Coyne and DeLongis 1986; Lieberman 1986); people evaluate the helpfulness of the same supportive gestures differently, depending on who made the gestures (Dakof and Taylor 1990); and the support people want from particular relationships cannot be replaced or compensated for by other relationships. For example, Brown and his colleagues (Brown et al. 1986) found that married mothers who anticipated receiving but failed to obtain crisis support from particular sources were more likely to experience an episode of depression than those who received the support they expected from these sources.

Emotions, Coping, and the Expression of Support

What determines whether and how social support is expressed? Did Bob somehow communicate the kinds of support he wanted or needed to the people around him? Did they base their behavior on anything Bob did or said? The interactional perspective on social support suggests that both parties influence whether and how support is expressed. The distressed party does this in two main ways: by revealing certain feelings and by dealing with his/her misfortune in particular ways.

As already mentioned, Bob showed his distress through expressing anger and dejection, especially in his interaction with his roommate and his basketball buddy. The two of them reacted in different ways. His roommate simply acknowledged and accepted Bob's anger and hurt, but Bob's basketball buddy at first acted as if he wasn't aware of these feelings, and then after Bob expressed them openly, behaved in ways that showed it was hard for him to deal with these feelings. He escaped from the unpleasant situation and said something that invalidated Bob's feelings ("It can't be that bad") and minimized the significance of his loss ("There's lots of fish in the sea").

Several studies suggest that people often miscarry their support, even when they know what kinds of support would be most helpful. For example, they may minimize or exaggerate an event's emotional impact, avoid open communication about the event, criticize the distressed party's ways of coping, put on a false cheerfulness, and encourage more rapid recovery. Lehman, Ellard, and Wortman (1986) speculate that the combined threat, anxiety, and feelings of responsibility aroused during face-to-face interaction with the distressed are responsible for these miscarried expressions of support. When people are made anxious by someone's distress, they often fall back on scripted responses, try to make someone feel better or cheer up, or, like the basketball buddy, simply try to get away from the uncomfortable interpersonal context. In fact, in a series of studies examining people's reactions to someone who is clinically depressed, it has been shown that the depressive mood is contagious; the would-be helper starts feeling depressed, and ends up withdrawing from, showing hostility toward, and even rejecting the depressed party (Coyne, Wortman, and Lehman 1988; Gotlib and Beatty 1985; Howes and Hokanson 1979).

In contrast, when would-be helpers can control their own emotions and accept the other party's distress rather than trying to ameliorate the feelings or shift the focus from them, both the support and the relationship outcomes are better. After all, if your goal is to make someone feel better, but you are unsuccessful because that person is not ready or able to feel better, then you will feel frustrated, inept and even more distressed, and probably want to avoid that person altogether. If you can accept someone's distress without expecting to improve his or her mood, then it's less likely you will come away feeling incompetent (Notarius and Herrick 1988). In fact, researchers in the fields of psychology and human communication have found that the most comforting and beneficial responses are those which facilitate ventilation and elaboration of the distressed party's perspective (Burleson and Samter 1985; Pennebaker 1989).

The helping process is affected not only by the emotions aroused in the interplay between the two parties, but also by the distressed person's coping behaviors. Sometimes we may withhold support from someone when we feel that he or she is not handling a problem in a way we approve of or in a way we would handle it. For example, if someone is coping with the pressure of final exams by procrastinating and taking drugs to relax, and we feel that he or she ought to buckle down and start studying, we are likely to decide that it would be a waste of our energy to invite him or her to study with us or to discuss strategies of preparing for an exam. That is because the help we are prepared to offer does not fit the coping strategies we observe. In fact, we might decide that this person doesn't even deserve our support because he or she has brought the problem on him or herself in the first place.

Two studies testify to the interdependence between social support and coping. According to one study, people were more likely to receive support when they engaged in ways of coping that involved doing something about the problem, such as making a plan of action and following it, rather than when they coped by denying and minimizing the problem or the feelings it aroused (Dunkel-Schetter, Folkman, and Lazarus 1987). The second study focused on parents of children who had serious chronic illnesses. My colleague and I found that the mothers, who were mainly responsible for the care of the children, were criticized by their husbands because they were coping in a way that was too emotional (Gottlieb and Wagner 1991). Threatened by their wives' open expression of distress about the illness and about the child's future, the husbands ridiculed their wives for their immaturity, chastised them for their lack of self-control, and even threatened to abandon them.

Returning to our scenario, we can see now that Bob's intense anger and depressed mood, along with his emotional way of coping, made it difficult for his roommate and his buddy to give him support. Later, once he had calmed down, it was less emotionally threatening to be around him, and he had begun to cope in a way that made it possible for him to discuss the subject of relationships with his dinner partner. Also, she offered support without calling attention to his need for it, and through a mutual exchange, Bob came away feeling better. In short, as time passed, Bob moved from the acute exposure stage and the runaway emotions accompanying it, to the calmer settling in stage, making his behavior and emotions more supportable. Only once he had regained a good measure of self-composure could he psychologically afford to break the news to his folks. He felt in greater control, and needed to show them, more than to anyone else, that he wasn't vulnerable, dependent or helpless. He could now shape their support in directions that would meet his needs without placing a huge burden of responsibility on them to rescue him from intense emotional turmoil.

The Impact of Social Support on Health and Relationships

Why study social support? The answer to this question depends on one's disciplinary affiliation. Sociologists have been mainly interested in understanding how social networks connect individuals to the larger social institutions of society, and how they communicate the norms and culture of the broader community. In addition, sociologists have shown that people who are more strongly integrated in society, through connections to voluntary organizations, paid employment, and a personal network of family and friends, have lower mortality rates than more socially isolated individuals (House, Landis and Umberson 1988). In contrast to this macro-level analysis, researchers in the communication field have studied the ways in which social support is actually expressed in human dialogue and through nonverbal interaction in groups and dyads. These micro-level analyses have concentrated on the ways in which people comfort one another, express esteem for one another, and help one another to make sense of stressful life events that they experience (Albrecht and Adelman 1987).

Impact on Health

Psychologists have largely tried to understand how social support affects people's efforts to cope when the going gets tough, and how it influences the quality and course of their relationships. For psychologists in my own particular area of specialization, which is called Community Mental Health, social support is of special interest because we are trying to identify the factors that keep people well rather than those which cause maladjustment and mental illness. The way we have learned that social support is indeed a critical resource for resisting stress is by examining people who are experiencing different kinds of stressful life events and transitions, and who differ in the amount and kinds of support they have. These studies show that people who actually receive social support, or just believe that they could obtain it if they wanted to, are at lower risk of maladjusting or becoming mentally or physically ill than those who lack social support.

In short, social support protects health because it buffers or cushions the impact of crises and chronic hardships (Cohen and Wills 1985). As you can see from the Bob Simpson scenario, the protective effect of social support lies in particular processes of social interaction that occur in particular relationships, not in the variable called social support. That is, social support is not a commodity or a resource that can be delivered; rather, it arises through the interactions occurring in our relationships.

There have been two kinds of studies linking social support to health: epidemiological studies which examine rates of death (mortality) and illness (morbidity) among large samples over a relatively lengthy period of time, and studies that examine particular stressful life events and transitions. The former is epitomized by Berkman's (1985) research in California. She discovered that people who had more personal and public (e.g., voluntary associations) social ties, and more frequency of contact with them, had subsequent (eight years later) mortality rates that were significantly lower than people who were more socially isolated. Other studies have confirmed this pattern of prospective association between social ties and mortality, even after controlling for biomedical risk factors such as smoking, diet, exercise, and initial health status (House, Landis, and Umberson 1988).

Examples of the studies examining particular life events include investigations of the mental health of women undergoing the transition to parenthood (Gottlieb and Pancer 1988), the adjustment of various samples of bereaved people, the adaptation of new immigrants, the adjustment of adults as well as children in the wake of marital separation, the stress resulting from job loss, and the extent of psychiatric symptomatology among women caring for elderly relatives at home. In fact, virtually every type of stressful event, including various medical diagnoses, has been subject to study to determine whether social support can mitigate its adverse effects, and the weight of evidence favors its protective impact.

Social support is not important only because of its protective function when people experience hardships. That would be tantamount to saying that our relationships are of value to us only because of the help they provide when adversity strikes. We also value our relationships because they contribute to our general well-being and life satisfaction. When people are surveyed about the domains of their life to which they attach greatest importance and satisfaction, they typically rank social relationships highly. Similarly, when people experience the loss of significant attachments, they are at greater risk of a range of adverse physical and mental health consequences. Our relationships validate our social roles and stabilize our personal identities, providing ongoing feedback about who we are and the appropriateness of our thoughts and feelings (Swann and Predmore 1985).

Impact on Relationships

Social support is also of great interest to psychologists who are trying to understand why relationships dissolve or grow stronger over time. After all, a relationship can be damaged if the support expected from it fails to materialize or if there is a significant asymmetry in the amount of support exchanged between the partners. Many marriages break down precisely because of lopsided patterns of support, because the partners grow insensitive to one another's support needs, or because one partner takes over the other's problems or is overprotective toward the other. For example, in two studies, one of heart patients and one of cancer patients, many patients reported that others were oversolicitous toward them, babying them and making them feel incapable of performing ordinary tasks. They came to resent these people, and even blamed them for complicating their life (Peters-Golden 1982; Wishnie, Hackett, and Cassem 1971).

Similarly, the course of relationships can be strengthened through the expression of support. If someone you had never expected to be there for you proved to be very supportive, would it not change your feelings about the relationship? Would it not signal something about that person's desire to have a closer relationship with you? Even when life is running a fairly smooth course, just knowing that there are people who you will be getting together with for some fun and relaxation can make you feel good. It is pleasurable to look forward to sharing the company of a good friend or going home to family for the weekend. In fact, a lot of the advertisements you see on television present their products in a social context where a group of people are having a good time together. This is especially true of the beer, soft drink, and fast food commercials that are pitched at the youthful market. It is as if these ads are saying, "You too can share the warm glow generated by the group camaraderie, if you buy this product."

How Social Support Works

Earlier in this chapter, social support was defined as a process of interaction in relationships which improves coping, esteem, belonging, and competence through actual or predictable exchanges of practical or psychosocial resources. Like most definitions of complicated social processes, this one still lacks specificity. First, it doesn't tell us whether social support is based on interaction with only one person or with several people. Second, it doesn't necessarily mean that a single interaction can accomplish any one or all the functions listed among its effects. Third, it doesn't tell us anything about the nature of the interactional process. And finally, and perhaps most important, it doesn't disclose how social support works.

Much is yet unknown about the mechanisms or processes whereby social support protects and promotes health, and about how it affects the conduct and course of our relationships. In order to develop a coherent theory of social support, we need to understand its mechanisms of action on human thought, emotions, behaviors, and relationships. At present, there are a number of hypotheses about these mechanisms of action, some based on speculation and some on social psychological theories that were formulated before the dawn of research on social support.

Social Support Mechanisms

For example, the epidemiological data linking social ties to decreased risk of illness and death have been explained in terms of the role that the social network plays in encouraging health promoting behaviors such as safe sex and proper sleep, diet, and exercise, and placing pressure on people to abandon health-injurious behaviors such as smoking and drug abuse. As already noted, the network may also act as an informal diagnostic system (Gottlieb 1982), detecting signs and symptoms of ill health or emotional imbalance, and referring people to professional practitioners or informal sources of help.

Hypotheses about how social support works—its mechanisms of action—have also been based on two well known theoretical perspectives in social psychology: social comparison theory (Festinger 1954) and attribution theory (Jones and Davis 1965). Studies of self-help and support groups suggest that the group provides opportunities for engaging in social comparisons. Members can make downward and upward comparisons on several dimensions. They can make downward comparisons with those whose problems are more severe than their own or who are not coping as well as themselves, and they can make upward comparisons with those who represent models of successful coping. Through both kinds of comparisons, participants can gain reassurance, a sense of optimism about their own prospects for recovery, and knowledge of effective coping strategies (Wood, Taylor, and Lichtman 1985).

Antze's (1976) studies of self-help and support groups revealed that these groups also develop ideologies which guide the members' attributions about the causes of their predicaments. In some instances these accounts steer members to reattribute their problems to factors outside their control, thereby relieving feelings of guilt and self-blame. This is exemplified in groups that point to genetic causes of illnesses (e.g., mothers who blame themselves for giving birth to a child with a chronic illness) or to causes that are rooted in cultural norms (e.g., slender images of femininity in groups for women with eating disorders). In other instances, these accounts emphasize the individual's role in creating the problem, reattributing the responsibility for change from situational factors to factors under the individual's control. This is exemplified in the ideology of Alcoholics Anonymous. It is noteworthy, however, that there is considerable debate about the effect of these different causal and control attributions on emotions, behavior, and self-perceptions. For example, Bulman and Wortman (1977) have argued that people can only take control of their coping if they believe that they had something to do with the cause of their problem in the first place.

Additional ideas about how social support works come from observations of self-help and support groups. Through comparing notes with one another, people's uncertainty about novel circumstances is reduced. By being exposed to veteran sufferers who have adjusted well to the same affliction or personal problem, hope and new ideas about coping are gained. At an even more basic level, peer support can offer validation and affirmation of new roles and identities following life transitions, normalize feelings, and counteract stigma. Additional ideas about how the support process helps the members of self-help groups to adjust include: their active participation in the role of helper; the way the group helps its members make meaning of their adversity; and the tendency for group members to form more personal relationships with one another. Over time, the boundary between the self-help group and the personal network of the participants gives way, making support more available in everyday life.

Using Support to Promote Human Welfare

Long before researchers in psychology, human communication, and epidemiology began to investigate the meaning and value of social support, there were social programs that tried to augment and improve the support that people gave to and received from others. Most people are familiar with the Big Brothers and Big Sisters agencies, which pair children with nonparental adult companions. And many university students have worked as volunteers or as coaches in tutoring programs, athletics, social service programs, and campus outreach initiatives. You may also be familiar with programs that involve friendly visits with people who live in institutions, foster grandparent programs, and programs in which someone serves as a mentor for a partner who is learning the ropes or needs some extra guidance and a good example to follow. In the film, "Return of the Jedi", the last of the "Star Wars" trilogy, Yoda was Luke Skywalker's mentor, showing him how to use "the Force". You may also recall that the "Karate Kid", in the movie of the same name, won out in the end thanks to his mentor.

Self-help and support groups have also proved to be very popular vehicles for exchanging support. Both medical and mental health professionals have formed support groups for people facing a wide range of disorders, afflictions, life events, and chronic hardships. There are groups for people with noxious habits (e.g., smoking; drug and alcohol use), groups for people with physical illnesses (e.g., cancer; colostomy; heart disease), groups for people living with or caring for someone with a serious illness (e.g., caregivers of persons with Alzheimer's Disease; friends and relatives of the mentally ill), and groups for people going through crises (e.g., death of a loved one; divorce) and developmental transitions (e.g., retirement; birth of a first child). A typical group is composed of eight to ten participants who meet for a fixed number of sessions, guided by a professional who supplements the members' experiential knowledge with expertise about the group's process, stressors the members face, and relevant coping strategies.

Hence, the topic of social support is of far more than academic interest. Professionals working in human services and health care, along with university psychologists who do intervention research are trying to engineer support in different ways and then evaluate the outcomes. For example, there are several studies of the impact of support groups for children whose parents have separated (Kalter et al. 1988) or died (Sandler et al. 1988), and there are programs in which home visitors establish supportive relationships with teenage mothers (Olds 1988), and telephone partners reach out to isolated elderly people (Heller et al. 1991). In these and other ways, efforts are being made to structure human relationships as systems of support, either by grafting new ties onto people's networks or by augmenting or improving the support people already exchange with members of existing natural networks.

Unlike the conventional individual or group therapy that professionals offer, programs that mobilize support try to create conditions that are conducive to the development of mutually responsive personal relationships. These programs are based on the idea that what people need more than anything else is to know that others are there for them—not just between the hours of 9:00 a.m. and 5:00 p.m.—but whenever the need arises. They are also based on the conviction that mutual exchanges of support, rather than the kind of one-way helping that occurs between a professional and a client, can be empowering. Instead of transferring the responsibility for change to a professional, people can become active agents of change themselves by showing caring, compassion, and commitment to one another.

Conclusion and Summary

In the end it is not a matter of choosing between the help provided by professionals on the one hand, and the support of our family and friends on the other. Each source of support can make a unique contribution to our welfare, depending on the needs we have at different times. There are occasions when nothing can substitute for close friends who, like Bob Simpson's roommate, hear us out and stay with us as long as we need them there. There are also occasions when our suffering exceeds the tolerance or helping skills of our associates, as proved to be the case for Bob's basketball buddy. In these instances, professional helpers may have the kind of specialized knowledge and training that equips them to offer expert judgements about the causes of our distress and insights about appropriate remedies. Moreover, there are times when we simply feel safer by seeking out the protective authority of professionals.

Perhaps the optimal support system is one which blends the contributions of professionals and the loved ones and companions who share our lives. By developing mutually respectful relationships and opportunities for mutual instruction between professional and informal supporters, we stand to learn and gain the most. We will learn that each of these sources of support has its fallibilities and its strengths, that each can make judicious use of the other, and that together, they comprise a durable and flexible safety net.

References

Albrecht, T. L., and M. B. Adelman. 1987. *Communicating social support.* Newbury Park, CA: Sage.

Antze, P. 1976. The role of ideologies in peer psychotherapy organizations. *Journal of Applied Behavioral Sciences,* 12:232–46.

Berkman, L. F. 1985. The relationship of social networks and social support to morbidity and mortality. In *Social support and health,* ed. S. Cohen and S. L. Syme, 241–62. Orlando, FL: Academic Press.

Brown, G. W., B. Andrews, T. Harris, Z. Adler, and L. Bridge. 1986. Social support, self-esteem and depression. *Psychological Medicine,* 16:211–30.

Bulman, R. J., and C. B. Wortman. 1977. Attributions of blame and coping in the 'real world': Severe accident victims react to their lot. *Journal of Personality and Social Psychology,* 35:351–63.

Burleson, B. R., and W. Samter. 1985. Consistencies in theoretical and naive evaluations of comforting messages. *Communication Monographs,* 52:103–23.

Clark, M. S. 1983. Some implications of close social bonds for help-seeking. In *New directions in helping, Vol. 1: Recipients' reactions to aid,* ed. J. D. Fisher, A. Nadler, and B. M. DePaulo, 205–27. New York: Praeger.

Cohen, S., and G. McKay. 1984. Social support, stress, and the buffering hypothesis: A theoretical analysis. In *Handbook of psychology and health, Vol 4,* ed. A. Baum, J. E. Singer, and S. E. Taylor, 253–267. Hillsdale, NJ: LEA.

Cohen, S., R. Mermelstein, T. Kamarck, and H. Hoberman. 1985. Measuring the functional components of social support. In *Social support: Theory, research, and applications,* ed. I. G. Sarason and B. R. Sarason. 73–94. The Hague: Martinus Nijhoff.

Cohen, S., and T. Wills. 1985. Stress, social support, and the buffering hypothesis. *Psychological Bulletin,* 98:310–57.

Coyne, J. C., and A. DeLongis. 1986. Going beyond social support: The role of social relationships in adaptation. *Journal of Consulting and Clinical Psychology,* 54:454–60.

Coyne, J. C., C. B. Wortman, and D. R. Lehmann. 1988. The other side of support: Emotional overinvolvement and miscarried helping. In *Marshaling social support: Formats, processes, and effects,* ed. B. H. Gottlieb. Beverly Hills, CA: Sage.

Cutrona, C. E., and D. W. Russell. 1990. Type of social support and specific stress: Toward a theory of optimal matching. In *Social support: An interactional perspective,* ed. B. R. Sarason, I. G. Sarason, and G. R. Pierce, 319–66. New York: Wiley.

Dakof, G. A., and S. E. Taylor. 1990. Victims' perceptions of social support: What is helpful from whom? *Journal of Personality and Social Psychology,* 58:80–89.

Dunkel-Schetter, C., S. Folkman, and R. S. Lazarus. 1987. Social support received in stressful situations. *Journal of Personality and Social Psychology,* 53:71–80.

Eckenrode, J., and E. Wethington. 1990. The process and outcome of mobilizing social support. In *Personal relationships and social support,* ed. S. Duck, 83–103. Newbury Park, CA: Sage.

Festinger, L. 1954. A theory of social comparison processes. *Human Relations,* 2:117–40.

Fisher, J. D., B. A. Goff, A. Nadler, and J. M. Chinsky. 1988. Social psychological influences on helpseeking and support from peers. In *Marshaling social support: Formats, processes, and effects,* ed. B. H. Gottlieb, 267–304. Newbury Park, CA: Sage.

Fisher, J. D., A. Nadler, and S. Whitcher-Alagna. 1982. Recipient reactions to aid. *Psychological Bulletin,* 91:27–54.

Gotlib, I. H., and E. Beatty. 1985. Negative responses to depression: The role of attributional style. *Cognitive Therapy and Research,* 9:91–103.

Gottlieb, B. H. 1982. Social support in the workplace. In *Community support systems and mental health,* ed. D. E. Biegel and A. J. Naparstek, 37–53. New York: Springer.

Gottlieb, B. H., and S. M. Pancer. 1988. Social networks and the transition to parenthood. In

The transition to parenthood: Current theory and research., ed. G. Y. Michaels and W. A. Goldberg. New Rochelle, CT: Cambridge University Press.

Gottlieb, B. H., and F. Wagner. 1991. Stress and support processes in close relationships. In *The social context of coping*, ed. J. Eckenrode, 165–88. New York: Plenum.

Heller, K., M. G. Thompson, P. E. Trueba, J. R. Hogg, and I. Vlacos-Weber. 1991. Peer support telephone dyads for elderly women: Was this the wrong intervention? *American Journal of Community Psychology*, 19:53–74.

House, J. S. 1981. *Work, stress and social support.* Reading, MA: Addison-Wesley.

House, J. S., K. R. Landis, and D. Umberson. 1988. Social relationships and health. *Science*, 241:540–45.

Howes, M. J., and J. E. Hokanson. 1979. Conversational and social responses to depressed interpersonal behavior. *Journal of Abnormal Psychology*, 88:625–34.

Jacobson, D. E. 1986. Types and timing of social support. *Journal of Health and Social Behavior*, 27:250–64.

Jones, E. E., and K. E. Davis. 1965. From acts to dispositions: The attribution process in person perception. In *Advances in experimental social psychology*, ed. L. Berkowitz, 2:219–66. New York: Academic Press.

Kalter, N., M. Schaefer, M. Lesowitz, D. Alpern, and J. Pickar. 1988. School-based support groups for children of divorce: A model of brief intervention. In *Marshaling social support: Formats, processes, and effects*, ed. B. H. Gottlieb, 165–86. Newbury Park, CA: Sage.

Lehman, D. R., J. H. Ellard, and C. B. Wortman. 1986. Social support for the bereaved: Recipients' and providers' perspectives on what is helpful. *Journal of Consulting and Clinical Psychology*, 54:438–46.

Lieberman, M. A. 1986. Social supports: The consequences of psychologizing: A commentary. *Journal of Consulting and Clinical Psychology*, 54:461–65.

Notarius, C. I., and L. R. Herrick. 1988. Listener response strategies to a distressed other. *Journal of Social and Personal Relationships*, 5:97–108.

Olds, D. 1988. The prenatal/early infancy project. In *Fourteen ounces of prevention*, ed. R. H. Price, E. L. Cowen, R. P. Lorion, and J. Ramos-McKay, 9–23. Washington, DC: American Psychological Association.

Pennebaker, J. W. 1989. Confession, inhibition, and disease. *Advances in Experimental Social Psychology*, 22:211–44.

Peters-Golden, H. 1982. Breast cancer: Varied perceptions of social support in the illness experience. *Social Science and Medicine*, 16:483–91.

Procidano, M. E., and K. Heller. 1983. Measures of perceived social support from friends and from family: Three validation studies. *American Journal of Community Psychology*, 11:1–24.

Sandler, I. N., J. C. Gersten, K. Reynolds, C. A. Kallgren, and R. Ramirez. 1988. Using theory and data to plan support interventions: Design of a program for bereaved children. In *Marshaling social support: Formats, processes, and effects*, ed. B. H. Gottlieb, 53–83. Newbury Park, CA: Sage.

Sarason, I. G., H. M. Levine, R. B. Basham, and B. R. Sarason. 1983. Assessing social support: The Social Support Questionnaire. *Journal of Personality and Social Psychology*, 44:127–39.

Steinberg, M., and B. H. Gottlieb. 1993. Appraisals of spousal support among women facing conflicts between work and family. In *The communication of social support: Messages, interactions, relationships, and community.* ed. B. Burleson, T. Albrecht, and I. Sarason. Newbury Park, CA: Sage.

Swann, W. B., and S. C. Predmore. 1985. Intimates as agents of social support: Sources of consolation or despair? *Journal of Personality and Social Psychology*, 49:1609–17.

Tardy, C. H. 1985. Social support measurement. *American Journal of Community Psychology*, 13:187–202.

Wishnie, H. A., T. P. Hackett, and N. H. Cassem. 1971. Psychological hazards of convalescence following myocardial infarction. *Journal of the American Medical Association*, 215:1292–96.

Wood, J. V., S. E. Taylor, and R. R. Lichtman. 1985. Social comparison in adjustment to breast cancer. *Journal of Personality and Social Psychology*, 49:1169–83.

Chapter 16

The Therapy Relationship

BARBARA A. WINSTEAD
Old Dominion University

VALERIAN J. DERLEGA
Old Dominion University

Outline

During first term of his senior year, Paul begins to have trouble finishing assignments. He has maintained a B average throughout college, but on his first tests this term he gets two Cs and a D. He tries to study and do homework assignments, but finds himself daydreaming. Time passes and the work is not done. On weekends friends ask him to join them in social activities. If he goes he feels bored or he drinks too much. Often he says he has too much to do and stays home or goes to the library. Good friends ask him, "What's wrong?" All he can say is, "It must be the 'senior blahs.'" He doesn't feel like talking, even to his close friends, about this problem. When he talks to his parents or visits them, he makes a special effort to seem cheerful. He has not told them about his test grades. He does not want them to worry. Finally, a close friend suggests that he go to the college counseling center to talk to someone. Feeling like he has to do something, he makes an appointment.

Why would someone seek help from a counselor or psychotherapist rather than talking to his friends or family? Sometimes, of course, individuals do not have good relationships with friends and family. For them going to a therapist may, in fact, be looking for a friend. As this chapter will explain, a good therapy relationship is not the same as having a good friendship. A positive therapy outcome for such individuals might be the ability to establish close relationships with persons outside of therapy.

Paul has close friends and good relations with his parents. Don't normal people get enough support in their close relationships so they do not need psychotherapy? It is often hard for individuals to talk openly with friends about personal problems, especially as in Paul's case when it is not clear what exactly the problem is. Paul may worry about burdening his friends with his concerns. He may figure that his friends' good advice to work harder during the week and relax on the weekend is not something that he can do. His friends may feel frustrated because they do not know how to help. Although his relationships with his parents are good, he does not want to worry them. Finally, no matter how much listening and advising friends and family are willing to do, they are a part of the situation. Paul may not want to tell his friends or parents about disappointments he feels about his relationships with them. Any advice they give may well reflect their own needs and concerns. His friends want him to go places and do things with them. His parents want him to finish school and get a job. A therapist is an outsider. She or he should be able to listen objectively to Paul's concerns without presuppositions about him, without feeling personally threatened by anything Paul says, and without an agenda about what Paul should be doing.

Is the Therapy Relationship a Close Personal Relationship?

Paul is going to talk with a therapist about his problems and, he hopes, get some relief from them. To understand thoroughly the nature of Paul's problems, the therapist will listen and ask questions. Paul is likely to reveal personal information to the therapist and may find that strong emotions are experienced during the therapy sessions. Clients often tell therapists things they have never told to anyone else; they often come to rely on therapists as a source of understanding and comfort. Although therapists reveal less, if any, personal information about themselves to clients and should not (for the clients' sake) depend on clients for support, they generally do feel caring and concern for their clients. The emotional intensity and shared experience of the therapy process make the therapy relationship a close relationship.

On the other hand, the therapy relationship is also a professional relationship (Reisman 1986). Unlike other close relationships in which partners expect reciprocity and equality, in the therapy relationship, the client self-discloses and the therapist listens; the client reveals weaknesses and personal problems, the therapist, generally, does not; the client pays a fee (directly or indirectly through insurance or student fees), the therapist provides a service. Whereas partners in close relationships usually get together whenever and wherever they choose, therapist and client meet at specified times and in a specified place (i.e., the therapist's office). Close relationships are expected to last as long as partners feel good about it, therapy relationships are successful when they end with both client and therapist feeling that it has been a good relationship. Despite its personal and emotional qualities, the therapy relationship is a task-oriented, working relationship. The goal is to improve the client's well-being.

The combination of personal and professional qualities in the therapy relationship makes it unique among relationships. Greenson in 1967 and Gelso and Carter in 1985 have discussed the therapy relationship as comprising three components: the working alliance, the transference-countertransference relationship, and the real relationship. The working or therapeutic alliance is the implicit, in some cases explicit, agreement between therapist and client that they are there to work on the client's problems.

Transference and countertransference are terms from psychoanalytic theory. Transference is a tendency for the client to establish a relationship with the therapist that is similar to relationships that the client has had with significant others. For example, if Paul tries hard to please his parents and is often afraid of disappointing them, then he will be likely to try to please and fear disappointing his therapist. Gelso and Carter (1985) call this component of the therapy relationship the unreal relationship because it "entails a misperception or misunderstanding of the therapist, whether positive or negative" (p. 170).

Countertransference refers to the misperceptions and misunderstandings of the client by the therapist. They may occur because the therapist lets her or his own personal issues influence reactions to the client. Paul's therapist may see in him characteristics that remind her or him of a younger sibling. Until the therapist recognizes the countertransference, she or he may treat Paul in a somewhat patronizing way, as she or he has sometimes treated this sibling. In another form of countertransference, Paul, in his eagerness to please, may evoke in the therapist a feeling of high expectations for Paul which Paul in turn will fear not living up to. Whenever countertransference occurs, it is the therapist's obligation to recognize and understand it and not let it interfere with therapy.

Transference and countertransference are unconscious processes; that is, client and therapist are not aware they are occurring when they first appear. It is the therapist's role to be vigilant for and correct countertransference, and to use transference for the benefit of therapy. In some therapies using transference may mean drawing the client's attention to it and analyzing it; in other therapies using the transference may mean maintaining a positive transference so that the client will comply readily with therapist interventions. Although transference and countertransference are terms associated with psychoanalytic therapy, they can occur in all therapies and are part of the therapy relationship.

In fact, misperceptions and misunderstandings based on previous relationship experiences occur in all relationships. Individuals enter relationships with hopes, fears, and expectations. They are likely to see their relationship partner in terms of their own personal concerns. Most people have had the experience of realizing that their partner has misunderstood them. A partner may believe that the relationship is more serious than we mean for it to be; or a partner may distrust us even though we have given them no reason to do so. The reciprocal self-disclosures that are characteristic in the development of a close relationship are partly an attempt to find out what our partner is really like and to communicate who we really are and what we want in a relationship and what we can be expected to give. Rather than seeking to understand the sources of these misperceptions or to use them in some way, in a nontherapy relationship we simply try to correct them. In the therapy relationship it is the therapist's responsibility to continuously correct their own misperceptions of the client and to manage the client's misperceptions in ways that are therapeutic.

There is also a real relationship between therapist and client based on accurate perceptions of one another and a willingness to be open and genuine with one another. The concept of the real relationship is associated with humanistic psychotherapy. Whereas in most close relationships the real relationship is what partners try to gain and keep, in the therapy relationship, when the real relationship component becomes predominant, psychotherapy has been successful and it is nearly time to end the relationship.

Types of Therapy Relationships

Paul does not know much about psychotherapy. He is a business major and does not remember much from the Introduction to Psychology course he took as a freshman. He takes the next available appointment at the counseling center. What is Paul in for?

To some extent what Paul will experience in psychotherapy depends on the type of therapist he sees and that therapist's clinical orientation. There are at least four categories of mental health professionals that do psychotherapy: clinical psychologists (M.S., Ph.D., or Psy.D. in clinical psychology), counseling psychologists (M.S. or Ph.D. in counseling psychology), clinical social workers (M.S.W.), and psychiatrists (M.D.). Clinical psychologists are trained in psychological assessment, therapy techniques, and research. Their training includes clinical experience with supervision as well as academic courses. Counseling psychologists receive similar training, but they often work with clients with less serious emotional problems. One would expect to find more clinical psychologists affiliated with inpatient facilities and more counseling psychologists in schools or work settings. The training of clinical social workers may focus more on couples, families, and communities. Psychiatrists are graduates of medical schools and, unlike other mental health professionals, can prescribe medication for psychological problems. In truth, although mental health professionals receive somewhat different training and may engage on average in somewhat different types of clinical practice, they all might do individual, group, or family therapy. An observer watching a psychotherapist in action would probably not be able to predict accurately his or her professional degree.

Paul's experience in psychotherapy will probably depend more on his therapist's theoretical orientation and on time limits for therapy than on his therapist's academic degree. There are three major orientations to psychotherapy: psychoanalytic/psychodynamic; humanistic/client-centered; and behavioral/cognitive. Psychoanalytic or psychodynamic psychotherapy is associated with the writing of Sigmund Freud although there have been many updates and modifications of Freud's ideas about therapy (cf. Blanck and Blanck 1974, on ego psychology and Cashdan 1988, and Greenberg and Mitchell 1983 on object relations theory and therapy). So important is the therapy relationship in psychoanalytic psychotherapy, that one might say the analysis of the therapy relationship is the therapy. The therapist adopts a neutral, listening stance towards the client. The client develops expectations of and feelings about the therapist that result from his or her experiences in other important relationships (e.g., relationships with parents). This is the transference. The therapist, rather than fulfilling these expectations, encourages the client to examine these expectations and feelings and to wonder where they came from. In this way the client usually gains insight into the developmental sources of her or his problems and also how misperceptions and false expectations influence current relationships.

If Paul's therapist is psychoanalytically oriented, he or she will encourage Paul to talk about his problems and his life saying whatever comes to mind. The therapist will ask few questions and give no advice. The therapist will be especially attentive to Paul's expression of thoughts and feelings about therapy. Perhaps after a few sessions Paul will wonder if he is doing good work in therapy. The therapist will help Paul explore the meaning of this and they may discover that Paul feels that the therapist, like his parents, must have very high expectations for him. With further investigation Paul may realize that his current malaise is the result, in part, of his feeling that if he does not succeed brilliantly, then there is no point in working at all. When he sees that neither his therapist, nor probably his parents, nor certainly he himself, need to have unreasonable expectations for his performance, then he begins to be able to work and relax as before. With further analysis Paul may discover that in addition to wanting to do very well, he also fears doing very well because he may outperform his father (in psychoanalytic terms, an Oedipal conflict). When he realizes that these fears are unrealistic, he may find that he can achieve As rather than Bs.

In humanistic/client-centered therapy, the therapy relationship is also a central ingredient of the therapy process. The therapy relationship is not, however, analyzed or interpreted. Therapists with this orientation believe the relationship itself, if it is authentic and accepting, will permit the client to change. Irving Yalom, a humanistic psychotherapist, wrote " 'It is the relationship that heals,' is the single most important lesson the psychotherapist must learn" (p. 401 1980). In 1951 and 1957 Carl Rogers described the essentials of client-centered therapy. The therapist, he wrote, must have unconditional positive regard for and empathic understanding of the client. Unconditional positive regard means that the therapist accepts the client as is, despite any negative traits, feelings, or impulses he or she might express. Rogers believed that if the therapist provided unconditional positive regard and empathic understanding in the therapy relationship, then the client would be free to examine his or herself without defenses or distortions. In relationship with another who expresses unconditional positive regard for her or him, the client will develop unconditional positive self-regard. For the humanistic therapist it is the real relationship, not transference, that is important.

If the therapist Paul sees is a client-centered therapist, she or he will not ask questions, give advice, or make interpretations. As Paul talks about his problems and experiences, the therapist will reflect back to Paul the feelings that he is expressing. By being attuned to Paul's feelings and completely accepting of them, Paul will feel free to express the anger he has felt about his parents' unrealistic expectations and his fears about disappointing them. He would then discover that he can accept himself as he is and whatever he becomes.

Although the humanistic or client-centered therapist is unlikely to reveal information about him or herself, Paul will feel that the therapist genuinely cares for him. Any misperceptions (transference) that Paul experiences in the relationship should automatically correct themselves as Paul freely explores his thoughts and feelings.

In behavioral or cognitive therapies, neither analysis of the therapy relationship nor the relationship per se is regarded as an active therapeutic ingredient. In these therapies, the therapist's role is to identify the client's behaviors and/or cognitions that are problematic and apply an intervention that will change them. The intervention may involve instruction, role-playing, and homework assignments. The therapist-client relationship should be warm and positive because this increases the probability that the client will follow through with the treatment. In 1974 Morris and Zuckerman demonstrated that "warm" therapists achieve better results than "cold" therapists using the same techniques.

If Paul sees a cognitive therapist, the therapist will help Paul identify irrational beliefs that interfere with his doing his work or having fun. They may decide that Paul believes that nothing he can do is good enough to please his parents. The therapist will encourage Paul to test this belief. Paul calls his parents and tells them about his grades this term. They are understanding. Paul reports back to his therapist that he realizes that his parents do accept his accomplishments. Paul decides that he feels that nothing he does is good enough for himself and that his friends are all going to get good jobs and he will not. The therapist has him list all the times he can remember feeling good about something he has done and to list his friends and the jobs he expects them to get. Paul sees that he does feel good when he knows he is working toward a goal and that realistically he and his friends have about the same job prospects.

The cognitive or behavioral therapist is more directive than other therapists. The relationship may seem somewhat like a teacher-student relationship. Because of the personal nature of the tasks, Paul is still likely to view the therapy relationship as close.

Development of the Therapy Relationship

Like all close relationships, the therapy relationship develops; it has a beginning, a middle, and, unlike some life-long close relationships, an end (i.e., termination). One variable affecting the development of the therapy relationship is its expected length. Increasingly psychotherapy is viewed as needing to be (largely for economic reasons) a short-term process (one to six months) rather than a long-term process (more than six months, perhaps years). In a 1980 study of therapist and client goals in short-term (less than fifteen sessions) and long-term (more than twenty sessions) psychotherapy, Horn-George and Archer (1982) found that therapist and client in short-term therapy placed greater value on support from the therapist and client conformity to therapist's recommendations. In other words, there was an emphasis on active participation in the therapy relationship by both therapist and client. Although most close relationships are ones that have lasted longer than six months, many individuals have had the experience of sharing a lot with another person during a short period of time and regarding the relationship with that person as a close one even if there is little or no contact with that person in the future. The amount of activity and exchange (support and conformity, in the therapy relationship) contained in the relationship rather than its duration contributes to the closeness of the relationship.

Irving Altman and Dalmas Taylor in 1973 (and Taylor and Altman 1987) argued in their social penetration theory that the process of development in close relationships is "gradual and orderly . . . from superficial to intimate levels of exchange" (1987, p. 259). It makes sense that you would test the water with a potential partner by first disclosing about relatively superficial information—for example, your opinions about music and entertainment. Then, if your partner responds well, you may feel confident about venturing a more personal disclosure, such as a story about an embarrassing experience or a secret hope of yours. In contrast to a gradual process of mutual disclosure that may occur in most close relationships, it is common, for clients in therapy to talk about very personal material in the first session without getting any personal disclosure from the therapist. In this way the therapy relationship seems to break the rules of normal intimacy.

Despite the fact that gradual mutual disclosure characterizes the development of close relationships, John Berg and Margaret Clark hypothesized in 1986 that relationships that will become close can be distinguished from those that will not at an early point in their development. For example, Berg (1984) found that the decision of roommates to stay together for the following school year could be predicted nearly as well by ratings of relationship quality made early in the year as by ratings made later in the year. In other studies of friendships (Hays 1984; 1985) and dating relationships (Berg and McQuinn 1986), researchers have found greater disclosure at early points in relationships that later became close compared to relationships that did not become close.

Several studies of the association between client, therapist, and relationship characteristics and the outcome of psychotherapy have similarly found a connection between positive perceptions and experiences early in the relationship and outcome months later. In 1985 Luborsky et al. reported that therapists' and clients' ratings of the therapy relationship made after the third therapy session were significantly related to therapy outcome assessed seven months later. In 1983 O'Malley, Suh, and Strupp reported that by the third session, ratings of client involvement in therapy were predictive of therapy outcome; and Marmar et al. reported in 1986 that measures of the therapeutic alliance obtained in sessions one and three were predictive of patients' and therapists' evaluations of overall change at the end of therapy (generally twenty sessions).

Thus, Paul entering psychotherapy will be sensitive to cues that indicate whether or not he will be comfortable revealing personal and, perhaps, upsetting or embarrassing information to this therapist. Even if his early impressions are not positive, Paul might hesitate to change therapists because he has been assigned or referred to this therapist, he does not know who else to go to, and he has already invested time, effort, and perhaps money in meeting with this therapist. In our opinion, based on the research literature showing that client ratings early in therapy predict outcome, Paul should heed his feelings about the quality of this therapy relationship and make the effort to change therapists if the relationship is not positive and productive.

The middle part of therapy is when a lot of the therapy work gets done. Client and therapist are familiar with one another and are on task. Even though much has been revealed by the client early on, clients often reveal even more personal and emotionally-charged information during the middle portion of therapy. In a good therapy relationship client and therapist feel close and in synchrony. As in other close relationships, client or therapist may feel angry or disappointed from time to time; but as in good close relationships, these feelings and the behaviors that contributed to them can be discussed openly. In most therapy clients are encouraged to talk about their feelings about the therapist and therapy. Therapists are generally discouraged from telling clients that they are angry or disappointed; but if clients regularly miss sessions, come late, fail to pay fees, forget homework assignments, etc., therapists do talk to clients about these behaviors.

In most close relationships, the relationship continues as long as it is rewarding to the participants. External circumstances may reduce its intensity (e.g., friends move away from one another; life events, such as marriage, childbirth, a new job, result in less time to invest in the relationship) or end it (death of a friend or partner); but these are not seen as deliberate efforts to change or end the relationships. A new attractive relationship or deterioration in the quality of an existing relationship are reasons that may lead a relationship partner to withdraw voluntarily from the close relationship. The therapy relationship, however, is a close relationship in which a goal of the relationship is that it should end. In fact, good therapy will end without the client seeking another therapy relationship (no attractive alternative) and still feeling good about the quality of the therapy relationship (no deterioration).

Many short-term therapies have a set termination date or a termination date set by circumstance (e.g., the end of the school year). As the date draws near the client, such as Paul, may increase his efforts to get all he can out of therapy. Near the end therapeutic accomplishments and tasks left only partly completed are reviewed. Paul and his therapist will discuss feelings of pride in accomplishments, disappointments and sadness regarding the termination. The therapy relationship is likely to end on a positive note.

In some short-term therapies and in all long-term therapies, the end of therapy is linked to client improvement. In a short-term therapy, improvement is expected only for the presenting complaint. In long-term therapy the improvement may represent broad changes in client behavior and personality. Especially in long-term therapy, which may have entailed years of regular sessions, the termination period is bound to involve feelings of sadness and acknowledgement of missing one another. It may be like saying goodbye to a friend moving a very long way away with the additional knowledge that this friendship, for the client, has changed her or his life. For the client in long-term therapy, extensive changes are expected, but Harold Searles (1975) has written about the therapeutic effects that clients can have on therapists as well, and he encouraged therapists to acknowledge these to clients.

Therapist Characteristics and the Therapy Relationship

If given the choice, should Paul choose a male or a female therapist? If Paul is African-American or Asian-American, should he choose a therapist from a similar ethnic background? Efforts have been made to study the effects of gender, race, and ethnicity of client and therapist on therapy outcome. Reviewing the studies examining sex bias in counseling and psychotherapy, Mary Smith concluded in 1980 that there was not evidence that sex of therapist or sex of client systematically influenced therapeutic outcome. Researchers have not, however, focused on the gender composition of the dyad: male therapist-male client; male therapist-female client; female therapist-female client; female therapist-male client. Work on close relationships would suggest that the dyad would be a more useful unit of assessment than the sex of client or therapist. Feminist therapists (e.g., Gilbert 1980), while acknowledging that men can be feminist therapists, nevertheless suggest that female clients are better understood and treated by female therapists.

In terms of the racial and ethnic background of therapist and client, Stanley Sue argued in 1988 that while there is no empirical evidence that racial/ethnic matching between client and therapist consistently improves therapy outcome, there is a moral issue of providing clients with freedom of choice and access. If most mental health professionals are not themselves minorities, the possibility for minority clients to choose a therapist from a similar background will not exist. Further, Sue argued that cultural similarity (e.g., language, beliefs, values, experiences) rather than ethnic category matching may be the more important variable in enhancing therapy outcome.

If Paul is an avid sports fan and his therapist shows no interest in or knowledge of sports, or if Paul uses rap lyrics to express his feelings and the therapist needs lengthy explanations of their meaning or, worse, appears to disapprove of them, then Paul will probably feel after a session or two that this therapist will not understand other things about him. The therapy relationship is unlikely to become a close relationship.

Although "similarity leads to likely" is a rule for interpersonal attraction (Byrne 1971), individuals from very different backgrounds continue to form close relationships. A therapist who knows nothing about sports or rap but is eager to listen and learn and who appreciates the importance of these in the life of her or his patient is a therapist with whom Paul could form a close relationship regardless of gender/ethnic/racial differences.

Problems in the Therapy Relationship

Close relationships are usually symmetrical. The partners in the relationships are interdependent and mutually self-disclosing. The therapy relationship is asymmetrical. The client talks about his or her feelings, thoughts, behaviors, personal history, and the therapist listens and comments. The therapy relationship is also imbalanced in power and authority. The client comes seeking help; the therapist, by virtue of training, knowledge, and experience, helps the client.

When the therapist has come to know many intimate details about the client, the client may naturally wish to know something about the therapist. Paul may find himself complaining after many sessions, "You know nearly everything about me, but I know almost nothing about you." Although therapists differ in the degree to which they reveal personal information to clients, Pope, Tabachnik, and Keith-Spiegel reported in 1987 that 90 percent of practicing psychologists use self-disclosure as a therapy technique at least on occasion. Still it is unlikely that a client will know a therapist as well as he or she is known by the therapist. The client may feel frustrated that someone as understanding and caring as her or his therapist can never be a friend in the ordinary sense.

The therapist may also feel the urge to form a close, but nontherapy, relationship with a client he or she has come to know well and to like. Establishing social, business, or sexual relationships with clients is unethical. Doing psychotherapy with clients with whom a therapist already has another relationship (e.g., as a student, supervisee, close friend, or relative) is also to be avoided. Whereas other types of close relationships may be combined (e.g., business partners become friends or lovers or vice versa), it is assumed that the therapy relationship is compromised when it is combined with other relationships. The therapist's special knowledge of and influence with a client is kept within the therapy relationship in order to avoid the risk of impairing the therapist's professional judgment or exploiting the client.

Sexual relationships between therapist and client or ex-client are generally damaging to the client. This possibility is less likely to happen to Paul than to a female client. Surveys of therapists have found that 5.5 to 9.5 percent of male therapists report having had sexual relations with clients and 0.6 to 2.5 percent of female therapists report having had sexual relations with clients (Holroyd and Brodsky 1977; Pope, Keith-Spiegel, and Tabachnik 1986). A female client propositioned by her former therapist two years after the end of her therapy stated, "It's taking unfair, personal advantage of knowledge he gained in a relationship of professional trust and confidence" (Finney 1975, p. 595). How much more damaging it must be when a therapist establishes a sexual relationship with a patient during therapy when she or he is feeling dependent and vulnerable. Although the incidence of therapist-client sexual relationships are less that 10 percent, 95 percent of male and 66 percent of female therapists report experiencing sexual feelings about their clients (Pope, Keith-Spiegel, and Tabachnick 1986), attesting to the closeness of the therapy relationships. Most, but not all, of the behaviors and feelings reported by therapists involve heterosexual dyads.

In addition to the trust that the client should be able to have that the therapist will not exploit him or her for the therapist's relationship or sexual needs, the client trusts that information shared with the therapist will be confidential. In any close relationship sharing personal information with a partner which is then passed on to others without the discloser's knowledge or permission is grounds for relationship problems. Clients often share information that is more personal than that shared in all but the most intimate relationships. The guidelines of the American Psychological Association state that a therapist reveals information only with the consent of the client or the client's legal representative, "except in the unusual circumstances in which not to do so would result in clear danger to the person or to others" (American Psychological Association 1981, p. 636). In research by Crowe et al. (1985) confidentiality was cited by clinical psychologists as their most important ethical duty. On the other hand, psychologists have also reported breaches in confidentiality to be their most frequent violation of ethical standards. Sixty-two percent report that they have unintentionally disclosed confidential information about clients and 76 percent say they have discussed clients (without names) with friends (Pope, Tabachnick, and Keith-Spiegel 1987). In a recent national survey of members of the American Psychological Association asking subjects to describe incidents that they found "ethically challenging or troubling," Kenneth Pope and Valerie Vetter (1992) found problems of confidentiality to be the most commonly reported (18 percent of all incidents). These findings clearly indicate that psychologists view issues of confidentiality to be both important and confusing.

Most therapists admit that they discuss cases with colleagues and (without names) with friends and spouses. Clients are, of course, free to discuss their therapist with whomever they please. Ordinarily our close relationships are embedded in a network of relationships. Close friends often know our other close friends; close friends know life partners and vice versa. Talking about our close relationships, both revealing information about our partners (e.g., "John is upset because he got a D on the midterm") and disclosing about our relationship with them (e.g., "We're talking again, but I can't believe how upset he was that I called Carl when it was just to get Susan's phone number"), is a typical aspect of conversations in close relationships. The professional nature of the therapy relationship prevents it from becoming a part of the social network of either therapist or client. Nevertheless, both clients and therapists may feel the need to talk with others about their close therapy relationship. Self-disclosing to others about the therapy relationship may provide client and therapist with the opportunity to clarify and validate the relationship and to receive feedback from others about it. Therapists must, however, balance their need to talk with colleagues or friends with the need to preserve confidentiality by not revealing names or identifying information about clients. These conversations about the therapy relationship may be a way of introducing the therapy relationship into the client's and therapist's social networks and may even make it more meaningful as a close relationship to both therapist and client.

Issues of confidentiality involving reporting information about the client to others occur in situations where the client may be a danger to self or others. Many states have mandatory reporting laws concerning information about child physical and sexual abuse. In those cases, if a therapist hears that the client or others have abused a child, they must report this information, however damaging it may be to the therapy relationship. Massachusetts now requires therapists to inform clients of the limits of confidentiality in psychotherapy. A brochure provided to clients lists eleven special disclosure situations. In a survey conducted by Miller and Thelen (1986) of public attitudes about confidentiality in therapy 42 percent of the respondents said being told before the first session that certain information is not confidential would have a negative effect and 27 percent indicated they would have ambivalent feelings. Therapists have an obligation to protect the client's confidentiality and privacy but also to protect others. Unlike partners in other relationships, the therapist may also be subject to ethical review by her or his professional organization and could be sued for malpractice either for breaching confidentiality or failing to do so when the client's or someone else's welfare was threatened.

Whereas problems in close relationships often involve tensions between the needs for intimacy and interdependence as opposed to the needs for autonomy and identity, problems in the therapy relationship often involve tensions between the personal and professional aspects of the relationship. Self-disclosures of the sort characteristic of the most intimate relationships are shared by the client, strong emotions are felt by both client and therapist, feelings of care and concern are experienced by the therapist. The client, perhaps naturally, thinks of the therapy relationship as a close and personal one. The therapist must preserve the professional aspects of the relationship, often reminding the client of the limitations of the relationship and of the benefits of maintaining these limits. These professional aspects of the relationship, i.e., the therapist's objective perspective and noninvolvement in the client's daily life, are, in fact, the very things that bring a client to therapy. If these aspects are lost, the therapy relationship loses its therapeutic focus and becomes some other kind of relationship.

Conclusions

Concerns about caring, trust, and confidentiality arise in most personal relationships. Personal relationships are also the arenas in which we are most likely to hope and expect to have social needs and wishes fulfilled and to fear rejection, loss, disapproval, and abandonment. Whether these hopes and fears are realistic or not depends on the nature of the relationship. Relationship partners normally spend time establishing their capacity to meet the others' needs (and/or setting limits as to which needs they can meet) and testing the others' willingness to meet their own needs. In developing close personal relationships there is a process of making oneself known and getting to know the other. Ideally, both partners will turn out to be caring and trustworthy, capable of meeting one another's needs, and capable of having their own needs met.

In the therapy relationship this mutual give and take, testing and demonstrating is missing. Therapists are supposed to provide the caring and trustworthiness; clients provide personal self-disclosure. Therapists ensure confidentiality (clients are free to talk about their therapy and therapist to whomever they like); clients reveal their hopes and fears. In most close relationships certain roles are interchangeable. This week John talks about personal problems and Mary listens and is supportive. Next week it is Mary who seeks support and advice and John who provides it. When Joe tells Mark something in confidence, he expects Mark not to tell others. Another time Mark may share a secret with Joe. This mutuality is a hallmark of close personal relationships; but it is missing in therapy relationships. The therapist stays in the role of provider of care and keeper of confidences; the client stays in the role of help seeker and revealer of secrets.

For clients the therapy relationship is a safe place where they are free to express whatever thoughts, feelings, or memories they have. They know their secrets will not be shared. Many also feel free to express their feelings about the therapist. One client said the therapy relationship was the first relationship in which she was able to tell someone directly that she was angry with them. She knew that the therapist would not retaliate, reject her, or feel hurt. The therapy relationship provided an opportunity for her not only to acknowledge her anger but also to learn how to express it effectively.

The therapist's responsibility to be empathic, understanding, trustworthy, and helpful is a difficult one, but one for which they have received training. Performing this role well also provides the therapist with a sense of professional pride. Therapists do not turn to clients for the help and support they need. They depend on their personal relationships and in many cases have been or are in therapy themselves. In their own psychotherapy, therapists can learn to identify and manage their own needs and fears so that they do not interfere with the therapy that they do.

The asymmetrical nature of the therapy relationship makes it different from most close personal relationships. It does, however, share this characteristic with other important relationships, such as parent-child, teacher-student, and coach-athlete relationships. Each of these relationships have their own unique qualities, but it is interesting to think about how they are like the therapist-client relationship described here.

Summary

The present chapter has noted the similarities and dissimilarities of the therapy relationship to a close relationship. As in close relationships, a high level of mutual trust and caring develops between client and therapist, and negative feelings such as anger, disappointment, and jealousy may be felt. Unlike a close relationship, however, the therapy relationship has features of a professional relationship. It is the client (and not the therapist) who self-discloses; the client pays a fee; and the client and therapist meet for a certain length of time (forty-five to fifty minutes), in a specific place and at a specific time.

A considerable literature exists in clinical and counseling psychology on the therapy relationship (e.g., the psychoanalytic, humanistic, and behavioral/cognitive approaches). On the other hand, social psychological concepts and research on close relationships (e.g., social attraction, development and decline of relationship, and confidentiality in self-disclosure of private information) may be useful in understanding how the therapy relationship is a type of personal relationship and how therapy outcomes are achieved.

References

Altman, I., and D. A. Taylor. 1973. *Social penetration: The development of interpersonal relationships*. New York: Holt, Rinehart & Winston.

American Psychological Association. 1981. Ethical principles of psychologists. *American Psychologist*, 36: 633–51.

Berg, J. H. (1984). The development of friendship between roommates. *Journal of Personality and Social Psychology*, 46: 346–56.

Berg, J. H., and M. S. Clark. 1986. Differences in social exchange between intimate and other relationships: Gradually evolving or quickly apparent? In *Friendship and social interaction*, ed. V. J. Derlega and B. A. Winstead, 101–28. New York: Springer-Verlag.

Berg, J. H. and R. D. McQuinn. 1986. Attraction and exchange in continuing and noncontinuing dating relationships. *Journal of Personality and Social Psychology*, 50: 942–52.

Blanck, G., and R. Blanck. 1974. *Ego psychology: Theory and practice*. New York: Columbia University Press.

Byrne, D. 1971. *The attraction paradigm*. New York: Academic Press.

Cashdan, S. 1988. *Object relations therapy*. New York: W. W. Norton & Co.

Crowe, M., J. Grogan, R. Jacobs, C. Lindsay, and M. Mark. 1985. Delineation of the roles of clinical psychology. *Professional Psychology: Research and Practice*. 16: 124–37.

Finney, J. C. 1975. Therapist and patient after hours. *American Journal of Psychotherapy*, 29: 593–602.

Gelso, C. J., and J. A. Carter. 1985. The relationship in counseling and psychotherapy: Components, consequences, and theoretical antecedents. *The Counseling Psychologist*, 13: 155–243.

Gilbert, L. A. 1980. Feminist therapy. In *Women and psychotherapy: An assessment of research and practice*, ed. A. M. Brodsky and R. T. Hare-Mustin, 245–265. New York: Guilford Press.

Greenberg, J. R., and S. A. Mitchell. 1983. *Object relations in psychoanalytic theory*. Cambridge, MA: Harvard University Press.

Greenson, R. 1967. *The technique and practice of psychoanalysis*. New York: International Universities Press.

Hays, R. B. 1984. The development and maintenance of friendship. *Journal of Social and Personal Relationships*, 1: 75–98.

———. 1985. A longitudinal study of friendship development. *Journal of Personality and Social Psychology*, 48: 909–924.

Holroyd, J. C., and A. M. Brodsky. 1977. Psychologists' attitudes and practices regarding erotic and nonerotic physical contact with patients. *American Psychologist*, 32: 843–49.

Horn-George, J. B., and K. N. Archer. 1982. Perceptions of the psychotherapy relationship in long- and short-term therapy. *Professional Psychology*, 13: 483–91.

Luborsky, L. A., T. McLellan, G. E. Woody, C. P. O'Brien, and A. Auerbach. 1985. Therapist success and its determinants. *Archives of General Psychiatry*, 42: 602–11.

Marmar, C. R., M. J. Horowitz, D. S. Weiss, and E. Marziali. 1986. The development of the Therapeutic Alliance Rating System. In *The psychotherapeutic process: A research handbook*, ed. L. S. Greenberg and W. M. Pinsof, 367–90. New York: Guilford Press.

Miller, D. J., and M. H. Thelen. 1986. Knowledge and beliefs about confidentiality in psychotherapy. *Professional psychology: Research and practice*, 17: 15–19.

Morris, R. J., and K. R. Zuckerman. 1974. Therapist warmth as a factor in automated systematic desensitization. *Journal of Consulting and Clinical Psychology*, 42: 244–50.

O'Malley, S. S., C. S. Suh, and H. H. Strupp. 1983. The Vanderbilt Psychotherapy Process Scale: A report on the scale development and process-outcome study. *Journal of Consulting and Clinical Psychology*, 51: 581–86.

Pope, K. S., P. Keith-Spiegel, and B. G. Tabachnick. 1986. Sexual attraction to clients: The human therapist and the (sometimes) inhuman training system. *American Psychologist*, 41: 147–58.

Pope, K. S., B. G. Tabachnick, and P. Keith-Spiegel. 1987. Ethics of practice: The beliefs and behaviors of psychologists as therapists. *American Psychologist*, 42: 993–1006.

Pope, K. D., and V. A. Vetter. 1992. Ethical dilemmas encountered by members of the American Psychological Association. *American Psychologist*, 47: 307–411.

Reisman, J. M. 1986. Psychotherapy as a professional relationship. *Professional Psychology: Research and Practice*, 17: 565–69.

Rogers, C. R. 1951. *Client-centered therapy*. Boston: Houghton Mifflin.

———. 1957. The necessary and sufficient conditions of therapeutic personality change. *Journal of Consulting Psychology*, 21: 95–103.

Searles, H. F. 1975. The patient as therapist to his analyst. In *Tactics and techniques in psychoanalytic therapy, vol. II: Countertransference*, ed. P. Giovacchini, 95–151. New York: Jason Aronson.

Smith, M. L. 1980. Sex bias in counseling and psychotherapy. *Psychological Bulletin*, 87: 392–407.

Sue, S. 1988. Psychotherapeutic services for ethnic minorities. *American Psychologist*, 43: 301–08.

Taylor, D. A. and I. Altman. 1987. Communication in interpersonal relationships: Social penetration processes. In *Interpersonal processes: New directions in communication research*, ed. M. E. Roloff and G. R. Miller, 257–77. Newbury Park, CA: Sage Publications.

Yalom, I. D. 1980. *Existential psychotherapy*. New York: Basic Books.

Chapter *17*

Close Relationships in Environmental Context

BARBARA B. BROWN
Environment and Behavior Area,
Department of Family and Consumer Studies

CAROL M. WERNER
Psychology Department
University of Utah

IRWIN ALTMAN
Psychology Department
University of Utah

Outline

Introduction

You're Getting Married

Imagine you have recently decided to get married. Although it is tempting to think of marriage as a dyadic event, an examination of a wedding highlights how a marriage goes beyond the dyad, involving a wide range of social relationships, material objects, places, and events. In the United States, prior to the wedding, it is customary to date a variety of others before becoming engaged to a personally chosen future spouse. Wedding preparations, if economically feasible, involve assembling a wide range of carefully chosen and meaningful paraphernalia—rings, flowers, wedding clothes, invitations, vows, etc. Although there may be disagreements about details such as the guest list, the ideal wedding is a joyous event. In addition, couples must prepare themselves for new tasks and roles to begin after the wedding, such as starting their own households and adjusting to new relationships as spouses and in-laws. This range of tasks facing a newly marrying couple underscores the fact that a close relationship is embedded in relationships with others—parents, relatives, and friends—and in the physical world of objects and places. Close relationships are also informed by cultural and historical patterns, and unfold in temporal routines and rhythms involving mundane daily events and occasional important ceremonies. The chapter will highlight how close relationships become real through the confluence of all of these aspects of relationships—physical environments and objects, social relationships, cultural and historical traditions, and temporal patterns.

A Dialectic and Transactional Approach to Close Relationships

This chapter will emphasize a dialectic approach to relationships between close partners and between partners and kin. A transactional perspective is used to guide the examination of a central dialectic theme of relationships.

Dialectics

A dialectic approach to relationships focuses on competing and opposite pressures that exist in the relationship. There is a tension between joining or identifying with others and keeping a degree of separateness or individuality. Although the particular pairs of opposites used in various dialectic approaches differ (e.g., individuality-communality, autonomy-connection; see Baxter 1988 and Montgomery 1990, for a review), many deal with the general theme of how smaller social units maintain their individuality while bonding with others to form larger social units (e.g., Montgomery 1990; Baxter 1990; Altman, Vinsel, and Brown 1981). Furthermore, the oppositional forces help to define one another, creating a unified interdependent system. A person does not lose individual identity when in a relationship; the personal identity and the relationship are interdependent, sustaining each other while in opposition. Finally, the tension creates changes as joining or separating forces ebb and flow over time, altering the character of the relationship. At some times individuality is emphasized, at other times the relationship is emphasized. This chapter addresses how, over the course of a relationship, members solve this basic dilemma of maintaining their individuality while simultaneously committing themselves to a larger social unit such as a dyad.

Transactionalism

Relationships, although often described in abstract terms by researchers, cannot exist apart from their contexts. A transactional approach emphasizes the inseparability of social relationships from their cultural, physical, and social contexts. Married couples, for example, meet in particular places, at particular times, while also managing their obligations to work, family and other commitments. The close relationship develops within the context of all of the other realities of life. Places, objects, routines, and cultural traditions are as embedded in the relationship as are feelings and other aspects of relationships. Because relationships are thoroughly embedded in these contexts, transactional researchers prefer to study relationships holistically, rather than focusing on one or two variables that are carved out of their natural contexts and studied in isolation (Altman and Rogoff 1987).

Themes of the Chapter

Although the goal of studying relationships in context is useful, in practical terms a student may wonder how to go about such a complex endeavor. Instead of requiring researchers to look at everything, the dialectic and transactional approaches suggest certain more specific guidelines for examining personal relationships.

First, a dialectic approach focuses us on opposing forces that act in a unified and dynamic way in relationships. So the examination will focus on how relationships over time involve different blends of togetherness or unity or linkage as well as separateness or uniqueness and autonomy.

Second, a transactional approach assumes that relationships can be examined at many levels of analysis. The central dialectic opposition between maintaining individuality and distinctiveness while simultaneously joining with relationship partners can apply to two or more embedded layers of relationships. This chapter will focus on two levels of analysis: the close male-female dyadic relationship and the couple-kin relationship. All of the examples so far have focused on the dyadic level—how men and women sustain their individual identities while engaged in a relationship with each other. We will also highlight a second level of analysis— how the couple maintains its unique and separate couple identity in relating to their families. The transactional approach also recognizes that these different levels of analysis are interdependent. A couple's identity is not only a function of the individuals involved and the relationships they create with each other, it also depends on relationships with extended family and friends.

Third, the holistic nature of transactional analysis suggests that the dialectic oppositions between individuality and connection can be seen in the contextual aspects of relationships. How do the activities, places, and objects within the relationship create, reflect, and communicate the dialectic nature of the relationship, with its tension between individuality and commonality? What practices are used by individuals and cultures to join partners together yet maintain their separate identities and contributions to the bond? How do friends and family accentuate the couple's relationship or, instead, demand loyalties which may threaten the couple's bond? The physical environment, culture, and social context will provide opportunities and constraints that favor some blend of relating and separating.

Because the cultural and physical aspects of close relationships have been relatively neglected in relationship research, this chapter will try to highlight these aspects in particular. Cultures vary a great deal in the relative importance placed on various relationships and the activities used to join or separate individuals. For example, in traditional Chinese society, the bond between a woman and her husband was less important for her well-being and daily activities than the bond she had with her mother-in-law. In general, the places and objects involved in relationships often reflect the nature of individuality and communality. For example, in many societies the roles of women and men are quite distinct; their distinctions are revealed in separate practices during wedding ceremonies and in their access to different places and objects in the home after the wedding.

Because this type of holistic examination of the life courses of relationships is rare in the United States, many of the rich details of cultural practices will come from ethnographic studies of societies around the world. Although many relationships exist, our review will emphasize those relationships that have received much research attention; unfortunately, this means that there will be little attention given to blended family relationships, homosexual relationships, cohabitation or other close relationships outside of heterosexual, first marriage relationships. As the reader will see, ethnographic studies emphasize cultural patterns, but have the disadvantage of giving less attention to individuals' understandings and interpretations of their ongoing relationships. In the ideal case, the transactional researcher would want to examine both cultural patterns and individual interpretations.

Change is a final aspect of dialectic and transactional analysis. The importance of change has long been highlighted in research on personal relationships from the time of social penetration (Altman and Taylor 1973), an approach that emphasized a particular course of change in dyadic relationships, to more recent approaches that reflect a variety of directions and ways of change in relationships (see Duck 1988). According to the transactional perspective, change and development are assumed to be intrinsic to life and relationships. Although oppositional forces co-exist and give meaning to one another, there is no optimal blend or balance point between the oppositions. The tension between opposites will be reflected in greater emphasis on individuality at one time, connection and involvement at another. These changes reflect both large scale historical changes and finer scale day-to-day changes in relationships. The chapter will follow the tensions over part of the life course of relationships, from the way couples meet to the creation of a dwelling for the newly married couple. The following review divides relationships into dating or courtship, wedding, and placemaking stages for convenience. Admittedly, not all stages may be salient in all cultures and the stages often overlap in time, such as when engaged couples begin making, buying or collecting gifts for the postmarriage home, thus beginning the process of placemaking even before they have a place.

Three Stages of Relationships

Dating and Courtship

Historical Background

In Western societies, families historically were more actively involved with their childrens' choices of marital partners than they are today. A daughter's preference might be discouraged if the prospective son-in-law was seen as a poor choice for continuing the family business, for example. To a greater extent than today a family's well-being depended on provisions by the younger generation. Currently, the availability of college educations, retirement funds, and other publicly accessible support systems mean that the economic well-being of any family is less closely tied to the continuation of a specific family business. Except for farming families or other segments of society where it is still important for families to continue particular businesses (Davis-Brown, Salamon, and Surra 1987), free choice is more the norm. Although this norm feels natural to many readers, it is important to remember that this is a fairly new cultural innovation in the West and not at all the tradition in many other societies.

In addition to a loosening of intergenerational obligations in the choice of spouses, a historical analysis by Bailey (1988) reveals that woman- and family-controlled courtship practices in the early 1900s shifted to the control of men. Before the change, middle to upper income women and their parents exerted a great deal of control over the progress of initial encounters. Women extended invitations to men to visit. If a man visited, he was not automatically welcomed, but left a calling card. The woman received this card in privacy and could decide whether she was at home or not. The visit took place in a parlor or front porch—areas very much under the control of the woman and her parents.

Later, when car ownership became widespread, the environmental possibilities for dating changed, and so did relations between men and women. Cars, along with changing social standards and new public entertainment options, moved dating from the protective turf of the woman's home. Cars and dating became synonymous, and as only men could afford cars, they began to take the initiative in dating. In more recent decades, it has become more acceptable for young people to move out of their parents' homes before marriage (Whyte 1990).

Young people who live in college dormitories or their own apartments or houses have even fewer parental influences on dating practices.

Current Western Patterns

The role of parents in the courtship initiation of their children is now often limited to fairly indirect measures. One subtle way in which parental values and ideals may influence their childrens' courtship is through the choice of a neighborhood. Physical proximity and routine contacts with others in the area may establish a pool of eligible dating partners their children are likely to meet. For example, in 1940, in New Haven, Connecticut, there was a one in three chance that one's marriage partner lived within three blocks and a 76 percent chance that the eventual spouse lived within twenty blocks (Kennedy 1943). Similar findings emerged from Philadelphia in 1931 and Seattle in 1964 (see Murstein 1986 for a review). A more recent study found that half of the marriages in a sample of Detroit residents occurred between individuals living less than three miles apart if they married in the 1925–1944 era, but this expanded to four miles in the 1945–1964 era, then to five miles in the 1965–1984 era (Whyte 1990). Thus the places that are closest to home are likely to give greatest opportunity for meeting one's spouse, although historical increases in mobility extend the geographic boundaries of the field of opportunities.

Within these broad geographical limits on opportunities, the freedom of the younger generation to select future spouses is clear. A review of five studies involving the United States, England, France and the former U.S.S.R. by Whyte (1990) shows that a majority of spouses meet directly rather than through introductions by friends or family. As noted in Bailey's (1988) historical analysis, younger generations now have access to a number of public, perhaps age-linked settings, where relationships begin. These include neighborhoods, schools, workplaces, parties, bars, leisure spots, and other public places. Even so, some cultural variations were evident. A third of English couples met at parties, dances, or weddings—a higher rate than other countries, such as the U.S.S.R., where over a quarter of couples met at bars or dance halls. In the United States, parents are not heavily involved in initiating courtships, although over one fourth of couples were introduced by friends, attesting to the power of peers in the early stages of relationships.

Once couples have had initial dates they may deepen their commitments to each other and withdraw their commitments from others (see Milardo and Lewis 1985). Couples may reveal their commitments with a variety of nonverbal presentations, such as hand-holding, that communicates their togetherness to others (Patterson 1988). In addition, the places of later dates may provide tangible evidence, both to the couple and to others, of deepened commitment. For example, introducing a dating partner to one's parents or taking the person on an extended family trip may signal that a dating relationship is getting serious.

Despite the absence of formal parental controls over children's courtships, kin and social network members are not passive onlookers to the budding relationships. Instead Lewis (see Milardo and Lewis 1985) proposed that network members create obstacles or supports to the newly developing relationship. Friends may either respect the couple's apparent seriousness or complain about their incompatibility or even the lessened commitment and attention they themselves receive. Parents may begin to respect the couple's privacy more, ask about the partner's well-being, note the partner's absence, and generally expect to see the partner more in the home. Thus the couples' individual and joint relationships to others relate to the waxing and waning of the dyadic bond.

As the relationship becomes more serious, the couple may gain more privacy from their family and others. Withdrawing from the public places of earlier dates may reinforce commitment by simply decreasing the availability of rivals, making the boundary between the couple and their peers stronger. An intensive study of Welsh courtships and marriages in the 1960s by Diana Leonard (1980) suggests that withdrawal also allows the couple time to experiment with spending longer periods of time together, allowing them to develop a wider range of shared experiences. Can they get along together without the interventions and distractions of the larger social and physical world? Are they able to maintain their compatibility and individual identities over long time periods? The increased privacy accorded the couple allows them to test out these realms of compatibility and is intrinsic to their deepening commitment.

In Wales, although the agreement to become engaged is usually made by the couple in private, there are public features to engagement as well. Couples may have small engagement dinners to celebrate the decision with close kin and friend, they may publish a newspaper announcement as a public statement of the decision, and the woman may wear a ring that members of the culture understand as an engagement ring. Family members may change their way of referring to the future son or daughter-in-law, calling her "our Judy" or in some way signalling their closeness to the family. The man may ask the woman's father for permission to marry, a remnant of the tradition that passes women as possessions from father to husband. In current times, this request is more of a formality, as the couple again has most say in their marital relationship and their families have less right to object. The combination of these practices give the force of public commitment to the private decision to marry; few couples break off their engagements.

In Wales, as in most Western societies, because marriage requires a large investment in housing and household goods, engaged couples strive to save money for their married life. Here again the places and activities accompanying engagement test and affirm the commitments of couples who remain together. The fiancés often take on overtime work or second jobs to finance their economic obligations of marriage. The fiancés spend more time with their families at home, perhaps working on wedding arrangements or crafting future household goods, while their fiancés work. Leisure time together is more likely to involve low cost evenings at her home instead of enjoyable but expensive public outings. These arrangements provide somewhat trying circumstances for the couple to test and affirm their commitments. The daughters are likely to discuss marriage and wedded life with their mothers, establishing a new area of interaction in their own relationship which may prepare the daughter for the tasks of married life.

The couple can see whether they can sustain their relationship given the stress of his long work hours and new, domestically oriented recreations.

Other Societies

To understand how cultures vary in the ways in which couples relate to their families and the physical environment a variety of examples from other societies will be described; original citations for the ethnographic work can be found in Altman et al. (1992). Sometimes courtship elsewhere also reflects the personal choices of young people. Amongst the Hagen of New Guinea, young people meet at public dances where they court by "turning heads," kneeling with their foreheads pressed together, swaying. Similarly Sioux Indian couples often met freely at community dances in public places free of parental control. Many non-European cultures involve kin more intimately in the choices of courting partners, places, and activities.

In many societies personal compatibility of couple members and an emphasis upon their independent dyadic bond takes a back seat to family interests. These may include concerns about economic compatibility, the wishes of parents, and the divination of wishes of the ancestors or cosmological forces. Many societies have extended financial negotiations between parents or with the help of a go-between. In India a fiancée must bring money and goods before the husband's family will accept her, therefore gifts are given from the fiancée's parents to the man's family, the couple, and their daughter. For the Lodabaga, an African society, separate gifts for the woman and the man prepare them for their distinct household duties. She gets cooking utensils, grains, and money from her kin while he receives chickens for breeding and arrows for hunting from his kin.

Perhaps the greatest departure from the Western emphasis on free choice occurs in societies where the parents select the younger generation's spouses. In traditional Taiwanese society, a father and mother shared their household with married sons. Marriage was less a matter of individual compatibility between couple members than group compatibility between the woman and her prospective extended family. Any prospective daughter-in-law was scrutinized for her economic status, in terms of what dowry she would bring into the family, and whether she was acceptable to the more powerful members of the family. The prospective groom was less active in courtship than his father and ancestors. First meetings of the couple took place in her home, after both sets of parents had greeted each other. The couple met when she served tea to the visitors, a fairly formalized pattern of interaction that revealed little about her personal identity. Amongst the Comoro islanders the local Muslim traditions dictated that young women covered themselves with cloth and ideally were not viewed by their husbands until the wedding ceremony. Courtship progress was more a matter of familial economic compatibility and satisfying cosmological concerns than discerning or developing personal compatibility. In many cultures the greater stake that families have in their children's matches is evident from their courtship practices. The physical objects, places, and activities give substance to and define the varied courtship relationships.

Marriage Ceremonies

Weddings often reveal personal and cultural understandings of marital and family relationships; the people, places and activities involved in the ceremony reflect husband-wife and couple-kin relationships.

Current Western Ceremonies

These societies often have ceremonies that emphasize the bringing together of two independent individuals and, to a lesser extent, their families. This emphasis is apparent in Welsh wedding activities in the late 1960s, which resemble many contemporary European and United States practices. Diana Leonard (1980) describes how the ceremony brings together separate individuals and publicly unites them in front of family and friends. Independence and separation from families are emphasized by traditions in which the bride and groom are expected to be separated from each other on the wedding day until the ceremony itself. Not only is it bad luck for the groom to see the bride on the wedding day before the ceremony, but he is not supposed to see her dress at any time before the ceremony. Separation is also evident in the wedding ceremony, with the bride and her kin taking the left side of the church, the groom and his kin the right. After the ceremony families intermingle, as the bride's father escorts the groom's mother from the church and both families interacting at the reception. The ceremony reflects the bonding of previously separated individuals and families.

Despite the mingling of families at the wedding, most of the focus on unity involves the couple themselves, not their families. Religious vows that pledge togetherness provide a very intense and serious mechanism for underscoring the bond. Ceremonial actions also emphasize bonding: the groom gives the bride a wedding ring, they leave the church together, and are feted at a reception which also emphasizes their joining. At the reception they are photographed, given wedding gifts, and toasted. These toasts are ways in which family and friends can give public recognition to the couple's union as well as the unique qualities the bride and groom bring to the marriage. Couple members then embark on a honeymoon, a time of leisure and togetherness. Their independence from the influence of family and friends is sometimes so extreme that the destination of the trip is kept secret. All of these practices underscore the Western tradition of viewing married couples as strongly bonded for reasons of personal preference, creating a dyad that is fairly free of parental authority. The within-dyad forces toward bonding are more salient than the dyad-kin forces, unlike many nonWestern wedding ceremonies.

Although the wedding joins two individuals, a dialectic analysis underscores that these individuals are neither fused nor interchangeable; they cultivate and maintain distinct identities that both keep them distinct partners and that contribute to the dyadic bond. As an example of the differences with the marital dyad, the Welsh wedding generally placed more emphasis on the bride than the groom. This is consistent with other aspects of Welsh society at that time. Paid work for women was less available and less remunerative, so a woman's economic well-being, but not a man's, depended heavily on the choice of a spouse. In addition, women usually quit their jobs upon marriage and devoted their attentions to the domestic wellbeing of the home, the husband, and the children; men maintained their jobs.

Greater salience of marriage in the lives of Swansea females was evident throughout their lives. At a young age, they often received gifts in preparation for an eventual marriage. In preparing for the wedding women were expected to buy or make elaborate new white dresses, to be used only for this ceremony (or passed down to their own daughters); the dresses were expected to make them look beautiful and also to symbolize purity and chastity. Men, in contrast, had fewer choices of costume design and often rented their ceremonial dress, which connoted class differences but nothing about his sexual purity. The brides' family organized most of the wedding and the bride herself received special ceremonial emphasis in a procession down the aisle of the church aisle with musical accompaniment, her father as escort, and bridesmaids following along behind. After the wedding the brides wrote the thank you notes and wore the wedding ring. Although these accounts have focused on Wales, many Western societies have ceremonies that also emphasize the joining of two individuals, each bringing unique and distinct contributions to the dyadic bond; in addition, the ceremonies underscore the fact that the dyad will become a fairly independent unit, maintaining their own household.

Other Societies

Ceremonies in other cultures often give less attention to the husband-wife bond and more attention to their individual or couple relations with kin. This is evident from the symbolically laden practices, places, and things that give expression to these bonds beyond the couple. For the nomadic Gabra, in Africa, the word "marriage" means to build a home. The wedding ceremony extends over four days during which a hut is built for the couple by their kin. The women from both the bride's and the groom's family camps bring specified material, including part of the bride's mother's hut, which is disassembled for this event. Over four days the hut is built and rebuilt. Finally, the groom builds a fire with sticks provided by his mother and anoints the home.

Many ceremonies reflect the fact that women's identities include lesser power vis-á-vis men. Wedding ceremonies often transfer the bride from the rule of her father in her family home to the rule of the groom and others in his home, as in New Guinea, China, and Java. In some societies this transfer takes the form of a symbolic bride abduction, creating a salient break in the bride's bonds with her family. Other cultures emphasize the obedience of the couple to religious figures, family ancestors, or the older generation. A traditional Korean practice had the woman kowtow to her in-laws, stretching out full length and face down on the floor in front of them as a gesture of respect and obedience. Many societies have a system of bridewealth, whereby the groom's family gives certain gifts to the bride's family. This bridewealth is often used to allow the bride's brother to obtain a wife, making the marriages of sisters interdependent with the marriages of their brothers (Goody 1973). Thus links between the bride, groom, or both and their parents, kin, or spiritual authorities are more central to the definition of marital relations in other societies.

Placemaking

Placemaking is the lifelong process of constructing, altering, embellishing and assigning meaning to places. Although most Western couples would agree that the most central place in their lives is their home, few researchers have examined how people turn houses and other dwellings into personally meaningful homes. The activities that transform a house into a home can also reflect in tangible and symbolic ways the nature of the bond between partners, and between the dyad and its family and kin. Placemaking activities include particular patterns of territoriality, privacy regulation, rituals, use of objects, and ongoing maintenance that contribute to a sense of identity and meaning in the world. For Kim Dovey (1985), being at home means that one experiences a particular spatial, temporal, and sociocultural order that contributes to one's sense of understanding self and world. Experiencing home involves establishing connectedness with the past, the physical home, and with individuals both inside and outside the home.

Prior to the wedding, placemaking can be central to marital negotiations, as families negotiate brideprices and dowries. Other placemaking activities may include financial savings, gift giving, accumulation of household supplies and objects, or construction, maintenance, or adaptation of a dwelling. The symbolic importance of placemaking activities is often highlighted by their inclusion in important celebrations or rituals, such as engagement and housewarming parties, the custom of carrying the bride over the threshold, house blessings, and decorations of homes on religious or social occasions.

Western Practices

In the United States the term "family" suggests an independently living unit. The walls of a household help to create what we think of as a natural separation between the household and the larger community, reinforcing the uniqueness and identity of the nuclear family. Inside the home the separate bedrooms for parents and children corresponds to our way of thinking of these relationships as having a certain degree of separation. The sharing of bedrooms and beds for spouses supports a view of spouses as intimate dyads and provides daily interaction opportunities to sustain this view. As we shall see later in the chapter, in other cultures households may regularly include grandparents or adult siblings, or they may separate husbands from wives, creating a different context for the conduct of husband-wife relationships. In those cultures, just as in North America, the physical environment suggests and reinforces a particular way of thinking about relationships and provides particular opportunities and constraints on interactions that sustain relationships.

Personal and cultural traditions for use of the environment also suggest connections and separations between people that help define relationships. Rules for appropriate behavior—"Don't enter without knocking," "Don't visit without phoning ahead," "Tell your spouse everything"—suggest what types of people have what types of access to one another. These rules help to support individuality and bonding although the rules vary cross culturally in terms of the types of bonds and the actors involved. In the United States, spouses rarely knock before entering their own shared bedrooms but may require their children to do so. Best friends or kin may drop in for unannounced visits but more distant relationships assume that they should call ahead to arrange access to the household.

For a newly married couple, the home helps the couple solidify their bonds to each other and to establish new ways of relating to their kin and friends. For example, new brides often invite their in-laws to dinner, which reveals their own domestic skills and communicates to in-laws the togetherness of the couple. Within the home, the couple often divides up the space into shared and private areas. The order and predictability of having one's toothbrush, clothes, hobby supplies and other materials in particular places helps to smooth the day to day activities in the home (Rosenblatt and Budd 1975) and may prevent squabbles between spouses. Although the preceding research involved married couples, it is also true that a wide range of groups use territoriality to create and sustain order in life (Brown 1987), although few studies have examined the residential context of non-heterosexual couples or other groups.

The layout of rooms in the home also creates settings for a variety of interactions. In United States homes, the living room is often formally decorated and used to welcome guests, setting a careful and scheduled stage for couple-kin or couple-friend interactions. In contrast, the family room may be more informally decorated and used (Altman and Chemers 1980), setting the stage for spontaneous and informal relationships among family members. Within the marital dyad, although space use in the home is not as strongly segregated by sex as some other cultures, women in the United States and Israel show distinct patterns of space use. They are less likely to have a private space and more likely to spend home time in the kitchen and with others than men (Sebba and Churchman 1983; Ahrentzen, Levine, and Michelson 1989), making them more available for relationships in the home than men.

Throughout the home the artifacts may reflect both individual and communal aspects of identity. Leonard (1980) noted that many young brides could go through the home and point out which relative or friend gave which wedding present. Thus in a tangible way young couples are reminded of their social networks even inside the home. Women's roles as family caregivers are reflected not only in their space use and interactions, but in the way they view symbolically important objects in the home. Women are more likely to decorate with objects that symbolize relationships (Vinsel et al. 1980). In a study of the meaning of special objects in the home, women were much more likely to treasure objects that symbolize relationships (Csikszentmihalyi and Rochberg-Halton 1981). For example, one man reported that he liked his fireplace, not because it connoted family togetherness and warmth, but because it reminded him of hunting and camping adventures. In contrast, one woman reported attachment to a sculpture because her son made it while another treasured a trunk because it was a family heirloom that reminded her of the links across the generations.

As suggested by a transactional approach, the daily and seasonal events in the home also reflects both individual and communal aspects of domestic relationships. A study of the daily experiences of couples showed that happy couples spent more time together at home, especially for leisure activities, than unhappy couples (Kirchler 1988). In 1973, Dreyer and Dreyer found that middle class families often had regular patterns of eating dinner that revealed things about family relationships. For example, the mother provided all the domestic work for dinner, which was geared to the father's arrival from work. Father took the head of the table while mother often sat next to small children who needed help. The oldest child offered prayers before the meal and discussions during the meal often serve to socialize the children and provide a family forum for discussing standards of behavior and discipline. These daily patterns can be seen from a dialectic perspective, revealing unique roles of children, as well as husband and wife, while simultaneously joining them together for a family event. In other cultures, the daily meal might separate generations and/or sexes, revealing different patterns of close relations in the home.

United States Christmas celebrations involve an intricate weaving together of particular artifacts and practices to draw kin together. In studying Christmas traditions, Theodore Caplow (1984) found that married couples often give gifts as a couple to their parents and other family members. So one way of connecting with in-laws is to give gifts as a couple, reinforcing the dyadic identity and establishing bonds between the generations. On the other hand, individuality is also recognized, because the gift givers will try to find or make gifts that demonstrate a special understanding of the recipient's unique interests. Many of these symbolic messages of Christmas are unstated. Celebrants might not reflect on the meaning of the symbols unless one of the unstated rules is violated, such as when an expected gift is not forthcoming. In sum, our home, objects, and cultural traditions are part of the individual and communal aspects of bonds between husband and wife and between the couple and their families.

Other Practices

Other societies are more likely to have extended family forms and the physical structures that complement those forms. In the ideal traditional Chinese family many generations shared a family compound that housed all the married sons and their wives. Labor was segregated by sex, and new brides spent more time with their mothers-in-law than with their husbands.

Individuals from other societies are more likely to participate in the actual creation of their homes, which also provides an opportunity to reveal important relationships in its creation. Recall that among the Gabra of Kenya, Africa, hut building is a community event. A newlywed couple's home blends parts of the bride's mother's home with new materials; it incorporates items and has symbolic involvement of the groom's family; the couple plays an important role, with the husband specifying the location of the home and sanctifying it, and the bride furnishing it.

In many societies, gender roles are often involved in home and artifact creation, ownership, and use, revealing the unique contributions of participants in relationships. For example, the Fulani and Nyansongo. African groups distinguish between male and female parts of the home or homestead. Husbands and wives engage in distinctive activities in certain places, and there are strong cultural norms about who has access to what place in the home for what purpose. The Hagen culture, New Guinea extends husband and wife role distinctions to include economic aspects of settings, including control over land, gardens and animals (Altman et al. 1992).

In sum, culturally conditioned relationships between husbands and wives and between married couples and others often achieve tangible expression in the use and meaning of home spaces. Although these points have been illustrated with historical and cross cultural examples, it is useful to recognize the profound changes occurring in today's relationships and to speculate on the ways in which the confluence of social, cultural, and physical aspects of relationships will change for the future.

Conclusion and Summary

Current Changes for Courtships, Wedding, and Placemaking

Currently, United States society is undergoing the types of changes that have historically been associated with changing experiences of home and family relationships. It is useful to review these trends in terms of changing individual and relational roles and to anticipate how society may cope with these changes in the future.

Since the 1970s there have been tremendous changes in the activities and groups who create households in the United States. In terms of activities, many women have entered the paid work force, taking them out of their traditional roles as full-time homemaker. In addition, the households headed by single individuals, single parents, and divorced parents have increased at a much more rapid rate than traditional two-parent with children households (Struyk, Turner, and Uneno 1988). Thus the path toward marriage is more optional and temporary today than in past generations. How do such changes relate to courtship, weddings, and placemaking?

A study of Detroit weddings of 1925 to 1984 revealed an increase in ceremonial elaboration of weddings over time (Whyte 1990). This occurred despite evidence of large scale changes in events associated with marriage. For example, weddings after 1945 were less likely to provide a rite of passage into adult sexual activity or represent the first move out of the family home. Nevertheless, the wedding still provided an important ceremony marking the joining of two distinct individuals and their families. Recent weddings were more likely to be celebrated with engagement rings, bachelor parties, wedding showers, and honeymoons than weddings of the 1925–1944 era. Greater attention to these ceremonial elements may in part reflect greater financial resources of working couples; but they also underscore the couple's autonomy and independence from the family.

In terms of placemaking, close relationships have experienced the privacy of the home to a greater extent now than at any other time in history (Laslett 1973). Suburban homes and neighborhoods were designed to support one particular family configuration. Many who occupy those homes no longer fit the traditional family mold. Thus it is useful to see how homes and neighborhoods serve placemaking for traditional and nontraditional households.

Dolores Hayden (1984), based on an examination of historical documents, argued that assumptions about proper home and family activities and values are integral to the physical structure of suburban housing. Suburban homes were to be nuclear family havens, supported financially by husbands who commute to work during the day and supported emotionally by wives who work without pay day and night in the home. Grandparents and other kin lived elsewhere, further isolating the nuclear family. Community intrusion into activities in the home should be minimal. Families were to work out both functional and dysfunctional aspects of their relationships in privacy, which serves to sustain whatever family relations are developed.

The physical structure of suburban housing reflects these concerns. Housing is physically separated by zoning laws from commercial or industrial areas. Homes themselves are often separated from neighbors by lawns and fences. Most equipment needed to sustain daily activities, such as washers, vacuum cleaners, stoves, and the like were to be privately purchased by each household and operated in isolation by the wife. As technology improved the ease of housework, standards for cleanliness also increased, maintaining the full-time efforts needed for housing upkeep (Forty 1986). Thus homes supported the separate roles that husbands and wives brought to the marriage and separated them from kin, neighbors, and others outside of the immediate nuclear family.

Placemaking for New Households

An examination of new households—dual career, divorced, single parent, and three generation households—shows how homes are moving away from their traditional uses. In general, these new households alter the role assignments of members of close relationships and/or begin to erode that strong buffer of privacy that used to surround couples in their homes.

Dual career couples are experiencing how difficult it is to live in a house designed to be cared for by a full time homemaker when the social reality is that both husband and wife work outside the home full-time. Wives in dual career couples often experience tension in trying to fulfill both work and family roles, reporting this type of conflict two to three times a week against once a week reported by their husbands (Emmons et al. 1990). These women feel like they do not spend enough time alone or with their husbands, but also feel that they spend less time on both housework and careers than they would like. This conflict illustrates the stresses involved with changing roles in relationships. Although paid employment can add to the individual experiences and strengths married women bring to relationships, and their choice to work may reflect their dedication to their families, the time demands of paid employment conflict with the tradition demands on homemakers to express their dedication to their families through home-based unpaid labor. The realities of life in a dual career family—getting to the store and the child care center, finding the time and energy for housework after the full-time job—suggest that large outlying suburban houses may only intensify the stresses for these new families. In the future, dual career couples may seek out housing that requires low maintenance and proximity to work and child care but also provides that same prestige and privacy as suburban housing currently offers.

Divorcing or remarrying couples may become acutely aware of placemaking when they try to transform their households to accommodate to single parent, blended family, or single person lifestyles. Changes are likely to involve the meaning and possession of objects within the household, negotiation between new partners and children about the design and management of places, etc. Single parent families, often headed by women, are more likely to be poor than other family forms. Divorcing women often face the stress of moving to a lower income area after the divorce, where the household itself is often noisy and disorderly (Chase-Lansdale and Hetherington 1990). Custodial fathers often have a difficult time maintaining good relationships with their children, although this difficulty is attenuated if he has a home they can visit overnight and they visit often (Chase-Lansdale and Hetherington 1990). Thus, providing places for relationships makes those relationships easier to sustain.

Single parent households, like many other dual parent households, would prefer low cost options for maintenance, child care, and affordable transportation to work or the option of working from home. In Scandinavia, co-housing has been developed to provide more of such needed services to new household forms. Co-housing is designed to blend the privacy options of single family housing with greater potential for community relationships. The units themselves are smaller, requiring less upkeep and expense. Expensive equipment for hobbies or laundry may be located in shared spaces jointly owned by the community. Cooking and child care cooperatives may relieve some of the time pressure and isolation of domestic labor. In cohousing, the design of community spaces to meet everyday needs diminishes the degree of independence and isolation characteristic of suburban communities. It is likely that couples need to negotiate their links with neighbors just as couples negotiate relationships with kin. Here, instead of close connections between husband and wife and separation between the couple and others, the trend is toward greater connection between neighbors.

A final trend that deserves comment involves the aging of the population, as individuals can live longer today but may need some help in daily tasks. Both elders and their children subscribe to the ideal of independent living—neither generation generally prefers the idea of extended generation households. As older individuals need more care, it is likely that daughters are the ones to provide it (Brody 1990). Research has shown that adults dislike caring for parents in the home if the parents interfere in areas that have traditionally been private family matters. Here, despite all the intervening years of independence, adult children still experience parental complaints or advice as a threat to their close relationships. One physical solution that may meet the independence needs of both generations despite the reality of dependence, is ECHO housing—detached independent units for elders that can be placed in the back yards of their children's home. The physical and psychological separation provided by the free standing unit may allow both adults and their parents a sense of independence, yet the adult is close enough to provide necessary care, thus allowing both parties to achieve desired autonomy and connection.

In sum, many important continuities and changes in the nature and dynamics of contemporary social relationships are intermeshed with placemaking processes. The present review of issues salient to the future has necessarily been incomplete. It would be useful to know how changing households mesh with wider social networks, especially after disruptions created by divorce or widowhood. Similarly, we know very little about how care for elders or children of former spouses are reflected in subsequent courtship and wedding activities. Very little is known about placemaking practices among nonmarital couples; most studies have concentrated on dormitories or other clearly temporary residences. It would be interesting to see how placemaking practices might create strong bases for relationships amongst homosexual or unmarried heterosexual couples. Perhaps homes operate not only to create order and symbolic significance but also to create a refuge against a social or cultural context that may not condone nonmarital alternatives. Finally, as noted above, it is challenging to understand how new households are constrained by and alter housing designed for different family forms.

Finally, it is important to remember that the physical context is integral to relationships. New understandings about close relationships may be developed in the abstract but they cannot be executed or maintained in the abstract. Changes in society involve changing material and cultural circumstances for relationships that must be figured into the meaning of each particular relationship. Studying the interdependent physical, social, and cultural contexts of husband-wife and couple-kin relationships can add significantly to our understanding of close relationships.

References

Ahrentzen, S., D. Levine, and W. Michelson. 1989. Space, time, and activity in the home: A gender analysis. *Journal of Environmental Psychology,* 9:89–101.

Altman, I., B. B. Brown, B. Staples, and C. M. Werner. 1992. A transactional approach to close relationships: courtship, weddings, and placemaking. In *Person-Environment Psychology,* ed. B. Walsh, K. Craik, and R. Price. Hillsdale, NJ: Erlbaum.

Altman, I., and M. M. Chemers. 1980. The American Home. *Culture and environment.* Belmont, CA: Wadsworth.

Altman, I., and B. Rogoff. 1987. World views in psychology: Trait, interactional, organismic, and transactional perspectives. In *Handbook of environmental psychology: Volume 1,* ed. D. Stokols and I. Altman, 1–40. New York: Wiley.

Altman, I. and D. A. Taylor. 1973. *Social penetration: The development of interpersonal relationships.* New York: Holt, Rinehart, and Winston.

Altman, I., A. Vinsel, and B. B. Brown. 1981. Dialectic conceptions in social psychology: An application to social penetration and privacy regulation. In *Advances in experimental social psychology: Volume 14,* ed. L. Berkowitz, 107–160. New York: Academic Press.

Bailey, B. L. 1988. *From front porch to back seat.* Baltimore, MD: Johns Hopkins University Press.

Baxter, L. A. 1988. A dialectic perspective on communication strategies in relationship development. In *Handbook of personal relationships,* ed. S. W. Duck, 257–73. New York: Wiley.

———. 1990. Dialectical contradictions in relationship development. *Journal of Social and Personal Relationships,* 7:69–88.

Brody, E. M. 1990. *Women in the middle: their parent care years.* New York: Springer.

Brown, B. B. 1987. Territoriality. In *Handbook of environmental psychology: Volume 1,* ed. D. Stokols and I. Altman, 505–31. New York: Wiley.

Caplow, T. 1984. Rule enforcement without visible means: Christmas gift giving in Middletown. *American Journal of Sociology,* 89:1306–23.

Chase-Lansdale, P. L., and E. M. Hetherington. 1990. The impact of divorce on life-span development: Short and long term effects. In *Life-span development and behavior, Vol. 10,* eds. P. B. Baltes, D. L. Featherman, and R. M. Lerner. Hillsdale, NJ: Erlbaum.

Csikszentmihalyi, M. and E. Rochberg-Halton. 1981. *The meaning of things: Domestic symbols and the self.* New York: Cambridge University Press.

Davis-Brown, K., S. Salamon, and C. A. Surra. 1987. Economic and social factors in mate selection: An ethnographic analysis of an agricultural community. *Journal of Marriage and the Family,* 49:41–55.

Dovey, K. 1985. Home and homelessness. In *Home environments. Vol.8. Human behavior and environment: Advances in theory and research,* ed. I. Altman and C. M. Werner, 33–64. New York: Plenum.

Dreyer, C. A., and A. S. Dreyer. 1973. Family dinner time as a unique behavioral habitat. *Family Process,* 12:291–301.

Duck, S. W. ed. 1988. *Handbook of personal relationships.* New York: Wiley.

Emmons, C., M. Biernat, L. B. Tiedje, E. L. Lang, and C. B. Wortman. 1990. Stress, support, and coping among women professionals with preschool children. In *Stress between work and family,* ed. J. Eckenrode and S. Gore. New York: Plenum.

Forty, A. 1986. Labour-saving in the home. *Objects of desire.* New York: Pantheon.

Goody, J. 1973. Bridewealth and dowry in Africa and Eurasia. In *Bridewealth and dowry,* ed. J. Goody and S. J. Tambiah, 1–58. Cambridge: Cambridge University Press.

Hayden, D. 1984. *Redesigning the American dream.* New York; W. W. Norton.

Kennedy, R. J. R. 1943. Pre-marital residential propinquity and ethnic endogamy. *American Journal of Sociology,* 48:580–84.

Kirchler, E. 1988. Marital happiness and interaction in everyday surroundings. *Journal of Social and Personal Relationships,* 5:375–82.

Laslett, B. 1973. The family as a public and private institution: an historical perspective. *Journal of Marriage and the Family,* 35:480–92.

Leonard, D. 1980. *Sex and generation.* London: Tavistock.

Milardo, R. M., and R. A. Lewis. 1985. Social networks, families, and mate selection: A transactional analysis. In *The handbook of family psychology and therapy, vol. 1,* ed. L. L'Abate, 258–85. Homewood, IL: Dorsey Press.

Montgomery, B. 1990. Communication at the interface between couples and culture. In *Communication Yearbook 15,* ed. S. Deetz. International Communication Association.

Murstein, B. I. 1986. *Paths to marriage.* Beverly Hills: Sage.

Patterson, M. L. 1988. Functions of nonverbal behavior in close relationships. In *Handbook of personal relationships,* ed. S. W. Duck, 41–56. New York: Wiley.

Rosenblatt, P. C., and L. G. Budd. 1975. Territoriality and privacy in married and unmarried cohabiting couples. *Journal of Social Psychology,* 97:67–76.

Sebba, R., and R. Churchman. 1983. Territories and territoriality in the home. *Environment and Behavior,* 15:191–210.

Struyk, R. J., M. A. Turner, and M. Uneno. 1988. *Future U. S. housing policy: Meeting the demographic challenge.* Washington, DC: Urban Institute Press.

Vinsel, A., B. B. Brown, I. Altman, and C. Foss. 1980. Privacy regulation, territorial displays, and the effectiveness of individual functioning. *Journal of Personality and Social Psychology,* 39:1104–15.

Whyte, M. K. 1990. *Dating, mating, and marriage.* New York: Aldine de Gruyter.

Chapter *18*

General Perspective on the Multi-Disciplinary Field of Personal Relationships

STEVE DUCK
University of Iowa

Outline

The social scientific study of relationships has been a long time coming, given the absolute centrality of relationships to people's lives. This centrality has been one of the givens of social life since we all emerged from the caves. The earliest commentaries about the conduct of relationships go back to the earliest known human records (Ginsburg 1988), and the most ancient documents contain advice (or commandments) about the ways in which relationships should be conducted (e.g., "Honor thy father and thy mother"). Most major literature and drama across the centuries have contained important depictions of relationships and their value to our lives. Of course, a lot of it says one thing and a lot says another, but there is nothing odd about there being contrasting views of relationships.

Despite the ready availability of this multitudinous guidance, it was not until the 1980s that there was apparently a dramatic boom in social science research in relationship. In fact, it is more accurate to say that the appearance of a boom was created by three underlying trends:

1) the bringing together of several previously independent sets of scholars from different disciplines into one interacting group that became more aware of one another's work as a result of the organizational changes;

2) the infiltration of new methods of research across disciplinary lines, as a result of a number of separate influences, one of them being a general desire in the 1980s to move away from simple laboratory manipulation and towards the study of real life experience;

3) the increased recruitment of a body of new and vigorous scholars from diverse backgrounds who began to see the ways in which personal relationships impinge on and influence almost every other aspect of human social experience.

Again, the generality of this realization was partly due to the fact that these researchers came from different parent backgrounds and brought their own disciplinary perspectives to their work—and yet began to find that they shared something in common with people from other backgrounds and could talk to them despite the differences. My own disciplinary background is illustrative here: my undergraduate degree was in Psychology and Philosophy, and I was then trained in social psychology. I did my Ph.D. in a mixture of Personality Psychology and Social Psychology, and now teach in a Communication Studies Department. I edit the international, interdisciplinary journal (*Journal of Social and Personal Relationships*) with Associate Editors in Community and Clinical Psychology, Communication, Developmental Psychology, Family Studies and Sociology, Personality and Individual Differences, and Social Psychology. No wonder the editors of this book gave me *this* chapter to write!

The (Very) Extended Family of Relationship Scholars

In the early 1980s the large number of people already doing research in relationships from the vantage point of different parent disciplines (such as sociology, personality psychology, communication, clinical work, women's studies, developmental, and social psychology) became more interactive. They began to recognize one another's work as a result of the organization and the initiation of series of conferences, the creation of the *Journal of Social and Personal Relationships*, the setting up of professional networks, and other programmatic forces that demonstrated the possibility of a tangible coherence.

Origins

There had always been clinical psychologists interested in relationships since at least the time of Freud. Developmental psychologists had always been interested in the relationships of infants and parents (and more recently, of children with one another). Sociologists had always been interested in the nature of the family. Anthropologists had always attended to the ways in which the form of relationships differs from one culture to another. Communication researchers at large had always been concerned about the relationship of speaker to audience, while interpersonal communication researchers, specifically, were also interested in the dynamics of communication between people who were known to one another. Social psychologists and sociologists had always had an interest in the emotions and motivational states through which relationships are typically explained.

Now many social psychologists have also begun to understand that many other social phenomena (whether the decision making of groups or the understanding of others' behavior, or the changing of attitudes), all have some links, often subtle links, to the nature of the relationships between people. For instance, groups perform differently when members like one another and when they do not, when the structure of relationships and communication between people is altered, and when a history of personal interaction between members precedes a particular decision-making meeting. Although much attitude change is conceived as a purely rational (or at least mental) activity, it has been recognised since Aristotle that one's likelihood of being persuaded by a person face-to-face depends to some extent on whether one likes the speaker. The apparent growth in research on relationships thus actually grew out of existing interests within different disciplines and it has become a coherent reality on the later 1980s and early 1990s [with the International Network on Personal Relationships growing from 75 members to over 900 in the last four years, as an example].

Methods

In addition to, and parallel with, the organizational growth which made the field a reality, methodological changes in the social sciences at large helped to make the study of relationships a more vibrant possibility than some of the tedious and unrealistic laboratory work of the 1960s and 1970s. The chapter here by Ickes gives a good idea of these developments and illustrates the sorts of changes that I mean, so I will not repeat the points. The organizational changes perhaps made people from different parent disciplines more aware of the generality of the movement towards more realistic research, however. The organizational changes also helped scholars in one parent discipline to see the advances made by scholars in other disciplines and so led to a greater adventurousness in research. For instance, instead of exploring the ways in which lab-based expectations of meeting someone could be manipulated according to an experimenter's beliefs about the situation, researchers began to uncover interesting and exciting ways in which people secretly found out about another person's interest in dating them (Douglas 1987). Alternatively, we also began to study the sorts of secret tests that real people used in order to difine whether a steady partner was as committed to the relationship as they were themselves (Baxter and Wilmot 1984). Although the latter research was originally published in a communication journal, it is now regularly discussed and quoted by scholars and students from many other disciplines, such as social psychology and sociology.

Changes of Style

Thirdly, the recruitment of a vigorous body of new researchers whose average age is in the mid-thirties, has meant that many old traditional styles of laboratory research have been eclipsed. In addition there is now much work from scholars with a hands on approach to real life, researchers who are versed in methods of naturalistic or ethnographic study (especially the study of everyday behavior and the assumptions that are built into it by way of rules, and norms and expectations). In keeping with the *social constructivist* approach to social psychology (e.g., Gergen and Gergen 1987), recent scholarship focuses on the ways in which people create social reality for themselves in their behavior. For instance, it is much more inclined to focus on the day-to-day management of relationships in real life than on the manipulation of special forms of behavior in the laboratory, whether it is done by social psychologists or by scholars from other disciplines (for example, chapters by Aron and Aron, Sprecher and McKinney, DeSteno and Salovey, Jones and Burdette, Marshall, and Weber and Harvey). Old textbooks of interpersonal attraction used to spend most of their space looking at attraction to strangers or at attraction as an attitude and so focused on processes pared down to the bone in order to make their study that much easier. More recent texts have chapters on such real life experiences as dissolution of relationships, maintenance of relationships, jealousy, and betrayal, and so focus on topics that are more familiar in their complexity, but more challenging to study.

A Personal Context for Understanding Relationships

The changes and improvements to the research focus now better reflect the reality of lived lives. Obviously we relate our way through life.

Everyone Has an Opinion

I have never met anyone who is not interested in relationships and the ways in which they work. By the same token I have never yet met a hairdresser (airline passenger, dental hygienist, other human being. . .) who, on finding out that I study relationships, does not have some idea about their explanation from his or her own perspective, just as the different disciplines do. Everyone has some ideas about how relationships work, but it is rather interesting to discover that these different barbers' (airline passengers', etc.) explanations are often quite different. For instance, I have had some haircuts from barbers who believe that it is all just a natural process, that birds, bees—even educated fleas—know how to do it and so do we. In recent months the haircuts have been more likely to be associated with comments about the breakdown of family values and the rising divorce rate—seeming to suggest that at least some people do not know how to do it and need to be told. But each snip of the scissors is associated with a viewpoint on human relationships. When it comes to thinking about relationships, we are all experts—at least on how other people should conduct their relationships.

If we run out of advice on our own or from the people we meet, then there are many other sources of commentary about relationships. This fact is not as trivial as it appears, since it provides a context for the ways in which we all become accustomed to thinking about relationships. For example, many popular songs are about relationships and the emotions that are appropriate in them or about the ways of conducting them. Television soap operas are all about the complex interweaving of relational fabric. Advertisements usually tell us new ways to be liked or admired by others (through purchase of this or that item), or demonstrate ways to make ourselves attractive to others (by buying this or that perfume, pair of jeans, hat, nail polish, car, . . .). News stories frequently offer us background information about the relationship lives of the rich and famous. Finally, anyone with in-laws or a room-mate knows that there is always a bottomless store of advice and experience about the conduct of relationships that is ever freely offered and given out generously with both hands by other people.

Some Opinions Are Worth More than Others

All the same, despite the ready availability of advice about relationships, most of us have experienced unsatisfactory relationships, have some enemies, have been betrayed or let down, have failed to get into, or have lost a relationship we wanted, or have felt the need to get out of a relationship at some time or another. It is also a familiar experience of teachers of relationship classes that many people in a given class would like some help with a relationship problem at some point in their life. People with relationship problems do not find them at all common sensical or easy to deal with. When people cannot talk to a relationship class instructor about their relationship problems, they usually turn to friends (see Gottlieb's chapter) or to professional counselors (see Winstead and Derlega's chapter). So there are many different sources of information about relationships based on social context and many different perspectives about them based on individual background.

Everyone Is Different . . . and Yet the Same

In some ways each person's relationship problem is different and yet the principles are often similar: trouble with a romantic partner, trouble with a close
relative, trouble with a dating partner or a roommate. Am I in too deep? Am I in
deep enough? Is my partner in deep enough? Can I trust my partner [ever again
after what she or he did to me]? It is quite striking that everyone feels that her or
his own relationship experience is unique, and yet everyone is also curious about
whether everyone else feels the same way about relationships. While some people
crave intimacy, others find it hard to deal with. Some like lots of relatively shallow
relationships and some prefer one really deep relationship. Some seek romantic
partners who are like their parents and others seek to avoid such resemblance at
all costs. Some people want advice about whether they are behaving correctly in
the relationship or whether they are normal to feel the way they do, or whether
they are feeling the way they should or whether they have a perfect relationship.

Such differences and similarities are particularly interesting because they
tacitly acknowledge that the individual emotions that we feel about relationships
are often not all that there is to the experience. Much of our behavior in close and
personal relationships is in fact guided by norms of behavior or by the opinions
of others in the social network that we inhabit. All the same there are always those
who say that "Our love is the best there has ever been and no-one else's is like it."
Almost everyone who has ever been in love feels that uniqueness at some time or
another—along with everyone else who is in love! Thus a full understanding of
relationships would require us to recognize that relationships are not simply
caused by emotion. They are not simply the result of attitudes or impersonal
forces of attraction, but are much more complex social processes. Obviously they
involve emotions and attitudes but that is by no means all there is to them.

The Value of Different Perspectives

What I draw from these casual observations is that individuals can take their own
perspectives and have their own models of relationships and relationship development but also have a commonality with other people in our culture in our
thoughts about relationships. We are also fundamentally affected by past relationship experiences and we never enter new relationships without some of our past
history hanging out like shirt-tails. While some people seek to copy past experiences, other people use them as a guide about the things that must be avoided or
emphasized in future relationships. We experience relationships as a part of life's
unfolding cloth and not as pieces of material separate from the rest of what we
know as individuals. Although we experience each relationship as an individual,
we are affected in that experience by factors from our past as well as from the
present. We are also, perhaps unknowingly, affected by a range of other social,
cultural, and contextual sources, such as norms and cultural beliefs about relationships. Thus we relate according to some general and shared principles that

reflect common elements in the human approach to close personal relationships. If this commonality of experience were not something that researchers could assume, then there would be no point in doing research on them. We would just be exploring the individual lives of persons and not discovering any underlying common factors that make the human approach to relationships the same for all of us. . . . And yet individuals do still have the feeling that our own relationships may be different and unique or that our perspective on relationships may be different from everyone else's.

Individual Affections and Cultural Cages

When we start to think about relationships we soon discover that the experiences that are felt as individual emotions are embedded in many other contexts that also require examination and explanation. For instance, if I love you, I feel certain physical feelings, but I am guided in my expression of them by some cultural factors and the shared metaphors that our society uses familiarly. For example, if I describe my love as like a feeling of burning fire, or say that I am head-over-heels in love with you, then listeners probably know what I mean by the metaphors. On the other hand, if I were to say that being in love is like having a crocodile on a spring, listeners would probably have to stop and think about it a bit. Some metaphorical terms have an immediate meaning to us in the description of love and some do not. Many linguists (Kovecses 1991) are now beginning to look at the ways in which our feelings of love are somehow channeled by the ways we learn to talk and think about the emotion within the particular culture that is our normal linguistic environment. Such research naturally adds considerably to the way we can understand the human experiences of love or friendship, since we usually talk to one another in order to demonstrate and reify emotions and relationships.

As another example that shows the multifarious nature of the conduct of relationships, recall an early Beatles' song about the expression of love: "I Want to Hold Your Hand." Why hold the hand? In some cultures the song would have to be "I Want to Rub Noses with You". It all depends where you live, not just on how you feel. The expression of emotions is culturally channeled in a way that needs explanation and research by such scholars as sociologists and anthropologists (or even cultural historians, since forms of emotional expression change across time in a given culture). If a close friend dies, why would I wear black to the funeral instead of white (as in China)? Why is it we believe that our romantic partner can be anyone in the world if we love the person and the person loves us, yet study after study after study has shown that most people marry others from the same country, the same social class, the same religious group, the same economic level, the same intelligence level, the same educational experience, the same race, and the same lifestyle? Incidentally, demographic research also shows that those for whom this is not the case stand an even higher chance of getting divorced. Such findings can hardly be explained by simple explanations of love in terms of internal emotions alone, for example, without taking account of the issues in which sociologists and demographers are expert. At the very least, we are forced to reflect on the fact that choices are not unlimited, not based on emotion alone, and not uninfluenced by social expectations.

Feelings and Places: How Context Affects Emotions

If love is just the strong positive feelings of one person for another, caused objectively by a favorable reaction to the other person's physical, mental, behavioral and personal characteristics, then why do we not all love the same people? After all, a lovable person should seem so to everyone who encounters him or her and there would be no personal preferences . . . no? Why do some cultures find one set of physical characteristics (say, obesity) appealing and another finds it appalling? How come you can insult a friend and the friend bursts out laughing and feels good, but the same words spoken to a stranger could get you a black eye?

Recall that "Attraction" is defined in the Simpson and Harris chapter as "A motivational state in which an individual is predisposed to think, feel, and usually behave, in a positive manner towards another person." However, the fact is that, besides being based on psychological responses to others, attraction is also influenced by social context, communicative rules, developmental experiences, and norms of behaviors. The very definition of a positive manner, for instance, depends at least on social context: I may embrace my romantic partner passionately at home, but cannot do it at a public place (as the Beatles pointed out when they asked in their "White album" song, "Why don't we do it in the road?") Thus, the same behavior can be acceptable or unacceptable depending on where it happens—its social context. Moreover, an insult can be taken as positively affectionate by persons who have already worked out in their relationship that such an insult is a tease. Yet when this relationship context has not been pre-established, the insult is just an insult.

Thus the same behavior can be either positive or negative depending on the circumstances that exist outside of the motivational state of the behaver: its meaning depends on its interpretation in context by the partner—in this case, the context of the relationship's history.

Also, for some persons (women) a flirtatious behavior is usually a generally friendly act while for others (men) it is usually a generally sexual act (Montgomery 1986). Thus one's comprehension of relationship behavior has to be moderated by an accounting of the sex of the target also: the behavior itself cannot be safely interpreted in terms of the intentions or motives of the behaver alone, but has meaning derived from context.

Finally, even when we like someone we may also be aware of the fact that they (just like we) have some negative qualities. Thus liking is not only the blind predisposition to feel positively about someone that is often suggested; it is possible to like and dislike at the same time—one may like the person but dislike some of the acts, for example.

These examples all make the same point: that the psychological exploration of the emotions and motives associated with liking or relating stops short of the whole story. In fact, my examples do not go very deeply to some of the issues here, and social psychologists are keenly aware of the importance of contextual influence (Duck, in press). Behavior in relationships has many different facets that require researching and illumination from many different viewpoints. The meanings applied at any time to a behavior are not absolute nor just definable in terms of the individual behaver, but instead they relate to a lot of other external contexts and can be interpreted only in those contexts.

Understanding Relationships as More than Feelings

The proper full study of relationships thus has to draw from an uncovering and understanding of the complex web of factors that create the contexts for them. We will never understand what is happening in relationships if we look only inside the heads of individuals, or only at the person's relational history, or only at the effects of social structure, any more that you can truly understand what a particular house would be like to live in if you look only at the realtor's single-angle photograph of it.

All the same, it is obviously right for each discipline to bring its own baggage along with it and hurl it into the pile of contributions to the study of relationships. The mistake occurs only if no-one else ever takes the time to open the baggage of other disciplines. For instance, those who study relationships from a psychological point of view are bound, as a result of their particular expertise and training, to make certain assumptions about the nature of individual persons and they are guided by those assumptions, yet need not stop there. There is no surprise that psychologists in various fields are likely to be concerned with personality as an influence on relationship activity or to find out how an individual makes judgements about others' behavior, or how a person is attracted to certain characteristics of others. Psychology is in the business of exploring the individual mind, and social psychology has a tradition of exploring the ways in which individual minds think about social events. For this reason, a psychologist is generally less likely than a sociologist would be to emphasize the relationship's place in the social structure, and to examine the ways in which social structure influence what people do when they are alone together. A sociologist is likely to pay attention to the fact that even our dyadic close personal relationships occur in a society that has rules about relationships ("You may not marry your brother"; "You cannot sell your children to buy groceries"). A sociologist may point to the fact that however people feel the emotions that a psychologist might attend to, their expression is guided by cultural and social norms. While one society places emphasis on the family as a nuclear structure consisting of a man, a woman, and their children, others see a family as an extended group of kin including grandparents, cousins, and some accept multiple definitions of family as they open themselves to the possibility of gay or lesbian families. (And in some cases, the nature of the family and family values are contentious issues that can be disputed within a given culture, as my various barbers have been making plain recently). Some societies see friends as those who are especially close and can be trusted to help you in times of need, while others insist that friends are people from another village who are nominated to be your friends, since you cannot trust anyone else in your own village (La Gaipa 1990). The Romans used to adopt one another's children into their own family while the parents were still alive and they did this in order to create political alliances, yet the adopted children became full-fledged members of the adoptive family and owed their allegiance to that family from that moment on. And so on and so on. The point is that one cannot assume that only one form of relationships needs explanation nor that human behavior at large is driven only by the principles explored in one culture or from one disciplinary perspective. This is one reason, why many methods being developed in personal relationships scholarship are now crossing traditional disciplinary boundaries.

Scholars in yet other disciplines can illuminate other features of relationship life. For instance a lifespan researcher (see Blieszner's chapter) would be interested in the different ways in which individuals have relationships in the course of the lifespan. Why do people have mostly same sex friends between the ages of five–fourteen? Why do most people's friends come from the work-place between the ages of thirty–fifty? Why do many parents become friends after their children begin to play together? A developmental psychologist may also be intrigued by the influence of early childhood experience on the ways in which a person's adult relational experience manifests itself. For instance, some developmental psychologists (Putallaz, Costanzo and Klein 1993) have recently begun to explore the ways in which a parent's experiences as a child influence the way in which the parent brings up his or her own children. Some parents, for example, recall nasty experiences from their own childhoods and seek to prevent those things from happening to their children. In some cases, parents can be very vigorous in steering their children away from such remembered pains or may deliberately organize the child's social world in a way that avoids them (e.g., if the parents were lonely and isolated in childhood, they may continually arrange for other children to come over and play with their own youngsters). Therefore, one person's set of relational experiences can be truly influential on another's experience. So it would clearly be incomplete to explain one person's relationships just by reference to the social psychological and motivational circumstances presently available to that individual—unless these are understood to include developmental history. Thus some researchers have become intrigued by the way in which a person's infantile attachment to a parent figure can affect and influence the sorts of adult romantic attachment that the person forms with other adults. In doing so, they have stressed the individual peculiarities that also act as a context for relational activity (see Shaver and Hazan's chapter).

Conclusion and Summary: Multiple Views of Multifarious Phenomena

I could summarize the above this way: I hope that my various hairdressers are also cutting the hair of sociologists, psychologists, anthropologists, and clinicians as well as of communication professors. That way they may get the fullest information about the sorts of factors that are important in relationships! Relationships are multifarious things and need illumination from multiple perspectives.

Social and personal relationships happen for people in a variety of ways and in a variety of contexts. This simple and obvious fact has been increasingly recognized since the 1980s relationship boom. This recognition has served to direct the ways in which the phenomena are studied, since relationships encompass an enormous range of different activities and experiences that cut right through most of the human adventure. Accordingly, such relationships present us with many different topics and issues to be studied.

In addition to topics reviewed in this volume, what else could we try to explain about relationships? We might be interested in the social forces that influence the nature of friendship in a given culture or subculture or in the pressures on men and women to be intimate in different ways (e.g. for women to express emotions more and for true men to be strong and silent!). We could explore the rules of cross-sex non-romantic friendship that are different from other personal relationships such as romantic relationships, or the idealized nature of relationships as perceived in a particular culture. If these are our interests then we could take either a psychological or a sociological approach to the questions (Allan 1993; Honeycutt 1993). Alternatively, we might be interested in how people persuade one another to go on a date, to get into a relationship or out of one, or how they indicate the degree of commitment they feel towards one another. If such were our interest then we would be inclined to set about the study of the creation of messages and strategies of influence and the ways in which people structure their talk with one another in order to attain certain goals (Dindia in press). We could look at the nonverbal behavior that is used to indicate relational feelings independently of talk (Keeley and Hart, in press), or we could explore the everyday discussions that people have with one another to achieve all this (see Montgomery's chapter or Duck, in press). In all of these cases, we may take account of the place of the individual in the social structure, his or her relationships to a larger functioning network of other people, or his or her developing roles in the friendships and other personal relationships that are created.

Furthermore, while the complete list of topics for study in personal relationships is probably inexhaustible, it is only recently that it has been pointed out that the research is typically biased toward the positive (Cupach and Spitzberg, in press; Spitzberg 1993). There are few studies of revenge, gossip, hatred, enemyship, back-biting, sabotage of relationships, and so on, all of which become more important to study once one has begun the focus on daily experience and on the communications that people have with one another in daily talk (Duck in press). Even more noticeable is the absence of extensive study of several relationships that are frequent in the real world, such as relationships with grandparents, reconfigured families, relationships of adults with their parents, sibling relationships, and some that are products of the technological advances of recent times, such as relationships conducted over electronic-mail by computer (see Wood and Duck in press; Duck and Wood in press).

All of these approaches and concerns are relevant to the study of close personal relationships as are many other sorts of interests and concerns not listed earlier. They assume greater importance as investigative work relies less on isolated experiments or single relationship events and moves to processes and contexts that take more account of lived lives. For example, once we are interested in what relationships are, rather than in what are some of the thoughts or behaviors that make them up, then we also start to look at how they function and how people balance their positive and negative or in their negative side effects (the binds that go with the bonds). Then we might become concerned with the obligations of relationships, the needs to be there to support others when they call upon us, and the tragic consequences of getting committed and involved with others who then leave, die, become less involved with us, or even betray our trust in them (see Jones and Burdette and Weber and Harvey chapters here).

Relationships are a phenomena that embrace our lives in enormous numbers of ways and provide a broad selection of completely fascinating topics for study by future generations of scholars of relationships. The ways are so enormous that we need a wide range of techniques and theoretical insights in order to grasp them fully. A complete understanding of relationships is quite beyond the scope of any one discipline to encompass satisfactorily. The only way to go in relationship studies is the multidisciplinary route. Research is best when it takes account of the special contribution that can be made to the overall picture by a given discipline, yet remains open to the valuable insights that are obtainable from broader scholarship. Different perspectives on relationships should not be regarded as competing but as complementary. Good scholars will strive to be aware of the work of other disciplines than their own and to find in it the illuminating discoveries on which they can build in their own work.

References

Allan, G. 1993. Social structure and relationships. In *Understanding relationship processes 3: Social contexts of relationships,* ed. S. W. Duck, Newbury Park, CA: Sage.

Baxter, L. A., and W. Wilmot, 1984. 'Secret tests: Social strategies for acquiring information about the state of the relationship.' *Human Communication Research,* 11:171–201.

Cupach, W. R., and B. H. Spitzberg, (Eds.) In press. *The dark side of interpersonal communication.* Hillsdale, NJ: LEA.

Dindia, K. (in press) The intrapersonal-interpersonal dialectical process of self-disclosure. In *Understanding relationship processes 4: Dynamics of interactions,* ed. S. W. Duck, Newbury Park: Sage.

Douglas, W. 1987 Affinity testing in initial interaction. *Journal of Social and Personal Relationships* 4:3–16.

Duck, S. W. (In press) Stratagems, spoils, and a serpent's tooth: On the delights and dilemmas of personal relationships. In *The dark side of interpersonal communication.* ed. W. R. Cupach and B. H. Spitzberg Hillsdale, NJ: LEA, in press.

Duck, S. W. and J. T. Wood, In press *Understanding relationship processes 5: Relationship challenges* Newbury Park: SAGE.

Gergen, K. J., and M. M. Gergen, 1987. Narratives of relationship. In *Accounting for relationships* ed. R. Burnett, P. McGhee, and D. D. Clarke (Eds.), (pp. 269–315). London: Methuen.

Ginsburg, G. P. 1988. Rules, scripts and prototypes in personal relationships. In *Handbook of personal relationships*, ed. S. W. Duck, 23–40. New York: John Wiley and Sons.

Honeycutt, J. M. 1993. Memory structures for the rise and fall of personal relationships. In *Understanding relationship processes 1: Individuals in relationships*, ed. S. W. Duck, Newbury Park, CA: Sage.

Keeley, M., and A. Hart, (In press). Nonverbal behavior in relationships. In *Understanding relationship processes 4: Dynamics of interactions*, ed. S. W. Duck Newbury Park: SAGE.

Kovecses, Z. 1991. A linguist's quest for love. *Journal of Social and Personal Relationships,* 8:77–98.

La Gaipa, J. J. 1990 The negative effects of informal support systems. In *Personal Relationships and Social Support,* ed., S. W. Duck with R. C. Silver, London: SAGE.

Montgomery, B. M. 1986. Flirtatious messages. Paper presented to the Third International Conference on Personal Relationships, Herzlia, Israel, July.

Putallaz, M., P. R. Costanzo, and T. P. Klein, (1993) Parental childhood social experiences and their effects on children's relationships. In *Understanding relationship processes 2: Learning about relationships,* ed. S. W. Duck, Newbury Park: SAGE.

Spitzberg, B. H. 1993. The dialectics of (in)competence. *Journal of Social and Personal Relationships,* 10, 137–158.

Wood, J. T., and S. W. Duck, In press *Understanding relationship processes 6: Off the beaten track.* Newbury Park, CA: SAGE.

Conclusion: Reflections and Perspectives

JOHN H. HARVEY
University of Iowa

ANN L. WEBER
University of North Carolina at Asheville

"We don't know one-hundredth of 1% about anything."
—Thomas Edison

We have come to the end of a volume that we believe is unique. It was aimed at audiences who are both beginning and more advanced in their study of close relationships. The authors and editors attempted to walk a fine line between state-of-the art scholarship on the topics covered and a more general review of theory and research that is the foundation for more recent contributions. This volume is unique for another principal reason, as well: It is one of the handful of texts now available in the social sciences that is multi-authored—with the "multi" here being more than thirty scholars! In developing the format for this text, we followed the lead of an introductory social psychology text that one of us (John H. Harvey) had contributed to in 1981, Drury Sherrod's edited *Social Psychology*, published by Random House. That text received good reviews based on its editing and bringing together of multiple perspectives. If a multi-authored text is well-edited, it has the potential of being superior in its competence of examination of topics, as compared to the more common type of text that is authored by one or two, or sometimes a few more, scholars.

We hope that you, the reader, will appreciate the editing of this text and the diversity of expertise on display. The field of close relationships is of such breadth that this kind of major collaborative enterprise may represent a promising new direction for books aimed at general audiences. Certainly, no one scholar in the field can expertly analyze and comment on the many relationship topics being explored. You, the reader, must be the judge of the adroitness of our attempted balancing act, in terms of level of scholarship and the value of the many voices heard among our various chapters.

In addition to the above questions for evaluation, readers of this text will discover major limitations. What is important in the field that was not covered in a chapter of the text? No one book can cover everything it should cover. Edison's quote to start this commentary may be a bit extreme, but it resonates with a probable state-of-affairs in the study of close relationships. Scholars in this field at the turn of the twenty-first century probably do not have a good understanding of more than a few percent of the totality of all that could be learned about how humans relate closely to one another. We make no apology for our ignorance or the fact that this text covered only a fragment of the terrain. Our objective was to be selective, but at the same time representative of interesting directions of work in this field.

Still, the issue of what is left out cannot be simply dismissed because no work can be completely comprehensive. There are some glaring omissions in our coverage. They include such topics as: friendship (a topic for which we tried unsuccessfully to get representation), gender differences, the family, homosexuality, relationships from a multi-cultural perspective, and the history of close relationships. For each of these topics, the reader could be directed toward a vast literature and might even seek a valuable supplementary text on a particular topic.

This issue of what we have had to omit takes us to another question: What will the future bring in terms of texts and learning materials in the field of close relationships? A sociological examination of this field of scholarship would reveal that it is exceedingly popular. It has appeal on all fronts, from books being produced to scholars joining up to work on relationship topics to students and a general public hungry to read what is known or theorized about relationship topics. Focusing just on the books being produced as one index of growth, some useful texts on close relationships already exist, and some are thriving in second and beyond editions. As this volume reveals, more are coming, and they likely will be presented in different formats. The problems we have encountered with available texts are mainly the same issues we raise about our own present text: level of writing, intended audience, and breadth of coverage. It remains to be seen whether any text can surmount these issues powerfully and still be useful across the several disciplines constituting the field of close relationships.

The supplementary market is doing quite well and will probably continue to reflect a major direction for writing in this field. Several series of works on close relationship topics are being published (e.g., the Sage Series edited by Susan and Clyde Hendrick, and the Guilford Series edited by Steve Duck are notable examples). Because these supplementary works can hone in on a particular topic so precisely, they do a splendid job of providing a menu of related works for the reader or instructor. Whether they are cost efficient for the classroom is a question that still must be asked. But they likely will remain viable for some time to come.

Quite apart from supplementary texts, books focusing on relationship topics such as relationship counseling, jealousy, relationship conflict and break-down, alternative lifestyles, love, hate, and sexuality now comprise a good percentage of all books being produced in the social and behavioral sciences every year.

We could go on at some length about possible future directions in teaching close relationships. One of us (Ann L. Weber) regularly organizes and leads round-table discussions on such directions at close relationship conferences. Teachers are learning how to combine different scholarly works, books, chapters, and journal articles with a menu of useful learning aids, including newspaper and magazine articles, videotaped presentations, and various types of group discussions—such as panels of people who deal with certain close relationship matters in their work (e.g., divorce lawyers and divorce mediators).

Close relationships represent a cauldron for all human experience. As this text aptly displays, within the contexts of our closest relationships, we often find the greatest joys and happiness of our existence. At the same time, however, within those same relationships, we often find the greatest pain, tragedy, and the darkest of human thought and action. When Fritz Heider, the founder of attribution theory in social psychology, was once asked about the future of the study of attribution, he suggested that it was bright because attribution was a part of the way people see, think about, and act toward their environment (Heider 1976). We believe that the same sentiment can be entertained regarding the future of the study of close relationships. It is a field that probably will be around for a long time, because we as humans are so intrinsically curious about it and simply do not know the answers to many key questions and concerns about our own personal relationships. Not only do we have a long way to go in learning about relationships, but also many of the sub-phenomena that we study are highly subject to historical and cultural forces, and thus they change in significant ways over time (e.g., divorce and remarriage trends). In the end, therefore, we celebrate the reality that the field of close relationships is developing so swiftly and in such multifaceted ways. Yet, we have barely begun the process of inquiry that may well continue as long as the human species exists and humans reach out to try to connect their lives with those of others.

Reference

Heider, F. 1976. A conversation with Fritz Heider. In *New directions in attribution research*, ed. J. H. Harvey, W. J. Ickes, and R. F. Kidd (vol. 1), 3–18. Hillsdale, NJ: Erlbaum.

Subject Index

Name Index